thomson com

changing the way the world learns℠

To get extra value from this book for no additional cost, go to:

http://www.thomson.com/wadsworth.html

thomson.com is the World Wide Web site for Wadsworth/ ITP® and is your direct source to dozens of on-line resources. *thomson.com* helps you find out about supplements, experiment with demonstration software, search for a job, and send e-mail to many of our authors. You can even preview new publications and exciting new technologies.

thomson.com: *It's where you'll find us in the future.*

The Religious Life in History Series

Charles Hallisey, *Series Editor*

The Way of Torah

An Introduction to Judaism

Sixth Edition

JACOB NEUSNER
University of South Florida
Bard College

Wadsworth Publishing Company
I(T)P® An International Thomson Publishing Company

Belmont, CA • Albany, NY • Bonn • Boston • Cincinnati • Detroit • Johannesburg • London • Madrid
Melbourne • Mexico City • New York • Paris • Singapore • Tokyo • Toronto • Washington

Religion Editor: Peter Adams
Assistant Editor: Clay Glad
Editorial Assistant: Greg Brueck
Marketing Manager: Dave Garrison
Project Editor: Jennie Redwitz
Print Buyer: Barbara Britton
Permissions Editor: Jeanne Bosschart
Copy Editor: Laura Larson
Cover: Craig Hanson
Compositor: Thompson Type
Printer: BookCrafters

Cover Image: Jewish Museum/Art Resource, NY. *Torah Shield.* Augsburg, c. 1715, by Zacharias Wagner (c. 1680–1733). Silver, repousse, cast, engraved and gilt. 42.2 x 30.3 cm. Gift of Dr. Harry G. Friedman, F70C. Jewish Museum, New York, New York, U.S.A.

Printed in the United States of America
1 2 3 4 5 6 7 8 9 10

For more information, contact Wadsworth Publishing Company, 10 Davis Drive, Belmont, California 94002, or electronically at http://www.thomson.com/wadsworth.html

International Thomson Publishing Europe
Berkshire House 168-173
High Holborn
London, WC1V 7AA
England

Thomas Nelson Australia
102 Dodds Street
South Melbourne 3205
Victoria, Australia

Nelson Canada
1120 Birchmount Road
Scarborough, Ontario
Canada M1K 5G4

International Thomson Publishing GmbH
Königswinterer Strasse 418
53227 Bonn, Germany

International Thomson Editores
Campos Eliseos 385, Piso 7
Col. Polanco
11560 México D.F. México

International Thomson Publishing Asia
221 Henderson Road
#05-10 Henderson Building
Singapore 0315

International Thomson Publishing Japan
Hirakawacho Kyowa Building, 3F
2-2-1 Hirakawacho
Chiyoda-ku, Tokyo 102, Japan

International Thomson Publishing
Southern Africa
Building 18, Constantia Park
240 Old Pretoria Road
Halfway House, 1685 South Africa

Library of Congress Cataloging-in-Publication Data

Neusner, Jacob
    The way of Torah : an introduction to Judaism / Jacob Neusner. —
    6th ed.
        p.   cm.—(The Religious life in history series)
    Includes bibliographical references and index.
    ISBN 0-534-51568-1
    1. Judaism. I. Title. II. Series.
BM565.N487   1997
296—dc20

96-39049

Contents

Three Important Doctrines

The Torah's Worldview

The Torah's Way of Life

Four Types of Judaic Piety

III   Classical Judaism in Modern Times   179

Reform, Orthodox, and Conservative Judaisms

The Practice of Judaism in Contemporary North America

Foreword

The Religious Life in History series introduces the richness and diversity of religious thought, practice, experience, and institutions as they are found in living traditions throughout the world.

Some of the religious traditions included in the Religious Life in History series are defined by geography and cultural arenas, while others are defined by their development across cultural and geographic boundaries. In all cases, however, the introductions seek to take full account of the variety within each tradition while keeping in sight the traits and patterns that encourage both scholars and members of various religious communities to distinguish a particular religious tradition from others around it. Moreover, as a set of introductions to quite different religious traditions, the series naturally invites comparison between different ways of being religious and encourages critical reflection on religion as a human phenomenon more generally. Thus, in addition to containing volumes on different religious traditions, the series also includes a core text on the study of religion, which is intended to aid the kinds of comparative inquiry and critical reflection that the series fosters through its introductions to religion in particular cultural and historical contexts.

The basic texts in the Religious Life in History series all provide narrative descriptions of a religious tradition, but each also approaches its subject with an interpretive orientation appropriate to its focus. Some traditions lend themselves more to developmental, others to more topical, studies. This lack of single interpretive stance in the series is itself instructive. It reflects the interpretive choices made by the different authors, choices informed by a deep knowledge of the languages and cultures associated with the religious tradition in question. It also displays the methodological pluralism that characterizes the contemporary study of religion. But perhaps most importantly, it can serve as a useful reminder that what is considered religiously important in one context may not be so in another; indeed, what is viewed as religious in one culture may not be so regarded elsewhere.

Many of the basic texts in the series have a complementary anthology of reading selections. These include translations of texts used by the participants of a tradition, descriptions of practices and practitioners' experiences, and brief interpretive studies of phenomena important in a given tradition. In addition, all of the basic texts present a list of materials for further readings, including translations and more in-depth examinations of specific topics.

The Religious Life in History series was founded more than two decades ago by Frederick J. Streng. While Streng was editor of the series, continuous efforts were made to update the scholarship and to make the presentation of material more effective in each volume. These efforts will continue in the future through the publication of revised editions as well as with the addition of new volumes to the series. But the aim of the series has remained the same since its beginning: As Frederick Streng said, we hope that readers will find these volumes "introductory" in the most significant sense—as introductions to new perspectives for understanding themselves and others.

Charles Hallisey
Series Editor

Preface

This introduction to Judaism provides a history of the principal system of that religion and an account of how the religion flourishes in the world today, with special emphasis on North America and the English-speaking world, where this textbook finds its readers. The history of a religion sorts out through time how various religious formulations of that religion's practices and beliefs took shape. It identifies the major periods in the life of a given religious system and proposes to show how what happened to that religious system correlates with what happened to the religious community—important events that demanded explanation, urgent issues that required attention—with the ongoing life of the system. In the case of Judaism, as of Christianity and Islam, a major problem concerns the very definition of the faith: what do we mean by Judaism? For, over time, various Judaic religious systems have taken shape, and diverse communities of the faithful, all of them calling themselves "Israel," defined Judaism for themselves. From the inside, those definitions set forth not "our Judaism" or "a Judaism" but simply "Judaism." From the observer's perspective, by contrast, each of the definitions, examined in the context of the life of the group that formulated it, tells us about a Judaism. Then what a history of Judaism will organize and explain is the picture of diverse Judaisms that competed in a given span of time and space. That picture is what I present in this sixth edition of my principal textbook.

The call for this edition, completely revised, after five prior editions, suggests that my approach to the academic study of religion, exemplified by the case of Judaism, will enjoy a reading well into the twenty-first century. My first effort to think through how to teach Judaism commenced in 1964, when I began my teaching career at Dartmouth College. There I formed many of my commitments to undergraduate education, on the one side, and much of my program of the academic study of Judaism, the religion, on the other. This book began, in its first edition, in 1969, emerging from conversations with colleagues and experience with students. The textbook has formed a companion to my personal and professional life. As my children, Samuel, Eli, Noam, and Margalit—to whom, to our great joy, are now added Jill, Samuel's wife, and Andrea, Noam's wife, and their daughter, Emma Rose—have grown and changed in the last quarter-century, so have my wife, Suzanne, in her art, and I in my labor of learning. I claim to remain always a learner, seeking to improve my understanding of matters and my presentation of what I understand. The fact that this book takes a fresh perspective on a subject on which I have worked so long testifies to my goal: to remain always a beginner, still a learner, seeing everything new and fresh every morning.

As in the five prior editions, the changes are many. The most important is that I have rewritten many chapters. I also have dropped some old chapters and added several entirely fresh chapters. These include new and more detailed presentations of Reform and Orthodox Judaism and altogether new chapters on Conservative Judaism and the practice of Judaism in North America. I mean to show how, at the cusp of the new century, Judaism sustains a vivid and influential life for itself, in both the diaspora and the State of Israel. By lengthening the book, I have enhanced its usefulness for courses on Judaism, simply providing much more information and a broader range of ideas than the prior editions. I hope to better serve a new range of students, while continuing to serve the kinds of students who, for more than twenty-five years, have found the book useful.

I now enjoy a dual academic appointment. My primary professorship remains at the University of South Florida, where I hold tenure. An additional, ongoing appointment is at Bard College. This book benefits from my experiences in both types of universities, each typifying the best in the remarkably diverse range of schools that comprise American higher education. One, Bard College, is a small liberal arts college in the Hudson Valley; the other, University of South Florida, a massive state university in a major metropolitan area. The first is select and elite, the other, mass-enrollment; the former, a truly distinguished liberal arts college; the other, a full-service university on the urban frontier. Everyone who loves teaching as I do will envy me for facing the challenges of teaching in two such diverse places. Each makes life interesting in its own way. And what they have in common is truly excellent, productive, and intellectually stimulating departments of religious studies and faculties encompassing academic superstars. I am proud to identify with both centers of higher learning.

If this revision shows merit and attracts a still larger readership than the prior editions, credit belongs to my new editor in this series, Charles Hallisey, to my colleagues at Bard and USF, and to my students.

Jacob Neusner
Distinguished Research Professor of Religious Studies
University of South Florida, Tampa
and
Professor of Religious Studies
Bard College
Annandale-on-Hudson, New York
July 28, 1996, my sixty-fourth birthday

Acknowledgments

This book has gone through four different publishing firms and many more editors, and now, a new series editor, Charles Hallisey, has come aboard. He has given me more help on this project than all the earlier publishers, editors, and series editors put together. When I completed my revisions, he took over and gave innumerable, valuable suggestions, all of them useful, some of them of considerable importance. If this book serves as a more effective classroom presentation of Judaism within the context of the study of religion, it is in formidable measure because of Mr. Hallisey's help. I take much pleasure in working with him and express thanks for his commitment to the book.

No work of mine can omit a word of gratitude for the exceptionally favorable circumstances in which I conduct my research. To the University of South Florida, I express my thanks for not only the advantage of a Distinguished Research Professorship, which must be the best job in the world for a scholar, but also of a substantial research expense fund, ample research time, and some stimulating and cordial colleagues, especially in the department of religious studies—every member of which is a publishing scholar of considerable merit. To Bard, I am indebted for a research grant as well.

I derived much benefit from the anonymous readers of the five prior editions of *The Way of Torah,* in both providing specific corrections and also offering more general comments on how to make this a still more useful textbook. I also thank the reviewers for this sixth edition: Ira Chernus, University of Colorado at Boulder; Daniel J. Evearitt, Toccoa Falls College; Sara R.

Horowitz, University of Delaware; David Timmer, Central College; Theodore Weinberger, Florida International University; and Tzvee Zahavy, University of Minnesota. Because learning proceeds apace and, as time passes, we gain a better grasp of things, there certainly will be a seventh edition, so I earnestly solicit the critical comments of colleagues, teachers, and students alike. These should be sent to me at the Department of Religious Studies, University of South Florida, Tampa FL 33620-5550.

I am considering adding a reader, with sources and discussions, as a companion to this textbook, and I solicit the suggestions of colleagues on what they would find useful in such a supplementary reader. These too should go to my office in Tampa.

I gratefully acknowledge permission to reprint the following copyrighted material:

From *The Grace after Meals,* trans. Judah Goldin (New York: Jewish Theological Seminary of America, 1955), pp. 9, 15ff.

From *Daily Prayerbook,* trans and ed. Philip Birnbaum (New York: Hebrew Publishing, 1949), p. 424.

From *Haggadah of Passover,* trans. Maurice Samuel (New York: Hebrew Publishing, 1949), pp. 9, 13, 26, 27.

From Israel Abrahams, *Hebrew Ethical Wills* (Philadelphia: Jewish Publication Society, 1948), pp. 207–218.

From *Weekday Prayer Book,* ed. Rabbinical Assembly of America Prayerbook Committee, Rabbi Gershon Hadas, chairman, and Rabbi Jules Harlow, secretary (New York: Rabbinical Assembly of America, 1962), pp. 42, 45–46, 50–54, 97–98.

From *A Rabbi's Manual,* ed. by Rabbi Jules Harlow (New York: Rabbinical Assembly of America, 1965), pp. 45, 96.

From A. S. Halkin, "The Judeo-Islamic Age," from *Great Ages and Ideas of the Jewish People*, ed. Leo Schwarz (New York: Random House, 1956).

From Isaak Heinemann, *Judah Halevi, Kuzari* (London: East & West Library, 1957).

From Franz Kobler, *Letters of Jews Through the Ages* (London: East & West Library, 1952), pp. 565–567. © Horovitz Publishing Co. Ltd., 1952.

From Bernard Martin, *Prayer in Judaism,* pp. 84–85, © 1968 by Basic Books, Inc., Publishers, New York. Reprinted by permission of HarperCollins Publishers, Inc.

From *Medieval Jewish Mysticism: The Book of the Pious,* trans. Sholom Alchanan Singer (Northbrook, IL: Whitehall, 1971), pp. 37–38.

From "The Mystical Elements of Judaism," by Abraham J. Heschel in *The Jews: Their History, Culture, and Religion*, ed. Louis Finkelstein, vol. II, pp. 932–951. © 1949, 1955, 1960, 1971 by Louis Finkelstein. By permission of HarperCollins, Publishers, Inc.

Table of Dates

1200 B.C.E.	Exodus from Egypt under Moses; conquest of Canaan under Joshua
1200–1050	Period of the Judges
ca. 1050	Samuel
ca. 1013–973	David, king of Judah and then also of Israel
973–933	Solomon
ca. 930	Kingdom divided
ca. 750	Amos
ca. 735	Hosea
ca. 725	Isaiah
722	Assyrians take Samaria, exile ten northern tribes
639–609	Josiah
620	Deuteronomic reforms
ca. 600	Jeremiah
ca. 590	Ezekiel

1000 ✳ (handwritten annotation)

586	Jerusalem temple destroyed; Judeans exiled to Babylonia
ca. 550	Second Isaiah
538	First return to Zion under Sheshbazzar
520	Zerubbabel, Haggai lay foundation for Temple
515	Temple completed
ca. 444	The priest, Ezra, comes from Babylonia, then under Persian rule, with the task assigned to him by the Persian government of taking over Jerusalem and establishing the Torah as the governing document for the Jews of Jerusalem and surrounding Judea
331	Alexander takes Palestine
168	Antiochus IV prohibits practice of Judaism; Maccabees revolt
165	Temple regained, purified by Maccabees
ca. 100	Community founded at Dead Sea, produces scrolls
63	Romans conquer Jerusalem, which becomes part of the Roman system
37–4	Herod rules as Roman ally
	Hillel
ca. 40 C.E.	Gamaliel I heads Pharisees
70	Destruction of Jerusalem by Romans
	Yohanan ben Zakkai founds center for legal study and judicial and administrative rule at Yavneh
ca. 80–110	Gamaliel heads academy at Yavneh
	Final canonization of Hebrew Scriptures
	Promulgation of Order of Prayer by rabbis
115–117	Diaspora Jewries revolt against Trajan
120	Aqiba leads rabbinical movement
132–135	Bar Kokhba leads messianic war against Rome
	Southern Palestine devastated
140	Rabbis reassemble in Galilee, restore Jewish government

ca. 200	Judah the Prince, head of Palestinian Jewish community, promulgates Mishnah
ca. 220	Babylonian academy founded at Sura by rab
ca. 250	Pact between Jews and Persian King, Shapur I: Jews to keep state law; Persians to permit Jews to govern selves, live by own religion
297	Founding of school at Pumbedita, in Babylonia, by Judah b. Ezekiel
ca. 330	Pumbedita school headed by Abbaye, then Rava, lays foundation of Babylonian Talmud
ca. 400	Talmud of the Land of Israel completed
ca. 400	R. Ashi begins to shape Babylonian Talmud; completed by 600
ca. 450	Genesis Rabbah, commentary out of Genesis on the meaning of Israel's history, and Leviticus Rabbah, historical laws of Israel's society developed out of the book of Leviticus, are completed
ca. 475–500	Pesiqta deRav Kahana, set of essays on the salvation of Israel in the Messianic time, expected fairly soon, worked out
630–640	Moslem conquest of Middle East
ca. 700	Saboraim complete the final editing of Babylonian Talmud
ca. 750	*Problems* of Ahai Gaon; compilation of legal discourses
ca. 780	Death of Anan b. David, leader of Karaite revolt against rabbinic Judaism
882	Birth of Saadya, leading theologian, author of *Doctrines and Beliefs*
ca. 950	*Book of Creation,* mystical work, brief statement on how phenomena of world evolved from God
1040	Birth of Rashi, greatest medieval Bible and Talmud commentator

1096	First Crusade; Jews massacred in Rhineland by crusader armies
1138	Birth of Moses Maimonides
1141	Death of Judah Halevi
1179	Third Lateran Council issues anti-Semitic decrees
1180	Maimonides completes code of Jewish law
1187	Saladin recaptures Jerusalem from crusaders
1190	Riots at Lynn; massacre of Jews at York, England
1233	Inquisition at Aragon
1244	Ritual burning of Talmuds at Paris by church authorities
1247	Papal bull against ritual murder libel
1264	Charter of Boleslav the Pious
1283–1287	Riots against Jews in Rhineland
1290	Expulsion of Jews from England
1298–1299	Riots against Jews of Germany in Rhindfleisch, 1320-1321, Pastoureaux; 1336–1337, Armleder
1306, 1311, 1322, 1349, 1394	Expulsions of Jews from France
1328	Massacres in Navarre
1348–1350	Black death; Jews massacred; migration to Poland begins en masse
1385	Spanish Jews forbidden to live in Christian neighborhoods
1391	Massacres of Spanish Jewry, forced conversions to Christianity
1492	Jews expelled from Spain
1496	Jews expelled from Portugal; mass conversions to Christianity
1506	Secret Jews (*Maranos*) killed in Lisbon

1516	Ghetto introduced at Venice; Jews forced to live in separate neighborhood
1520	First printed edition of Babylonian Talmud
1521	Jewish migrations to Palestine
1542–1543, 1546	Luther preaches against Jews
1553	Talmud burned in Italy
1567	Publication of *Shulhan Arukh,* code of Jewish law, by Joseph Karo
1624	Ghetto law instituted at Ferrara, Italy
1648	Massacres of Polish and Ukrainian Jews
1654	Jewish community founded in New Amsterdam (New York)
1655	Jews readmitted to England by Oliver Cromwell
1658	Newport, RI, Jewish community founded
1665	Sabbetai Zevi proclaimed Messiah in Smyrna, Turkey
1670	Jews expelled from Vienna
1712	First public synagogue in Berlin
1760	Death of Baal Shem Tov, founder of Hasidism
1772	Rabbis of Vilna oppose Hasidism
1786	Death of Moses Mendelssohn, philosopher of Jewish Enlightenment
1789	U.S. Constitution guarantees freedom of religion
1791	Jews receive full citizenship in France
1796	Jews receive full citizenship in Batavia (Holland)
1807	Sanhedrin called by Napoleon
1812	Jews receive partial citizenship in Prussia
1815	Polish Constitution omits Jewish rights
1825	Jews granted full citizenship in Maryland
1832	Jews receive full rights in Canada

1847	Birth of Solomon Schechter, leader of Conservative Judaism in the United States
1866	Emancipation of Jews of Switzerland
1868	Emancipation of Jews of Austria-Hungary
1870	Unification of Italy; ghettos abolished
1873	Founding of Union of American Hebrew Congregations (Reform)
1874	Death of Abraham Geiger, founder of German Reform
1881	Beginning of mass immigration of East European Jews to the United States, Britain, Canada, Australia, South Africa, Argentina
1882	Bilu Movement—beginning of Jewish immigration into Palestine
1885	Pittsburgh Platform of Reform Rabbis renounces hope to return to Zion; affirms reason, progress
1886	Jewish Theological Seminary founded to train conservative rabbis
1888	Death of Samson R. Hirsch, leader of German Orthodoxy
1892	Anti-Semites elected to German Reichstag
1896	Herzl publishes *The Jewish State,* urging the creation of a Jewish State as the solution to the problem of the anti-Semitic politics developing in Europe.
1897	Zionist movement founded at Basel, Switzerland
	The Bund, Jewish Workers Union, founded in Poland as the Jewish section of the international workers' movement; identifies the Yiddish language as its principal instrument of culture
1909	Tel Aviv founded, first Hebrew-speaking city in the world since ancient times
1917	Balfour Declaration favors founding of Jewish national home in Palestine

1933	Hitler becomes chancellor of Germany, Jews begin to lose rights
1935	Nuremberg Laws in Germany; Jews lose all rights
1937	Columbus Platform of Reform Rabbis reaffirms Zionism, Jewish peoplehood
1938	Every synagogue in Germany burned down, November 9
1939–1945	Deportation to death camps and mass starvation, massacres of Jews of Europe
1942	"Final Solution" adopted by German government, systematically to exterminate in death factories created for the purpose of mass-murdering all Jews in German-occupied Europe. Nearly six million are ultimately put to death
1943	Warsaw ghetto revolt
1945	World War II ends; Jews in displaced persons camps
1948	Palestine partitioned; State of Israel created in Jewish part; Jews prohibited from sacred shrines in Jordanian Jerusalem
1967	Jerusalem reunited; ancient Temple wall recovered for Jewish veneration
1973	Yom Kippur War both calls into question the messianic spirit generated in 1967 and intensifies the messianic hope associated with the State of Israel and Jerusalem
1982	Invasion of Lebanon; Christian Lebanese massacre of Palestinian women and children precipitates moral crisis in State of Israel; Kahan commission report invokes Scripture, Talmud in dealing with the matter and condemning it on the basis of collective responsibility
1984	First woman ordained as a Conservative rabbi by the Jewish Theological Seminary of America
1986	Orthodox rabbinical leader addresses Reform rabbis, vice versa, amid talk of schism in Judaism on account of

changes in law of personal status to treat the child of a Jewish father and a non-Jewish mother as a born Jew; established law regards only the child of a Jewish mother as a Jew by birth

1996   U.S. Reform rabbis (Central Conference of American Rabbis) votes to conduct same-sex marriages and to exclude from Reform religious schools children who simultaneously attend Judaic and Christian religious schools

Religious political parties in the State of Israel win more than 20 percent of the vote for the Israeli parliament (the Knesset) and take over major ministries of state: Education, Religion, Interior, and others

PART I

Defining Judaism, the Religion

1

Defining a Religion

RELIGION AS AN ACCOUNT OF
THE SOCIAL ORDER

Judaism is a religion. In general, people define religions by describing what people believe. A definition of Judaism, therefore, could begin with the statement that Judaism believes God is one, unique, and concerned for us and our actions. Thus, Judaism is "ethical" monotheism. But belief is too small a conception of what a religion is and accomplishes. Religion transcends matters of belief, because it shapes behavior and makes a difference when it accounts for the life of the social group that professes that religion. But defining religion mainly in terms of what people do also tells only part of the story. Religion in the abstract invokes definitions that appeal to the inner life and social ethics, to psychology and sociology, to public history and private attitudes. But, then, religion in the abstract does not exist in the everyday world. There we see religions concrete and immediate, but not in the abstract. And when religions take shape, it is always in community: "we" believe, and the "I" belongs to that "we." That is the point at which religion becomes public and factual, not merely private, personal, and idiosyncratic—something we can study, not merely set forth as a matter of fact beyond all analysis and any rational inquiry.

So a definition of propositions and practices without close attention to their social context in the everyday world proves necessary but insufficient. Where religion makes a difference in the world, such that we can study and analyze concrete facts, is in the social reality of specific religions—in history, in community, in the here and now of public action. In this context, then, religion matters for several reasons. First, religion is public; it is social, something people do together; and what people believe tells us only about what individuals think or are supposed to think. Second, religion governs what we do, telling us who we are and how we should live, whereas what people believe tells us only about attitudes. Religion therefore encompasses not only beliefs or attitudes—matters of mind and intellect—but also actions and conduct.

Religion thus combines these two: belief or attitude, worldview, which we may call *ethos,* and also behavior or way of life or right action, which we may call in a broad and loose sense *ethics.* But because religion forms the basis of life of not only or mainly individuals or families but people otherwise unrelated to one another, it must be seen as an account of a social entity or group—for instance, a church, a holy people, or a nation. In that sense, religion explains the social world made up by people who believe certain things in common and act in certain aspects of their lives in common, and so religion accounts for the social entity, which we may call, for the sake of symmetry, *ethnos.* These three things together—ethos, ethics, and ethnos—define religion, which forms the foundation of the life of many social entities in humanity. Indeed, only when we understand that religion does its work in the social world can we begin to grasp why religion is the single most powerful social force in the life and politics of the world today, as in nearly the whole of recorded history. That definition of religion as public and communal serves especially well when we come to Judaism, which, as we shall see, frames its entire message in the setting of the life of a group that calls itself "Israel," meaning the heirs of the holy people of whom the Hebrew Scriptures or Old Testament speak.

How does religion work? A religious system—way of life, worldview, theory of the social entity that lives by the one and believes in the other—identifies an urgent and ongoing question facing a given social group, and it provides an answer that for the faithful is self-evidently valid. To study any vital religion is to address a striking example of how people explain to themselves, by appeal to God's will, word, or works, who they are as a social entity. Religion as a powerful force in human society and culture is realized in society, not only or mainly in theology; religion works through the social entity that embodies that religion. Religions form social entities—"churches," "peoples," "holy nations," monasteries, communities—that, in the concrete, constitute the "us," versus "the nations" or merely "them." And religions carefully explain, in deeds and words every day, who that "us" is. To see religion in this way is to take religion seriously as a way of realizing, in classic documents, a large conception of the world.

RELIGION AS TRADITION OR SYSTEM

Religions may often represent themselves as a tradition, meaning the increment of the ages. They trace their origins to remote beginnings, even to the creation of the world, and set forth their doctrines as unchanging through eternity. They portray themselves as the sole, linear heir of ancient and pure truth. This approach forms one way of validating the faith. Or they may come forth as systems, setting out a cogent statement, a well-crafted set of compelling answers to urgent questions. This approach forms a different, other-than-historical way of validating the faith.

Many religions lay claim to constituting traditions, some to setting forth systems. A religious tradition covers whatever the received sedimentary process has handed on. History then is invoked to justify the religion. A religious system addresses in an orderly way a worldview, a way of life, and a defined social entity. Logic, order, compelling insight—these validate the system, without considering time, location, or circumstance. And both processes of thought, the traditional and the systematic, obey their own rules. The life of intellect may commence morning by morning. Or it may flow from an ongoing process of thought, in which one day begins where yesterday left off, and one generation takes up the task left to it by its predecessors.

A system of thought by definition starts fresh, defines first principles, and augments and elaborates them in balance, proportion, and, above all, logical order. In a traditional process, by contrast, we never start afresh but only add to an ongoing increment of knowledge, doctrine, and mode of making judgment. And, in the nature of such an ongoing process, we never start afresh but always pick, in a received program, the spot we choose to augment. The former process, the systematic one, works from the beginning in an orderly, measured, and proportioned way to produce a cogent and neatly composed statement; a philosophy, for instance. Tradition by its nature is supposed to describe not a system, whole and complete, but a process of elaboration of a given, received truth: exegesis, not fresh composition. And, in the nature of thought, what begins in the middle is unlikely to yield order and system and structure laid forth *ab initio*. In general terms, systematic thought is philosophical in its mode of analysis and explanation, and traditional thought is historical in its manner of drawing conclusions and providing explanations.

So far as "tradition" refers to the matter of process, it invokes, specifically, an incremental and linear process that step-by-step transmits out of the past statements and wordings that bear authority and are subject to study, refinement, preservation, and transmission. In such a traditional process, by definition, no one starts afresh to think things through. Each participant in the social life of intellect makes an episodic and ad hoc contribution to an agglutinative process, yielding, over time, a cumulative deposit. The opposite process we may call systematic, in that, starting as if from the very beginning and working out the fundamental principles of things, the intellect, unbound by received perspectives and propositions, constructs a free-standing and well-proportioned system. The difference is like that between a city that just grows and one that is planned; a scrapbook and a fresh composition; a composite commentary and a work of philosophical exposition.

The one thing a traditional thinker in religion, versus a system builder in religion, knows is that he or she stands in a long process of thought, with the sole task of refining and defending received truth. And the systematic thinker affirms the task of starting afresh, seeing things all together, all at once, in the right order and proportion; a composition, not merely a composite, held together by an encompassing logic. A tradition requires exegesis; a system, exposition. A tradition demands the labor of harmonization and elaboration of the given; a system begins with its harmonies in order and requires not elaboration but merely a repetition, in one detail after another, of its main systemic message. A tradition does not repeat but only renews received truth; a system always repeats because it is by definition encompassing, everywhere saying one thing, which, by definition, is always new. A system in its own terms has no history; a tradition defines itself through the authenticity of its history.

This distinction brings us to Judaism in particular, a set of well-honed religious systems, most of them claiming to set forth the single, received, traditional truth of Sinai—that is, God's revelation to Moses of the Torah. The task of studying Judaism is problematic in the fact that many Judaisms flourish; no single "tradition" predominates. In the United States we know Orthodox, Reform, Conservative, and Reconstructionist Judaisms, all well organized into synagogues and national organizations. In addition flourish New Age Judaisms, synagogues made up of lesbians and homosexual men, and diverse forms of Orthodox Judaisms, some segregated from gentiles, others integrated, each alleging that it alone preserves the true faith of the Torah. Moreover, large numbers of Jews practice no religion at all, and, in recent times, Christians of Jewish ethnic origin ("Messianic Jews") claim to belong to the Jewish community but reject Judaism (and are rejected by all Judaisms and the organized Jewish community as apostates). So the picture is complicated in both social and religious terms—and it should be, for the same complications affected Christianity in the United States. Even among Judaisms, how are we to sort out the theological situation when all Judaisms allege of themselves a linear connection to the Torah—the revelation—of Sinai? No incremental, linear, harmonious history links any Judaism to Sinai, and two or more Judaisms flourish side-by-side at the same time, each with its own community of the faithful.

Two questions will occupy our attention. First, how do we compare and contrast one Judaism with some other, a process that will occupy us in particular when we come to modern and contemporary times? Second, how do we define Judaism in such a way as to take account of the vitality of Judaisms? That issue comes to the fore in the remainder of Part I.

2

Defining Judaism, the Religion

Sorting Out the Religious from the Ethnic

ETHNIC AND RELIGIOUS,
JEWISH AND JUDAIC

Before we can even begin to ask questions about Judaism, the religion, we must confront the single fact about Judaism that most people who know anything at all about Judaism take for granted: Judaism is identified as the religion of the Jews. But, as we will soon see, the Jews in Western democracies form an ethnic group, and in the State of Israel they constitute a nation, and, as a matter of acknowledged fact, not all Jews practice Judaism or any other religion. So at the very outset, we have to identify that about which we are studying—and those who present us with pertinent facts for analysis. We are studying Judaism, the religion, and those Jews who practice Judaism, the religion, supply information about that religion—and not the ethnic or secular Jews who do not practice Judaism though remain good Jews in the ethnic or national context in which they live.

Why does that fact present a problem to the study of Judaism? It is because people confuse the religion, practiced by a determinate group of people, with ethnic opinion at large. If religion speaks for a "we," then those who count themselves in the "we" tell us about the religion, and others do not. But when people confuse an ethnic group with a religious community, then they will take random, individual opinion as a definitive fact for the beliefs of the faith. Then Judaism is the sum total of the opinions held by individual Jews—a mass of confusion and contradiction. We cannot study the religion, Judaism, if we are constantly confronted with the confusion created by the routine claim "But I'm Jewish and I don't believe that" or "But I'm Jewish and I'm not religious at all." Now the importance of recognizing the social character of a religion, its power to explain a particular group's life, comes to the fore: when it comes to describing a religion in its own integrity, there is no "I" but only a "we."

In Chapter 1, "religion" was defined so that when we speak of "Judaism, the religion," we know the genus, a species of which is constituted by Judaism. "Religion" specifies what we study when we study Judaism (or, in light of what has been said, a Judaism), which is the most urgent and abstract. It requires our distinguishing secular Jews, who practice no religion, from religious Jews, who practice a form of Judaism. The former we call simply "Jews," and the latter, the invented term, "Judaists," that is, Jews who practice

Judaism. Once we know both what we want to know and also what does not pertain to our subject at all, we can begin the solid work.

Let us unpack this idea that religion and ethnicity, although often combined, have to be distinguished for the purpose of studying religion. In the United States and Canada, Western Europe and Hispanic America, the Jews form an ethnic group, part of which also practices the religion Judaism. In the State of Israel, the Jews form the vast majority of the population of a nation, only part of which also practices the religion Judaism. Judaism is not the culture of an ethnic group, nor is it the nationalism of a nation-state, even though it is nourished by and helps define both. And there we identify the most subtle but important point of distinction.

If we are to study the religion on its own terms, we must distinguish between the religious and the ethnic and the cultural, for Jews outside the State of Israel, and the national and the cultural, for Jews in the State of Israel. For instance, certain food in certain places is regarded as "Jewish," meaning, a Jewish ethnic specialty. At one time bagels were a Jewish food, so (as I recall from sixth grade) Jews were called "bagel eaters," just as in ancient times they called themselves "garlic eaters." But if we know how to bake bagels, we do not know anything about how Judaism, the religion, views God or virtue or salvation.

The ethnic group and the religion shape the life of one another, but the fate of Judaism as a religion is not the same as the fate of the Jews as a group. If the Jews as a group grow few in numbers, the life of the religion, Judaism, may yet flourish among those who practice it. And if the Jews as a group grow numerous and influential but do not practice the religion Judaism (or any other religion), or practice a religion other than Judaism, then the religion Judaism will lose its voice, even while the Jews as a group flourish. The upshot is simple. A book (that is, a set of religious ideas, divorced from a social entity) is not a Judaism, but the opinions on any given subject of every individual Jew also do not add up to a Judaism. To have a Judaism we require a group of Jews who together set forth a way of life, a worldview, and a theory of who and what they are. Many of the great debates among Judaisms focus on the definition of the word *Israel,* meaning not the nation-state, the State of Israel of our own day, but the people, Israel, of which Scripture speaks. The debate is not a question of the here and now but an issue of what it means to form the people descended from the saints and prophets of that "kingdom of priests and holy people" that God calls into being at Sinai, that defines itself within the Torah. This matter of "what is 'Israel'" and "who is a 'Jew,' meaning who belongs to 'Israel,'" will occupy our attention, much as it is a center of ongoing, contemporary debate among Judaisms and Jews.

We therefore distinguish Jews' opinions as individuals from the system of Judaism as a coherent statement—way of life, worldview, theory of the social entity "Israel." In Chapter 3 we shall ask about the requirements that any religious system claiming to constitute (a) Judaism must meet. Here it suffices to underscore the fact that the ethnic group does not define the religious system. We cannot study Judaism if we identify the history of the Jews with the history of Judaism, just as we cannot study Judaism if we regard the faith as a set of ideas quite divorced from the life of the people who hold those ideas. We have to define our terms and make sure we know precisely that about which, when we study the religion Judaism, we are concerned.

Our problem now is to make sense of this statement: all Judaists—those who practice the religion Judaism—are Jews, but not all Jews are Judaists. That is, all those who practice the religion Judaism, by definition fall into the ethnic group "the Jews," but not all members of the ethnic group practice Judaism. In Parts IV and V, we shall speak only of Judaists in the setting of how Judaism transforms and enchants the everyday life. Before the nineteenth century, no one imagined a person could be a Jew but not practice Judaism; that is, there was no such thing as a "secular Jew" or a "godless Jew."

In modern times—the age in which one can be a secular Jew, remaining Jewish but not practicing Judaism—we must refer to both Jews and Judaists. What we shall see in Chapters 28, for Reform Judaism, and 29, for Orthodox Judaism, is that the political crisis represented by the development of the nation-state, which treated all persons the same, namely, as citizens, required a response. Is Judaism so all-embracing that Jews cannot be citizens? Or does Judaism leave a place in life that is untouched by the sacred, a place for secularity, including citizenship? With the advent of the idea that all citizens are equal before the law, not judged as distinct groups, each with its own definitive traits, the distinction between the religious and the secular leads to the definition of "Judaism" as a religion, a sector of life, but not the whole of life. Raising these issues here may be premature, but it is important at the very outset to recognize that, in the modern sense of "religion" as distinct from "culture," Judaism had to be turned into a religion as much as Christianity did.

TWO COMPLICATIONS
IN STUDYING JUDAISM

Two complications require attention at the outset, both of them involving the Jews as a secular, ethnic group. First comes the paradox that is central to Judaism. Here is a religion that addresses all humanity with a message of what God wants of all creation but is identified with a particular ethnic group, the Jews. The universality of its focus, the religion's concern for the entire history and destiny of the human race, and its message of salvation are framed in terms that involve a specific group of people. When everyone that belonged to that people believed in God and practiced Judaism, then that "people" corresponded, in Judaism, to "the Church, the mystical body of Christ," in Christianity; that is, "people" stood for "holy community," a religious group. Then, everyone understood, to form "Israel" was not the same thing as to form a nation or an ethnic, secular community. It meant to form a holy community, a church in Christian terms. But in modern times some Jews gave up the practice of Judaism without adopting any other religion and furthermore, by everyone's lights, remained part of the group, which, consequently, lost its clear-cut character as a religious community like other religious communities and came to be seen as an ethnic group. The group defined itself by common traits of ethnicity, for instance, customs and ceremonies, rather than by a common religion involving divine commandments and sacred rites. But within the group, many continue to practice Judaism. Not only so, but as we shall see, people convert to the religion, Judaism, and as a matter of common practice, that conversion admits them also to the ethnic group. And Jews who give up Judaism for another religion are regarded as having left the ethnic group. Clearly, matters are complicated.

Studying Judaism carries us to an everyday and familiar religion, so we begin with the single most puzzling problem that anyone faces in dealing with Judaism, which is, the relationship between the religion, Judaism, and the ethnic group, the Jews. The puzzle comes about because only some of the Jews practice Judaism, but all of them regard all those who practice Judaism as not only "Judaists" ("people who observe the Judaic religion") but also as "Jews" (members of the ethnic community). To study Judaism the religion, therefore, we must distinguish the religion from the ethnic group and identify the former as the object of our study.

Second, for the vast majority of those who read this book, there is the Christian problem. It is the fact that not only do people not always realize that secular Jews do not represent Judaism, but they bring to the Jews and Judaism attitudes framed within Christianity, which attributes to Judaism negative traits. Jews and Judaism stand in a special relationship to Christians and Christianity (sometimes called "its daughter religion") because the founders of Christianity—Jesus, the evangelists, and apostles—all considered themselves part of "Israel" the holy people or, in our language, Jews who practiced and taught Judaism. The reason that that special relationship poses particular problems for studying Judaism is simple. Christianity, originating among Jews in the world of Judaism, has for the whole of its history set forth doctrines that concern Judaism. Later we shall consider some of the main lines of the relationship between Judaism and Christianity. Even at the outset, however, we have to recognize that the special relationship puts obstacles in the way of academic study, which involves accurate description, objective analysis, and informed interpretation of the religion in its own terms.

For nearly the whole of its history, until the middle of the twentieth century, Christianity declared Judaism a dead religion, superseded by Christianity. Christianity further taught that "the Jews killed Christ" and treated the Jews' loyalty to their own religion as a mark of perfidy and unbelief in Christianity. Deep, poisoned wells of hatred watered the soil of Christianity for nearly the whole of its history, and anti-Judaic (against the religion) and anti-Semitic (against the group) doctrines and attitudes have impeded, and today impede, Christian study of Judaism. The Holocaust was perpetrated by pagans but also by Christians. While many Catholic and Orthodox priests and Protestant ministers were imprisoned and even killed, with the German armies and their allies marched Christian chaplains, and they sang "Silent Night" at Auschwitz and the other German concentration camps and death factories for several Christmases, in the midst of the everyday murder of millions of people, most of them Jews. That is why the principal Christian churches have reviewed their doctrine of Judaism and reconsider that religion.

That Jews and Christians live in sufficient numbers so that most people who read these pages will also know Jews as friends, neighbors, coworkers, and fellow students therefore forms both an advantage and a disadvantage. Judaism is familiar to Christians in a way in which, at this time, Islam or Hinduism or Buddhism is not, because of, first, the social integration that marks the situation of the Jews in most Western countries, and, second, the widespread representation of Judaism, the religion, among the religions of the Western countries. Prior knowledge, established impressions—these help in the academic study of the religion. We move from the known to the unknown.

THE UNIVERSAL RELIGION
OF AN ETHNIC GROUP

Of the two problems—the confusion of the ethnic and the religious, the heritage of negative opinion about Judaism and anti-Semitism against the Jews as a group—the former poses the more formidable obstacle to studying Judaism. Often what we know we have learned from Jewish friends or neighbors, and their opinions or impressions of Judaism may not correspond to any of the expressions of Judaism, the religion, past or present, about which you will learn in these pages. The reason is that not all Jews practice a religion at all; some are quite secular. And confusion also results from the several forms of Judaism that are practiced. The former—the fact that not all Jews practice Judaism or any other religion—creates a great deal of confusion. Knowing secular Jews leaves the impression that Judaism, the religion, is dead, which is far from the truth. Knowing Jews whose practices are personal and marginal to the received faith, in any of its contemporary formulations, leaves puzzling impressions about the actuality of the religion. For Judaism, like all religions, is a community of faith, public and social, not just the personal idiosyncrasy of this one or that one.

If that fact is obvious, a further consequence of the secularity of some Jews and the religiosity of others has now to come to the fore. It is the confusion of the ethnic and Jewish with the religious and Judaic that characterizes not only gentiles' but also Jews' impressions of the state of affairs. Not all Jews practice Judaism or any other religion. Hence, not all Jews provide authentic information on the religion Judaism. But many think they do. Right at the outset, therefore, studying about Judaism must address the confusion of the ethnic with the religion, the personal and impressionistic with the public, communal, and doctrinal. Otherwise, as we just noted, we shall end up confusing personal opinion with public faith. All religions deal with the gap between

what the books say and what the faithful do; everyone knows that most
Catholics practice birth control, which Church doctrine condemns, for example. But in the case of Judaism, that quite familiar fact—the gap between
the official faith (in its several formulations) and everyday practice—is joined
by a second one, which is not routine.

No one confuses the Catholic faith with the ethnic culture of Italians,
Poles, Austrians, Spaniards, Germans, or Brazilians—Catholics all. To be a
Lutheran is not necessarily also to be a Finn, Dane, Swede, Norwegian, or
German. Everyone understands that there is a Catholic or a Lutheran faith
that is distinct from the various ethnic cultures that take shape in dialogue
with that faith, that transcends the particularities of circumstance. Brazilian
and American Pentecostals know the difference between nationality and religion. So, too, Judaism is not an ethnic religion, and the opinions of an ethnic
group cannot serve to define that religion. Practice of the singular faith takes
diverse forms in different circumstances, so that the national culture of the
State of Israel, infused though it is with Judaism, is not the same thing as Judaism, nor is the ethnic culture of American Jews.

You would be misled, however, if you suppose that, among Jews, the ethnic and the religious are as readily sorted out as they are among Catholics,
Lutherans, or Pentecostals. The reason is that, in the United States and
Canada, the Jews themselves confuse the ethnic with the religious, hence random opinions of Jews with Judaism, the religion. No one can study Judaism
without addressing this question, because, if we ignore the confusion, what
we learn in the classroom and what we see in the streets will not cohere. We
shall have no way of understanding the public realities of a complex community: faithful and secular joined together in various ways and varying proportions. It is a waste of time to study a religion if out of the study we do not
understand the workaday world of that religion. So before we address the traits
of Judaism, the religion, we must address the relationship of the ethnic to the
religious in the social world in which Judaism takes place.

PUBLIC RELIGION VERSUS
PERSONAL RELIGIOSITY: WHAT IS
AT STAKE IN DISTINGUISHING
RELIGION FROM ETHNICITY?

When ethnic attitudes are confused with religious doctrines, the opinion of a
given Jew, based on secular opinion or merely personal considerations and not
in dialogue with the holy books of Judaism, is taken to speak for the religion
Judaism. But, in fact, the holy books of Judaism and the great body of believers may not hold such a view at all. Some simple examples make the point.
Some Jews may declare themselves atheists. But Judaism teaches that one,
unique God created the world and gave the Torah. Other Jews may not

believe in the resurrection of the dead. But Judaic worship, whether Orthodox or Reform (matters we shall consider much later), affirms that God raises
the dead and "keeps faith with those that sleep in the dust." A public opinion
poll might produce broad Jewish consensus in favor of abortion. Judaism, the
religion, in its classical formulation condemns abortion from the ninetieth
day after conception. (Some contemporary Judaic formulations do not concur.) So, too, many Jews regard "Judaism" as the foundation for liberal opinion, even quoting verses of Scripture to prove their point. But among the
faithful—that is, among those who practice a Judaism of one kind or
another—considerable debate takes place on whether Judaism is conservative
or liberal or even whether these contemporary political categories apply at all.
Because of these simple facts, the confusion of the ethnic and the religious
must be addressed head-on. Otherwise, the representation of Judaism in these
pages, based as it is on the classical sources of Judaism and contemporary practice of Judaism in synagogues by the faithful, will conflict with the impressions
we gain from everyday life.

How come personal opinion takes the place of public religious doctrine?
The reason is that in North America, Europe, Latin America, the South Pa-
cific, and South Africa, Judaism, the religion, finds itself wrapped around by
Jewishness, the ethnic identity of persons who derive from Jewish parents and
deem "being Jewish" to bear meaning in their familial and social life and cultural world. In considering the facts of Judaism that the world presents, therefore, we have always to remember that the Jews form a community, only part
of which practices Judaism. Some may even join synagogues and attend public
worship mainly to be with other Jews, not to engage in public worship. They
may wish to use the synagogue to raise their children "as Jews," whereas in
their homes they practice no form of Judaism. A key institution of Judaism,
the Sabbath, is praised by a secular thinker in these words: "More than Israel
has kept the Sabbath, the Sabbath has kept Israel." That is, the Sabbath is
treated as instrumental, Israel the secular group as principal. But in Judaism,
the Sabbath is a holy day, sanctified by Israel, the holy people, and not a means
for some ethnic goal of self-preservation.

To explain the mixture of ethnic and religious, a simple case serves for illustration. The word *Israel* today generally refers to the overseas political nation, the State of Israel. When people say, "I am going to Israel," they mean a
trip to Tel Aviv or Jerusalem, and when they speak of Israeli policy or issues,
they assume they refer to a nation-state. But the word *Israel* in Scripture and
the canonical writings of the religion Judaism speaks of the holy community
that God has called forth through Abraham and Sarah, to which God has given
the Torah ("teaching") at Mount Sinai, of which the Psalmist speaks when he
says, "The One who keeps Israel does not slumber or sleep." The Psalmists
and the Prophets, the sages of Judaism in all ages, the prayers that Judaism
teaches, all use the word *Israel* to mean "the holy community." "Israel in Judaism forms the counterpart to the Church, the mystical body of Christ" in
Christianity. Among most Judaisms, to be "Israel" means to model life in the
image, after the likeness, of God, who is made manifest in the Torah. Today

"Israel" in synagogue worship speaks of that holy community, but "Israel" in Jewish community affairs means "the State of Israel."

That example of the confusion of this-worldly nation with holy community by no means ends matters. In the Jewish world outside the State of Israel, Jews form a community, and some Jews (also) practice Judaism. To enter the Jewish community, which is secular and ethnic, a gentile adopts the religion Judaism; his or her children are then accepted as native-born Jews, without distinction, and are able to marry other Jews without conversion. So the ethnic community opens its doors not by reason of outsiders' adopting the markers of ethnicity, the food or the association or the music, but by reason of adopting what is not ethnic but religion. And to leave the Jewish community that is ethnic, one takes the door of faith. Here comes a further, but not important, complication. Although not all Jews practice Judaism, in the iron consensus among contemporary Jews, Jews who practice Christianity cease to be part of the ethnic Jewish community, whereas those who practice Buddhism remain within. Buddhism, not a monotheism (not even theistic), is viewed as a philosophy, not a competing religion. Christianity, monotheist as is Judaism, reaching back to the same Scriptures, viewing the history of humanity within the same structures, sharing much in traditions of ethics, is a competing religion. For Jews and the diverse Judaisms, moreover, the long and bloody record of Christian antipathy to the Jews and Judaism, the massacres and pogroms and "Christ-killer" epithets, the annual Passion narratives with their dreadful portrayal of "the Jews"—these serve to place Christianity outside the range of commitments that the Jewish ethnic community can tolerate. And, as to those that practice Judaism, to adopt any other theistic religion is to apostatize, pure and simple.

The upshot is that the ethnic and the religious in the world of the Jews present confusion. Our task here is to sort out the confusion by identifying the religion Judaism in particular. This we do by describing the teachings and practices of the faith as these are set forth in the holy books, on the one side, and in the attitudes and actions of the faithful, on the other. In that way, Judaism, the religion, takes its place, for comparison and contrast, beside other religions, described within the same framework.

3

The Ecology of Judaism

JUDAISMS AND JUDAISM

When we deal with Judaism, we pay close attention to the various groups of Jews who do practice the religion they call Judaism, while respecting the differences that separate these groups from one another. This approach requires that we learn how to respect the plurality of Judaic religious systems and speak of Judaisms or "a Judaism" when we mean a specific Judaism religious system.

The change in our normal way of speaking—from Judaism to Judaisms—will prove less jarring if we remember that, when we speak of Christianity, we ordinarily mean, a particular Christian religious system. Christianity encompasses a remarkably diverse set of religious systems that have some qualities in common—belief in Jesus Christ—but also differ deeply, especially about matters on which they seem at first glance to concur. For example, who, exactly, was, and is, Jesus Christ? No one imagines that by describing a single common denominator Christianity tells us about one unitary religion. Catholic, Protestant, and Orthodox, Methodist, Mormon, and Lutheran—each is comprised by clearly delineated groups of Christians, all of them with their respective systems of belief and behavior. Just from the very beginning, when Peter and Paul contended about absolutely fundamental issues of faith, as the world knows Christianities, but no single Christianity, so the world has known, and today recognizes, diverse Judaisms, but no single Judaism.

If we were studying Christianity, we would differentiate Catholic from Protestant, noting that Italian, Hispanic, German, and Irish Catholics practice a common religion but differ on ethnic grounds, so when studying Judaism we differentiate one Judaism from another, noting that the ethnic group, the Jews, also thrives partly concentric with but partly beyond the circles of the faithful.

What holds all Judaisms together and permits us to speak of not only Judaisms but Judaism? The answer has two parts. First, all Judaisms address a common set of questions, those that derive from the situation of the Jews in the world. Second, all Judaisms recapitulate—go over, in one way or another—a single pattern, one that Scripture initially set forth and that, in one language or another, each Judaism reworks in its own context and terms. That does not mean there ever was, or is, a single Judaism, all Judaisms concurring on that common-denominator definition of matters. It does mean that, viewed all together and all at once, all Judaisms do work on some questions in common, and all of them do conform to a single pattern.

What emerges, therefore, is a set of responses to a single ecological circumstance. Here is where the ethnic and the religious, the Jewish and the Judaic, come together and where diverse Judaisms meet and become Judaism. Let me explain a point that governs all that follows in these pages.

THE ECOLOGY OF RELIGION

Ecology is a branch of science concerned with the interrelationships of organisms and their environments. By "ecology of…," I mean the study of the interrelationship between the religious world a group constructs for itself and the social and political world in which that same group lives. I refer to the interplay between a particular, religious system's way of viewing the world and living life, and the historical, social, and especially political situation of the people who view the world and live life in accord with the teachings of their religion. The Jewish people form a very small group, spread over many countries. One fact of Jews' natural environment is that they form a distinct group in diverse societies. A second is that they constitute solely a community of fate and, for many, of faith, but that alone, in that they have few shared social or cultural traits. A third is that they do not form a single political entity. A fourth is that they look back on a very long and in some ways exceptionally painful history. The Holocaust—the murder of millions of Jews in Europe in German death factories—has intensified Jews' sense of themselves as a persecuted group and obscured the long history of stable, secure life that they have enjoyed in various times and places, a thousand years in Poland, for example, and long centuries in much of the Muslim world. But Scripture itself presents its account of the people of Israel as the story of disaster and destruction.

A worldview suited to the Jews' social ecology must make sense of their unimportance and explain their importance. It must explain the continuing life of the group, which in important ways marks the group as different from others, and persuade people that their forming a distinct and distinctive community is important and worth carrying on. The interplay between the political, social, and historical lives of the Jews and their conceptions of themselves in this world and the next (that is, their worldview, contained in their canon, their way of life, explained by the teleology of the system, and the symbolic structure that encompasses the two and stands for the whole all at once and all together) define the focus for the inquiry into the ecology of a Judaism.

Obviously, by using the word *ecology*, borrowed from the natural sciences, I want to introduce an unusual metaphor into the study of religions. Ecology is a branch of science concerned with the interrelationship of organisms and their environments. By "ecology of religions," I mean the study of the interrelationship between a religious way of viewing the world and living life, and the historical and social situation of the people who view the world and live life in accord with the teachings of their religion. The Jewish people are a very small group, spread over many countries.

Judaism cannot be studied, or even defined, outside the historical experience of the Jewish people. But it also cannot be studied solely within that experience—as if there is no such thing as Judaism, but merely the this-worldly culture of the Jewish group. There *is* such a thing as (a) Judaism, which may stand definition and analysis in the same way that any other religion may be defined and analyzed. A Judaism is no less difficult to define and describe than any other religious system. It holds no mysteries accessible only to people who originate in a Jewish family, and nothing about Judaism is inaccessible to the accepted methods and procedures of the academic study of religions.

THE ECOLOGY OF JUDAISM:
COMPARING JUDAISMS

When we recognize that an ahistorical idea of religion gives way to the reality of religions as they exist in history, we also find insight by comparing one religion to another. This gives perspective on each, allows us to see the choices that face various, kindred religions, and underscores what makes each religion distinct. The same is so when we recognize that within a given religion we discern differences of such importance as to require us to differentiate one religious system from another within a family of such systems. So a labor of comparison and contrast between Judaisms is called for. How shall we carry it out? The task of analyzing a Judaism requires four steps. First, we need to ask about the context of that Judaism: where, when, how come it came into being. Second, we require a description of the worldview at hand, which allows us to identify the urgent question to which a given Judaic system responds. Third, we want an account of the way of life as well: what do people do because of the worldview that motivates them? Finally, because a Judaism is deemed by its participants to set forth teaching that is self-evidently true, we ask about the basis for the allegation that the system at hand enjoys the status of a Judaism of self-evidence. When we consider the various Judaic religious systems that took shape in modern times, we shall follow this program of comparing and contrasting Judaisms. And that leads to the final, and critical, question of systemic description and analysis: what turns all Judaisms into one family of religious systems, or, in simple terms, species of a common genus?

THE ECOLOGY OF JUDAISM:
WHAT HOLDS THE WHOLE TOGETHER

We cannot reduce all Judaisms to a single common denominator. But we can point to traits that will characterize a Judaism and no other religious system.

One idea predominates in nearly all Judaic religious systems: the conception that the Jews are in exile but have the hope of coming home to their own

land, which is the Land of Israel (a.k.a. Palestine). The original reading of the
Jews' existence as exile and return derives from the Pentateuch, the Five Books
of Moses, which were composed as we now have them (out of earlier materials, to be sure) in the aftermath of the destruction of the Temple in 586 B.C.E.
In response to the exile to Babylonia, the experience selected and addressed
by the authorship of the document is that of exile and restoration. But that
framing of events into the pattern at hand represents an act of powerful imagination and interpretation. That experience taught lessons people claimed to
learn from the events they had chosen and from the Pentateuch, which took
shape in 450 B.C.E. when some Jews returned from Babylonia to Jerusalem, for
their history:

> The life of the group is uncertain, subject to conditions and stipulations.
> Nothing is set and given, all things a gift: land and life itself. But what ac-
> tually did happen in that uncertain world—exile but then restoration—
> marked the group as special, different, select.

There were other ways of seeing things, and the Pentateuchal picture was
no more compelling than any other. Those Jews who did not go into exile
and those who did not "come home" had no reason to take the view of matters that characterized the authorship of Scripture. The life of the group need
not have appeared more uncertain, more subject to contingency and stipula-
tion, than the life of any other group. The land did not require the vision that
imparted to it the enchantment, the personality, that, in Scripture, it received:
"The land will vomit you out as it did those who were here before you." And
the adventitious circumstance of Iranian imperial policy—a political happenstance—did not have to be recast into return. So nothing in the system of
Scripture—exile for reason, return as redemption—followed necessarily and
logically. The religion does not simply describe how things are. It imposes its
own vision on the everyday and makes sense of the world by appeal to that vision. Judaism forms an act of interpretation, not of description, of the life of
Israel.

That experience of the uncertainty of the life of the group in the century
or so from the destruction of the First Temple of Jerusalem by the Babylonians in 586 to the building of the Second Temple of Jerusalem by the Jews,
with Persian permission and sponsorship returned from exile, formed the paradigm. With the promulgation of the "Torah of Moses" under the sponsorship of Ezra, the Persians' viceroy, in approximately 450 B.C.E., all future Israels
would then refer to that formative experience as it had been set down and
preserved as the norm for Israel in the mythic terms of that "original" Israel—
the Israel not of Genesis and Sinai and the end at the moment of entry into
the promised land, but the "Israel" of the families that recorded as the rule
and the norm the story of both the exile and the return. In that minority genealogy, that story of exile and return, alienation and remission, imposed on
the received stories of preexilic Israel, adumbrated time and again in the Five
Books of Moses, and addressed by the framers of that document in their work
overall, we find that paradigmatic statement in which every Judaism, from

then to now, found its structure. What we are dealing with is a kind of language that people use to make sense of the world, a language that names the things of the world and imposes a relationship on those things. The language does not just replicate the world out there but makes it intelligible. In our terms, religion supplies an account of the deep syntax of social existence, the grammar of its intelligible message.

No Judaism recapitulates any other, and none stands in a linear and incremental relationship with any prior one. But all Judaisms recapitulate that single paradigmatic experience of the Torah of "Moses," the authorship that reflected on the meaning of the events of 586–450 selected for the composition of history and therefore interpretation. That experience (in theological terms) rehearsed the conditional moral existence of sin and punishment, suffering and atonement and reconciliation, and (in social terms) the uncertain and always conditional national destiny of disintegration and renewal of the group. That moment captured within the Five Books of Moses—that is, the judgment of the generation of the return to Zion, led by Ezra—about its extraordinary experience of exile and return would inform the attitude and viewpoint of all the Israels beyond.

Let me now spell out this theory accounting for the character and definition of all of the diverse Judaisms that have taken shape since the destruction of the first Temple of Jerusalem in 586 and the return to Zion, building of the second Temple of Jerusalem, and writing down of the Torah, a process complete in 450 B.C.E. Because the formative pattern imposed that perpetual, self-conscious uncertainty, treating the life of the group as conditional and discontinuous, Jews have asked themselves who they are and invented Judaisms to answer that question. Accordingly, on account of the definitive paradigm affecting their group life in various contexts, no circumstances have permitted Jews to take for granted their existence as a group. Looking back on Scripture and its message, Jews have ordinarily treated as special, subject to conditions and therefore uncertain, what (in their view) other groups enjoyed as unconditional and simply given. Why the paradigm renewed itself is clear: this particular view of matters generated expectations that could not be met; hence, it created resentment and then provided comfort and hope that made possible coping with that resentment. To state my thesis with appropriate emphasis: *Promising what could not be delivered, then providing solace for the consequent disappointment, the system at hand precipitated in age succeeding age the very conditions necessary for its own replication.*

There have been many Judaisms, each with its indicative symbol and generative paradigm, each pronouncing its worldview and prescribing its way of life and identifying the particular Israel that, in its view, is Israel, bearer of God's original promise. But each Judaism retells in its own way and with its distinctive emphases the tale of the Five Books of Moses, the story of a no-people that becomes a people, that has what it gets only on condition, and that can lose it all by virtue of its own sin. That is a terrifying, unsettling story for a social group to tell of itself, because it imposes acute self-consciousness, chronic insecurity, on what should be the level plane and firm foundation of society. That is, the collection of diverse materials joined into a single tale on the occasion of the original exile and restoration because of the repetition in age succeeding age also precipitates the recapitulation of the interior experience of exile and restoration—always because of sin and atonement.

So it is the Pentateuch that shaped Jews' imagination wherever they lived, and it is their social condition as a small and scattered group that made the question raised by the Pentateuchal narrative urgent, and it is the power of the Pentateuch both to ask and to answer the question that made the answer compelling whenever and wherever Jews (that is, "Israel") lived. Now that we have formulated a theory of the history of Judaism, let us turn from the historical and contemporary context of the Judaic religious system to its contents. Each Judaism sets forth the way of Torah—God's teaching. But to define "Torah" precisely, we must pay attention to each Judaism in turn.

4

The History of Judaism

Brief Definitions

SOCIAL ENTITY, WAY OF LIFE,
WORLDVIEW: ETHNOS, ETHICS, ETHOS

In an everyday encounter with diverse Jews (which could take place in any large American city or in London, Paris, Tel Aviv, Johannesburg, or Sydney), the first thing you would notice is that some wear head coverings and others do not. Among those that do, some cover their head with a skull cap and others wear a hat. Once you get to know Jews, you will discover that some observe the Sabbath and others do not. Some do so by attending services but otherwise conduct themselves in an ordinary way; others spend the day in ways different from the ordinary routine. If all tell you they practice Judaism, then you face the challenge of sorting out the data that they supply: this one eats this, not that, and that one eats everything—and so on through tens of thousands of facts. Our job, then, is to learn how to classify the facts so as to see the generalizations that they yield. These generalizations, deriving from the facts properly classified, will allow us to differentiate one Judaism from another.

How shall we know when we have a Judaism? The answer to that question draws us to the data—the facts—we must locate and describe, analyze and interpret.

Israel

The first requirement is to find a group of Jews who see themselves as "Israel," that is, the Jewish People who form the family and children of Abraham, Isaac, Jacob, Sarah, Rebecca, Leah, and Rachel, the founding fathers and mothers. That same group must tell us that it uniquely constitutes "Israel," not *an* Israel, the descriptive term we use.

Worldview/Torah

The second requirement is to identify the forms through which that distinct group expresses its worldview. Ordinarily, we find that expression in writing, so we turn to the authoritative holy books that the group studies and deems God given—that is, the group's Torah or statement of God's revelation to Israel. Because we use the word *Torah* to mean biblical books, starting with the

Five Books of Moses (Genesis, Exodus, Leviticus, Numbers, and Deuteronomy), we must remind ourselves that the contents of the Torah have varied from one Judaism to the next. Some groups regard as holy what other groups reject or ignore.

A more suitable word than *Torah,* therefore, is *canon,* meaning the collection of authoritative writings. The canon contains much of the group's worldview and describes its way of life. We err, of course, if we treat as our sole source of facts only what is in writing.

Way of Life/Commandments

A group expresses its worldview in many ways: through dance, drama, rite and ritual; through art and symbol; through politics and ongoing institutions of society; through where it lives, what it eats, what it wears, what language it speaks, and the opposites of all these—what it will not eat, where it will not live. Synagogue architecture and art bear profound, powerful, visible messages. The life cycle, from birth through death, the definition of time and the rhythm of the day, the week, the month, and the year—all of these testify to the worldview and way of life of the social group that, all together, all at once, constitute a Judaism.

In the long history of the Jews, groups of people who regarded themselves as "Israel," that is, groups of Jews, have framed many Judaisms. What permits us to make sense of the history of these Judaisms is the fact that, over time, we are able to identify periods in which a number of Judaisms competed and other times in which a single Judaism predominated. The historical perspective therefore permits us to sort out the Judaisms that have flourished, keeping each by itself for the purpose of description, analysis, and interpretation, and also to hold the Judaisms together in a single continuum, over time and space, of the whole of which, all together and all at once, we can make sense. By recognizing that a given Judaism came into existence at a time in which Judaisms competed, and by understanding that, at another point, a single Judaism defined the Jews' way of life, worldview, and social existence as a distinct entity, we may understand how the diverse facts—writings, theologies, definitions of what matters in the everyday life, doctrines of the end of time and the purpose of life—fit together, when they cohere or do not fit together, and when, in fact, they prove discrete.

DIVERSE HISTORIES OF JEWS:
THE HISTORY OF JUDAISM

In studying the history of Judaism, we concentrate not on the Jews as an ethnic group but on the Judaic religious systems that various groups in diverse times and places have set forth as an account of the social world that diverse ethnic groups, all of them regarding themselves as "Jewish" or as "Israel," have adopted. The Jews as a people have not had a single, unitary, and continuous history. They have lived in many places, centuries here, centuries there, and what happened in one place rarely coincided with what happened in some other place. When Jews in the Iberian Peninsula flourished, those in other parts of Western Europe (for example, England, France, and Germany) perished; when, in 1492 and 1497, respectively, the Spanish and Portuguese governments expelled Muslims and Jews, Jews in Poland and the Turkish empire flourished. Only rarely did the histories of many distinct and different communities of Jews coincide (for example, during the horror of the mass extermination of European Jews between 1933 and 1945 in Germany and German-occupied Europe).

But if the ethnic group proves too diverse and distinct to treat as whole and harmonious (except as a matter of theology in the conception of Israel, God's first love, or as a matter of ideology in the conception that the Jews form a people, one people), we can treat as a coherent whole, harmonious and unitary, the history of the Judaic religious system, or Judaism. Let me specify the periods of the history of Judaism: first, an age of diversity; then an era of definition; third, a time of essential cogency; and, finally, a new age of diversity. I will discuss these in greater detail in the next chapter.

THE FIVE FACTS THAT DEFINE THE HISTORY OF JUDAISM—THE ENTIRE HISTORIES OF ALL JUDAISMS

Because the definition rests on historical facts of the life of Israel, the Jewish people, I must list the five facts of political history that mark off everything else. These facts derive from the histories of various groups of Jews, in diverse times and places, and govern the history of the Jews and also Judaism from the beginning to the present. In the next chapter, we shall treat these same secular facts as major indicators of the several periods in the history of Judaism.

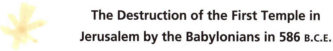 The Destruction of the First Temple in Jerusalem by the Babylonians in 586 B.C.E.

The ancient Israelites, living in what they called the Land of Israel, produced Scriptures that reached their present form in the aftermath of the destruction of their capital city and Temple. Whatever happened before that time was reworked in the light of that event and the meaning imputed to it by authors who lived afterward. All Judaisms, from 586 forward, appeal to the writings produced in the aftermath of the destruction of the first Temple. These writings encompass the Pentateuch—Genesis, Exodus, Leviticus, Numbers, and Deuteronomy—and also important prophetic works. Therefore, we must regard the destruction of that Temple as the date that marks the beginning of the formation of Judaism(s).

The Destruction of the Second Temple
in Jerusalem by the Romans in 70 C.E.

The Jews' leaders—the political classes and priesthood—after 586 were taken to Babylonia, the homeland of their conquerers, where they settled down. A generation later, Babylonia fell under the rule of the Persians, who permitted Jews to return to their ancient homeland. A small number did so, where they rebuilt the Temple and produced the Hebrew Scriptures. The second Temple of Jerusalem lasted from about 500 B.C.E. to 70 C.E., when the Romans—by that time ruling the entire Middle East, including the Land of Israel, mainly through their own friends and allies—put down a Jewish rebellion and, in the war, destroyed Jerusalem again. The second destruction proved final and marked the beginning of the Jews' history as a political entity defined in social and religious terms, but not in territorial ones. That is, the Jews formed a distinct religious-social group, but all of them did not live in any one place, and some of them lived nearly everywhere in the West, within the lands of Christendom and Islam alike.

The Conquest of the Near and Middle East
and North Africa by the Muslims in 640 C.E.

The definition of the world in which the Jews would live was completed when the main outlines of Western civilization had been worked out. These encompassed Christendom, in Western and Eastern Europe, inclusive of the world west of the Urals in Russia; and Islam, in command of North Africa and the Near and Middle East, later destined to conquer India and much of the Far East, Malaysia, and Indonesia in particular, as well as sub-Saharan Africa. During this long period, the Jews in Christendom and Islam alike ordinarily enjoyed the status of a tolerated but subordinated minority, and they were free to practice their religion and sustain their separate group existence. Of still greater importance, both Christianity and Islam affirmed the divine origin of the Jews' holy book, the Torah, and acknowledged the special status, among the nations, of Israel, the Jewish people.

The American Constitution (1789)
and the French Revolution (1787)

The American Constitution in the United States and the French Revolution in Western Europe marked the beginning of an age in which political change reshaped the world in which the West, including Western Jewries, lived. Politics became essentially secular, and political institutions no longer acknowledged supernatural claims of special status accorded to either a church or a religious community. The individual person, rather than the social group, formed the focus of politics. In the case of the Jews, the turning meant that the Jews would be received as individuals and given rights equal to those of all others, at the same time that "Israel" as a holy people and community no longer would enjoy special status and recognition.

The Destruction of the Jews in Europe ("the Holocaust")
and the Creation of the State of Israel, 1933–1948

In 1933 Germany chose the National Socialist Party to govern. A principal doctrine of that party was that various groups among humanity, called races, possess traits that are inherent in the genes and passed on through time: racial characteristics. Some races have good traits, others, bad; and the worst of all of these "races" are the Jews. To save humanity from this dreadful "curse," all of the Jews of the world have to be murdered, which will constitute "the final solution of the Jewish problem." This racist doctrine, broadly held in Europe and elsewhere during World War II, from 1939 to 1945, led to the Germans' murder of nearly six million European Jews. In the aftermath of World War II, seeking a home for the remnants who had survived, the United Nations voted in 1947 to create a Jewish and an Arab state in what was then Palestine. The Jewish state came into being on May 15, 1948, as the State of Israel.

These events defined an entirely new ecology for Judaism. On the one hand, the problem of evil was restated with great intensity. On the other hand, the social and political life of the Jews was entirely redefined. The issue of "exile and return," paramount at the outset, was framed with fresh urgency, but with a new resolution. The formation of the State of Israel in the aftermath of the Holocaust opened a new chapter in the history of Judaism, but that chapter's story is not yet clear.

5

The Four Periods in
the History of Judaism

How shall we organize the histories of various Judaisms, each with its beginning, middle, and (in some cases) end, into a single history of Judaism? The answer is to survey the long history of Judaisms and find the traits of the periods into which that history breaks down. One paramount fact imposes structure on the history of Judaism: for a long time, a single Judaism, rabbinic Judaism, predominated. Its success in defining the normative faith for nearly the whole Jewish world is marked in two ways. First, that Judaism absorbed into its own system new modes of thought and piety—philosophy and mysticism being the main ones. Second, that same Judaism defined the terms by which its competition—"heresies"—defined themselves. That is, the competition adopted doctrines antithetical to those of rabbinic Judaism, rather than building fresh and free-standing systems of its own. To define the issues of debate means to dominate, and rabbinic Judaism dominated, specifically, from ancient times to nearly our own day, for nearly 1,800 years. When we speak of Judaisms, in both ancient and modern times, we must not lose sight of the fact that, through most of the history of Judaism into contemporary times, rabbinic Judaism defined the norm.

In fact, the history of Judaism is the story of how diverse Judaisms before 70 C.E. gave way to that single Judaism that predominated from 70 onward and of how, in the modern age, rabbinic Judaism broke up into derivative Judaisms and lost its commanding position as the single, defining force in the life of the Jews as a social group. Here we consider the history of Judaism as a whole. In later units we return to important chapters in that history, examined in detail, with an emphasis on modern times. Seen whole, the history of Judaism the religion divides into the following four principal periods. (Note that in place of B.C., "before Christ," and A.D., "in the year of the Lord," we use the secular terms B.C.E., "before the Common Era," and C.E., "in the Common Era." They mean the same.)

The first age of diversity	About 586 B.C.E.–70 C.E.
The age of definition	About 70–640 C.E.
The age of cogency	About 640–1800 C.E.
The second age of diversity	About 1800–present

The first age of diversity begins with the writing down, in more or less their present form, of the Scriptures of ancient Israel, beginning with the Five

Books of Moses. Drawing upon writings and oral traditions of the period before the destruction of the first Temple of Jerusalem in 586, the authors of the
surviving leadership of that Temple and court, the priests, produced most of
the books we now know as the Hebrew Bible (the "Old Testament" or
"Tanakh")—specifically, the Pentateuch or Five Books of Moses; the prophetic
writings from Joshua and Judges through Samuel and Kings and Isaiah, Jeremiah, and Ezekiel; the twelve smaller books of prophetic writings; and some
of the other Scriptures as well. During this same period, several diverse groups
of Jews, living in the Land of Israel and Babylonia, to the east, and in Alexandria, Egypt, to the west, took over these writings and interpreted them in various ways. Hence, during the period from the formation of the Torah to the
destruction of the second Temple, there were many Judaisms.

The age of definition, beginning with the destruction of the second
Temple in 70, saw the diverse Judaisms of the preceding period give way, over
a long period of time, to a single Judaism. That was the system worked out by
the sages who, after 70, developed a system of Judaism linked to Scripture but
enriched by an autonomous corpus of holy writings in addition. This Judaism
is marked by its doctrine of the dual media by which the Torah was formulated and transmitted, in writing on the one side, in formulation and transmission by memory, hence, orally, on the other. The doctrine of the dual Torah,
written and oral, then defined the canon of Judaism. The written Torah encompassed pretty much the same books that Christians know as the Old Testament. The oral Torah added the writings of the sages, beginning with the
Mishnah—a philosophical law code produced in approximately 200 C.E.—and
two massive commentaries on the Mishnah—the two Talmuds, one produced
in the Land of Israel and called the Yerushalmi, or Jerusalem Talmud, circa
400 C.E., the other in Babylonia and called the Bavli, or Talmud of Babylonia,
circa 600 C.E. In that same age, alongside Mishnah commentary, systematic
work on Scripture yielded works organized around particular books of the
written Torah, parallel to works organized around particular tractates of the
Mishnah: Sifra, to the book of Leviticus; Sifré, to Numbers; and another Sifré,
to Deuteronomy. Also written during this time were works containing statements attributed to the same authorities who stand behind the Mishnah, to be
dated sometime between 200 and 400; Genesis Rabbah and Leviticus Rabbah, discursive works on themes in Genesis and Leviticus, edited between 400
and 450; Pesiqta deRav Kahana, a profoundly eschatological treatment of topics in pentateuchal writings, of about 450; and similar works. These writings
all together—organized around, first, the Mishnah, and, then, Scripture—
comprised the first works of the oral Torah. That is, the teachings of the sages,
originally formulated and transmitted in memory, were the written contents
of the oral Torah that God had revealed (so the system maintained) to Moses
at Sinai. During the age of definition, that Judaism of the dual Torah reached
its literary statement and authoritative expression.

The age of cogency is characterized by the predominance, from the far
West in Morocco, to Iran and India, and from Egypt to England, of the
Judaism of the dual Torah. During this long period, the principal question

facing Jews was how to explain the success of Christianity and Islam, which claimed to replace the Judaism of Sinai with a new testament, on the one side, or a final and perfect prophecy, on the other. Both religions affirmed but then claimed to succeed Judaism, and the Judaism of the dual Torah enjoyed success, among Jews, in making sense of the then-subordinated status of the enduring people and faith of Sinai. While heresies took shape during this long period, the beliefs of the new systems responded to the structure of the established one.

   The second age of diversity is marked not by the breaking apart of the received system but by the development of competing systems of Judaism. In this period, new Judaisms came into being that entirely ignored the categories and doctrines of the received system, responding not to its concerns but to other issues altogether. Now the principal question addressed by new systems concerned matters other than those found urgent by the received Judaism of the dual Torah, with its powerful explanation of the Jews' status in the divine economy. The particular points of stress, the self-evident answers to urgent questions, came at the interstices of individual life. Specifically, Jews needed to explain to themselves how as individuals, able to make free choices on their own, they found a place also, within the commanded realm of the holy way of life and worldview of the Torah of Judaism. The issue again was political, but it concerned not the group but the individual. Judaisms produced in modern times answered the urgent question of individual citizenship, just as the Judaism of the long period of Christian and Muslim hegemony in Europe, Africa, and western Asia had taken up the (then equally pressing) question of a subordinated, but in its own view holy, society's standing and status as Israel in Islam or Christendom.

THE FIRST AGE OF DIVERSITY
(circa 586 b.c.e.–70 c.e.)

The destruction of Jerusalem in 586 B.C.E. produced a crisis of faith, because ordinary folk supposed that the god of the conquerors had conquered the God of Israel. Israelite prophets saw matters otherwise. Israel had been punished for its sins, and it was God who had carried out the punishment. God was not conquered but vindicated. The pagans were merely his instruments. God could, moreover, be served anywhere, not only in the holy and promised Land of Israel. Israel in Babylonian exile continued the cult of the Lord through worship, psalms, and festivals; the synagogue, a place where God was worshipped without sacrifice, took shape. The Sabbath became Israel's sanctuary, the seventh day of rest and sanctification for God. When, for political reasons, the Persians chose to restore Jewry to Palestine and many returned (about 500 B.C.E.), the Jews were not surprised, for they had been led by prophecy to expect that with the expiation of sin through suffering and atonement, God would once more show mercy and bring them homeward. The prophets' message was authenticated by historical events.

In the early years of the Second Temple (about 450 B.C.E.), Ezra, the priest-scribe, came from Babylonia to Palestine and brought with him the Torah, the collection of ancient scrolls of law, prophecy, and narrative. Jews resolved to make the Torah the basis of national life. The Torah was publicly read on New Year's Day in 444 B.C.E., and those assembled pledged to keep it. Along with the canonical Scriptures, oral traditions, explanations, instructions on how to keep the law, and exegeses of Scripture were needed to apply the law to changing conditions of everyday life. A period of creative interpretation of the written Torah began, one that has yet to end in the history of Judaism. For that time forward, the history of Judaism became the history of the interpretation of Torah and its message for each successive age.

THE AGE OF DEFINITION
(circa 70–640 c.e.)

The next great event in Jews' history was the destruction of the Second Temple in 70 C.E.. A political and military event, its religious consequences were drawn by Yohanan ben Zakkai and other great rabbis of the age. These rabbis, heirs of the tradition of oral interpretation and instruction in Torah and the continuators of the prophets of old, taught that the God of Israel could still be served by the Jewish people, who had not been abandoned by God but once more chastised. The rabbis in the following Talmudic story—told not after 70 but after a deep disappointment three hundred years later—taught that by obedience to Torah, Israel would again be restored to its land:

> When a disciple of Yohanan ben Zakkai wept at seeing the Temple mount in ruins, Yohanan asked him, "Why do you weep, my son?"
>
> "This place where the sins of Israel were atoned is in ruins, and should I not weep?" the disciple replied.
>
> "Let it not be grievous to your eyes, my son," Yohanan replied, "for we have another means of atonement, as effective as Temple sacrifice. It is deeds of loving-kindness, as it is said [Hosea 6:6], *For I desire mercy and not sacrifice.*"

In our own century, we have seen how historical events—the destruction of European Jewry, the creation of the State of Israel—defined the issues that Judaic religious systems would have to address. So we cannot find it surprising that once again a historical event produced a major religious revolution in the life of Judaism. That revolution is embodied in the pages of the Palestinian and Babylonian Talmuds, compendia of Judaic law, lore, and theology produced by the rabbis of Palestine and Babylonia on the basis of the ancient oral tradition and finally edited in the fifth and sixth centuries C.E. Once and for all, the rabbis defined "being Jewish" in terms of laws universally applicable, laws that might be kept by Jews living in every civilization. Wherever Jews might go, they could serve God through prayer, study of Torah, practice of the commandments, and acts of loving-kindness. All Jews were able to study.

No clerical class was required—only learned men. So rabbis took the priests' place as teachers of the people.

The Jews thus formed a commonwealth within an empire, a religious nation within other nations, living in conformity with the laws of alien governments, but in addition carrying out their own Torah. It was a commonwealth founded on religious belief, a holy community whose membership was defined by obedience to laws believed to have been given at Sinai and interpreted and applied by rabbinical sages to each circumstance of daily life.

We see, therefore, that the first age of diversity, the age from the formation of the Pentateuch in about 500, to before the first century C.E., was a period in which religious experiences and beliefs of various kinds, among diverse groups, took shape among the Jewish people, the people of ancient (and modern) Israel. One principal development in that long period was the Hebrew Scriptures, called by Christians the Old Testament and by Jews *Tanakh* (for the letters beginning the Hebrew words for the three parts of the document: *Torah* or Pentateuch, *Nebi'im* or Prophets, and *Ketubim* or Writings—hence *T–N–K*). As we must realize, the Hebrew Scriptures are a mosaic of different kinds of books, about different sorts of religious experiences and teachings, all addressed to a single group of people, ancient Israel, and all brought together and united solely by their common audience.

The formative generations of rabbinic Judaism, the next period, drew upon more than the ancient Hebrew Scriptures. The formative generations flowed out of particular groups in the world of Judaism that read these Scriptures in a particular way and that had a distinctive approach to the religious life of the community of Israel. Three main components of Jews' religious life in the last two centuries B.C.E. and the first century C.E. deserve our attention. These components, not mutually exclusive, are (1) the priests, with their commitment to the Temple of Jerusalem and its sacred offerings and to governance of the people of Israel in accord with the orderly world created by and flowing out of the Temple; (2) the scribes, with their commitment to the ancient Scriptures and their capacity to interpret and apply these Scriptures to the diverse conditions of the life of the people (later on, the heirs of the scribes would gain the honorific title of "rabbi," which was not distinctive to their group of Jews or even to the Jews); and (3) the messianic Zealots, who believed that God would rule the Jews when foreign rulers had been driven out of the Holy Land. Obviously, these three components were talking about different things to different people.

Of these three groups, one predominated in the shaping of events in the first century C.E., and the other two fused thereafter. Until the destruction of the Temple of Jerusalem in 70 C.E., the messianic Zealots were the most powerful force in the history of the Jews. For they precipitated the single most important event of the time: the war fought against Rome from 66 to 73 C.E., climaxed by the fall of Jerusalem in 70 C.E. And the messianic Zealots must have remained paramount for another three generations, because the next major event in the Jews' history was yet a second, and still more disastrous, holy and messianic war against Rome fought under the leadership of Ben

Kosiba (also called Bar Kokhba, the Star's Son) from 132 to 135 C.E. That war surely was a mass uprising, which tells us that a large part of the population was attracted to the Zealot way of thinking.

The other two groups—the priests and the scribes—with their interest in continuity, order, and regularity lost out both times. The priests of the Temple saw the destruction of their sanctuary in 70 C.E. and realized after 135 C.E. that it would not be rebuilt for a long time. The scribes who taught Scriptures and administered their law witnessed the upheavals of society and the destruction of the social order that war inevitably brings in its aftermath. Although both groups doubtless shared in the messianic hopes, they most certainly could not have sympathized with the policies and disastrous programs of the messianic Zealots.

THE AGE OF COGENCY
(circa 640–1800 C.E.)

The age of cogency ran on into the nineteenth century, which does not mean no other Judaic systems existed. It means that the Judaism of the dual Torah set the standard. A heresy selected its "false doctrine" by defining in a way different from the Judaism of the dual Torah a category emerging in that Judaism of the dual Torah. Such a group was the Karaites, who believed that the Torah of Sinai encompassed only the written part and rejected the authority of the books that rabbinic Judaism called "the Oral Torah" (discussed later). Shifts and changes of all sorts occurred. But the Judaism of the dual Torah absorbed into itself and its structure powerful movements, such as philosophy, on the one side, and mysticism (called Qabbalah), on the other, and found strength in both of them. The philosopher defended the way of life and worldview of the Judaism of the dual Torah. The mystic observed the faith defined by that same way of life as the vehicle for gaining his or her mystical experience. So when we see the Judaism of the dual Torah as cogent for nineteen centuries, it is not because the system remained intact and unchanged but because it was forever able to take within itself, treat as part of its system of values and beliefs, a wide variety of new concepts and customs. This span is an amazingly long time for something so volatile as a religion to have remained essentially stable and to have endured without profound shifts in symbolic structure, ritual life, or modes of social organization for the religious community.

The Judaism that predominated during that long period and that has continued to flourish in the nineteenth and twentieth centuries bears a number of names: *rabbinic* because of the nature of its principal authorities, who are rabbis; *Talmudic* because of the name of its chief authoritative document after the Hebrew Scriptures, which is the Talmud; *classical* because of its basic quality of endurance and prominence; or, simply, *Judaism* because no other important alternative was explored by Jews.

What proved the stability and essential cogency of rabbinic Judaism during the long period of its predominance was the capacity of rabbinic Judaism—its modes of thought, its definitions of faith, worship, and the right way to live life—to take into itself and to turn into a support for its own system a wide variety of separate and distinct modes of belief and thought. Of importance were, first, the philosophical movement and, second, the mystical one. Both put forward modes of thought quite distinct from those of rabbinic Judaism.

Philosophers of Judaism raised a range of questions and dealt with those questions in ways essentially separate from the established and accepted rabbinic ways of thinking about religious issues. But all of the philosophers of Judaism not only lived in accord with the rabbinic way of life; all of them were entirely literate in the Talmud and related literature, and many of the greatest philosophers were also great Talmudists. The same can be said of the mystics. Their ideas about the inner character of God, their quest for a fully realized experience of union with the presence of God in the world, their particular doctrines, with no basis in the Talmudic literature produced by the early rabbis, and their intense spirituality were all thoroughly "rabbinized"—that is, brought into conformity with the lessons and way of life taught by the Talmud. In the end, rabbinic Judaism received extraordinary reinforcement from the spiritual resources generated by the mystic quest. Both philosophy and mysticism found their way into the center of rabbinic Judaism. Both of them were shaped by minds that, to begin with, were infused with the content and spirit of rabbinic Judaism.

THE SECOND AGE OF DIVERSITY
(circa 1800–THE PRESENT)

Only in modern times have other religious consequences been drawn from cataclysmic historical events. Because Judaism had developed prophecy and rabbinic leadership, it was able to overcome the disasters of 586 B.C.E. and 70 C.E. The challenge of modern times comes not only from the outside but also from within: the nurture of new religious leadership for Jews facing a world of new values and ideals. Religion provides a particularly subtle problem for students of the process of modernization. In other areas such as politics and economics, that which is "modern" may meaningfully be set apart and against that which is "traditional," but in religion the complexities of the process of social change become most evident, the certainties less sure.

What happened in modern times is that new questions arose that rabbinic Judaism did not address. In the nineteenth century, continuator-Judaisms, referring to the same authoritative books as rabbinic Judaism but finding in them answers to questions not previously addressed, came to the fore. They did not replace rabbinic Judaism in its historical forms; they simply took shape as other Judaisms, alongside that Judaism and related to it in fundamental ways. The new Judaisms of the nineteenth century all wanted to know how people could be both "Israel"—God's holy people—and also other things, citizens of the nation-state in which they lived, for example. All of them differentiated a religious from a secular part of everyday life, making space in that secular corner for Jews' other commitments and concerns besides religion. Reform, integrationist-Orthodox, and Conservative Judaisms all responded to the critical issues Jews in Western countries wished to address.

In the twentieth century, essentially secular systems responded to yet another set of questions. These questions derived not from the challenges of other religions but rather from the political crisis represented by the rise of racist anti-Semitism, which identified the Jews as the source of all evil and denied them the right to live at all. Zionism in the first half of the twentieth century and the Judaism of Holocaust and Redemption in the second half responded to that crisis by explaining the conditions under which Jews could endure. From the last third of the nineteenth century onward, many Jews began to understand that the promises of Enlightenment and emancipation would never be kept; indeed, they were false to begin with. Western civilization had no place for the Jews, who had to build their own state as a refuge from the storms that were coming upon them. These Jews rejected that fundamental teleological optimism, rationalism, yielding patience, and quietism with which classical Judaism had viewed the world. They did not believe that the world was so orderly and reliable as Judaism had supposed. They regarded Judaism as a misleading and politically unwise view of the Jewish people and their worldly context. What was needed was not prayer, study of Torah, and a life of compassion and good deeds.

What the hour demanded was renewed action, a reentry into politics, and the repoliticization of the Jewish people. Zionism was the movement that redefined the Jewish people into a nation and revived the Jews' ancient political status. So far as Zionism saw the world as essentially irrational and unreliable, unable to proceed in the orderly, calm, reasonable fashion in which Judaism assumed the world would always do its business, Zionism marked an end to Judaism as it had been known. The fact that Zionism would in time take up the old messianic language and symbolism of Judaism and make over these ancient vessels into utensils bearing new meaning is not to be ignored. But at its beginning, Zionism marked a break from Judaism, not because of Zionism's messianic fervor but because of its rejection of the quiet confidence, rationalism, and optimism of rabbinic Judaism.

Thus, these two things—the promise of emancipation and the advent of racist and political anti-Semitism—fell so far outside the worldview of rabbinic Judaism that they could not be satisfactorily interpreted and explained within the established system. The result was the breakdown of the Judaic system for many, many Jews. The system of Judaism was not overturned; for these people, it simply had become implausible. It had lost the trait of self-evidence. To state matters very simply: rabbinic Judaism was and is a system of balance between cosmic, teleological optimism and short-term skepticism—a system of moderation and restraint, of rationalism and moderated feeling. Just as it came into being in response to the collapse of unrestrained Messianism, feelings unleashed and hopes unbounded by doubt, so it came to an end, where and when it did come to an end, in a renewed clash with those very emotions and aspirations that, in the beginning, it had overcome: passionate hope and unrestrained, total despair. A system of optimistic skepticism and skeptical optimism, a world grasped with open arms and loved with a breaking heart, could never survive those reaches toward the extremes, those violations of the rules and frontiers of moderate and balanced being, that characterize modern times.

THE HISTORY OF JUDAISM AND
THE HISTORY OF THE JEWS

The Jews have written a diverse history that exhibits no single, continuous narrative. In each area of the world where Jews have lived, what happened to them in that place and time is to be examined in its own terms. Thus, at the same time that, in one part of the world, one group of Jews lived in peace and security, another, elsewhere, did not. In 1492, for example, with the Christian reunification of Spain, the Jews and Moors (Muslims) were expelled from the country, and in 1497, Portugal did the same. Jews had lived in Spain and Portugal from Roman times, so the end of nearly fifteen centuries of continuous history marks a considerable calamity. At the same time, however, Jews found a safe home in the Turkish Empire, which extended throughout the Middle East and into the Balkans. A history of the Jews in that part of the world would tell a very different story. That is why a single, unitary, harmonious, and linear history of the Jews, treating the history of diverse groups in various places as one story, is misleading.

The various Judaisms too have had their own histories, though, as we have seen, one of those Judaisms, the rabbinic, has enjoyed the longest continuous history and the greatest influence. A uniform and continuous history of a single Judaism would require us to treat as coherent and whole a vast variety of conflicting convictions and practices. In addition, we would then miss what made these convictions and practices important in their own distinctive settings. To understand a given Judaism, we need not tell everything that was happening to the Jews in all parts of the world of the age of that Judaism, let alone everything that came before or afterward. The history of rabbinic Judaism cannot be told by an account of the facts of the life of the Jews in Poland, Germany, Spain, or North Africa. As a matter of fact, no unitary, single history of the Jewish people, from the beginning to now, has ever succeeded in holding together in a sound, proportionate manner the remarkably diverse and distinctive histories of the Jews in Poland, Germany, Spain, or North Africa, let alone North America and Hispanic America. If the Jews have written no single, linear history, a number of Judaisms have; among them, the critical one, rabbinic Judaism, does cohere from its origins in ancient times to today.

At the same time, what has happened to the Jews—their diverse histories in various times and places—has shaped the histories of Judaisms in all times and places, because Jews bring to the Torah the concerns and challenges that everyday life presents. During prosperity, the issue of the purpose of the good life will predominate. In a society that accords Jews equality and welcomes them as part of society, the issue of why Jews should remain separate and distinct takes priority. The Holocaust made urgent the problem of evil—how could an all-powerful, loving God permit such things to happen? Every Judaism found itself required to frame an answer to that question. Hence, although we recognize the difference between the ethnic and the secular, and the religious and the sacred, we also must keep in mind how the Jews' experience as an ethnic group formulates for any Judaism a set of urgent questions, emerging from everyday life, that all Judaisms of that time and place must address.

In the following pages, we consider the religion Judaism, with special emphasis on the paramount Judaism, the one defined by "our sages of blessed memory" or rabbis—thus rabbinic Judaism. At the same time, when we study the history of that Judaism (among all Judaisms), we also want to know how what was happening to the Jews made an impact on the issues of Judaism, the religion. This consideration becomes especially important when we come to the splitting of that single, rabbinic Judaism in modern times into a number of distinct Judaisms, all of them deriving from the rabbinic one. Then the history of the Jews emerges as a defining force in the history of Judaism. In this book, Part II presents Judaism in the ages of formation and cogency, and Part III portrays the second age of diversity.

6

Defining Judaism

Why Don't the Jews Believe in Christ?

ere we step aside from the narrative of the history of rabbinic Judaism to address a question every Christian reader brings to this book: Why Judaism at all? Why, in other words, did the Jews of the first century not accept Jesus as Christ or Messiah, and why do the Jews over time, to the present day, persist in practicing Judaism rather than Christianity? These are not questions that Judaism has to answer for itself or that belong in an account of that religion, but they naturally occur to students of Judaism. People tend to frame the question in terms of origins: "Why didn't the Jews accept Christ?" This they may reframe as "Why don't the Jews believe in Christ (today)?" The truth is, Christianity finds it necessary to formulate a judgment on Judaism, but Judaism does not have to formulate a judgment on Christianity or Islam. Nonetheless, we gain perspective on the history of Judaism by raising questions of contrast and comparison, and in the real world of competing religions, the study of religion should take up the basis for competition and conflict. And no two religions have coexisted for so long or so intimately as the two religions that emerge out of ancient Israel and its Scriptures.

THE JUDEO–CHRISTIAN
CONFLICT OVER SCRIPTURE

But Christians ask, and their question deserves serious attention. To answer the question very simply: the Jews who practice Judaism do not believe in Jesus as Christ because they believe in the Torah of Moses. They have a religion too, and it is not Christianity but Judaism. The Judaic faithful do not meet God Incarnate in Jesus Christ because they meet God in the Torah as expounded by "our sages of blessed memory." They do not practice Christianity because they practice Judaism. They have a religion of their own, which they believe to be true. That's why.

The circumstance that Christianity reveres the sacred writings that Judaism knows as the Written Torah and Christianity as the Old Testament is only part of the reason that the question proves chronic. The other part is that, as everyone knows, the earliest Christians were Jews and saw their religion as normative and authoritative: (a) Judaism. A natural question troubling believing Christians, therefore, is why Judaism as a whole remains a religion that believes other things, or, as Christians commonly ask, "Why did the Jews not 'accept Christ'?" or "Why, after the resurrection of Jesus Christ, is there Judaism at all?" Often asked negatively, the question turns on why the Jews do not believe rather than on what they do believe. Yet it is a constructive question, for it leads us deeper into an understanding of not only the differences between one religion and the other but also the traits of the religion under study. In other words, it is a question of comparison—even though the question is not properly framed.

In their shared Scriptures, Judaism and Christianity meet and separate. Thus, any account of Judaism written in a context in which Christianity forms the predominant religion must deal with the conflict over Scripture that in part defines the context in which Judaism reads its own holy books. For, we now realize, the Torah, oral and written, in Judaism corresponds to the Bible, Old and New Testaments, in Christianity, and although the two faiths share the written Torah/Old Testament, they also differ radically on its meaning. What they have in common is what divides them. Not only so, but Christianity always recognized in the oral Torah, particularly the Talmud of Babylonia, the most formidable obstacle standing in the way of the conversion of the Jews. During the Middle Ages, Christian authorities outlawed, condemned, and burned the Talmud, on a single occasion, in Paris in 1290, collecting hundreds of ox carts of documents and committing them to the flames. It makes sense, therefore, to consider the relationship of Judaism and Christianity in the setting of the holy books of Judaism, which, Judaic and Christian faithful concur, have made all the difference.

THE ORAL TORAH AND THE CHALLENGE OF CHRISTIANITY

Christianity—with its fully articulated Bible, made up of the Old Testament and the New Testament, with its claim to succeed and replace the old Israel, with its proof for the kingship of Jesus as Christ in the Christian empire, and with its dismissal of Israel after the flesh as now rejected and set aside by God—presented a powerful challenge to Judaism as the sages defined matters. They countered with the dual Torah, with the reaffirmation of holy Israel as God's first love, with the claim that the Messiah will come in the future and that the prophetic promises have not yet been fulfilled. Just as Christianity found in the Bible ample proof for its claim, so sages found in the Torah probative evidence on behalf of theirs. The issue became urgent in the fourth century, when Christianity could no longer be ignored by the sages, as, in general, it had been. Christianity became licit, then favored, and, finally, the official religion of the Roman Empire.

With the triumph of Christianity through Constantine and his successors in the West, from the legalization of Christianity in 312 to its establishment as religion of the state by the end of the fourth century, Christianity's explicit claims, now validated in world-shaking events of the age, demanded a reply. The sages of the two Talmuds provided it. At those very specific points at which the Christian challenge met head-on old Israel's worldview, sages' doctrines responded. What did Israel's sages have to present as an answer to the cross? It was the Torah.

The Torah took three forms. It was defined in the doctrine, first, of the status, as oral and memorized revelation of the Mishnah and, by implication, other rabbinic writings. The Torah was also presented as the encompassing symbol of Israel's salvation. Finally, the Torah was embodied in the person of the Messiah who, of course, would be a rabbi. The Torah in all three modes confronted the cross, with its doctrine of the triumphant Christ, Messiah and king, ruler now of Earth as of heaven. The dual Torah formed the generative symbol for the Judaism that triumphed: it dealt with the urgent and critical question that had to be confronted, and it provided an answer that, to believers, was self-evidently valid—both points necessary and sufficient. When we come to modern times, we shall see how when Christianity met competition from secular sources of truth, so did Judaism.

A FAMILY QUARREL,
AN ISRAELITE CIVIL WAR

Because both Christians and Judaists claim to inherit the ancient Israelite Scriptures and the promises God made to Israel of old, the conflict between Judaism and Christianity takes place within Israel: an Israelite civil war. It goes without saying that each party to the debate pointed to verses of Scripture that proved its point and disproved the point of the other side. Both parties found it easy, moreover, to address the other side's proof and dismiss it. The upshot is that each group talked to its adherents about its points of urgent concern—that is, different people talking about different things to different people. Incomprehension marks relations between Judaism and Christianity in the first century as much as in the twentieth, yet then as now the groups were two sectors of the same people. Each addressed its own agenda, spoke to its own issues, and employed language distinctive to its adherents. Neither exhibited understanding of what was important to the other. Recognizing that fundamental inner-directedness may enable us to interpret the issues and the language used in framing them. For if each party perceived the other through a thick veil of incomprehension, the heat and abuse that characterized much of their writing about one another testify to a truth different from that which conventional interpretations have yielded. If the enemy is within, if I see only the mote in the other's eye, it matters little whether there is a beam in my own.

The key is this: the incapacity of either group to make sense of the other. We have ample evidence for characterizing as a family quarrel the relationship between the two great religious traditions of the West. Only brothers can hate so deeply, yet accept and tolerate so impassively, as have Judaic and Christian brethren both hated yet taken for granted each other's presence. Christianity wiped out unbelievers but under ordinary circumstances adhered to the doctrine that the Jews were not to be exterminated. Nevertheless, from the first century onward, the echoes of Matthew's Pharisees as hypocrites and John's Jews as murderers poisoned the Christian conscience. Jews grudgingly recognized that Christianity was not merely another paganism. But then they knew the truth and rejected it. So maintained a first-century rabbi, Tarfon. He said in so many words that Christians knew God but denied him, knew the Torah but did violence against its meaning. Today we recognize in these implacably negative projections signs of frustration, anger at someone who should know better than to act as he does, a very deep anger indeed. That anger corresponds to Christian impatience with what it deemed Israel's "unbelief."

THE PHARISEES

The Pharisees are represented in some of the Gospels as leading critics of Jesus, and they also formed one of the principal groups that created the Mishnah and hence founded the Judaism of the dual Torah. The kind of Judaism that emerges from the first century—rabbinic Judaism—thus draws heavily on the methods and values imputed to the Pharisees in the later rabbinic literature. Some of the same authorities identified in the New Testament as Pharisees occur in the Mishnah as sages, notably, Gamaliel. So let us narrow our discussion to that group among first-century Judaisms that in the event contributed substantially to the Judaism that later became normative. And when we speak of Christianity, let us, following the same principle, specify a particular aspect of the rich and various belief of the church represented in the writings of the evangelists. That aspect, the common denominator of the Gospels, finds full expression in the simple claim that Jesus Christ came to save humanity. Hence, we shall center on the salvific aspect of the Christianity represented by the Gospels (though not by them alone).

What was at issue between Jesus and the Pharisees? It was, in simple words, salvation versus sanctification. The Judaism defined by the system and method of the Pharisees (whom we met in the person of Yohanan ben Zakkai in connection with the destruction of the Second Temple by the Romans in 70) addressed the issue of the sanctification of Israel, whereas Christianity as defined by the evangelists took up the question of Israel's salvation. Both were expressions of Israel's religion; one spoke of one thing, the other of something else. In retrospect, although they bear some traits in common, the two groups appear in no way comparable. Why not? The Gospels portray the first Christians as the family and followers of Jesus. So, as a social group, Christianity represented at its outset in a quite physical, familial, and genealogical way "the body of Christ." The Pharisees, by contrast, hardly formed a special group at all. It is easier to say what they were not than what they were. How so? Although the Pharisees appear as a political group by the first century in Josephus's writings about Maccabean politics, the Gospels and the rabbinic traditions concur

(handwritten margin note: written afterwards to make Jews look bad)

that what made an Israelite a Pharisee was not exclusively or even mainly politics. The Pharisees were characterized by their adherence to certain cultic rules. They were not a member of a family in any natural or supernatural sense. Their social affiliations in no way proved homologous.

The Christians carried forward one aspect of Scripture's doctrine of Israel, and the Pharisees another. The Hebrew Scriptures represent Israel as one very large family, descended from a single set of ancestors. The Christians adopted that theory of Israel by linking themselves, first, to the family of Jesus and his adopted sons, the disciples, and second—through him and them to his ancestry—to David and on backward to Abraham, Isaac, and Jacob (hence the enormous power of the genealogies of Christ). The next step—the spiritualization of that familiar tie into the conception of the church as the body of Christ—need not detain us. But Scripture did not restrict itself to the idea of Israel as family; it also defined Israel as a kingdom of priests and a holy people. That is the way taken by the Pharisees. Their Israel found commonality in a shared, holy way of life, required of all Israelites—so Scripture held. The Mosaic Torah defined that way of life in both cultic and moral terms, and the prophets laid great stress on the latter. What made Israel holy—its way of life, its moral character—depended primarily on how people lived, not on their shared genealogy.

Both Christians and Pharisees belonged to Israel but chose different definitions of the term. The Christians saw Israel as a family; the Pharisees saw it as a way of life. The Christians stressed their genealogy; the Pharisees their ethos and ethics. The Christian family held things in common; the holy people held in common a way of life that sanctified them. At issue in the argument between them are positions that scarcely intersect held by groups whose social self-definitions are incongruent.

Christians were a group composed of the family of Israel, talking about salvation; Pharisees were a group shaped by the holy way of life of Israel, talking about sanctification. The two neither converse nor argue. For groups unlike one another in what, to begin with, defines and bonds them, groups devoid of a common program of debate, have no argument. They are different people talking about different things to different people. Yet, as is clear, neither group could avoid recognizing the other. What ensued was not a discussion, let alone a debate, but only a confrontation of people with nothing in common pursuing programs of discourse that do not in any way intersect. Not much of an argument.

DIFFERENT PEOPLE TALKING ABOUT
DIFFERENT THINGS TO DIFFERENT PEOPLE

Christianity (represented by Jesus in the Gospels) and Judaism (represented by the Pharisees) each took over the inherited symbolic structure of Israel's religion. Each, in fact, did work with the same categories as the other. But, in the hands of each, the available and encompassing classification system found wholly new meaning. The upshot was two religions out of one, each speaking within precisely the same categories, but so radically redefining the substance of these categories that conversation with the other became impossible.

What is the similarity? Christ embodies God, just as the Talmudic sage, or rabbi, in later times would be seen to stand for the Torah incarnate. What is the difference? Christ brought salvation, and, for the ages to come, the Talmudic sage promised salvation.

Salvation, in the nature of things, concerned the whole of humanity; sanctification, equally characteristic of its category, spoke of a single nation, Israel. To save, the messiah saves Israel amid all nations, because salvation categorically entails the eschatological dimension and so encompasses all of history. No salvation, after all, can last only for a little while or leave space for time beyond itself. To sanctify, by contrast, the sage sanctifies Israel in particular. Sanctification categorically requires the designation of what is holy against what is not holy. To sanctify is to set apart. No sanctification can encompass everyone or leave no room for someone in particular to be holy. One need not be "holier than thou," but the *holy* requires the contrary category, the *not-holy*. So, once more, how can two religious communities understand one another when one raises the issue of the sanctification of Israel, and the other the salvation of the world? Again, different people talking about different things to different people.

Mutual comprehension becomes still more difficult when the familiar proves strange, when categories we think we understand we turn out not to grasp at all. Using the familiar in strange ways was the most formidable obstacle to resolving the Jewish–Christian argument in the first century. Both Christians and Pharisees radically revised existing categories. To understand this transvaluation of values, let us examine the principal categories of the inherited Israelite religion and culture. Once their picture is clear, we can readily grasp how, in both Christianity and Judaism, each category undergoes revision, in both definition and content.

PRIEST, SAGE, PROPHET: ANCIENT ISRAEL'S HERITAGE IN CHRISTIAN AND JUDAIC RECONSTRUCTION

Ancient Israel's heritage yielded the cult with its priests, the Torah with its scribes and teachers, and the prophetic and apocalyptic hope for meaning in history and an eschaton mediated by messiahs and generals. From these derive Temple, school, and (in the apocalyptic expectation) battlefield on Earth and in heaven. To seek a typology of the modes of Israelite piety, we must look for the generative symbol of each mode: an altar for the priestly ideal, a scroll of Scripture for the scribal ideal of wisdom, a coin marked "Israel's freedom: year 1" for the messianic modality. In each of these visual symbols we perceive things we cannot touch, hearts and minds we can only hope to evoke. We seek to enter into the imagination of people distant in space and time. We must strive to understand the way in which they framed the world and encapsulated their worldview in some one thing: the sheep for the priestly sacrifice, the memorized aphorism for the disciple, the stout heart for the soldier of light. Priest, sage, soldier—each stands for the whole of Israel. When all would meld into one, a fresh and unprecedented Judaism would emerge, whether among the heirs of Scribes and Pharisees or among the disciples of Christ.

The symbols under discussion—Temple-altar, sacred scroll, victory wreath for the head of the messiah-king—largely covered Jewish society. We need not reduce them to their merely social dimensions to recognize that on them was founded the organization of Israelite society and the interpretation of its history. Let us now rapidly review the social groups envisaged and addressed by the framers of these symbols.

The **priest** viewed society as organized along structural lines emanating from the Temple. His caste stood at the top of a social scale in which all things were properly organized, each with its correct name and proper place. The inherent sanctity of the people of Israel, through the priests' genealogy, came to its richest embodiment in the high priest. Food set apart for the priests' rations, at God's command, possessed the same sanctity; so, too, did the table at which priests ate. To the priest, for the sacred society of Israel, history was an account of what happened in, and (alas) on occasions to, the Temple.

To the **sage,** the life of society demanded wise regulations. Relationships among people required guidance by the laws enshrined in the Torah and best interpreted by scribes; the task of Israel was to construct a way of life in accordance with the revealed rules of the Torah. The sage, master of the rules, stood at the head.

Prophecy insisted that the fate of the nation depended on the faith and moral condition of society, a fact to which Israel's internal and external history testified. Both sage and priest saw Israel from the viewpoint of externity, but the nation had to live out its life in this world, among other peoples coveting the very same land, and within the context of Roman imperial policies and politics. The messiah's kingship would resolve the issue of Israel's subordinate relationship to other nations and empires, establishing once and for all the desirable, correct context for priest and sage alike.

Implicit in the messianic framework was a perspective on the world beyond Israel for which priest and sage cared not at all. The priest perceived the Temple as the center of the world: beyond it he saw in widening circles the less holy, then the unholy, and, further still, the unclean. All lands outside the Land of Israel were unclean with corpse uncleanness; all other peoples were unclean just as corpses were unclean. Accordingly, in the world life abided within Israel; in Israel, within the Temple. Outside, in the far distance, were vacant lands and dead peoples, comprising an undifferentiated wilderness of death—a world of uncleanness. From such a perspective, no teaching about Israel among the nations, no interest in the history of Israel and its meaning, was apt to emerge.

The wisdom of the sage pertained in general to the streets, marketplaces, and domestic establishments (the household units) of Israel. What the sage said was wisdom as much for gentiles as for Israel. The universal wisdom proved international, moving easily across the boundaries of culture and language, from eastern to southern to western Asia. It focused, by definition, on human experience common to all and undifferentiated by nation, essentially unaffected by the large movements of history. Wisdom spoke about fathers and sons, masters and disciples, families and villages, not about nations, armies, and destiny.

Because of their very diversity, these three principal modes of Israelite existence might easily cohere. Each focused on a particular aspect of the national life, and none essentially contradicted any other. One could worship at the Temple, study the Torah, and fight in the army of the Messiah, and some did all three. Yet we must see these modes of being and their consequent forms of piety as separate. Each contained its own potential to achieve full realization without reference to the others.

The symbolic system of cult, Torah, and messiah demanded choices. If one thing was most important, others must have been less important. Either history matters, or it happens, without significance, "out there." Either the proper conduct of the cult determines the course of the seasons and the prosperity of the land, or it is "merely ritual"—an unimportant external and not the critical heart. (We hear this judgment in, for example, the prophetic polemic against the cult.) Either the messiah will save Israel, or he will ruin everything. Accordingly, though we take for granted that people could have lived within the multiple visions of priest, sage, and messiah, we must also recognize that such a life was vertiginous. Narratives of the war of 66–73 emphasize that priests warned messianists not to endanger their Temple. Later sages—Talmudic rabbis—paid slight regard to the messianic struggle led by Bar Kokhba, and after 70 they claimed the right to tell priests what to do.

The way in which symbols were arranged and rearranged was crucial. Symbol change is social change. A mere amalgam of all three symbols hardly serves by itself as a mirror for the mind of Israel. The particular way the three were bonded in a given system reflects an underlying human and social reality. That is how it should be, because the three symbols—with their associated myths, the worldviews they projected, and the way of life they defined—stood for different views of what really matters. In investigating the existential foundations of the several symbolic systems available to Jews in antiquity, we penetrate to the bedrock of Israel's reality, to the basis of the life of the nation and each Israelite, to the ground of being, even to the existential core that we the living share with them.

Let us unpack the two foci of existence: public history, and the private establishment of the home and heart. We may call the first "time." Its interest is in one-time, unique *events* that happen day by day in the here and now of continuing history. We may call the other focus "eternity." Its interest is in the recurrent and continuing patterns of life—birth and death; planting and harvest; the regular movement of the sun, moon, stars in heaven; night and day; Sabbaths, festivals and regular seasons. The two share one existential issue: How do we respond to the ups and downs of life?

The events of individual life—birth, maturing, marriage, death—do not make history, except for individuals. But the events of group life—the formation of groups, the development of social norms and patterns, depression and prosperity, war and peace—do make history. When a small people coalesces and begins its course through history in the face of adversity, one of two things can happen. Either the group may disintegrate in the face of disaster and lose its hold on its individual members, or the group may fuse, being strengthened by trial, and so turns adversity into renewal.

The modes around which Israelite human and national existence coalesced—those of priests, sages, and messianists (including prophets and apocalyptists)—emerged, we must remember, from national and social consciousness. The heritage of the written Torah (the Hebrew Scriptures or "Old Testament") was carried forward in all three approaches to Judaism. The Jewish people knew the mystery of how to endure through history. In ancient Israel, adversity elicited self-conscious response. Things did not merely *happen* to Israelites. God made them happen to teach lessons to Israel. The prophetic and apocalyptic thinkers in Israel shaped, reformulated, and interpreted events, treating them as raw material for renewing the life of the group.

History was not merely "one damn thing after another." It was important, teaching significant lessons. It had a purpose and was moving somewhere. The writers of Leviticus and Deuteronomy, of the historical books from Joshua through Kings, and of the prophetic literature agreed that, when Israel did God's will, it enjoyed peace, security, and prosperity; when it did not, it was punished at the hands of mighty kingdoms raised up as instruments of God's wrath. This conception of the meaning of Israel's life produced another question: How long? When would the great events of time come to their climax and conclusion? And as one answer to that question, the hope arose for the messiah, the anointed of God, who would redeem the people and set them on the right path forever, thus ending the vicissitudes of history.

THE PARTING OF THE WAYS

We may now return to our starting point, where Judaic and Christian religious life led in different directions. Judaic consciousness in the period under discussion had two competing but not yet "contradictory" symbol systems: the altar/scroll of the Pharisees and scribes, and the wreath of the messiah-king. What made one focus more compelling than the other? The answer emerges when we realize that each kind of piety addressed a distinctive concern; each spoke about different things to different people.

We may sort out the types of piety by returning to our earlier observations. Priests and sages turned inward, toward the concrete everyday life of the community. They addressed the sanctification of Israel. Messianists and their prophetic and apocalyptic teachers turned outward, toward the affairs of states and nations. They spoke of the salvation of Israel. Priests saw the world of life

in Israel, and death beyond. They knew what happened to Israel without concerning themselves with a theory about the place of Israel among the nations.
For priests, the nations formed an undifferentiated realm of death. Sages, all
the more, spoke of home and hearth, fathers and sons, husbands and wives,
the village and enduring patterns of life. What place was there in this domestic scheme for the realities of history—wars and threats of wars, the rise and
fall of empires? The sages expressed the consciousness of a singular society
amid other societies. At issue for the priest/sage was being; for the
prophet/messianist the issue was becoming.

The radical claims of the holiness sects, such as Pharisees and Essenes, of
professions such as the scribes, and of followers of messiahs—all expressed aspects of Israel's common piety. Priest, scribe, messiah—all stood together with
the Jewish people along the same continuum of faith and culture. Each expressed in a particular, intense way one mode of the piety that the people as a
whole understood and shared, which is why the description of the common
faith in first-century Israel can move from the particular to the general. That
common faith, we hardly need argue, distinguished Israel from all other peoples of the age, whatever the measure of "hellenization" in the country's life.
As far as Israel was concerned, there was no "common theology of the ancient Near East."

No wonder that the two new modes of defining Judaic piety that issued
from the period before 70 and thrived long after that date—the Judaism
framed by sages from before the first to the seventh century, and Christianity
with its paradoxical king-messiah—redefined that piety while remaining true
to emphases of the inherited categories. Each took over the established classifications—priest, scribe, and messiah—but infused them with new meaning.
Though in categories nothing changed, in substance nothing remained what
it had been. Both Christian and Judaic thinkers thus reread the received Scriptures—"the Old Testament" to the one, "the written Torah" to the other—
and produced, respectively, "the New Testament" and the "Oral Torah." The
common piety of the people of Israel in its land defined the program of religious life for both the Judaism and the Christianity that emerged after the
caesura of the destruction of the Temple. The bridge to Sinai—worship, revelation, national and social eschatology—was open in both directions.

Thus, Christ as perfect sacrifice, teacher, prophet, and Messiah-King in
the mind of the church brought together but radically recast the three foci of
what had been the common piety of Israel in Temple times. Still later on, the
figure of the Talmudic sage would encompass but redefine all three categories
as well.

How so? After 70, study of the Torah and obedience to it became a temporary substitute for the Temple and its sacrifice. The government of the
sages—in accord with "the one whole Torah of Moses, our rabbi," revealed by
God at Sinai—carried forward the scribes' conception of Israel's proper government. The Messiah would come when all Israel, through mastery of the
Torah and obedience to it, had formed that holy community that, to begin
with, the Torah prescribed in the model of Heaven revealed to Moses at Sinai.

Jesus as perfect priest, rabbi, Messiah, was a protean figure. So was the Talmudic rabbi as Torah incarnate, priest for the present age, and, in the model of (Rabbi) David, progenitor and paradigm of the Messiah. In both cases, we find an unprecedented rereading of established symbols through the fresh interpretation of the received Scriptures. And that point brings us to the oral part of the Torah, which is what makes Judaism not simply "the religion of the Old Testament" or "the religion that is not Christianity" but very much a religion on its own.

PART II

49-73

Classical Judaism

7

The Mishnah

From what time may they recite the Shema in the evening? From the hour that the priests enter [their homes] to eat their heave offering, "until the end of the first watch," the words of R. Eliezer. But sages say, "Until midnight." Rabban Gamaliel says, "Until the rise of dawn." There was the case in which his [Gamaliel's] sons returned from a banquet hall [after midnight]. They said to him, "We did not [yet] recite the Shema." He said to them, "If the dawn has not yet risen, you are obligated to recite [the Shema]. And [this applies] not only [in] this [case]. Rather, [as regards] all [commandments] which sages said [may be performed] "Until midnight," the obligation [to perform them persists] until the rise of dawn." [For example,] the offering of the fats and entrails—their obligation [persists] until the rise of dawn [see Leviticus 1:9, 3:3–5]. And all [sacrifices] which must be eaten within one day, the obligation [to eat them persists] until the rise of dawn. If so why did sages say [that these actions may be performed only] until midnight? In order to protect man from sin.

MISHNAH-TRACTATE BERAKHOT
CHAPTER 1, PARAGRAPH 1, THE OPENING LINES OF THE MISHNAH

So begins the Mishnah, a principal holy book of Judaism. Not a very promising start! To someone who has never seen the writing before, the Mishnah must cause puzzlement. From the first line to the last, discourse takes up questions internal to a system that is never introduced. The Mishnah provides information without establishing context. It presents disputes about facts hardly urgent outside a circle of faceless disputants. Consequently, we start with the impression that we join a conversation already long under way about topics we can never grasp anyhow. Even though the language is our own, the substance is not. We shall feel as if we are in a transit lounge at a distant airport. We understand the words people say but are baffled by their meanings and concerns—above all, by the urgency in their voices.

DEFINING THE MISHNAH: THE FIRST HOLY BOOK, AFTER THE HEBREW SCRIPTURES, IN RABBINIC JUDAISM

Defining the Mishnah presents difficulties, because the Mishnah does not identify its authors. It permits only slight variations, if any, in its authorities' patterns of language and speech, so there is no place for individual characteristics of expression. It nowhere tells us when it speaks. It does not address a particular place or time and rarely speaks of events in its own day. It never identifies its prospective audience. There is scarcely a *you* in the entire mass of sayings and rules. The Mishnah begins nowhere. It ends abruptly. There is no predicting where it will commence or explaining why it is done. Where, when, why the document is laid out and set forth are questions not deemed urgent and not answered.

Indeed, the Mishnah contains not a hint about what its authors conceive their work to be. Is it a law code? Is it a schoolbook? Because it makes statements describing what people should and should not do, or rather, do and do not do, we might suppose it is a law code. Because, as we shall see in a moment, it covers topics of both practical and theoretical interest, we might suppose it is a schoolbook. But the Mishnah never expresses a hint about its authors' intent. The reason is that the authors do what they must to efface all traces not only of individuality but even of their own participation in the formation of the document. So it is not only a letter from utopia to whom it may concern. Nor should we fail to notice, even at the outset, that while the Mishnah clearly addresses Israel, the Jewish people, it is remarkably indifferent to the Hebrew Scriptures. The Mishnah makes no effort at imitating the Hebrew of the Hebrew Bible, as do the writers of the Dead Sea Scrolls. The Mishnah does not attribute its sayings to biblical heroes, prophets, or holy men, as do the writings of the pseudo-epigraphs of the Hebrew Scriptures. The Mishnah does not claim to emerge from a fresh encounter with God through revelation, as is not uncommon in Israelite writings of the preceding four hundred years; the Holy Spirit is not alleged to speak here. So all the devices by which other Israelite writers gain credence for their messages are ignored. Perhaps the authority of the Mishnah was self-evident to its authors. But, self-evident or not, they in no way take the trouble to explain to their document's audience why people should conform to the descriptive statements contained in their holy book.

If then we turn to the contents of the document, we are helped not at all in determining the place of the Mishnah's origination, the purpose of its formation, or the reasons for its anonymous and collective plane of discourse and monotonous tone of voice. For the Mishnah covers a carefully defined program of topics. But the Mishnah never tells us why one topic is introduced and another is omitted, or what the agglutination of these particular topics is meant to accomplish in the formation of a system or imaginative construction. Nor is there any predicting how a given topic will be treated, why a given set of issues will be explored in close detail, and another set of possible issues ignored. Discourse on a theme begins and ends as if all things are self-evident, including the reason for beginning at one point and ending at some other. In all, one might readily imagine, on first glance at this strange and curious book, that what we have is a rule book. It appears on the surface to be a book lacking all traces of eloquence and style, revealing no evidence of system and reflection, serving no important purpose. First glance indicates in hand is yet another shard from remote antiquity no different from the king lists inscribed on the ancient shards, the random catalogue of (to us) useless, meaningless facts: a cookbook, a placard of posted tariffs, detritus of random information, accidentally thrown up on the currents of historical time. Who would want to have made such a thing? Who would now want to refer to it?

The answer to that question is deceptively straightforward: the Mishnah is important because it is a principal component of the canon of Judaism. Indeed, that answer begs the following question: Why should some of the ancient Jews of the Holy Land have brought together these particular facts and rules into a book and set them forth for the Israelite people? Why should the Mishnah have been received, as much later on it certainly was received, as a half of the "whole Torah of Moses at Sinai"? The Mishnah was represented, after it was compiled, as the part of the "whole Torah of Moses, our rabbi," which had been formulated and transmitted orally, so it bore the status of divine revelation right alongside the Pentateuch. Yet it is already entirely obvious that little in the actual contents of the document evoked the character or the moral authority of the written Torah of Moses. Indeed, because most of the authorities named in the Mishnah lived in the century and a half before the promulgation of the document, the claim that things said by men known to the very framers of the document in fact derived from Moses at Sinai through a long chain of oral tradition contradicted the well-known facts of the matter. So this claim presents a paradox even on the surface: How can the Mishnah be deemed a book of religion, a program for consecration, a mode of sanctification? Why should Jews from the end of the second century to our own day have deemed the study of the Mishnah to be a holy act, a deed of service to God through the study of an important constituent of God's Torah, God's will for Israel, the Jewish people?

In fact, the Mishnah is precisely that, a principal holy book of Judaism. The Mishnah has been and now is memorized in the circle of all those who participate in the religion Judaism. Of still greater weight, the two great documents formed around the Mishnah and so shaped as to serve, in part, as commentaries to the Mishnah—namely, the Babylonian Talmud and the Palestinian Talmud—form the center of the curriculum of Judaism as a living religion. Consequently, the Mishnah is necessary to the understanding of Judaism. It hardly needs saying that people interested in the study of religions surely will have to reflect on the same questions I have formulated within the context of Judaism, namely, how such a curious compilation of materials may be deemed a holy book. And, self-evidently, scholars of the formative centuries of Christianity, down to the recognition of Christianity as a licit religion in the fourth century, will be glad to have access to a central document of the kind of Judaism taking shape at precisely the same time as the Christianity studied by them was coming into being. In all, we need not apologize for our interest in this sizable monument to the search for a holy way of life for Israel represented, full and whole, in this massive thing, the Mishnah.

DESCRIBING THE MISHNAH:
ITS CONTENTS AND CONTEXT

Let me now briefly describe the Mishnah. It is a six-part code of descriptive rules formed toward the end of the second century C.E. by a small number of Jewish sages and put forth as the constitution of Judaism under the sponsorship of Judah the Patriarch, the head of the Jewish community of the Land of Israel at the end of that century. The reason the document is important is that the Mishnah forms the foundation for the Babylonian and Palestinian Talmuds. It therefore stands alongside the Hebrew Bible as the holy book on which the rabbinic Judaism of the past nineteen hundred years is constructed. The six divisions are (1) agricultural rules; (2) laws governing appointed seasons (for example, Sabbaths and festivals); (3) laws on the transfer of women and property along with women from one man (father) to another (husband); (4) the system of civil and criminal law (corresponding to what we today should regard as "the legal system"); (5) laws for the conduct of the cult and the Temple; and (6) laws on the preservation of cultic purity both in the Temple and under certain domestic circumstances, with special reference to the table and bed. These divisions define the range and realm of reality.

The world addressed by the Mishnah is hardly congruent to the worldview presented in the Mishnah. Consider the time and context in which the document took shape. The Mishnah is made up of sayings bearing the names of authorities who lived in the later first and second centuries. (The book contains very little in the names of people who lived before the destruction of the Temple of Jerusalem in 70 C.E.) These authorities generally fall into two groups, namely, two distinct sets of names, each set of names randomly appearing together but rarely, if ever, with names of the other set. The former set of names is generally supposed to represent authorities who lived between the destruction of the Temple in 70 and the advent of the second war against Rome, led by Simeon Bar Kokhba, in 132. The latter set of names belongs to authorities who flourished between the end of that war, circa 135, and the end of the second century. The Mishnah itself is generally supposed to have come to closure at the end of the second century, and its date, for conventional purposes only, is about 200 C.E.

Now, of these two groups, from 70 to 130 and from 135 to 200, the latter is represented far more abundantly than the former. Approximately two thirds of the named sayings belong to mid-second-century authorities. This is not surprising, because these are the named authorities whose (mainly unnamed) students collected, organized, and laid out the document as we now have it. So, in all, the Mishnah represents the thinking of Jewish sages who flourished in the middle of the second century. It is that group that took over whatever they had in hand from the preceding century, and from the whole legacy of Israelite literature even before that time, and revised and reshaped the whole into the Mishnah. Let us briefly consider their world.

In the aftermath of the war against Rome in 132–135, the Temple was declared permanently prohibited to Jews, and Jerusalem was also closed off to them. So there was no cult, no Temple, no holy city, to which the description of the Mishnaic laws applied at this time. We observe at the very outset, therefore, that a sizable proportion of the Mishnah deals with matters to which the sages had no material access or practical knowledge at the time of their work. For we have seen that the Mishnah contains a division on the conduct of the cult, namely, the fifth, as well as one on the conduct of matters so as to preserve the cultic purity of the sacrificial system along the lines laid out in the book of Leviticus, the sixth division. In fact, a fair part of the second division, on appointed times, takes up the conduct of the cult on special days (such as the sacrifices offered on the Day of Atonement, Passover, and the like). Indeed, what the Mishnah wants to know about appointed seasons concerns the cult far more than it does the synagogue. The fourth division, on civil law, presents an elaborate account of a political structure and system of Israelite self-government, in tractates Sanhedrin and Makkot, not to mention Shebuot and Horayot. This system speaks of king, priest, Temple, and court.

But it was not the Jews, their kings, priests, and judges but the Romans who conducted the government of Israel in the Land of Israel in the time when the second-century authorities did their work. So it would appear that well over half of the document before us speaks of cult, Temple, government, and priesthood. Moreover, the Mishnah takes up a profoundly priestly and Levitical conception of sanctification. When we consider that, in the very time when these authorities did their work, the Temple lay in ruins, the city of Jerusalem was prohibited to all Israelites, and the Jewish government and administration that had centered on the Temple and based its authority on the holy life lived there were in ruins, the fantastic character of the Mishnah's address to its own catastrophic day becomes clear. Much of the Mishnah speaks of matters not in being in the time in which the Mishnah was created, because the Mishnah wishes to make its statement on what really matters.

In the age beyond catastrophe, the problem is to reorder a world off course and adrift, to gain reorientation for an age in which the sun has come out after the night and the fog. The Mishnah is a document of imagination and fantasy, describing how things "are" out of the shards and remnants of reality but, in larger measure, building social being out of beams of hope. The Mishnah tells us something about how things were but everything about how a small group of men wanted things to be. The document is orderly, repetitious, careful in both language and message. It is small-minded, picayune, obvious, dull, routine—everything its age was not. The Mishnah stands in contrast with the world to which it speaks. Its message is one of small achievements and modest hope. It means to defy a world of large disorders and immodest demands. The heirs of heroes build an unheroic folk in the new and ordinary age. The Mishnah's message is that what a person wants matters in important ways. It states that message to an Israelite world that can shape affairs in no important ways and speaks to people who by no means will the way things now are. The Mishnah therefore lays down a practical judgment on, and in favor of, the imagination and will to reshape reality, regain a system, and reestablish that order on which trustworthy existence is to be built.

Now the Judaism shaped by the Mishnah consists of a coherent worldview and comprehensive way of living. It is a worldview that speaks of transcendent things, a way of life in response to the supernatural meaning of what is done, a heightened and deepened perception of the sanctification of Israel in deed and deliberation. Sanctification means two things: first, distinguishing Israel in all its dimensions from the world in all its ways; second, establishing the stability, order, regularity, predictability, and reliability of Israel at moments and in contexts of danger. Danger means instability, disorder, irregularity, uncertainty, and betrayal. Each topic of the system as a whole takes up a critical and indispensable moment or context of social being. Each orders what is disorderly and dangerous. Through what is said in regard to each of the Mishnah's principal topics, what the system as a whole wishes to declare is fully expressed. Yet if the parts severally and jointly give the message of the whole, the whole cannot exist without all of the parts, so well joined and carefully crafted are they all.

THE MISHNAH'S JUDAISM

Let me now describe and briefly interpret the six components of the Mishnah's system. The critical issue in the economic life, which means farming, is in two parts, revealed in the first division. First, Israel, as tenant on God's holy Land, maintains the property in the ways God requires, keeping the rules that mark the Land and its crops as holy. Next, the hour at which the sanctification of the Land comes to form a critical mass, namely, in the ripened crops, is the moment ponderous with danger and heightened holiness. Israel's will so affects the crops as to mark a part of them as holy, the rest of them as available for common use. The human will is determinative in the process of sanctification.

Second, in the second division, what happens in the Land at certain times, at Appointed Times, marks off spaces of the Land as holy in yet another way. The center of the Land and the focus of its sanctification is the Temple. There the produce of the Land is received and given back to God, the one who created and sanctified the Land. At these unusual moments of sanctification, the inhabitants of the Land in their social being in villages enter a state of spatial sanctification; that is, the village boundaries mark off holy space, within which one must remain during the holy time. This is expressed in two ways. First, the Temple itself observes and expresses the special, recurring holy time. Second, the villages of the Land are brought into alignment with the Temple, forming a complement and completion to the Temple's sacred being. The advent of the Appointed Times precipitates a spatial reordering of the Land, so that the boundaries of the sacred are matched and mirrored in village and in

Temple. At the heightened holiness marked by these moments of Appointed Times, therefore, the occasion for an affective sanctification is worked out. Like the harvest, the advent of an Appointed Time, a pilgrim festival, also a sacred season, is made to express that regular, orderly, and predictable sort of sanctification for Israel that the system as a whole seeks.

If for a moment we now leap over the next two divisions, the third and fourth, we come to the counterpart of the divisions of Agriculture and Appointed Times. These are the fifth and sixth divisions, namely, Holy Things and Purities, those that deal with the everyday and the ordinary versus the special moments of harvest, on the one side, and special time or season, on the other.

The fifth division is about the Temple on ordinary days. The Temple, the locus of sanctification, is conducted in a wholly routine and trustworthy, punctilious manner. The one thing that may unsettle matters is the intention and will of the human actor. This is subjected to carefully prescribed limitations and remedies. The division of Holy Things generates its companion, the sixth division, the one on cultic cleanness, Purities. The relationship between the two is like that between Agriculture and Appointed Times: the former locative, the latter utopian; the former dealing with the fields, the latter with the interplay between fields and altar.

Here, too, in the sixth division, once we speak of the one place of the Temple, we address, too, the cleanness that pertains to every place. A system of cleanness—taking into account what imparts uncleanness and how this is done, what is subject to uncleanness, and how that state is overcome—is fully expressed, once more, in response to the participation of the human will. Without the wish and act of a human being, the system does not function. It is inert. Sources of uncleanness, which come naturally and not by volition, and modes of purification, which work naturally and not by human intervention, remain inert until human will has imparted susceptibility to uncleanness, that is, introduced into the system, that food and drink, bed, pot, chair, and pan that to begin with form the focus of the system. The movement from sanctification to uncleanness takes place when human will and work precipitate it.

This point now brings us back to the middle divisions, the third and fourth, on Women and Damages. They take their place in the structure of the whole by showing the congruence, within the larger framework of regularity and order, of human concerns of family and farm, politics and workaday transactions among ordinary people. For without attending to these matters, the Mishnah's system does not encompass what, at its foundations, it is meant to comprehend and order. So what is at issue is fully cogent with the rest.

In the case of Women, the third division, attention focuses on the point of disorder marked by the transfer of that disordering anomaly, woman, from the regular status provided by one man, to the equally trustworthy status provided by another. That is the point at which the Mishnah's interests are aroused: once more, predictably, the moment of disorder.

In the case of Damages, the fourth division, two important concerns emerge. First, there is the paramount interest in preventing, so far as possible, the disorderly rise of one person and fall of another and in sustaining the status quo of the economy, the house and household, of Israel, the holy society in eternal stasis. Second, there is the necessary concomitant in the provision of a system of political institutions to carry out the laws that preserve the balance and steady state of persons.

The two divisions that take up topics of concrete and material concern— the formation and dissolution of families and the transfer of property in that connection, the transactions, both through torts and through commerce, that lead to exchanges of property and the potential dislocation of the state of families in society—are both locative and utopian. They deal with the concrete locations in which people make their lives, household and street and field, the sexual and commercial exchanges of a given village. But they pertain to the life of all Israel, both in the Land and otherwise. These two divisions, together with the household ones of Appointed Times, constitute the sole opening outward toward the life of utopian Israel, that diaspora in the far reaches of the ancient world, in the endless span of time. From the Mishnah's perspective, this community is not only in exile but unaccounted for, outside the system, for the Mishnah declines to recognize and take it into account. Israelites who dwell in the land of (unclean) death instead of in the Holy Land simply fall outside the range of (holy) life. Priests, who must remain cultically clean, may not leave the Land, and neither may most of the Mishnah.

So much for the Mishnah. What about its amplification and extension in the Mishnah commentary called "the Talmud"?

8

The Mishnah and the Talmud

THE TALMUD AS A COMMENTARY TO THE MISHNAH

The Talmud is a commentary on the Mishnah. In fact, there are two Talmuds, one produced in the Land of Israel and completed at about 400 C.E., called "the Talmud of the Land of Israel" or "the Yerushalmi (Jerusalem) Talmud," the other produced in Babylonia, in the Iranian Empire (present-day Iraq) and completed at about 600, called "the Talmud of Babylonia" or, in Hebrew, "the Bavli." Each of these extensive documents selected tractates—topical expositions—of the Mishnah for comment. But the two Talmuds are quite distinct from one another; they differ in their choices of tractates that require analysis, and their treatment of the tractates they do choose is quite distinct. The Talmud of the Land of Israel deals with thirty-nine tractates of the Mishnah's sixty-two, and the Talmud of Babylonia, thirty-seven.

To sample the kind of religious writing we find in the Talmud's reading of the Mishnah, we consider the single most important statement of that book. It is the rule of the Mishnah that defines who is, and who is not, a Jew—that is, "Israel, the holy people." It does so by explaining who belongs and who does not: "All Israel" will not die but will rise from the dead at the end of days; then those who do not "have a portion in the world to come" will not be part of Israel in the resurrection. Excluded are those who deny the resurrection of the dead, or deny that the Torah teaches that the dead will live, or that the Torah was given by God ("does not come from Heaven"), or a person who denies the principles of the faith ("an Epicurean"):

Mishnah-tractate Sanhedrin 11:1–2

A. All Israelites have a share in the world to come,

B. as it is said, "your people also shall be all righteous, they shall inherit the land forever; the branch of my planting, the work of my hands, that I may be glorified" (Isaiah 60:21).

C. And these are the ones who have no portion in the world to come:

D. He who says, the resurrection of the dead is a teaching which does not derive from the Torah, and the Torah does not come from Heaven; and an Epicurean.

The Babylonian Talmud to this passage begins with two questions in mind. First, is the rule of the Mishnah fair? Second, how on the basis of the written

[handwritten margin note: More questioning to commentary]

Torah do we know the fact taken for granted by the oral Torah—namely, that the resurrection of the dead will take place and that the Torah itself says so? First comes the justification of God's way:

Babylonian Talmud Tractate
Sanhedrin Folio Pages 90A–B

I. A. [With reference to the Mishnah's statement, "And these are the ones who have no portion in the world to come":] Why all this [that is, why deny the world to come to those listed]?

B. On Tannaite authority [it was stated], "Such a one denied the resurrection of the dead, therefore he will not have a portion in the resurrection of the dead.

C. "For all the measures [meted out by] the Holy One, blessed be he, are in accord with the principle of measure for measure."

What someone denies shall be denied to that person; hence, it is only fair that someone who does not believe in the resurrection will not live when the dead are raised up. But where in Scripture do we find that fact? The Talmud proceeds to many pages of proofs, among which the following provide a taste of the discussion:

IV. A. It has been taught on Tannaite authority:

B. R. Simai says, "How on the basis of the Torah do we know about the resurrection of the dead?

C. "As it is said, 'And I also have established my covenant with [the patriarchs] to give them the land of Canaan' (Exodus 6:4).

D. "'With you' is not stated, but rather, 'with *them*,' indicating on the basis of the Torah that there is the resurrection of the dead."

V. A. *Minim* [believers, sectarians, sometimes identified as Jews who believed in Jesus as the Messiah, hence, Christian Jews] asked Rabban Gamaliel, "How do we know that the Holy One, blessed be he, will resurrect the dead?"

B. He said to them, "It is proved from the Torah, from the Prophets, and from the Writings." But they did not accept his proofs.

C. He said to them, "From the Torah: for it is written, 'And the Lord said to Moses, Behold, you shall sleep with your fathers and rise up' (Deuteronomy 31:16)."

D. They said to him, "But perhaps the sense of the passage is, 'And *the people* will rise up' (Deuteronomy 31:16)?"

E. He said to them, "From the Prophets: as it is written, 'Thy dead men shall live, together with my dead body they shall arise. Awake and sing, you that live in the dust, for your dew is as the dew of herbs, and the earth shall cast out its dead' (Isaiah 26:19)."

F.   They said to him, "But perhaps that refers to the dead whom Ezekiel raised up."

G.   He said to them, "From the Writings, as it is written, 'And the roof of your mouth, like the best wine of my beloved, that goes down sweetly, causing the lips of those who are asleep to speak'(Song of Songs 7:9)."…

H.   [The *minim*—in this case, heretic Jews who did not believe in the resurrection of the dead—would not concur in Gamaliel's view] until he cited for them the following verse: "'Which the Lord swore to your fathers to give to them'(Deuteronomy 11:21)—to *them* and not to you, so proving from the Torah that the dead will live."

We see how the Talmud of Babylonia has faithfully expounded the Mishnah's teaching, so forming an expansion and explanation of the oral Torah's claim.

THE TALMUD AND THE MISHNAH AS PART OF THE ORAL TORAH

Now let us step back and examine the importance of the Talmuds in the history of Judaism, beginning with their reading of the Mishnah. The most important statement concerning the Mishnah made by the two Talmuds is not set forth in so many words but is contained in every page of the two writings. It is that the Mishnah is part of the Torah, and in commenting on the Mishnah, the authors of the two Talmuds were explaining the meaning of the Torah. This was expressed in a simple way. The framers of the two Talmuds tried to show how most of the rules of the Mishnah derive from statements in the Scriptures. So the Mishnah was shown to depend on the written Torah.

Not only so, but in the first important piece of writing after the Mishnah was closed, a collection of sayings attributed to sages of the Mishnah called "The Sayings of the Fathers" (in Hebrew: *Pirqé Abot*), the Mishnah is shown to form part of the chain of tradition that began at Sinai. This proposition is contained in a rather subtle exposition. First, it is alleged that when God gave the Torah at Sinai to Moses, he handed on a tradition that was to be memorized and repeated, master to disciple, for all time. This other medium by which the Torah was revealed was oral; hence, "the Oral Torah" referred to the part of the Torah formulated and handed on in memory. The story of this other part of the Torah, the oral part, is contained in a few words of a document called "The Sayings of the Founders" (Hebrew: *Pirqé Avot*), a writing of about 250 C.E. read in the synagogue, chapter by chapter, as a principal part of Torah study.

Moses received Torah at Sinai and handed it on to Joshua, Joshua to elders, and elders to prophets. And prophets handed it on to the men of the great assembly. They said three things: "Be prudent in judgment. Raise up many disciples. Make a fence for the Torah." Simeon the Righteous was one of the last survivors of the great assembly. He would say, "On three things does the world stand: On the Torah, and on the Temple service, and on deeds of loving-kindness."

Mishnah-tractate Abot 1:1–2

What is striking in this statement is three allegations. First, we find the claim that there is a tradition from God's revelation to Moses at Sinai that continues beyond the figures we know in the holy scriptures of ancient Israel ("the Old Testament"), specifically, Joshua and the prophets. The "men of the great assembly" and Simeon the Righteous stand in the chain of tradition from Sinai, but they are not figures out of the Old Testament. It follows that there is that other Torah, one not in writing, hence the orally formulated and orally transmitted part of the Torah. The second claim is that this other Torah comes down through the relationship of master to disciple, who becomes a master later on. The third striking fact is that what is stated is not a citation of Scripture but a saying that stands on its own. Simeon's saying is part of that Torah from Sinai, for example, but it does not refer to or quote Scripture. This same chapter then goes on to include sayings by various other sages, onward to figures who are cited many times in the pages of the Mishnah itself, Hillel and Shammai. By citing these figures within the chain of tradition from Sinai, the framer of the passage was able to show that the Mishnah contains part of the Torah of Sinai, the oral part.

Certainly the single most important figure in the chain of tradition from Sinai onward to the sages who created the Mishnah itself is Hillel, a sage who flourished at about the same time as Jesus and to whom is attributed a statement strikingly like the Golden Rule: "What is hateful to yourself, do not do to anybody else. That is the whole of the Torah. All the rest is commentary. Now go learn." Both the teaching of Hillel and that of Jesus in the Golden Rule—"Do unto others as you would have them do unto you"—state in other language the commandment of the Torah at Leviticus 19:18: "You shall love your neighbor as yourself," and many great sages of Judaism have maintained that that statement summarizes the whole of Judaism. A further statement in Hillel's name forms the foundation of the morality of Judaism:

If I am not for myself, who is for me? And when I am for myself, what am I? And if not now, when?

Mishnah-tractate Abot 1:13

The collection of sayings gathered in "The Sayings of the Founders" appears now as part of the most important holy book of Judaism after the written Torah, which is the Mishnah, a philosophical law code written in about 200 C.E.

Scripture, the written Torah, and the Mishnah, the oral Torah, received extensive commentaries. Books of the written Torah, such as Genesis, Exodus, Leviticus, Numbers, and Deuteronomy, were given extensive commentaries, called in Hebrew *midrashim* (plural of *midrash*). The Mishnah too was given its extensive commentary. This is called, in Hebrew, a *talmud* (plural: *talmudim*), and there are two of them, the Talmud of the Land of Israel, of about 400 C.E., and the Talmud of Babylonia, of about 600 C.E. The fact that the written Torah and the Mishnah are treated in precisely the same way, that is, are read closely and carefully so as to discover their meaning for the world today, proves that the Mishnah enjoyed a unique position as part of the Torah. The two Talmuds then provided an authoritative explanation of what the oral part of the Torah meant and how it was to be observed.

TORAH IN TWO MEDIA, WRITTEN AND ORAL

The conception of another form of the Torah, an oral, memorized form, is expressed by the Talmud of the Land of Israel in the following passage of the Talmud of the Land of Israel, where we find the theory that there is a tradition separate from and in addition to the written Torah. This tradition it knows as "the teachings of scribes." The Mishnah is not identified as the collection of those teachings.

III. A. Associates in the name of R. Yohanan: "The words of scribes are more beloved than the words of Torah and more cherished than words of Torah: 'Your palate is like the best wine'(Song of Songs 7:9)."

B. Simeon bar Ba in the name of R. Yohanan: "The words of scribes are more beloved than the words of Torah and more cherished than words of Torah: 'For your love is better than wine' (Song of Songs 1:2)."...

D. R. Ishmael repeated the following: "The words of Torah are subject to prohibition, and they are subject to remission; they are subject to lenient rulings, and they are subject to strict rulings. But words of scribes all are subject only to strict interpretation, for we have learned there: He who rules, 'There is no requirement to wear phylacteries,' in order to transgress the teachings of the Torah, is exempt. But if he said, 'There are five partitions in the phylactery, instead of four,' in order to add to what the scribes have taught, he is liable [Mishnah-tractate Sanhedrin 11:3]."

E. R. Haninah in the name of R. Idi in the name of R. Tanhum b. R. Hiyya: "More stringent are the words of the elders than the words of the prophets. For it is written, 'Do not preach'—thus they preach—one should not preach of such things (Micah 2:6). And it is written, '[If a man should go about and utter wind and lies, saying,] "I will preach to you of wine and strong drink," he would be the preacher for this people!' (Micah 2:11).

F.   "A prophet and an elder—to what are they comparable? To a king who sent two senators of his to a certain province. Concerning one of them he wrote, 'If he does not show you my seal and signet, do not believe him.' But concerning the other one he wrote, 'Even though he does not show you my seal and signet, believe him.' So in the case of the prophet, he has had to write, 'If a prophet arises among you…and gives you a sign or a wonder…' (Deuteronomy 13:1). But here [with regard to an elder:] '…according to the instructions which they give you…' (Deuteronomy 17:11) [without a sign or a wonder]."

Talmud of the Land of Israel Tractate Abodah Zarah 2:7

What is important in the foregoing anthology is the distinction between teachings contained in the Torah and teachings in the name or authority of "scribes." These latter teachings are associated with quite specific details of the law and are indicated in the Mishnah's rule itself. Further, at E we have "elders" (that is, sages) as against prophets. What happens to the Mishnah in the two Talmuds shows us how the later sages viewed the Mishnah.

That view may be stated very simply. The Mishnah rarely cites verses of Scripture in support of its propositions. The two Talmuds routinely adduce scriptural bases for the Mishnah's laws. The Mishnah seldom undertakes the exegesis of verses of Scripture for any purpose. The two Talmuds consistently investigate the meaning of verses of Scripture and do so for a variety of purposes. Accordingly, the two Talmuds, subordinate as they are to the Mishnah, regard the Mishnah as subordinate to, and contingent on, Scripture. That is why, in the two Talmuds' view, the Mishnah requires the support of Scriptural proof texts.

A broad shift was taking place in the generations that received the Mishnah, that is, over the third and fourth centuries. If the sages of the second century, who made the Mishnah as we know it, spoke in their own names and in the name of the logic of their own minds, those who followed (certainly the ones who flourished in the later fourth century and onward to the sixth, who produced the two Talmuds) took a quite different view. Reverting to ancient authority like others of the age, they turned back to Scripture, deeming it the source of certainty about truth.

The result for rabbinic Judaism may be stated very briefly. The history of Judaism then proceeded in three stages: the written Torah, defining the basic issues of Israel's life; then the Mishnah, contributing to the dual Torah the revision of the theory of Israel's sanctification in response to the destruction of the Second Temple; and, third, the two Talmuds and related writings, adding to the complete account of Israel's supernatural life the reaffirmation of salvation in response to the advent of triumphant Christianity. These second and third phases in the formation of the one whole Torah show us, in the Mishnah, a version of the Judaism of the dual Torah that reached writing before Christianity made an impact on the Judaic sages, whereas the two Talmuds and their associates show us the changes that were made in the encounter with

Christianity as the triumphant religion of the Roman state. The Judaism that took shape in the Land of Israel in the fourth century, attested by documents brought to closure in the fifth, responded to that Christianity and in particular to its challenge to the Israel of that place and time and flourished, in Israel, the Jewish people, so long as the West was Christian. That, sum and substance, is the story of the most important Judaic system of all times.

9

The Midrash

WHAT IS MIDRASH?

The Judaism of the dual Torah produced a commentary on the Oral Torah in the form of the two Talmuds. It also produced a commentary on the written Torah, in the form of collections of scriptural explanation that are called *midrashim*. *Midrash* in Hebrew means investigation, and, when applied to Scripture, *midrash* means investigation of the meaning of Scripture, hence, interpretation. There are three types of interpretation of Scripture characteristic of midrash compilations. In the first, the focus of interest is on individual verses of Scripture, and interpreting those verses, in the sequence in which they appear, forms the organizing principle of sustained discourse. In the second, the center of interest attends to the testing and validating of large-scale propositions, which, through the reading of individual verses, an authorship wishes to test and validate. In that rather philosophical trend in rabbinic Bible interpretation, the interpretation of individual verses takes a subordinated position, the appeal to facts of Scripture in the service of the syllogism at hand. The third approach directs attention not to concrete statements of Scripture, whether in sequences of verses or merely individual verses or even words or phrases, but to entire compositions of Scripture: biblical themes, stories. This investigation of Scripture's meaning generates midrash as narrative: the imaginative recasting of Scripture's stories in such a way as to recast those stories and to make new and urgent points through the retelling.

Rabbinic Bible interpretation read the Hebrew Scriptures as one half, the written half, of the whole Torah—that is, the dual Torah revealed in two media, writing and memory, by God to Moses at Sinai. The other half of that same Torah, the oral part, derives from oral formulation and oral transmission of God's word, finally preserved in the teachings of the Judaic sages themselves. Midrash so works as to lead us into the world of the Hebrew Bible as that holy Scripture entered into Judaism. For the Holy Scriptures were transformed by the Judaic sages or rabbis of the formative centuries of Western civilization, from the first century to the seventh. *Through the workings of midrash the Hebrew Bible became the written half of the one whole Torah, oral and written, revealed by God to Moses our Rabbi at Mount Sinai.* Midrash works in three dimensions: first, as explanation of meaning imputed to particular verses of Scripture; second, as a mode of stating important propositions, syllogisms of thought, in conversation with verses or sustained passages of Scripture; and, third, as a way of retelling scriptural stories in such a way as to impart to those stories new immediacy.

By the word *midrash,* the Hebrew word for "investigation," people commonly mean one of three things. First comes the sense of midrash as the explanation, by Judaic interpreters, of the meaning of individual verses of Scripture. The result of the interpretation of a verse of Scripture is called a *midrash exegesis.* The result of the interpretation of Scripture is collected, second, in midrash compilations or what I call a *midrash document.* Third, the process of interpretation, for instance, the principles that guide the interpreter, is called *midrash method.* Let us now proceed to a simple definition for the word *midrash,* with close attention to the context, in literature and society, in which the writings of midrash are produced and the techniques of midrash exegesis. The best definition derives from Gary G. Porton,[1] who states:

> Midrash is "a type of literature, oral or written, which has its starting point in a fixed, canonical text, considered the revealed word of God by the Midrashist and his audience, and in which this original verse is explicitly cited or clearly alluded to."... For something to be considered Midrash it must have a clear relationship to the accepted canonical text of Revelation. Midrash is a term given to a Jewish activity which finds its locus in the religious life of the Jewish community. While others exegete their revelatory canons and while Jews exegete other texts, only Jews who explicitly tie their comments to the Bible engage in Midrash.

What is important in Porton's definition are three elements: (1) exegesis, (2) starting with Scripture, and (3) ending in community. Porton identifies five types of midrashic activity: the rabbinic (discussed in Part III); the midrash found in the Hebrew Scriptures themselves—for example, Deuteronomy's rewriting of Exodus, Numbers, and Leviticus; translations (called in Hebrew and Aramaic *targumim*); the rewriting of the biblical narrative; and the *Pesher-* midrash of an apocalyptic order. Porton writes:

> Rabbinic Midrash represents an independent phenomenon, for the rabbis are a distinct class within the Jewish community of Late Antiquity. The definitive characteristic of the ancient rabbi was his knowledge and how he attained it. What a rabbi knew distinguished him from the rest of the Jewish community, and the fact that he had gained his information by studying with another rabbi who participated in a chain of tradition which stretched back to God and Moses on Mount Sinai also set him apart in his larger environment. A rabbi's knowledge began with the Written Torah, the five books of Moses, the public record of the perfect revelation from the perfect God, and from there it moved into the Oral Torah, that part of revelation which had been handed down from God to Moses our Rabbi and from Moses our Rabbi, through an unbroken chain, to the rabbis of Late Antiquity. The Oral Torah is the record of rabbinic attempts to solve problems encountered in the Written Torah, for among other things it filled in the details, explained unclear matters and expanded upon enigmatic passages found in the Written Torah. The Oral Torah also offered the rules and methods according to which the

Written Torah was to be interpreted and upon which an understanding of it should be based. In short, the Oral Torah provided the guidelines that made possible the understanding of and the application of Scripture's lessons in contemporary life. The Oral Torah was the key to unlocking the mysteries of the Written Torah, and the rabbis were the only ones who possessed this key. Rabbinic Midrash is the type of Midrash produced by this small segment of the Jewish population of Palestine and Babylonia during the first seven centuries of the common era.

Rabbinic Midrash is based on several presuppositions. The rabbis believed that the Written Torah was the accurate and complete public record of a direct revelation from the One, Unique, and Perfect God to His people; therefore, nothing in the Bible was unimportant or frivolous. Every letter, every verse, and every phrase contained in the Bible was important and written as it was for a specific reason. The Bible contained no needless expressions, no "mere" repetitions, and no superfluous words or phrases. The assumption that every element of the biblical text was written in a specific way in order to teach something underlies the Midrashic activity of the rabbis. Furthermore, the rabbis believed that everything contained in Scriptures was interrelated. Often, one verse is explained by reference to another verse. A section of the Prophets may be used to explain a verse from the Torah, or a portion of the Torah may explain a passage from the Writings.

These form some of the principal technical aspects of how sages read a verse of Scripture. We move now to the theological side of matters.

ONE EXAMPLE OF MIDRASH: HOW THE SAGES OF JUDAISM READ THE BOOK OF GENESIS AS A PARABLE FOR THEIR OWN TIME

From this definition, let us turn to a concrete example of how the sages of the midrash read Scripture. Our case in point is the book of Genesis, which is examined in the midrash compilation, Genesis Rabbah, a document that took shape in the century beyond Constantine, in about 400–450. The sages who composed Genesis Rabbah read Scripture's account of creation and the beginnings of Israel: God set forth to Moses the entire scope and meaning of Israel's history among the nations and salvation at the end of days. Genesis drew their attention more than any other book of the Pentateuch—the five books of Moses. Sages read Genesis not as a set of individual verses, one by one, but as a single and coherent statement, whole and complete.

Sages read Scripture so that things were not what they seemed to be but meant something else altogether. For in general people read the book of Genesis as the story of how Israel saw the past, not the future: the beginning of the world and of Israel, humanity from Adam to Noah, then from Noah to Abraham, and the story of the three patriarchs and four matriarchs of Israel—Abraham, Isaac, Jacob, Sarah, Rebecca, Leah, and Rachel—and finally, Joseph and his brothers—from creation to the descent into Egypt. But to the rabbis who created Genesis Rabbah, the book of Genesis tells the story of Israel, the Jewish people, in the here and now. The principle was that what happened to the patriarchs and matriarchs signals what will happen to their descendants: the model of the ancestors sends a message for the children. So the importance of Genesis, as the sages of Genesis Rabbah read the book, derives not from its lessons about the past but from its message for Israel's present and, especially, future.

In the way in which the sages of Genesis Rabbah dealt with this crisis, we follow in concrete terms what it means to see things as other than what they seem. Specifically, sages conceded that Christian Rome required attention in a way in which pagan Rome had not. Furthermore, they appealed to their established theory of who Israel is to find a place for Rome. They saw Israel as one big family, children of Abraham, Isaac, Jacob. To fit Rome into the system, they had to locate for Rome a place in the family. Scripture (we now recognize) speaks of deeper truths. Hence, when Scripture told the story of certain members of the family, "we" who understand Scripture know that what is meant is a member whom only now we recognize. Specifically, Rome now is represented by Esau, then: Jacob's brother, Jacob's enemy. Or Rome may be Ishmael or Moab. "And we? We are Israel." Scripture therefore tells the story of Esau and Jacob, who are, in today's world, Rome and Israel. And Jacob supplants, Jacob wins the blessing and the patrimony and the birthright—and Jacob will again. Things are not what they seem; Scripture speaks of other things than those on the surface; and midrash exegesis, working out this mode of midrash process, collected in midrash documents, tells that story.

That is an example of reading one thing in light of something else and everything as though it meant something other than what it said. Identifying Rome as Esau is a fresh idea. In the mishnah, two hundred years earlier, Rome appears as a place, not as a symbol. But in Genesis Rabbah Rome is symbolized by Esau. Why Esau in particular? Because Esau is sibling: relations, competitor, enemy, brother. In choosing Rome as the counterpart to Israel, sages simply opened Genesis and found there Israel—that is, Jacob—and his brother, his enemy, in Esau. Why not understand the obvious? Esau stands for Rome, Jacob for Israel, and their relationship represents then what Israel and Rome would work out even now, in the fourth century, the first century of Christian rule. Esau rules now, but Jacob possesses the birthright. Esau/Rome is the last of the four great empires (Persia, Media, Greece, Rome). On the other side of Rome? Israel's age of glory. And why is Rome now brother? Because, after all, the Christians do claim a common patrimony in the Hebrew Scriptures and do claim to form part of Israel. That claim was not ignored, it was answered: yes, part of Israel, the rejected part. Jacob bears the blessing and transmits the blessing to humanity, Esau does not.

That concession—Rome is a sibling, a close relative of Israel—represents an implicit recognition of Christianity's claim to share the patrimony of Judaism, to be descended from Abraham and Isaac. So how are we to deal with the glory and the power of our brother, Esau? And what are we to say about the claim of Esau to enthrone Christ? And how are we to assess today the future history of Israel, the salvation of God's first, best love? It is not by denying Rome's claim but by evaluating it, not by turning a back to the critical events of the hour but by confronting those events forcefully and authoritatively. In this instance, we see how rabbinic midrash resorted to an allegorical or parabolic reading of Scripture to bring to Scripture the issues of the age and to discover God's judgment of those issues. We now turn to a detailed examination of how sages spelled out what Scripture really means. To sages Genesis reported what really happened. But, as we see throughout, Genesis also spelled out the meanings and truth of what happened. In the following passage, we have Esau in place of Rome:

Genesis Rabbah LXI:VII

2. A. *"[But to the sons of his concubines, Abraham gave gifts, and while he was still living,] he sent them away from his son Isaac, eastward to the east country]"* (Genesis 25:6):

B. He said to them, "Go as far to the east as you can, so as not to be burned by the flaming coal of Isaac."

C. But because Esau came to make war with Jacob, he took his appropriate share on his account: *"Is this your joyous city, whose feet in antiquity, in ancient days, carried her afar off to sojourn? Who has devised this against Tyre, the crowning city?"* (Isaiah 23:7).

D. Said R. Eleazar, "Whenever the name of Tyre is written in Scripture, if it is written out [with all of the letters], then it refers to the province of Tyre. Where it is written without all of its letters [and so appears identical to the word for enemy], the reference of Scripture is to Rome. [So the sense of the verse is that Rome will receive its appropriate reward.]"

Section 2 carries forward the eschatological reading of the incident. Israel's later history is prefigured in the gift to Isaac and the rejection of the other sons. The self-evidence that Esau's reward will be recompense for his evil indicates that the passage draws on sarcasm to make its point. Sages essentially looked in the facts of history for the laws of history. We may compare them to social scientists or social philosophers, trying to turn anecdotes into insight and to demonstrate how we may know the difference between impressions and truths. Genesis provided facts. Careful sifting of those facts will yield the laws that dictated why things happened one way, rather than some other. The language, as much as the substance, of the narrative provided facts demanding careful study. We understand why sages thought so if we call to mind their basic understanding of the Torah. To them (as to many today, myself included), the Torah came from God and in every detail contained revelation of God's truth. Accordingly, just as we study nature and derive facts demanding explanation and yielding law, so we study Scripture and find facts susceptible of explanation and yielding truth.

Let us consider an exemplary case of how sages discovered social laws of history in the facts of Scripture. What Abraham did corresponds to what Balaam did, and the same law of social history derives proof from each of the two contrasting figures.

Genesis Rabbah LV:VIII

1. A. *"And Abraham rose early in the morning, [saddled his ass, and took two of his young men with him, and his son Isaac, and he cut the wood for the burnt offering and arose and went to the place that God had told him]"* (Genesis 22:3):

    B. Said R. Simeon b. Yohai, "Love disrupts the natural order of things, and hatred disrupts the natural order of things.

    C. "Love disrupts the natural order of things we learn from the case of Abraham: '... *he saddled his ass.*' But did he not have any number of servants? But that proves love disrupts the natural order of things.

    D. "Hatred disrupts the natural order of things we learn from the case of Balaam: *'And Balaam rose up early in the morning and saddled his ass'* (Numbers 22:21). But did he not have any number of servants? But that proves hatred disrupts the natural order of things.

    E. "Love disrupts the natural order of things we learn from the case of Joseph: *'And Joseph made his chariot ready'* (Genesis 46:29). But did he not have any number of servants? But that proves love disrupts the natural order of things.

    F. "Hatred disrupts the natural order of things we learn from the case of Pharoah: *'And he made his chariot ready'* (Exodus 14:6). But did he not have any number of servants? But that proves hatred disrupts the natural order of things."

The social law about the overriding effect of love or hatred is proven by diverse cases, as we see. Now we move from the laws of social history to the rules that govern Israel's history in particular.

2. A. Said R. Simeon b. Yohai, "Let one act of saddling an ass come and counteract another act of saddling the ass. May the act of saddling the ass done by our father Abraham, so as to go and carry out the will of him who speak and brought the world into being counteract the act of saddling that was carried out by Balaam when he went to curse Israel.

B. "Let one act of preparing counteract another act of preparing. Let Joseph's act of preparing his chariot so as to meet his father serve to counteract Pharaoh's act of preparing to go and pursue Israel."

C. R. Ishmael taught on Tannaite authority, "Let the sword held in the hand serve to counteract the sword held in the hand.

D. "Let the sword held in the hand of Abraham, as it is said, *'Then Abraham put forth his hand and took the knife to slay his son'* (Genesis 22:10) serve to counteract the sword taken by Pharoah in hand: *'I will draw my sword, my hand shall destroy them'* (Exodus 15:9)."

We see that the narrative is carefully culled for probative facts, yielding laws. One fact is that there are laws of history. The other is that laws may be set aside, by either love or hatred. Yet another law of history applies in particular to Israel, as distinct from the foregoing, deriving from the life of both Israel and the nations, Abraham and Balaam.

Here is an exercise in the recurrent proof of a single proposition that Abraham foresaw the future history of Israel, with special reference to the rule of the four monarchies—Babylonia, Media, Greece, then Rome—before the rule of Israel:

Genesis Rabbah XLIV:XVII

4. A. *"[And it came to pass, as the sun was going down,] lo, a deep sleep fell on Abram, and lo, a dread and great darkness fell upon him"* (Genesis 15:12):

B. *"...lo, a dread"* refers to Babylonia, as it is written, *"Then was Nebuchadnezzar filled with fury"* (Genesis 3:19).

C. *"...and darkness"* refers to Media, which darkened the eyes of Israel by making it necessary for the Israelites to fast and conduct public mourning.

D. *"...great..."* refers to Greece....

E. *"...fell upon him"* refers to Edom [Rome], as it is written, *"The earth quakes at the noise of their fall"* (Jeremiah 49:21).

I find this a particularly moving tableau, with darkness descending and dread falling on Jacob. That accounts, also, for the power of the ideas at hand. Section 4 successfully links the cited passage once more to the history of Israel. Israel's history falls under God's dominion. Whatever will happen carries out God's plan. The fourth kingdom is part of that plan, which we can discover by carefully studying Abraham's life and God's word to him. In the following selection, we see an explicit effort to calculate the time at which the end will come and Israel will be saved:

Genesis Rabbah XLIV:XVIII

1. A. *"Then the Lord said to Abram, 'Know of a surety [that your descendants will be sojourners in a land that is not theirs, and they will be slaves*

there, and they will be oppressed for four hundred years; but I will bring judgment on the nation which they serve, and afterward they shall come out with great possessions']" (Genesis 15:13–14):

B. *"Know"* that I shall scatter them.

C. *"Of a certainty"* that I shall bring them back together again.

D. *"Know"* that I shall put them out as a pledge [in expiation of their sins].

E. *"Of a certainty"* that I shall redeem them.

F. *"Know"* that I shall make them slaves.

G. *"Of a certainty"* that I shall free them.

2. A. *"...that your descendants will be sojourners in a land that is not theirs and they will be slaves there, and they will be oppressed for four hundred years":*

B. It is four hundred years from the point at which you will produce a descendant. [The Israelites will not serve as slaves for four hundred years, but that figure refers to the passage of time from Isaac's birth.]

C. Said R. Yudan, "The condition of being outsiders, the servitude, the oppression in a land that was not theirs all together would last for four hundred years, that was the requisite term."

Section 1 parses the cited verse and joins within its simple formula the entire history of Israel, punishment and forgiveness alike. Section 2 parses the verse to follow, trying to bring it into line with the chronology of Israel's later history.

The single most important paradigm for history emerged from the deed at Moriah, the binding of Isaac on the altar as a sacrifice to God. We shall see, in Chapter 14, how the binding of Isaac forms a critical motif in synagogue art also, as the philosopher-artists of synagogue decoration created their midrash as well. Here is how sages derive enduring rules of history and salvation from the story of the willingness of Abraham to sacrifice even his son to God:

Genesis Rabbah LVI:I

1. A. *"On the third day Abraham lifted up his eyes and saw the place afar off"* (Genesis 22:4):

B. *"After two days he will revive us, on the third day he will raise us up, that we may live in his presence"* (Hosea 16:2).

C. On the third day of the tribes: *"And Joseph said to them on the third day, 'This do and live' "* (Genesis 42:18).

D. On the third day of the giving of the Torah: *"And it came to pass on the third day when it was morning"* (Exodus 19:16).

E. On the third day of the spies: *"And hide yourselves there for three days"* (Joshua 2:16).

F. On the third day of Jonah: *"And Jonah was in the belly of the fish three days and three nights"* (Jonah 2:1).

G. On the third day of the return from the Exile: *"And we abode there three days"* (Ezra 8:32).

H. On the third day of the resurrection of the dead: *"After two days he will revive us, on the third day he will raise us up, that we may live in his presence"* (Hosea 16:2).

I. On the third day of Esther: *"Now it came to pass on the third day that Esther put on her royal apparel"* (Esther 5:1).

J. She put on the monarchy of the house of her fathers.

K. On account of what sort of merit?

L. Rabbis say, "On account of the third day of the giving of the Torah."

M. R. Levi said, "It is on account of the merit of the third day of Abraham: *'On the third day Abraham lifted up his eyes and saw the place afar off'* (Genesis 22:4)."

The third day marks the fulfillment of the promise, at the end of time of the resurrection of the dead and, at appropriate moments, of Israel's redemption. The reference to the third day at Genesis 22:2 then invokes the entire panoply of Israel's history. The relevance of the composition emerges at the end. Before the concluding segment, the passage forms a kind of litany and falls into the category of a liturgy. Still, the recurrent hermeneutic that teaches that the stories of the patriarchs prefigure the history of Israel certainly makes its appearance. Our final example makes the point still more explicitly, and here we close:

Genesis Rabbah LVI:II

4. A. *"...and we will worship [through an act of prostration] and come again to you"* (Genesis 22:5):

   B. He thereby told him that he would come back from Mount Moriah whole and in peace [for he said that *we* shall come back].

5. A. Said R. Isaac, "And all was on account of the merit attained by the act of prostration.

   B. "Abraham returned in peace from Mount Moriah only on account of the merit owing to the act of prostration: *'...and we will worship [through an act of prostration] and come [then, on that account] again to you'* (Genesis 22:5).

   C. "The Israelites were redeemed only on account of the merit owing to the act of prostration: *'And the people believed...then they bowed their heads and prostrated themselves'* (Exodus 4:31).

   D. "The Torah was given only on account of the merit owing to the act of prostration: *'And worship [prostrate themselves] you afar off'* (Exodus 24:1).

E. "Hannah was remembered only on account of the merit owing to the act of prostration: *'And they worshipped before the Lord'* (1 Samuel 1:19).

F. "The exiles will be brought back only on account of the merit owing to the act of prostration: *'And it shall come to pass in that day that a great horn shall be blown and they shall come that were lost…and that were dispersed…and they shall worship the Lord in the holy mountain at Jerusalem'* (Isaiah 27:13).

G. "The Temple was built only on account of the merit owing to the act of prostration: *'Exalt you the Lord our God and worship at his holy hill'* (Psalms 99:9).

H. "The dead will live only on account of the merit owing to the act of prostration: *'Come let us worship and bend the knee, let us kneel before the Lord our maker'* (Psalms 95:6)."

Section 3 draws a lesson from the use of *thus* in the cited verses. The sizable construction at section 4 makes a simple point, to which our base verse provides its modest contribution. But its polemic is hardly simple. The entire history of Israel flows from its acts of worship ("prostration") and is unified by a single law. Every sort of advantage Israel has ever gained came about through worship. Hence, what is besought, in the elegant survey, is the law of history. The Scripture then supplies those facts from which the governing law is derived. The lesson that Israel commands its own destiny through obedience to God emerges in every line of Genesis as sages' midrash interprets the book. In the hands of the sages of Genesis Rabbah, the book of the beginnings tells the tale of the end time. Reading Genesis in this way typifies how "our sages of blessed memory" received and valued the written Torah. Rabbinic Judaism then reads Scripture as the Torah, the written part through the prism of the oral part.

NOTE

1. Gary G. Porton, "Midrash: The Palestinian Jews and the Hebrew Bible in the Greco-Roman Period," in Hildegard Temporini and Wolfgang Haase (eds.), *Aufstieg und Niedergand der romischen Welt* (Berlin: de Gruyter, 1979), II.19.2, 104. See also his "Defining Midrash," in Jacob Neusner (ed.), *The Study of Ancient Judaism I: Mishnah, Midrash, Siddur* (Hoboken, NJ: Ktav, 1981), 55–92, and *Understanding Rabbinic Midrash: Text and Commentary* (Hoboken, NJ: Ktav, 1985).

10

Women in Judaism
The Evidence of the Mishnah

FROM DOCUMENT TO DOCTRINE

The documents we have considered set forth ideas as well as interpretations of Scripture, but the ideas do not reach us in a systematic way. But if we are to grasp the whole of rabbinic Judaism, we must examine some of its main ideas or doctrines—the principles of the faith that comprise the worldview of that Judaism. We must, then, ask ourselves, How do we move from the documents of Judaism to the doctrines of Judaism? What steps do we take to generalize on the basis of episodic statements, to seek to view the whole that the parts comprise? That is an important task in studying any religion, for, in general, religions deliver their most eloquent messages through the details, but then it is our task to identify the generalization implicit in those details.

Here we take three important questions and ask how they are answered in the Torah, oral and written. The first concerns women; the second, the conception of Israel; and the third, the Messiah. For the present purpose, these correspond to the categories that we have already considered in general terms: way of life, worldview, theory of the social entity comprised by the group. Here we see how the study of the Torah's law and scriptural interpretation allows us to construct an account of the teachings of the Torah on critical questions: way of life, concerning women; theory of the social order, concerning Israel; and worldview, concerning the meaning and end of history. In these matters we propose to see how this Judaism's system of the social order of its holy Israel actually deals with fundamental issues, what doctrines embody the system in a concrete way. Clearly, rabbinic Judaism possesses many doctrines, and some of these—the principal theological ones—are expressed in the liturgy that will occupy our attention in the next part of the book. But if we wish to experiment, on our own, with the problem of describing a religion, in our case, a Judaism, we have to ask, How would we translate the abstract conceptions of worldview, theory of the social order, and way of life into concrete data? In this and the next two chapters, we do just that.

In examining any topic of rabbinic Judaism, our starting point is the Mishnah, and we proceed from there to examine how the Mishnah is interpreted and augmented in subsequent documents. The unfolding of the documents over time also conveys the history of ideas of rabbinic Judaism that those doctrines convey. So, in this account of doctrines, of how important ideas unfolded, first comes the Mishnah, then the later documents. We recall, also, our stress that a system says the same thing about everything, and what the system does is answer an urgent question with a response that, to the faithful, is self-evidently valid. Knowing the urgent question and the self-evidently valid answer of the system, we can predict what the system has to say about any topic it chooses to treat.

This brings us to the first and most interesting question—the way of life of rabbinic Judaism, as its thinking about women conveys its larger conception of the social order: the classes of society and how they relate, the crises of the social life and how these are to be resolved. The social vision of the Mishnah's Judaism encompasses issues of gender, social structure and construction, wealth and transactions in property, the organization of the castes of society. In all these matters the system seeks the principles of order and proper classification, identifying as problems the occasions for disorder and improper disposition of persons or resources. The fact that we can find our document saying one thing about many things tells us that the document stands for a well-considered view of the whole, and, when we come to the theological and philosophical program of the same writing, that consistent viewpoint will guide us to what matters and what is to be said about what matters.

WOMEN AS THE INDICATOR OF THE CHARACTER OF A RELIGIOUS SYSTEM

The principal focus of a social vision framed by men, such as that of the Mishnah, not only encompasses but focuses on woman, who is perceived as abnormal in a world to which men are normal. But to place the Mishnah's vision of woman in perspective, we have to locate woman within the larger structure defined by the household, for two reasons. First, as a matter of definition, woman forms the other half of the whole that is the householder. Second, because the household forms the building block of the social construction envisioned by the Mishnah's framers, it is in that setting that every other component of the social world of the system must situate itself.

In the conception at hand, which sees Israel as made up, on Earth, of households and villages, the economic unit also framed the social one, and the two together composed, in conglomerates, the political one, hence a political economy (*polis, oekos*), initiated within an economic definition formed out of the elements of production. That explains why women cannot be addressed outside the framework of the economic unit of production defined by the household. For, throughout, the Mishnah makes a single cogent statement that the organizing unit of society and politics finds its definition in the irreducible unit of economic production. The Mishnah conceives no other economic unit of production than the household, though it recognizes that such existed; its authorship perceived no other social unit of organization than the household and the conglomeration of households, though that limited vision omitted all reference to substantial parts of the population perceived to be present (for example, craftspeople, the unemployed, the landless, and the like). But what about woman in particular?

The framers of the Mishnah, for example, do not imagine a household headed by a woman; a divorced woman is assumed to return to her father's household. The framers make no provision for the economic activity of isolated individuals, out of synchronic relationship with a household or a village composed of householders. Accordingly, craftspeople and day laborers or other workers, skilled and otherwise, enter the world of social and economic transactions only in relationship to the householder. The upshot, therefore, is that the social world is made up of households, and, because households may be composed of many families (for example, husbands, wives, children), all of them dependents on the householder, households in no way are to be confused with the family. The indicator of the family is kinship; that of the household, "propinquity or residence." And yet, even residence is not always a criterion for membership in the household unit, because the craftspeople and day laborers are not assumed to live in the household compound at all. Accordingly, the household forms an economic unit, with secondary criteria deriving from that primary fact.

The Mishnaic law of women defines women's position in the social economy of Israel's supernatural and natural reality—God's perspective in Heaven, man's perspective on Earth. That position acquires definition in relationship to men, who give form to the Israelite social economy. It is effected through both supernatural and natural, this-worldly action. What man and woman do on Earth provokes a response in Heaven, and the correspondences are perfect. So the position of women is defined and secured in Heaven and here on Earth, and that position, always and invariably relative to men, is what comes into consideration. The principal point of interest on Mishnah's part is the times at which a woman changes hands, that is, when she enters and leaves the marital union. These transitional points in the relationships of women and men are frequently disorderly and therefore, as I suggested earlier, dangerous to society.

Five of the seven tractates of the Mishnah that pertain to women and family are devoted to the transfer of women, the formation and dissolution of the marital bond. Of them, three treat what is done by man here on Earth, that is, formation of a marital bond through betrothal and marriage contract and dissolution through divorce and its consequences: Qiddushin (betrothals), Ketubot (marriage contracts), and Gittin (writs of divorce). One of them is devoted to what by woman is done here on Earth: Sotah (the wife accused of adultery, in line with Numbers 5). Yebamot (levirate marriages, in line with Deuteronomy 25:1–5), greatest of the seven in size and informal and substantive brilliance, deals with the corresponding Heavenly intervention into the formation and dissolution of marriage: the effect of death on the marital bond and the dissolution, through death, of that bond. The other two tractates, Nedarim (vows) and Nazir (the special vow of the Nazirite, in line with Numbers 6), draw into one the two realms of reality, Heaven and Earth, as they work out the effects of vows—generally taken by married women and subject to the confirmation or abrogation of the husband—to Heaven. These vows make a deep impact on the marital relationship of the woman who has taken such a vow. So, in all, we consider the natural and supernatural character of the woman's relationship to the social economy framed by men: the beginning, end, and middle of that relationship.

PROPER CONDUCT WITH WOMEN

One of the many important issues worked out with special reference to women concerns proper conduct with women. Here we see how the Mishnah sets forth its ideas on avoiding improper sexual relations.

Mishnah-tractate Qiddushin 4:12

A. A man should not remain alone with two women, but a woman may remain alone with two men.

B. R. Simeon says, "Also: One may stay alone with two women, when his wife is with him.

C. "And he sleeps with them in the same inn,

D. "Because his wife keeps watch over him."

E. A man may stay alone with his mother or with his daughter.

F. And he sleeps with them with flesh touching.

G. But if they [the son who is with the mother, the daughter with the father] grew up, this one sleeps in her garment, and that one sleeps in his garment.

M. Qiddushin 4:12

4:13–14

A. An unmarried man may not teach scribes.

B. Nor may a woman teach scribes.

C. R. Eliezer says, "Also: He who has no wife may not teach scribes."

M. Qiddushin 4:13

A. R. Judah says, "An unmarried man may not herd cattle.

B. "And two unmarried men may not sleep in the same cloak."

C. And sages permit it.

D. Whoever has business with women should not be alone with women.

E. And a man should not teach his son a trade which he has to practice among women.

M. Qiddushin 4:14

Mishnah Qiddushin 4:13 refers to teachers of young children. They should not be brought into close association with the mothers or fathers of the children. The formal and substantive traits of what follows require no comment.

To appreciate these rules, we have to remember that, what the Mishnah's authors say about one thing, they say about all things. Hence, if we want to understand how the Mishnah's Judaism treats women, we have to ask how the Mishnah's Judaism deals with any important subject. We see that the Mishnah wants men and women to preserve relationships that are chaste and dignified. The authors of the document know full well that each sex desires the other—that is the foundation of the social order: family, home, household. But a well-ordered society is a predictable one, which keeps in check the natural desires of women and men.

A STEADY-STATE WORLD OF
PERMANENCE AND ORDER

What the Mishnah really wants is for nothing to happen. The Mishnah presents a tableau, a wax museum, a diorama. It portrays a world fully perfected and so fully at rest. The one thing the Mishnah does not want to tell us is about change, how things come to be what they are. That is why there can be no sustained attention to the priesthood and its rules, the scribal profession and its constitution, the class of householders and its interests. The Mishnah's pretense is that all of these have come to rest. They compose a world in stasis, perfect and complete, made holy because it is complete and perfect. It is an economy—again in the classic sense of the word—awaiting the divine act of sanctification that, as at the creation of the world, would set the seal of holy rest on an again-complete creation, just as in the beginning. There is no place for the actors when what is besought is no action whatsoever, but only perfection, which is unchanging. There is room only for a description of how things are: the present tense, the sequence of completed statements and static problems. All the action lies within, in how these statements are made.

Essentially, the Mishnah's authorship aimed at the fair adjudication of conflict, worked out in such a way that no party gained, none lost, in any transaction. The task of Israelite society, as they saw it, is to maintain perfect stasis, to preserve the prevailing situation, to secure the stability of not only relationships but status and standing. To this end, in the interchanges of buying and selling, giving and taking, borrowing and lending, transactions of the market and exchanges with artisans and craftspeople and laborers, it is important to preserve the essential equality, not merely equity, of exchange. Fairness alone does not suffice. *Status quo ante* forms the criterion of the true market, reflecting as it does the exchange of value for value, in perfect balance. That is the way that, in reference to the market, the systemic point of urgency, the steady state of the polity, therefore also of the economy, is expressed. The upshot of their economics is simple. No party in the end may have more than what he had at the outset, and none may emerge as the victim of a sizable shift in fortune and circumstance. All parties' rights to and in the stable and unchanging political economy are preserved. When, therefore, the condition of a person is violated, the law will secure the restoration of the antecedent status.

Critical to the social system of the Mishnah is its principal social entity, the village, imagined as a society that never changes in any important way, comprising households; and the model, from household to village to "all Israel," comprehensively describes whatever of "Israel" the authorship at hand has chosen to describe. We must therefore identify as systemically indicative the centrality of political economy—"community, self-sufficiency, and justice"— within the system of the Mishnah. It is no surprise, either, that the point of originality of the political economy of the Mishnah's system is its focus on the society organized in relationship to the control of the means of production— the farm, for the household is always the agricultural unit.

In the context of a world of pervasive diversity, the Mishnah's authorship set forth a fantastic conception of a simple world of little blocks formed into big ones: households into villages, no empty spaces, but also no vast cities. In the conception of the authorship of the Mishnah, community or village is made up of households, and the household constitutes the building block of both society or community and also economy. It follows that the household forms the fundamental, irreducible, and, of course, representative unit of the economy, the means of production, the locus and unit of production. We should not confuse the household with class status—for example, thinking of the householder as identical with the wealthy. The opposite is suggested on every page of the Mishnah, in which householders vie with craftspeople for ownership of the leavings of the loom and the chips left behind by the adze. The household, rather, forms an economic and a social classification, defined by function, specifically, economic function. A poor household was a household, and (in theory, the Mishnah's authorship knows none such in practice) a rich landholding that did not function as a center for a social and economic unit (such as a rural industrial farm) was not a household. The household constituted the center of the productive economic activities we now handle through the market. Within the household all local (as distinct from cultic, economic, therefore social) activities and functions were held together. For the unit of production comprised also the unit of social organization and, of still greater import, the building block of all larger social, now also political, units, with special reference to the village.

In identifying the householder as the building block of society, to the neglect of the vast panoply of "others," "nonhouseholders" (including that half of the whole of the Israelite society composed of women), the Mishnah's authorship reduced the dimensions of society to only a single component: the male landowner engaged in agriculture. But that is the sole option open to a system that, for reasons of its own, wished to identify productivity with agriculture, individuality in God's image with ownership of land, and social standing and status, consequently, with ownership and control of the land that constituted the sole systemically consequential means of production. Now if we were to list all of the persons and professions who enjoy no role in the system or who are treated as ancillary to the system, we have to encompass not only workers (the entire landless working class!) but also craftspeople and artisans, teachers and physicians, clerks and officials, traders and merchants, the whole of the commercial establishment, not to mention women as a caste.

Fair and just to all parties, the authorship of the Mishnah nonetheless speaks in particular for the Israelite landholding, proprietary person. The Mishnah's problems are the problems of the householder; its perspectives are his. Its sense of what is just and fair expresses his sense of the givenness and cosmic rightness of the present condition of society. These are men of substance and of means, however modest, aching for a stable and predictable world in which to tend their crops and herds, feed their families and dependents, keep to the natural rhythms of the seasons and lunar cycles, and, in all, live out their lives within strong and secure boundaries on Earth and in Heaven. Only when we understand the systemic principle concerning God in relationship to Israel in its land shall we come to the fundamental and generative conception that reaches concrete expression in the here and now of the householder as the centerpiece of society.

In this regard, therefore, the Mishnah's social vision finds its definition of the realm to which "economics" applies within its encompassing conception of who forms the community and who merely occupies space within the community. In the Mishnah's social vision, the householder is systemically the active force, and women, among all other components of the actual economy (as distinct from the economics), prove systemically inert. As such, of course, the Mishnah's social vision ignores most of the actuality of the Jewish people in the Land of Israel in the first and second centuries. But then what of the economically active members of the polis, those who had capital and knew how to use it? If they wished to enter that elevated "Israel" that formed the social center and substance of the Mishnah's Israel, they had to purchase land. The Mishnah's social vision thus describes a steady-state society.

THE HOUSEHOLD, THE
FAMILY, AND WOMEN

For the Mishnah, the center and focus of interest lie in the village, the household and family and home, a patriarchal conception. The village is made up of households, each a unit of production in farming. The households are constructed by and around the householder, father of an extended family, including his sons and their wives and children, his servants, his slaves (bondsmen), and the craftspeople to whom he entrusts tasks he chooses not to do. The concerns of householders are in transactions in land. Their measurement of value is expressed in acreage of top, middle, and bottom grade. Through real estate, critical transactions are worked out. The marriage settlement depends on real property. Civil penalties are exacted through payment of real property. The principal transactions to be taken up are those of the householder who owns beasts that do damage or suffer it; who harvests his crops and must set aside and so by his own word and deed sanctify them for use by the castes scheduled from on high; who uses or sells his crops and feeds his family; and who, if he is fortunate, will acquire still more land. It is to householders that the Mishnah is addressed: the pivot of society and its bulwark, the units of which the village is composed, the corporate component of the society of Israel in the limits of the village and the Land. The householder, as I said, is the building block of the house of Israel, of its economy in the classic sense of the word in Greek, *oikos* (household), which yields our word, *economics*. To that conception of the household, the woman is essential. But it would be many centuries before women would take a central role in Judaism: only in the twentieth century have women been ordained as rabbis, and then not in the Judaism that claimed to be authentic to the Mishnah and the Talmud, Orthodox Judaism, but in the Judaism that proclaimed itself a reforming movement, Reform Judaism, and, in its path, Reconstructionist and Conservative Judaisms too.

Through its six divisions, the Mishnah sets forth a coherent worldview and comprehensive way of living for holy Israel. It is a worldview that speaks of transcendent things, a way of life in response to the supernatural meaning of what is done, a heightened and deepened perception of the sanctification of Israel in deed and deliberation. Sanctification means two things: first, distinguishing Israel in all its dimensions from the world in all its ways; second, establishing the stability, order, regularity, predictability, and reliability of Israel at moments and in contexts of danger. Danger means instability, disorder, irregularity, uncertainty, and betrayal. Each topic of the system as a whole takes up a critical and indispensable moment or context of social being. Each orders what is disorderly and dangerous. Through what is said in regard to each of the Mishnah's principal topics, what the system as a whole wishes to declare is fully expressed. These writers are obsessed with order and compelled by a vision of a world in which all things are in their right place, each bearing its own name, awaiting the benediction that comes when, everything in order, God pronounces the benediction and brings about the sanctification of the whole.

FEMININE ISRAEL, MASCULINE ISRAEL, ANDROGYNOUS ISRAEL

Our story of rabbinic Judaism's treatment of women is partial, because the oral Torah contains a further conception that is critical. It is that Israel itself serves God best through adopting the virtues that the Torah deems feminine. Indeed, when Israel adopts the feminine virtues, assigning to God the masculine ones, God appreciates Israel and responds by bringing the Messiah, at which point Israel completes its sexual identity with masculine virtues as well. So Israel must become androgynous, feminine now, masculine at the end of days. More to the point, feminine Israel is represented as God's great love, and God is represented as feminine Israel's masculine lover. This complex picture of the sexuality of Israel's and God's passionate love affair comes to full expression in the sages' interpretation of the Song of Songs (a.k.a. the Song of Solomon).

The dual Torah, beginning to end, taught that the Israelite was to exhibit the moral virtues of subservience, patience, endurance, and hope. These would translate into the emotional traits of humility and forbearance. And they would yield to social virtues of passivity and conciliation. The hero was one who overcame impulses; and the truly virtuous person, the one who reconciled others by giving way before the opinions of others. All of these acts of self-abnegation and self-denial, accommodation rather than rebellion, required to begin with the right attitudes, sentiments, emotions, and impulses. The single most dominant motif of the rabbinic writings, start to finish, is their stress on the right attitude's leading to the right action, the correct intentionality's producing the besought decision and, above all, accommodating in one's heart to what could not be changed by one's action—which means the world as it was. Sages prepared Israel for the long centuries of subordination and alienation by inculcating attitudes that best suited people who could govern little more than how they felt about things.

In the definitive writings of Judaism, "our sages of blessed memory," who defined the Judaism of the dual Torah of Scripture and the Mishnah and explained and expanded both into the enduring religious worldview and way of life for Israel, the Jewish people, taught what Israel is supposed to feel. And, classified in accord with the indicators set forth in Chapter 4, these emotions are feminine, not masculine. The feminine traits, according to Song of Songs Rabbah, are patience, submission, deep trusting, conciliation, and accommodation; Israel is represented as feminine, therefore accepting and enduring. What, in concrete terms, does it mean for androgynous Israel to feel the feelings of a woman, and how do we know which emotion is feminine, which masculine? Israel is to cultivate the virtues of submission, accommodation, reconciliation, and self-sacrifice—the virtues we have now seen are classified as feminine ones. But, later on, having realized the reward for these virtues, Israel will resume the masculine virtues—again, in accord with the classification just now set forth—of aggression and domination.

A brief selection suffices to show the feminization of Israel. In the following passage, the relationship of Israel to God is the same as the relationship of a wife to the husband, which is explicit here:

Song of Songs Rabbah to Song 7:10

7:10 I am my beloved's, and his desire is for me.

XCIX:i.1 A. "I am my beloved's, and his desire is for me:"

    B. There are three yearnings:

    C. The yearning of Israel is only for their Father who is in heaven, as it is said, "I am my beloved's, and his desire is for me."

    D. The yearning of a woman is only for her husband: "And your desire shall be for your husband" (Genesis 3:16).

    E. The yearning of the Evil Impulse is only for Cain and his ilk: "To you is its desire" (Genesis 4:7).

F. R. Joshua in the name of R. Aha: "The yearning of rain
is only for the earth: 'You have remembered the earth and
made her desired, greatly enriching her' (Psalms 65:10).

G. "If you have merit, the rains will enrich it, but if not,
they will tithe it [the Hebrew words for *enrich* and *tithe* differ by a single letter], for it will produce for you one part
for ten of seed."

Here, therefore, we find that gender relationships are explicitly characterized
and, with them, the traits associated with the genders. The same analogy is
stated even more explicitly in the next quote, which reviews the principal
points of the marriage liturgy in describing Israel's and God's marriage:

Song of Songs Rabbah to Song 4:10

4:10 How sweet is your love, my sister, my bride! how much better
is your love than wine, and the fragrance of your oils than any
spice!

LIV:i.1. A. "How sweet is your love, my sister, my bride! how much
better is your love than wine:"

B. R. Berekhiah and R. Helbo in the name of R. Samuel b.
R. Nahman said, "There are ten passages in which Israel is
called bride, six here [in the Song of Songs] and four in the
prophets.

C. "Six here: 'Come with me from Lebanon, my bride; come
with me from Lebanon. Depart from the peak of Amana,
from the peak of Senir and Hermon, from the dens of lions,
from the mountains of leopards' (Song of Songs 4:8); 'You
have ravished my heart, my sister, my bride, you have ravished
my heart with a glance of your eyes, with one jewel of your
necklace' (Song of Songs 4:9); 'How sweet is your love, my
sister, my bride! How much better is your love than wine, and
the fragrance of your oils than any spice!' (Song of Songs
4:10); 'Your lips distill nectar, my bride; honey and milk are
under your tongue; the scent of your garments is like the
scent of Lebanon' (Song of Songs 4:11); 'A garden locked is
my sister, my bride, a garden locked, a fountain sealed' (Song
of Songs 4:12); 'I come to my garden, my sister, my bride, I
gather my myrrh with my spice, I eat my honeycomb with
my honey, I drink my wine with my milk. Eat, O friends, and
drink; drink deeply, O lovers!' (Song of Songs 5:1).

D. "And four in the prophets: 'The voice of mirth and the
voice of gladness, the voice of the bridegroom and the voice
of the bride' (Jeremiah 7:34); 'And as a bride adorns herself
with jewels' (Isaiah 61:10); 'And gird yourself with them like
a bride' (Isaiah 59:18); 'And as the bridegroom rejoices over
the bride' (Isaiah 62:5).

E. "And, correspondingly, the Holy One, blessed be he, puts on ten [nuptial] robes: 'The Lord reigns, he is clothed in majesty' (Psalms 93:1); 'The Lord is clothed' (Psalms 93:1); 'He has girded himself' (Psalms 93:1); 'And he put on righteousness as a coat of mail' (Isaiah 59:17); 'And he put on garments of vengeance' (Isaiah 59:17); ' 'For clothing' (Isaiah 59:17); 'This one who is glorious in his apparel' (Isaiah 63:1); 'Wherefore is your apparel red' (Isaiah 63:2); 'You are clothed with glory and majesty' (Psalms 104:1).

F. "This is so as to exact punishment from the nations of the world, who kept from the Ten Commandments the Israelites, who are [Simon] bound closely around them like the ornaments of a bride."

The concluding lines alert us to a rather subtle shift, which we shall consider presently: Israel's relationship to God undergoes change, so too, its relationship to the world; and, as we shall see, Israel proves androgynous, female now, male in the age to come, female to God, male to the nations of the world. Because the entire composition, we cannot overemphasize, derives from men, the metaphor proves remarkably daring and much more nuanced than we should realize were we to conclude that Israel here is only feminine, God only masculine.

The midrash exegesis turns to everyday experience—the love of husband and wife—for a metaphor for God's love for Israel and Israel's love for God. Then, when Solomon's song says, "O, that you would kiss me with the kisses of your mouth! For your love is better than wine" (Song 1:2), sages of blessed memory think of how God kissed Israel. Reading the Song of Songs as a metaphor, the Judaic sages as a matter of fact state in a systematic, orderly way their entire structure and system and, along the way, permit us to identify the traits they associate with feminine Israel and masculine God, respectively. What is important here, however, is not the document's doctrinal message but its implicit and tacit affirmations. The document does not set forth a great many explicit doctrines but delivers its message through the description of attitudes and emotions. And our particular interest lies in the identification of the system's designative as feminine and masculine of clearly defined attitudes and emotions. The writers mean to paint word pictures, evoke feelings, speak empathetically rather than only sympathetically. Song of Songs Rabbah tells how to think and feel, forming sensibility in the formation of the heart at one with God. That makes a survey of the taxonomic characterization of traits all the more promising.

What sages accomplished in formulating an androgynous system was to conciliate two distinct constituencies to a single policy concerning gender relationships. On the one side, women had not only to accept but to affirm and embody for the coming generations the legal position of subordination that the law prescribed for them. On the other, men had to find virtue in the political status of inferiority that history accorded to them as their lot. The solution to these distinct problems lay in the explicit androgyneity we have considered. Men must feel like women, women must act like (true, authentic, Israelite) men. But they can act like men, because the authentic Israelite man exhibits virtues that, for women, come quite naturally. What was asked of the women was no more than the men themselves accepted at the hand of the nations. What was demanded of the men was no more than the relationship that their wives endured with them, which was identical to that which Israel affirmed with God. The circle then is closed: God is to Israel as the nations are to Israel as man is to woman—for now. But, of course, as we have seen, that is only now; then matters will right themselves. By its femininity now, Israel will regain its masculinity.

Why did the system succeed so remarkably as it did? It was because the patriarchal gender doctrine of androgyneity, the dual Torah's unique formulation of *halakhah* and *aggadah* (the laws we examined, the exegesis of the Song of Songs that is before us now) successfully persuaded each Jew to accept what all Jews had to do to endure. Necessity defined virtue. Persuade the heart, not only the mind. Then each one privately would feel what everyone publicly had in any case to think. That accounts for not the mere persistence of sages' wise teachings but for their mythopoeic power. Sages' views on temper, their sagacious counsel on conciliating others and seeking the approval of the group—these not only made life tolerable; they in fact defined what life would mean for Israel. Society, in the canonical writings, set the style for the self's deepest sentiments. So the approved feelings retained approval for so long because emotions, in the thought of the sages of the canon at hand, followed rules. Feelings laid down judgments. Affections therefore constituted not mindless effusions but deliberate constructions. Whether the facts then conformed to sages' views we do not know.

When, in the Mishnah, women marry, they go into exile, leaving their father's house and going to their husband's, meaning leaving their own family and joining some other. That is why the halakhah has to guarantee the woman's right to return home at specified intervals and to maintain her relationships with her own home(land). And that is what happened to Israel too. Life in "exile," viewed as living in other peoples' countries and not in their own land, meant life as a woman, not as a man. And that meant for Israel, as Judaism conceived Israel, a long span of endurance, a test of patience to end only with the end of time. That required Israel to live in accord with the will of others. Under such circumstances the virtues of the independent citizen, sharing command of affairs of state, the gifts of innovation, initiative, independence of mind, proved beside the point. From the end of the Second Revolt against Rome in 135 to the creation of the State of Israel in 1948, Israel, the Jewish people, faced a different task. The human condition of Israel therefore defined a different heroism, one filled with patience, humiliation, self-abnegation. Israel's heroes would exhibit the feminine virtues.

To turn survival into endurance, pariah status into an exercise in godly living, the sages' affective program served full well. Israel's hero saw power in submission, wealth in the gift to be grateful, wisdom in the confession of ignorance. Like the cross, ultimate degradation was made to stand for ultimate power. Like Jesus on the cross, so Israel in exile served God through suffering. True, the cross would represent a scandal to the nations and foolishness to some Jews. But Israel's own version of the doctrine at hand endured and defined the nation's singular and astonishing resilience.

If I had to set forth in a single passage what I believe is at stake in androgynous Judaism, it is the system's account of God's most profound preference, which is for those traits that the system knows as feminine but wishes to nurture also in men's hearts and minds. This comes to expression in the simple statement "God favors the pursued over the pursuer."

1. A. "God seeks what has been driven away" (Qoheleth 3:15).

    B. R. Huna in the name of R. Joseph said, "It is always the case that 'God seeks what has been driven away' [favoring the victim].

    C. "You find when a righteous man pursues a righteous man, 'God seeks what has been driven away.'

    D. "When a wicked man pursues a wicked man, 'God seeks what has been driven away.'

    E. "All the more so when a wicked man pursues a righteous man, 'God seeks what has been driven away.'

    F. "[The same principle applies] even when you come around to a case in which a righteous man pursues a wicked man, 'God seeks what has been driven away.' "

2. A. R. Yosé b. R. Yudan in the name of R. Yosé b. R. Nehorai says, "It is always the case that the Holy One, blessed be he, demands an accounting for the blood of those who have been pursued from the hand of the pursuer.

    B. "Abel was pursued by Cain, and God sought [an accounting for] the pursued: 'And the Lord looked [favorably] upon Abel and his meal offering' [Genesis 4:4].

    C. "Noah was pursued by his generation, and God sought [an accounting for] the pursued: 'You and all your household shall come into the ark' [Genesis 7:1]. And it says, 'For this is like the days of Noah to me, as I swore [that the waters of Noah should no more go over the earth]' [Isaiah 54:9].

    D. "Abraham was pursued by Nimrod, 'and God seeks what has been driven away': 'You are the Lord, the God who chose Abram and brought him out of Ur' [Nehemiah 9:7].

    E. "Isaac was pursued by Ishmael, 'and God seeks what has been driven away': 'For through Isaac will seed be called for you' [Genesis 21:12].

    F. "Jacob was pursued by Esau, 'and God seeks what has been driven away': 'For the Lord has chosen Jacob, Israel for his prized possession' [Psalms 135:4].

G. "Moses was pursued by Pharaoh, 'and God seeks what has been driven away': 'Had not Moses His chosen stood in the breach before Him' [Psalms 106:23].

H. "David was pursued by Saul, 'and God seeks what has been driven away': 'And he chose David, his servant' [Psalms 78:70].

I. "Israel was pursued by the nations, 'and God seeks what has been driven away': 'And you has the Lord chosen to be a people to him' [Deuteronomy 14:2].

J. "And the rule applies also to the matter of offerings. A bull is pursued by a lion, a sheep is pursued by a wolf, a goat is pursued by a leopard.

K. "Therefore the Holy One, blessed be he, has said, 'Do not make offerings before me from those animals that pursue, but from those that are pursued: 'When a bull, a sheep, or a goat is born'" (Leviticus 22:27).

Leviticus Rabbah XXVII:V

The pursuer imposes, demands, insists; the pursued negotiates, yields, pleads. Both parts of the Torah state explicitly that, in gender relationships, man is the pursuer (seeking his rib back), woman the pursued, so the pertinence of this powerful passage to this book is self-evident. That right relationship is the one that is not coerced, not manipulated, not one defined by a dominant party on a subordinated one. It is a relationship of mutuality, negotiation, response to what is freely given through what cannot be demanded but only volunteered. Israel should relate to God in accord with these virtues, which sages explicitly classify as feminine—and urge on Israel.

11

The Doctrine of "Israel"
in Rabbinic Judaism

A RELIGIOUS STRUCTURE AND
ITS COMPREHENSIVE METAPHOR

Rabbinic Judaism defines its Israel in supernatural terms, deeming the so-cial entity to form a transcendental community, by faith. That is shown by the simple fact that a gentile of any origin or status, slave or free, Greek or barbarian, may enter its "Israel" on equal terms with those born into the community, becoming children of Abraham and Sarah. The children of converts are Israelite without qualification. Because that fact bears concrete and material consequences (for example, in the right to marry any other Is-raelite without distinction by reason of familial origin), it follows that the "Is-rael" of rabbinic Judaism must be understood in a wholly theological framework. This Judaism knows no distinction between children of the flesh and children of the promise and therefore cannot address a merely ethnic "Is-rael," because for rabbinic Judaism, "Israel" is always and only defined by the Torah received and represented by "our sages of blessed memory" as the word of God, never by the happenstance of secular history.

That does not mean that this Judaism's Israel ignored this-worldly facts of the life of everyday Israel after the flesh. As we saw in Chapter 10, the funda-mental social unit in Israelite society (so matters now appear) was the house-hold, encompassing the large-scale economic unit of the farmer, his wife and children, slaves, dependent craftspeople and artisans, reaching outward to other such households to form a neatly composed social unit, the village—villages, in turn, reaching outward to other like villages. But rabbinic Judaism's sys-temic social entity transformed the extended family into a representation, in the here and now, of mythic "Israel."

In that way, the social unit adopted for itself and adapted for its purposes the social entity of Scripture and identified itself with the whole life and des-tiny of that entity. Clearly, therefore, rabbinic Judaism set forth a theory of the ethnic entity that invoked a metaphor to explain the group and identify it. That fundamental act of metaphorization, from which all else follows, was the comparison of persons—Jews—of the here and now to the "Israel" of which the Hebrew Scriptures—"the Torah"—speak, and the identification of those Jews with that "Israel." Treating the social group—two or more persons—as other than they actually are in the present, as more than a (mere) given, means that the group is something else than what it appears to be.

"ISRAEL" IN THE MISHNAH'S
JUDAISM WITHOUT CHRISTIANITY

The Mishnah took shape at a time when Christianity formed a minor irritant, perhaps in some places a competing Judaism, but not a formative component of the social order, and certainly not the political power that it was to become. Hence, the Mishnah's framers' thinking about "Israel" in no way took account of the competing claim to form the true Israel put forth by Christianity; "Israel" remained intransitive, bearing no relationships to any other distinct social entity. The opposite of "Israel" in the Mishnah is "the nations," on the one side, or "Levite, priest," on the other: always taxonomical, never defined out of relationship to others within the same theoretical structure. The opposite of "Israel" in the Yerushalmi became "Rome," and Israel found itself defined as a family, with good and bad seed. Now the nations were differentiated, and a different world order was conceived; Israel entered into relationships of comparison and contrast, not merely hierarchy, because Christianity, sharing the same Scriptures, now called into question the very status of the Jews to constitute "Israel."

As the Mishnah defines "Israel," the category bears two identical meanings: the "Israel" of (all) the Jews now and here, but also the "Israel" of which Scripture—the Torah—spoke. And that encompassed both the individual and the group, without linguistic differentiation of any kind. Thus, in the Mishnah "Israel" may refer to an individual Jew (always male) or to "all Jews," that is, the collectivity of Jews. The individual woman is nearly always called *bat yisrael,* daughter of (an) Israel(ite). The sages in the Mishnah did not merely assemble facts and define the social entity as a matter of mere description of the given. Rather, they portrayed it as they wished to. They imputed to the social group, Jews, the status of a systemic entity, "Israel." To others within Jewry, it was not at all self-evident that "all Jews" constituted one "Israel" and that that one "Israel" formed the direct and immediate continuation, in the here and now, of the "Israel" of holy writ and revelation. The Essene community at Qumran did not come to that conclusion, and the sense and meaning of "Israel" proposed by the authorships of the Mishnah and related writings did not strike Philo as the main point at all. Paul, for his part, reflected on "Israel" within categories not at all symmetrical with those of the Mishnah.

The Mishnaic identification of Jewry in the here and now with the "Israel" of Scripture therefore constituted an act of metaphor, comparison, contrast, identification, and analogy. It is that Judaism's most daring social metaphor. Implicitly, moreover, the metaphor excluded a broad range of candidates from the status of (an) "Israel," the Samaritans for one example, the scheduled castes of Mishnah-tractate Qiddushin Chapter 4 for another. Calling (some) Jews "Israel" established the comprehensive and generative metaphor that gives the Mishnaic system its energy. From that metaphor all else derived momentum.

The Mishnah defines "Israel" in antonymic relationships of two sorts: first, "Israel" as against "not-Israel," gentile; and second, "Israel" as against "priest" or "Levite." "Israel" serves as a taxonomic indicator, specifically part of a more encompassing system of hierarchization; "Israel" defined the frontiers, on the outer side of society, and the social boundaries within, on the other. To understand the meaning of "Israel" as the Mishnah and its associated documents of the second and third centuries sort matters out, we consider the sense of "gentile." The authorship of the Mishnah does not differentiate among gentiles, who represent an undifferentiated mass. To the system of the Mishnah, whether a gentile is a Roman or an Aramaean or a Syrian or a Briton does not matter. That is, differentiation among gentiles rarely, if ever, makes a difference in systemic decision making.

To the system of the Mishnah, in the relationship at hand "Israel" is not differentiated, either. The upshot is that just as "gentile" is an abstract category, so is "Israel." "Kohen" (another social caste) is a category, and so is "Israel." For the purposes for which Israel/priest are defined, no further differentiation is undertaken. That is where for the Mishnaic system matters end. But to the Judaic system represented by the Yerushalmi and its associated writings, "gentile" (in the collective) may be Rome or other-than-Rome, for instance, Babylonia, Media, or Greece. That act of further differentiation—we may call it "speciation"—makes a considerable difference in the identification of gentile. In the Israel of the Mishnah's authorship, therefore, we confront an abstraction in a system of philosophy.

The village then comprised "Israel," as much as did the region, the neighborhood, the corporate society people could empirically identify, the theoretical social entity they could only imagine—all formed "all Israel," viewed under the aspect of Heaven; and, of still greater consequence, each household—that is, each building block of the village community—constituted in itself a model of, the model for, "Israel." The utter abstraction of the Mishnah had left "Israel" as individual or as "all Israel," thus without articulated linkage to the concrete middle range of the Jews' everyday social life. Dealing with exquisite detail and the intangible whole, the Mishnah's system had left that realm of the society of Jews in the workaday household and village outside the metaphorical frame of "Israel" and "Israel" viewed in the image, after the likeness of family made up that omitted middle range. In the Mishnah's "Israel," we confront an abstraction in a system of philosophy, one centered on issues of sanctification.

"ISRAEL" IN THE TALMUD'S
JUDAISM DESPITE CHRISTIANITY

Two metaphors, rarely present and scarcely explored in the writings of the first stage (circa 70–300 C.E.) in the formation of the Judaism of the dual Torah came to prominence in the second stage (circa 400–600 C.E.). These were, first, the view of "Israel" as a family, the children and heirs of the man, Israel;

second, the conception of Israel as *sui generis*. Whereas "Israel" in the first phase of the formation of Judaism perpetually finds definition in relationship to its opposite, "Israel" in the second phase constituted an intransitive entity, defined in its own terms and not solely or mainly in relationship to other comparable entities. The enormous investment in the conception of "Israel" as *sui generis* makes that point blatantly. But "Israel" as family bears that same trait of autonomy and self-evident definition.

The "Israel" in the second stratum of the canon of the Judaism of the dual Torah bears a socially vivid sense. Now "Israel" forms a family, and an encompassing theory of society, built on that conception of "Israel," permits us to describe the proportions and balances of the social entity at hand, showing how each component both is an "Israel" and also contributes to the larger composite. "Israel" as *sui generis* carried in its wake a substantial doctrine of definition, a weighty collection of general laws of social history governing the particular traits and events of the social group.

In comparing transitive to intransitive "Israel," we move from "Israel" as not-gentile and "Israel" as not-priest to powerful statements of what "Israel" is. Now to specify in concrete terms the reasons adduced to explain the rather striking shift before us. Two important changes account for the metaphorical revolution at hand, one out at the borders, the other within the Jews' group. By claiming that "Israel" constituted "Israel after the flesh," the actual, living, present family of Abraham and Sarah, Isaac and Rebekah, Jacob and Leah and Rachel, the sages met head-on the Christian claim that there was—or could ever be—some other "Israel," of a lineage not defined by the family connection at all, and that the existing Jews no longer constituted "Israel." Moreover, by representing "Israel" as *sui generis*, the sages focused on the systemic teleology, with its definition of salvation, in response to the Christian claim that salvation is not of Israel but of the Church, now enthroned in this world as in Heaven. The sage, model for Israel, in the model of Moses, our rabbi, represented on Earth the Torah, which had come from Heaven. Like Christ, in Earth as in Heaven, like the Church, the body of Christ, ruler of Earth (through the emperor) as of Heaven, the sage embodied what Israel was and was to be. So Israel as family in the model of the sage, like Moses our rabbi, corresponded in its social definition to the Church of Jesus Christ, the New Israel, of salvation of humanity. The metaphors given prominence in the late fourth- and fifth-century writings of "our sages of blessed memory" then formed a remarkable counterpoint to the social metaphors important in the minds of significant Christian theologians, as both parties reflected on the political revolution that had taken place.

In response to the challenge of Christianity, the sages' thought about "Israel" centered on the issues of history and salvation, issues made not merely chronic but acute by the political triumph. That accounts for the unprecedented reading of the outsider as differentiated, a reading contained in the two propositions concerning Rome, first, as Esau or Edom or Ishmael, that is, as part of the family; second, of Rome as the pig. Differentiating Rome from other gentiles represented a striking concession indeed, without counterpart in the Mishnah. Rome is represented as only Christian Rome could have been represented: it looks kosher, but it is unkosher. Pagan Rome could not ever have looked kosher, but Christian Rome, with its appeal to ancient Israel, could and did and moreover claimed to. It bore some traits but lacked others that validate.

The metaphor of the family proved equally pointed. The sages framed their political ideas within the metaphor of genealogy, because to begin with they appealed to the fleshly connection, the family, as the rationale for Israel's social existence. A family beginning with Abraham, Isaac, and Jacob, Israel could best sort out its relationships by drawing into the family other social entities with which it found it had to relate. So Rome became the brother. That affinity came to light only when Rome had turned Christian, and that point marked the need for the extension of the genealogical net. But the conversion to Christianity also justified the sages' extending membership in the family to Rome, for Christian Rome shared with Israel the common patrimony of Scripture—and said so. The character of the sages' thought on Israel therefore proved remarkably congruent to the conditions of public discourse that confronted them.

THE METAPHOR OF THE FAMILY, "ISRAEL'S CHILDREN"

When the sages wished to know what (an) "Israel" was, in the fourth century they reread the scriptural story of "Israel's" origins for the answer. To begin with, as Scripture told them the story, "Israel" was a man, Jacob, and his children are "the children of Jacob." That man's name was also "Israel," and, it followed, "the children of Israel" composed the extended family of that man. By extension, "Israel" formed the family of Abraham and Sarah, Isaac and Rebekah, Jacob and Leah and Rachel. "Israel" therefore invoked the metaphor of genealogy to explain the bonds that linked persons unseen into a single social entity; the shared traits were imputed, not empirical. That social metaphor of "Israel"—a simple one and easily grasped—bore consequences in two ways.

First, children in general are admonished to follow the good example of their parents. The deeds of the patriarchs and matriarchs therefore taught lessons on how the children were to act. Of greater interest in an account of "Israel" as a social metaphor, "Israel" lived twice, once in the patriarchs and matriarchs, a second time in the life of the heirs as the descendants relived those earlier lives. The stories of the family were carefully reread to provide a picture of the meaning of the latter-day events of the descendants of that same family. Accordingly, the lives of the patriarchs signaled the history of Israel.

The polemical purpose of the claim that the abstraction "Israel" was to be compared to the family of the mythic ancestor lies right at the surface. With another "Israel," the Christian Church, now claiming to constitute the true one, the sages found it possible to confront that claim and to turn it against the other side. "You claim to form 'Israel after the spirit.' Fine, and we are Israel after the flesh—and genealogy forms the link, that alone." (Converts did not present an anomaly because they were held to be children of Abraham and Sarah, who had "made souls," that is, converts, in Haran, a point repeated in the documents of the period.) That fleshly continuity formed a single family of all of "us," rendering spurious the notion that "Israel" could be other than genealogically defined. But that polemic seems to me adventitious and not primary for the metaphor provided a quite separate component to the sages' larger system.

The metaphor of Israel as family supplied an encompassing theory of society. It not only explained who "Israel" as a whole was but also set forth the responsibilities of Israel's social entity, its society. The metaphor defined the character of that entity; it explained who owes what to whom and why, and it accounted for the inner structure and interplay of relationship within the community, here and now, constituted by Jews in their villages and neighborhoods of towns. Accordingly, "Israel" as family bridged the gap between an account of the entirety of the social group, "Israel," and a picture of the components of that social group as they lived out their lives in their households and villages. An encompassing theory of society, covering all components from least to greatest, holding the whole together in correct order and proportion, derived from "Israel" viewed as extended family.

That theory of "Israel" as a society made up of persons who, because they constituted a family, stood in a clear relationship of obligation and responsibility to one another corresponded to what people much later would call the social contract, a kind of compact that told families and households in palpable ways how in the aggregate they formed something larger and tangible. The web of interaction spun out of concrete interchange now was formed not of the gossamer thread of abstraction and theory but by the tough hemp of family ties. "Israel" formed a society because "Israel" was compared to an extended family. That, sum and substance, supplied to the Jews in their households (themselves a made-up category that, in the end, transformed the relationship of the nuclear family into an abstraction capable of holding together quite unrelated persons) an account of the tie from household to household, from village to village, encompassing ultimately "all Israel."

The power of the metaphor of "Israel" as family hardly requires specification. If "we" form a family, then we know full well what links us, the common ancestry, the obligations imposed by common ancestry on the cousins who make up the family today. The link between the commonplace interactions and relationships that make "us" into a community, on the one side, and that encompassing entity, "Israel," "all Israel," now is drawn. The large comprehends the little; the abstraction of "us" overall gains concrete reality in the "us" of the here and now of home and village, all together, all forming a "family." In that fundamental way, the metaphor of "Israel" as family therefore provided the field theory of "Israel" linking the most abstract component, the entirety of the social group, to the most mundane, the specificity of the household. One theory, framed in that metaphor of such surpassing simplicity, now held the whole together. That is how the metaphor of family provided an encompassing theory of society, an account of the social contract encompassing all social entities, Jews' and gentiles' as well, that no other metaphor accomplished.

"Israel" as family comes to expression in, among other writings of the fifth century, the document that makes the most sustained and systematic statement of the matter, Genesis Rabbah. In this theory we should not miss the extraordinary polemical utility, of which we have already taken note in passing. "Israel" as family also understood itself to form a nation or people. That nation-people held a land, a rather peculiar, enchanted or holy, land—one that, in its imputed traits, was as *sui generis* as Israel also was in the metaphorical thought of the system. Competing for the same territory, Israel's claim to what it called the Land of Israel—thus, of Israel in particular—now rested on right of inheritance such as a family enjoyed, and this claim was made explicit. The following passage shows how high the stakes were in the claim to constitute the genealogical descendant of the ancestors:

Genesis Rabbah LXI:VII

1. A. "But to the sons of his concubines, Abraham gave gifts, and while he was still living, he sent them away from his son Isaac, eastward to the east country" (Genesis 25:6):

    B. In the time of Alexander of Macedonia the sons of Ishmael came to dispute with Israel about the birthright, and with them came two wicked families, the Canaanites and the Egyptians.

    C. They said, "Who will go and engage in a disputation with them?"

    D. Gebiah b. Qosem [the enchanter] said, "I shall go and engage in a disputation with them."

    E. They said to him, "Be careful not to let the Land of Israel fall into their possession."

    F. He said to them, "I shall go and engage in a disputation with them. If I win over them, well and good. And if not, you may say, 'Who is this hunchback to represent us?' "

    G. He went and engaged in a disputation with them. Said to them Alexander of Macedonia, "Who lays claim against whom?"

    H. The Ishmaelites said, "We lay claim, and we bring our evidence from their own Torah: 'But he shall acknowledge the first-born, the son of the hated' (Deuteronomy 21:17). Now Ishmael was the first-born. [We therefore claim the land as heirs of the first-born of Abraham.]"

    I. Said to him Gebiah b. Qosem, "My royal lord, does a man not do whatever he likes with his sons?"

    J. He said to him, "Indeed so."

    K. "And lo, it is written, 'Abraham gave all that he had to Isaac' (Genesis 25:2)."

L. [Alexander asked,] "Then where is the deed of gift to the other sons?"

M. He said to him, " 'But to the sons of his concubines, Abraham gave gifts, [and while he was still living, he sent them away from his son Isaac, eastward to the east country]' (Genesis 25:6)."

N. [The Ishmaelites had no claim on the land.] They abandoned the field in shame.

The metaphor as refined, with the notion of Israel today as the family of Abraham, as against the Ishmaelites, also of the same family, gives way. But the theme of family records persists. The power of the metaphor of family is that it can explain not only the social entity formed by Jews but the social entities confronted by them. All fell into the same genus, making up diverse species. The theory of society before us thus accounts for all societies and, as we shall see when we deal with Rome, does so with extraordinary force.

O. The Canaanites said, "We lay claim, and we bring our evidence from their own Torah. Throughout their Torah it is written, 'the land of Canaan.' So let them give us back our land."

P. Said to him Gebiah b. Qosem, "My royal lord, does a man not do whatever he likes with his slave?"

Q. He said to him, "Indeed so."

R. He said to him, "And lo, it is written, 'A slave of slaves shall Canaan be to his brothers' (Genesis 9:25). So they are really our slaves."

S. [The Canaanites had no claim to the land and in fact should be serving Israel.] They abandoned the field in shame.

T. The Egyptians said, "We lay claim, and we bring our evidence from their own Torah. Six hundred thousand of them left us, taking away our silver and gold utensils: 'They despoiled the Egyptians' (Exodus 12:36). Let them give them back to us."

U. Gebiah b. Qosem said, "My royal lord, six hundred thousand men worked for them for two hundred and ten years, some as silversmiths and some as goldsmiths. Let them pay us our salary at the rate of a denar a day."

V. The mathematicians went and added up what was owing, and they had not reached the sum covering a century before the Egyptians had to forfeit what they had claimed. They abandoned the field in shame.

W. [Alexander] wanted to go up to Jerusalem. The Samaritans said to him, "Be careful. They will not permit you to enter their most holy sanctuary."

X. When Gebiah b. Qosem found out about this, he went and made for himself two felt shoes, with two precious stones worth twenty thousand pieces of silver set in them. When he got to the mountain of the house [of the Temple], he said to him, "My royal lord, take off your shoes and put on these two felt slippers, for the floor is slippery, and you should not slip and fall."

Y. When they came to the most holy sanctuary, he said to him, "Up to this point, we have the right to enter. From this point onward, we do not have the right to enter."

Z. He said to him, "When we get out of here, I'm going to even out your hump."

AA. He said to him, "You will be called a great surgeon and get a big fee."

The same metaphor serves both "Israel" and "Canaan." Each formed the latter-day heir of the earliest family, and both lived out the original paradigm. The mode of thought imputes the same genus to both social entities, and then makes its possible to distinguish among the two species. We shall see the same mode of thought (the family, but which wing of the family?) when we consider the confrontation with Christianity and Rome, in each case conceived in the same personal way. The metaphor applies to both and yields its own meanings for each. The final claim in the passage before us moves away from the metaphor of family. But the notion of a continuous, physical descent is implicit here as well. "Israel" has inherited the wealth of Egypt. Because the notion of inheritance forms a component of the metaphor of family (a conception critical, as we shall see in the next section, in the supernatural patrimony of the "children of Israel" in the merit of the ancestors), we survey the conclusion of the passage.

ISRAEL AS *SUI GENERIS*: THE RULES OF NATURE, THE RULES OF HISTORY, AND SUPERNATURAL GOVERNANCE OF ISRAEL IN LEVITICUS RABBAH

The definition of "Israel" comes to us not only in what people expressly mean by the word but also in the implicit terms yielded by how they discuss the social entity. In Leviticus Rabbah (a commentary on the book of Leviticus that reached closure in the mid-fifth century, about half a century after the conclusion of the first Talmud), the conception of "Israel" as *sui generis* is expressed in an implicit statement that Israel is subject to its own laws, which are distinct from the laws governing all other social entities. These laws may be discerned in the factual, scriptural record of "Israel's" past, and that past, by definition, belonged to "Israel" alone. It followed, therefore, that by discerning the regularities in "Israel's" history, implicitly understood as unique to "Israel," the sages recorded the view that "Israel," like God, was not subject to analogy or comparison. Accordingly, although not labeled a genus unto itself, Israel is treated in that way.

To understand how this view of "Israel" comes to expression, we have to trace the principal mode of thought characteristic of the authorship of Leviticus Rabbah. It is an exercise in proving hypotheses by tests of concrete facts. The hypotheses derive from the theology of Israel. The tests are worked out by reference to those given facts of social history that Scripture, for its part, contributes. As with the whole range of ancient exegetes of Scripture, rabbinic authorships treated Scripture as a set of facts. These facts concerned history, not nature, but they served, much as the facts of nature availed the Greek natural philosophers did, to prove or disprove hypotheses. The hypotheses concerned the social rules to which Israel was subjected, and the upshot was that Israel was subject to its own rules, revealed by the historical facts of Scripture. The single most common way in which the sages made the implicit statement that "Israel" is *sui generis* derives from their "as-if" mode of seeing "Israel's" reality. The sages read "Israel's" history not as it seems (that is, not as it would appear when treated in accord with the same norms as the histories of other social entities) but as a series of mysteries. The facts are not what appearances suggest. The deeper truth is not revealed in those events that happen, in common, to "Israel" and (other) nations around the world. What is happening to "Israel" is wholly other, different from what seems to be happening and what is happening to ordinary groups. The fundamental proposition pertinent to "Israel" in Leviticus Rabbah is that things are not what they seem. "Israel's" reality does not correspond to the perceived facts of this world.

Now if we ask ourselves the source of this particular mode of thinking about "Israel," we find no difficulty in identifying the point of origin. The beginning of seeing "Israel" as if it were other than the here-and-now social group people saw lay in the original metaphorization of the social group. When people looked at themselves, their households and villages, their regions and language group, and thought, "What more are we? What else are we?" they began that process of abstraction that took the form of an intellectual labor of comparison, contrast, analogy, and, as is clear, consequent metaphorization. The group is compared to something else (or to nothing else) and hence is treated as not fully represented by the here and now but as representative, itself, of something else beyond. And that very mode of seeing things, lying in the foundations of the thought of the Mishnah's authorship, implicit in the identification of the survivors as the present avatar of Scripture's "Israel," yielded an ongoing process of metaphorization.

The original use of the metaphor "Israel" to serve as the explanation of who the surviving groups were made it natural, from that time forward, to see "Israel" under the aspect of the "as-if." How this mode of thought worked itself out in the documents is clear. The exegetes maintained that a given statement of Scripture, in the case of Leviticus, stood for and signified something other than that to which the verse openly referred. If—as was a given for these exegetes—water stands for Torah, the skin disease mentioned in Leviticus 13, in Hebrew called *sara'at* and translated as leprosy, stands for, is caused by, evil speech, the reference to some thing to mean some other thing entirely, then the mode of thought is simple.

And what is decisive for our inquiry is that that mode of thought pertained to "Israel" alone. Solely in the case of "Israel" did one thing symbolize another, speak not of itself but of some other thing entirely. When other social entities (for example, Babylonia, Persia, or Rome) stood for something else, it was in relationship to "Israel" and in the context of the metaphorization of Israel. When treated in a neutral context, by contrast, we find no metaphors; for example, Alexander of Macedonia is a person, and no symbol stands for that person. When Greece appears in the sequence of empires leading finally to the rule of "Israel," then Greece may be symbolized by the hare. And there is another side of the matter too. Other things—the bear, the eagle—could stand for the empires, but, in that metaphorical context, "Israel" stands only for itself. Whichever way we have it, therefore, implicit in that view and mode of thought is the notion of "Israel" as *sui generis,* lacking all counterpart or parallel entity for purposes of comparison and contrast. The importance of the mode of reading Scripture "as if" it meant something else than what it said, in the case of the exegesis of Leviticus Rabbah, should not be missed. What lies beneath or beyond the surface is the true reality, the world of truth and meaning, discerned through metaphorical thinking.

12

The Messiah

The Evidence of the Talmud

THE ADVENT OF THE MESSIAH:
THE TALMUD OF THE LAND OF ISRAEL

When constructing their systematic account of Judaism (that is, the worldview and way of life for Israel presented in the Mishnah) the philosophers of the Mishnah did not make extensive use of the Messiah theme in the construction of a teleology for their system.[1] They found it possible to present a statement of goals for their projected life of Israel that was entirely separate from appeals to history and eschatology. Because they certainly knew, and even alluded to, long-standing and widely held convictions on eschatological subjects, beginning with those in Scripture, the framers thereby testified that, knowing the larger repertoire, they made choices different from others before and after them. Their document accurately and ubiquitously expresses these choices, both affirmative and negative.

The Messiah theme, trivial in the Mishnah, moves to the forefront in the Yerushalmi, which correlates with the same document's keen interest in history and its patterns. If the Mishnah provided a teleology without eschatology, the framers of the Yerushalmi and related midrash compilations could not conceive of any but an utterly eschatological goal for themselves. Historical events entered into the construction of a teleology for the Yerushalmi's system of Judaism as a whole. What the law demanded reflected the consequences of wrongful action on the part of Israel. So, again, Israel's own deeds defined the events of history.

But this notion of determining one's own destiny should not be misunderstood. The framers of the Talmud of the Land of Israel were not telling the Jews to please God by doing commandments in order that they should thereby gain control of their own destiny. To the contrary, the paradox of the Yerushalmi's system lies in the fact that Israel can free itself of control by other nations only by humbly agreeing to accept God's rule. The nations—Rome, in the present instance—rest on one side of the balance, whereas God rests on the other. Israel must then choose between them. There is no such thing for Israel as freedom from both God and the nations, total autonomy and independence. There is only a choice of masters, a ruler on Earth or a ruler in Heaven.

Keeping the commandments as a mark of submission, loyalty, humility before God is the rabbinic system of salvation. So Israel does not "save itself."

Israel never controls its own destiny, either on Earth or in Heaven. The only choice is whether to cast one's fate into the hands of cruel, deceitful men or to trust in the living God of mercy and love. The stress that Israel's arrogance alienates God, Israel's humility and submission win God's favor, cannot surprise us; this is the very point of the doctrine of emotions that defines rabbinic Judaism's ethics. Now the same view is expressed in a still more critical area. We shall now see how this position is spelled out in the setting of discourse about the Messiah in the Talmud of the Land of Israel.

The failed Messiah of the second century, Bar Kokhba, above all exemplifies arrogance against God. He lost the war because of that arrogance. His emotions, attitudes, sentiments, and feelings form the model of how the virtuous Israelite is not to conceive of matters. In particular, he ignored the authority of sages:

Yerushalmi Taanit 4:5

X. J. Said R. Yohanan, "Upon orders of Caesar Hadrian, they killed eight hundred thousand in Betar."

K. Said R. Yohanan, "There were eighty thousand pairs of trumpeters surrounding Betar. Each one was in charge of a number of troops. Ben Kozeba was there and he had two hundred thousand troops who, as a sign of loyalty, had cut off their little fingers.

L. "Sages sent word to him, 'How long are you going to turn Israel into a maimed people.'

M. "He said to them, 'How otherwise is it possible to test them?'

N. "They replied to him, 'Whoever cannot uproot a cedar of Lebanon while riding on his horse will not be inscribed on your military rolls.'

O. "So there were two hundred thousand who qualified in one way, and another two hundred thousand who qualified in another way."

P. When he would go forth to battle, he would say, "Lord of the world! Do not help and do not hinder us! 'Hast thou not rejected us, O God? Thou dost not go forth, O God, with our armies'"[Psalms 60:10].

Q. Three and a half years did Hadrian besiege Betar.

R. R. Eleazar of Modiin would sit on sackcloth and ashes and pray every day, saying "Lord of the ages! Do not judge in accord with strict judgment this day! Do not judge in accord with strict judgment this day!"

S. Hadrian wanted to go to him. A Samaritan said to him, "Do not go to him until I see what he is doing, and so hand over the city [of Betar] to you. [Make peace...for you.]"

T. [The Samaritan] got into the city through a drainpipe. He went and found R. Eleazar of Modiin standing and praying. He pretended to whisper something in his ear.

U. The townspeople saw [the Samaritan] do this and brought him to Ben Kozeba. They told him, "We saw this man having dealings with your friend."

V. [Bar Kokhba] said to him, "What did you say to him, and what did he say to you?"

W. He said to [the Samaritan], "If I tell you, then the king will kill me, and if I do not tell you, then you will kill me. It is better that the king kill me, and not you.

X. "[Eleazar] said to me, 'I should hand over my city.' ['I shall make peace…']"

Y. He turned to R. Eleazar of Modiin. He said to him, "What did this Samaritan say to you?"

Z. He replied, "Nothing."

AA. He said to him, "What did you say to him?"

BB. He said to him, "Nothing."

CC. [Ben Kozeba] gave [Eleazar] one good kick and killed him.

DD. Forthwith an echo came forth and proclaimed the following verse:

EE. "Woe to my worthless shepherd, who deserts the flock! May the sword smite his arm and his right eye! Let his arm be wholly withered, his right eye utterly blinded! [Zecharian 11:17].

FF. "You have murdered R. Eleazar of Modiin, the right arm of all Israel, and their right eye. Therefore may the right arm of that man wither, may his right eye be utterly blinded!"

GG. Forthwith Betar was taken, and Ben Kozeba was killed.

That kick—an act of temper, a demonstration of untamed emotions—tells the whole story. We notice two complementary themes. First, Bar Kokhba treats Heaven with arrogance, asking God merely to keep out of the way. Second, he treats an especially revered sage with a parallel arrogance. The sage had the power to preserve Israel. Bar Kokhba destroyed Israel's one protection. The result was inevitable.

The Messiah, the centerpiece of salvation history and hero of the tale, emerged as a critical figure. The historical theory of this Yerushalmi passage is stated very simply. In its view, Israel had to choose between wars, either the war fought by Bar Kokhba or the "war for Torah." "Why had they been punished? It was because of the weight of the war, for they had not wanted to engage in the struggles over the meaning of the Torah" (Yerushalmi Taanit 3:9 XVI:I). Those struggles, which were ritual arguments about ritual matters, promised the only victory worth winning. Then Israel's history would be written in terms of wars over the meaning of the Torah and the decision of the law.

In the Talmud's theory of salvation, the framers provided Israel with an account of how to overcome the unsatisfactory circumstances of an unredeemed present, so as to accomplish the movement from here to the much-desired future. When the Talmud's authorities present statements on the promise of the law for those who keep it, therefore, they provide glimpses of the goal of the system as a whole. These invoked the primacy of the rabbi and the legitimating power of the Torah, and in those two components of the system we find the principles of the Messianic doctrine. And these bring us back to the argument with Christ triumphant, as the Christians perceived him.

MESSIAH IN CONTEXT:
THE CHRISTIAN CHALLENGE

In line with stress on the study of a religion as a problem of social ecology, now we ask about the relationship of text to context, finding in the circumstance a way of explaining the substance of the functioning system before us. The context in which the Talmud of the Land of Israel and related midrash compilations restated the received Messiah theme, defining the Messiah as a humble sage finds its definition in the triumph of Christianity. The government's adoption of Christianity as the state religion was taken to validate the Christian claim that Jesus was, and is, Christ. Indeed, every page of Eusebius' writing bears the message that the conversion of Constantine proves the Christhood of Jesus: his messianic standing. History—the affairs of nations and monarchs—yields laws of society, proves God's will, and matters now speak for themselves.

For Judaism the dramatic shift in the fortunes of the competing biblical faith raised a simple and unpleasant possibility: perhaps Israel had been wrong after all. Because the Jews as a whole, and sages among them, anticipated the coming of the Messiah promised by the prophets, the issue could be fairly joined. If history proves propositions, as the prophets and apocalyptic visionaries had maintained, then how could Jews deny the Christians' claim that the conversion of the emperor, then of the Empire, demonstrated the true state of affairs in Heaven as much as on Earth?

John Chrysostom, who can stand for Christianity on the messianic issue, typifies the Christian theologians' concern that converts not proceed to the synagogue or retain connections with it. For the burden of his case was that since Christ had now been proved Messiah, Christians no longer could associate themselves with the synagogue. Judaism had lost, Christianity had won, and people had to choose the one and give up the other. At stake for Chrysostom, whose sermons on Judaism, preached in 386–387, provide for our purpose the statement of Christianity on the messianic issue, was Christians' participation in synagogue rites and Judaic practices. He invoked the Jews' failure in the fiasco of the proposed rebuilding of the Temple in Jerusalem only a quarter of a century earlier. He drew on the failure of that project to demonstrate that Judaic rites no longer held any power. He further cited that incident to prove that Israel's salvation lay wholly in the past, in the time of the return to Zion, and never in the future. So the happenings of the day demonstrated proofs of the faith. The struggle between sages and theologians concerned the meaning of important contemporary happenings, and the same happenings, read in light of the same Scripture, provoked discussion of the same issues: a confrontation.

The messianic crisis confronting the Christian theologians hardly matches that facing the Judaic sages. The one dealt with problems of triumph; the other, despair; the one had to interpret a new day; the other, to explain disaster. Scripture explicitly promised that Israel would receive salvation from God's anointed Messiah at the end of time. The teleology of Israelite faith, in the biblical account, focused on eschatology and, within eschatology, on the salvific, therefore the messianic, dimension. On the other hand, the Mishnah had for its part taken up a view of its own on the issue of teleology, presenting an ahistorical and essentially nonmessianic teleology. Sages' response to the messianic crisis had to mediate two distinct and contradictory positions. Sages explained what the messianic hope now entailed and how to identify the Messiah, who would be a sage. They further included the messianic issue in their larger historical theory. So we cannot address the question at hand as if the Christians defined the agendum. True, to Israel all they had to say was "Why not?" But sages responded with a far-reaching doctrine of their own, deeming the question, in its Christian formulation, trivial.

But the issue confronting both Judaic sages and Christian theologians was one and the same: precisely what difference the Messiah makes. To state matters as they would be worked out by both parties, in the light of the events of the day: What do I have to do because the Messiah has come (Christian) or because I want the Messiah to come (Judaic)? That question encompasses two sides of a single issue. On the issue of the Messiahship of Jesus all other matters depended. It follows that one party believed precisely the opposite of the other on an issue shared in identical definition by both. For Christians, the sole issue—belief or unbelief—carried a clear implication for the audience subject to address. When debate would go forward, it would center on the wavering of Christians and the unbelief of Jews. Our exemplary figure, Chrysostom, framed matters in those terms, drawing on the events of his own day for ample instantiation of the matter. The Christian formulation thus focused all argument on the vindication of Jesus as Christ. When Christians found attractive aspects of Judaic rite and belief, the Christian theologians invoked the fundamental issue: Is Jesus Christ? If so, then Judaism fails. If not, then Christianity fails. No question, therefore, drew the two sets of intellectuals into more direct conflict; none bore so immediate and fundamental consequences. Christians did not have to keep the Torah—that was a principal message of Chrysostom in context.

IDENTIFYING THE MESSIAH,
HASTENING HIS ADVENT

In the Talmud of the Land of Israel, circa 400 c.e., we find a fully exposed doctrine not only of a Messiah (for example, a kind of priest or general) but of *the* Messiah, the one man who will save Israel: who he is, how we will know him, what we must do to bring him. It follows that the Talmud of the Land of Israel presents clear evidence that the Messiah myth had found its place within that larger Torah myth that characterized Judaism in its later formative literature. A clear effort to identify the person of the Messiah and to confront the claim that a specific, named individual had been, or would be, the Messiah—these come to the fore. This means that the issue had reached the center of lively discourse in at least some rabbinic circles. The disposition of the issue proves distinctive to sages: the Messiah will be a sage, and the Messiah will come when Israel has attained that condition of sanctification, marked also by profound humility and complete acceptance of God's will, that signifies sanctification.

These two conditions say the same thing twice: sages' Judaism will identify the Messiah and teach how to bring him nearer. In these allegations we find no point of intersection with issues important to Chrysostom, even though the Talmud of the Land of Israel reached closure at the same time as Chrysostom's preaching. For Chrysostom dealt with the Messiah theme in terms pertinent to his larger system, and sages did the same. But the issue was fairly joined. In Chrysostom's terms, it was that Jesus is Christ, proved by the events of the recent past. In sages' terms, it was that the Messiah will be a sage, coming when Israel fully accepts, in all humility, God's sole rule. The first stage in the position of each hardly matches that in the outline of the other. But the second does: Jesus is Christ; therefore, Israel will have no other Messiah. The Messiah will come, in the form of a sage; therefore, no one who now claims to be the Messiah is in fact the savior.

Once the figure of the Messiah has come on stage, discussion arises on who, among the living, the Messiah might be. The identification of the Messiah begins with the person of David himself: "If the Messiah-King comes from among the living, his name will be David. If he comes from among the dead, it will be King David himself" (Yerushalmi Berakhot 2:3 V:P). A variety of evidence announced the advent of the Messiah as a figure in the larger system of formative Judaism. The rabbinization of David constitutes one kind of evidence. Serious discussion, within the framework of the accepted documents of Mishnaic exegesis and the law, concerning the identification and claim of diverse figures asserted to be Messiahs, presents still more telling proof.

Yerushalmi Berakhot 2:4 (translated by T. Zahavy)

A. Once a Jew was plowing and his ox snorted once before him. An Arab who was passing and heard the sound said to him, "Jew, loosen your ox and loosen the plow and stop plowing. For today your Temple was destroyed."

B. The ox snorted again. He [the Arab] said to him, "Jew, bind your ox and bind your plow, for today the Messiah-King was born."

C. He said to him, "What is his name?"

D. "Menahem."

E. He said to him, "And what is his father's name?"

F. The Arab said to him, "Hezekiah."

G. He said to him, "Where is he from?"

H. He said to him, "From the royal capital of Bethlehem in Judea."

I. The Jew went and sold his ox and sold his plow. And he became a peddler of infant's felt-cloths [diapers]. And he went from place to place until he came to that very city. All of the women bought from him. But Menahem's mother did not buy from him.

J. He heard the women saying, "Menahem's mother, Menahem's mother, come buy for your child."

K. She said, "I want to bring him up to hate Israel. For on the day he was born, the Temple was destroyed."

L. They said to her, "We are sure that on this day it was destroyed, and on this day of the year it will be rebuilt."

M. She said to the peddler, "I have no money."

N. He said to her, "It is of no matter to me. Come and buy for him and pay me when I return."

O. A while later he returned to that city. He said to her, "How is the infant doing?"

P. She said to him, "Since the time you saw him a spirit came and carried him away from me."

Q. Said R. Bun, "Why do we learn this from [a story about] an Arab? Do we not have explicit scriptural evidence for it? 'Lebanon with its majestic trees will fall' [Isaiah 10:34]. And what follows this? 'There shall come forth a shoot from the stump of Jesse' [Isaiah 11:1]. [Right after an allusion to the destruction of the Temple, the prophet speaks of the messianic age.]"

This is a set-piece story, adduced to prove that the Messiah was born on the day the Temple was destroyed. The Messiah was born when the Temple was destroyed; hence, God prepared a better fate for Israel than had appeared.

A more concrete matter—the identification of the Messiah with a known historical personality—was associated with the name of Aqiba. He is said to have claimed that Bar Kokhba, leader of the second-century revolt, was the Messiah. The important aspect of the story, however, is the rejection of Aqiba's view. The discredited Messiah figure (if Bar Kokhba actually was such in his own day) finds no apologists in the later rabbinic canon. What is striking in what follows, moreover, is that we really have two stories. At *G* Aqiba is said to have believed that Bar Kokhba was a disappointment. At *H–I,* he is said to have identified Bar Kokhba with the Messiah-King. Both cannot be true, so what we have is simply two separate opinions of Aqiba's judgment of Bar Kokhba/Bar Kozebah.

Yerushalmi Taanit 4:5

X. G. R. Simeon b. Yohai taught, "Aqiba, my master, would interpret the following verse: 'A star (*kokhab*) shall come forth out of Jacob [Numbers 24:17], a disappointment (*Kozeba*) shall come forth out of Jacob.'"

H. R. Aqiba, when he saw Bar Kozeba, said, "This is the King Messiah."

I. R. Yohanan ben Toreta said to him, "Aqiba! Grass will grow on your cheeks before the Messiah will come!"

The important point is not only that Aqiba had been proved wrong. It is that the very verse of Scripture adduced in behalf of his viewpoint could be treated more generally and made to refer to righteous people in general, not to the Messiah in particular. And that leads us to the issue of the age, as sages had to face it: what makes a Messiah a false Messiah? The answer, we recall, is arrogance.

The climax of the matter comes in an explicit statement that the practice of conduct required by the Torah will bring about the coming of the Messiah. That explanation of the purpose of the holy way of life, focused now on the end of time and the advent of the Messiah, must strike us as surprising. For the framers of the Mishnah had found it possible to construct a complete and encompassing teleology for their system with scarcely a single word about the Messiah's coming when the system would be perfectly achieved. So with their interest in explaining events and accounting for history, third- and fourth-century sages represented in the units of discourse at hand invoked what their predecessors had at best found of peripheral consequence to their system. The following contains the most striking expression of the viewpoint at hand:

Yerushalmi Taanit 1:1

X. J. "The oracle concerning Dumah. One is calling to me from Seir, 'Watchman, what of the night? Watchman, what of the night?' (Isaiah 21:11)."

K. The Israelites said to Isaiah, "O, our Rabbi, Isaiah, what will come for us out of this night?"

L. He said to them, "Wait for me, until I can present the question."

M. Once he had asked the question, he came back to them.

N. They said to him, "Watchman, what of the night? What did the Guardian of the ages tell you?"

O. He said to them, "The watchman says, 'Morning comes; and also the night. If you will inquire, inquire; come back again' (Isaiah 21:12)."

P. They said to him, "Also the night?"

Q. He said to them, "It is not what you are thinking. But there will be morning for the righteous, and night for the wicked, morning for Israel, and night for idolaters."

R. They said to him, "When?"

S. He said to them, "Whenever you want, He too wants [it to be]—if you want it, he wants it."

T. They said to him, "What is standing in the way?"

U. He said to them, "Repentance: 'Come back again' (Isaiah 21:12)."

V. R. Aha in the name of R. Tanhum b. R. Hiyya, "If Israel repents for one day, forthwith the son of David will come.

W. "What is the Scriptural basis? 'O, that today you would hearken to his voice!' (Psalms 95:7)."

X. Said R. Levi, "If Israel would keep a single Sabbath in the proper way, forthwith the son of David will come.

Y. "What is the Scriptural basis for this view? 'Moses said, Eat it today, for today is a Sabbath to the Lord; today you will not find it in the field' (Exodus 16:25).

Z. "And it says, 'For thus said the Lord God, the Holy One of Israel, 'In returning and rest you shall be saved; in quietness and in trust shall be your strength. And you would not' (Isaiah 30:15)."

The discussion of the power of repentance would hardly have surprised a Mishnah sage. What is new is at *V–Z,* the explicit linkage of keeping the law with achieving the end of time and the coming of the Messiah. That motif stands separate from the notions of righteousness and repentance, which surely do not require it. So the condition of "all Israel," a social category in historical time, comes under consideration, and not only the status of individual Israelites in life and in death. The latter had formed the arena for Abot's account of the Mishnah's meaning. Now history as an operative category, drawing in its wake Israel as a social entity, comes once more on the scene. But, except for the Mishnah's sages, it had never left the stage.

We must not lose sight of the importance of this passage, with its emphasis on repentance, on the one side, and the power of Israel to reform itself, on the other. The Messiah will come any day that Israel makes it possible. If all Israel will keep a single Sabbath in the proper (rabbinic) way, the Messiah will come. If all Israel will repent for one day, the Messiah will come. "Whenever you want...," the Messiah will come. Now, two things are happening here. First, the system of religious observance, including study of Torah, is explicitly invoked as having salvific power. Second, the persistent hope of the people for the coming of the Messiah is linked to the system of rabbinic observance and belief. In this way, the austere program of the Mishnah, with no trace of a promise that the Messiah will come if and when the system is fully realized, finds a new development. A teleology lacking all eschatological dimension here gives way to an explicitly messianic statement that the purpose of the law is to attain Israel's salvation: "If you want it, God wants it too." The one thing Israel commands is its own heart; the power it yet exercises is the power to repent. These suffice. The entire history of humanity will respond to Israel's will, to what happens in Israel's heart and soul. And, with the Temple in ruins, repentance can take place only within the heart and mind.

A discussion of the power of repentance would hardly have surprised a Mishnah sage. What is new is at *V–Z*, the explicit linkage of keeping the law with achieving the end of time and the coming of the Messiah. That motif stands separate from the notions of righteousness and repentance, which surely did not require it. We must not lose sight of the importance of this passage, with its emphasis on repentance, on the one side, and the power of Israel to reform itself, on the other. The Messiah will come any day that Israel makes it possible. Let me underline the most important statement of this large conception: *If all Israel will keep a single Sabbath in the proper (rabbinic) way, the Messiah will come. If all Israel will repent for one day, the Messiah will come.* "Whenever you want...," the Messiah will come.

NOTE

1. This chapter reviews the results of *The Foundations of Judaism: Method, Teleology, Doctrine* (Philadelphia: Fortress, 1983–1985), I–III:*II. Messiah in Context: Israel's History and Destiny in Formative Judaism,* 2d ed. (Lanham, MD: University Press of Amer-ica, 1988), Studies in Judaism series; and *Judaism and Christianity in the Age of Constantine: Issues of the Initial Confrontation* (Chicago: University of Chicago Press, 1987). A full bibliography and references are supplied in those monographs.

13

Discerning a Religious Worldview Through the Prayers People Say

We move from three specific doctrines to the more encompassing question: What is the worldview of the Judaism of the dual Torah? We focus now on how the authoritative theology of this Judaism comes to full expression. Although some claim that "Judaism has no theology," in fact rabbinic Judaism takes up a considerable theological position, covering how we know God and what we know about God. Specifically, through Creation, the Torah, and Redemption, we know God—in the here and now. The great themes of the Judaic theology, then, are God in creation, revelation, and redemption—that is, in nature, direct encounter in this world, and history and its conclusion with the coming of the Messiah.

But how do we know that this vast theological vision speaks to everyone, not just the sages of the Talmud? Specifically, what sort of evidence will lead us into the views that engaged everybody, not just religious virtuosi? The answer is to examine important prayers, which tell us what words people used when they spoke to God. In the elevated liturgy of the synagogue, we seek evidence of the worldview of the religious system before us. Moreover, the texture of the way of life, not only the worldview, is woven on the loom of worship: the ideals people set for themselves in the here and now, as much as the ideas they held concerning God. For in a history of nearly forty centuries, the Jews have produced rich and complex religious phenomena. Indeed, Judaic religious and historical data, like those of other religions, may seem at the outset to defy adequate description. The varieties of historical settings, rituals, intellectual and religious expressions, exegetical and theological literature can scarcely be satisfactorily apprehended in the modest framework of a lifetime of study. In working toward a definition of any religion, we must confront the same formidable complexities. Here we consider how theology comes to expression in worship, and in our consideration of the Torah's way of life (Chapter 19), we return to liturgy for an account of the life's ideal of the same system.

Our operative criteria of selection ought to be, What phenomena are most widely present and meaningful? What, further, is important as a representation of the reality both viewed and shaped by Judaism? The answers surely cannot be found in only philosophical, legal, mystical, or theological literature produced by and for a religious elite. We cannot suppose sophisticated conceptions of extraordinary people were fully grasped by common folk. Theological writings, although important, testify to the conceptions of reality held by only a tiny minority. The legal ideals and values of Judaism were first shaped by the rabbis, a class of religious virtuosi, and then imposed on the life of ordinary people. Excluding learned theological and legal writings, the religious materials best conforming to our criteria are liturgical. The myths conveyed by prayer and associated rituals are universal, everywhere present and meaningful in the history of Judaism. Of greatest importance, they provide the clearest picture of how Jews in archaic times envisioned the meaning of life and of themselves.

Before proceeding, we had best clarify the meaning of "mythic structure." By myth, historians of religion do *not* mean something that is not true. They mean truth that is conveyed in the medium of a narrative, rather than through doctrine, creed, proposition, and the like. If a myth is present, it must infuse all details of the faith, for it carries the worldview that comes to expression in the way of life, the pattern of deeds, of the faith, somehow hidden in every ceremony and rite, every liturgy, every sacred gesture and taboo. We must be able to locate it in commonplace, not merely extraordinary, events of piety. Liturgy provides the clearest and most reliable evidence of the structure of Judaic myth, because the prayers were said everywhere in pretty much the same structure and substance. They constituted the centerpiece of the religious life of expression. They carried the message of the faith, its view of the world, of history and of Israel, of the individual and of the holy community, and that message came to expression in emotionally powerful language and song, gesture and dance, procession and proclamation. The way of the Torah carries us to the synagogue, to stand before the ark, as the doors open wide and reveal, inside, the Torah scroll that stands for, symbolizes, the Torah: "This is the Torah that Moses set forth before the People, Israel, at the instruction of Lord." Here is the proclamation of the faith: stated, sung, acted out as the Torah is raised and shown, word for word, to the believing congregation.

The overall mythic structure of the Judaism of the dual Torah, which we now begin to describe, has three principal components: a story of creation, one of revelation, and one of redemption. God created the world, revealed the Torah, and will redeem the people of Israel—to whom God revealed the Torah—at the end of time through the sending of the Messiah, as we saw in Chapter 12. Sometimes the same elements will be given the shape of a story about God, Israel (the Jewish people), and the covenant effected through the keeping of the Torah—that is, through doing God's will for Israel. This set of mythic statements is called by the New Testament scholar E. P. Sanders "covenantal nomism," meaning the keeping of the religious requirements of the Torah as an expression of loyalty to the covenant between God and Israel.[1] In many of the religious statements we shall see, the main themes again and again are God's creation of the world, revelation of the Torah, and redemption of Israel. Naturally, it is possible to express these same themes in diverse ways, so that creation takes the form of the Garden of Eden story, redemption is symbolized by the going forth from Egypt, and revelation is reflected throughout in the use of Torah symbols.

We shall consider several sorts of liturgies, for the Judaic Prayerbook—the *Siddur*—constitutes the corpus of Judaic dogma, rite, and myth for the Judaism of the dual Torah and its continuators and successors in contemporary Orthodoxy, Reform, Conservatism, and Reconstructionism. First comes the *Shema,* containing the fundamental principles of faith. Then we shall turn to the marriage liturgy to see how the vital myth reshapes a private experience into a moment of public and communal meaning. Third, we shall consider two disparate liturgies of self-consciousness, the family together at the Passover *seder* and the community on the threshold of going forth from worship. Each prayer tells us about how the Jew sees and defines him- or herself in, and apart from, the world. We shall see, in the Grace after Meals, how the land and Jerusalem enter the Judaic imagination. We shall read a folk song, a message of prophecy, a stanza of a modern nationalist anthem, and a messianic prayer in the daily service, all addressed to the question "How long, O Lord?"

As we proceed in our study, we draw on materials from the Hebrew Scriptures (for instance, Psalms) as much as from documents generally credited to Talmudic rabbis, just as the rabbis themselves drew on the Scriptures for a definition of Judaism. What we see in the profoundly biblical orientation of Judaism is that the Talmudic rabbis did not start something essentially new but reshaped something that had been in existence for a very long time. That means that the ecological framework to be interpreted by Judaism—that is, the context framed and shaped in the life of the Jewish people—remained fairly stable, so that old ideas continued to be found plausible and self-evident. In this respect, the claim of the rabbinic version of Judaism to continue the Torah of Moses, "our rabbi," formed a statement through myth of a claim to form the authentic tradition. And (it goes without saying) the fact that a great many sources we shall adduce in evidence of the inner life of Judaism are not distinctive to rabbinic perspectives of Judaism changes nothing. These are materials Talmudic rabbis found congenial to their conceptions. And they found them so because they could and did read them as statements of ideas particular to the Talmudic rabbis themselves.

Why should this expression of Judaism—that is, the worldview expressed through the symbols of creation, revelation, and redemption—have made sense and proved plausible for the Jews over a long period of time? The reason is that the critical issues of the Jews' historical life—Why do we matter? Why should we go forward? How long will this situation last?—are dealt with in a profound and transcendent way. Keep in mind that the Jews have had to suffer for their faith and accept the condition of a despised minority, a pariah people, everywhere they have lived. Even in the United States today many people look down on the Jews and think ill of them. The Jews, for their part, have always had the choice of accepting the dominant religion of their place of residence—Christianity in the West, Islam in the Middle East—and so of leaving their condition as a pariah people. And some did. But most did not, just as the Jews of the modern period chose and continue to choose to be Jews, no matter what. Why should they do this? Why do they do this? And what does it mean? This barrage of questions deserves a simple answer.

In the classical myth, the meaning is found in the correspondence of Heaven and Earth. The world was created for the sake of the Torah; the Torah was revealed for the sake of Israel; and Israel, keeping the covenant through the Torah, will be redeemed in the end of time. To the world, the Jews may seem to be pariahs, but Judaism knows they are God's children—princes and princesses. The life of the Torah is a sweet and serene life. The rhythms of creation and Sabbath, revelation and Torah study, and redemption and the festivals (Passover, Tabernacles, Pentecost) join the lives of individual men and women to the patterns of the transcendent and the holy. From the perspective of Judaism lived by the Jewish people, the suffering has been the proof and vindication of the faith of the Torah. The very regularity of creation—the waves on the ocean, the majesty and permanence of the mountains and the valleys—stands as witness to the truth of the faith of the Torah. These are the lines of thought to be explored: the relationship between the Jews' historical and social realities and their self-understanding as shaped and expressed through their religion, Judaism.

NOTE

1. E. P. Sanders, *Paul and Palestinian Judaism* (Philadelphia: Fortress, 1977), *passim*.

14

"Hear, O Israel"
The Unity of God

Evening and morning, the pious Jew proclaims the unity and uniqueness of God. The proclamation is preceded and followed by blessings. The whole constitutes the credo of the Judaic tradition. It is "what the Jews believe." Components recur everywhere. Let us first examine the prayer called *Shema* (Hear). The recital of the Shema is introduced by a celebration of God as Creator of the world. In the morning, one says:

Praised are You, O Lord our God, King of the universe.
You fix the cycles of light and darkness;
You ordain the order of all creation
You cause light to shine over the Earth;
Your radiant mercy is upon its inhabitants.
In Your goodness the work of creation
Is continually renewed day by day....
O, cause a new light to shine on Zion;
May we all soon be worthy to behold its radiance.
Praised are You, O Lord, Creator of the heavenly bodies.[1]

The corresponding prayer in the evening refers to the setting of the sun:

Praised are You....
Your command brings on the dusk of evening.
Your wisdom opens the gates of heaven to a new day.
With understanding You order the cycles of time;
Your will determines the succession of seasons;
You order the stars in their heavenly courses.
You create day, and You create night,
Rolling away light before darkness....
Praised are You, O Lord, for the evening dusk.[2]

Morning and evening, the Jew responds to the natural order of the world with thanks and praise of God who created the world and who actively guides the daily events of nature. Whatever happens in nature gives testimony to the sovereignty of the Creator. And that testimony is not in unnatural disasters but in the most ordinary events: sunrise and sunset. These, especially, evoke the religious response to set the stage for what follows.

For the Jew, God is not merely Creator but purposeful Creator. The works of creation serve to justify and testify to the Torah, the revelation of Sinai. The

Torah is the mark not merely of divine sovereignty but of divine grace and love, source of life here and now and in eternity. So goes the second blessing:

> Deep is Your love for us, O Lord our God;
> Bounteous is Your compassion and tenderness.
> You taught our fathers the laws of life,
> And they trusted in You, Father and king,
> For their sake be gracious to us, and teach us,
> That we may learn Your laws and trust in You.
> Father, merciful Father, have compassion upon us:
> Endow us with discernment and understanding.
> Grant us the will to study Your Torah,
> To heed its words and to teach its precepts....
> Enlighten our eyes in Your Torah,
> Open our hearts to Your commandments....
> Unite our thoughts with singleness of purpose
> To hold You in reverence and in love....
> You have drawn us close to You;
> We praise You and thank You in truth.
> With love do we thankfully proclaim Your unity.
> And praise You who chose Your people Israel in love.[3]

Here is the way in which revelation takes concrete and specific form in the Judaic tradition: God, the Creator, revealed his will for creation through the Torah, given to Israel his people. That Torah contains the "laws of life."

The Jew, moved to worship by the daily miracle of sunrise and sunset, responds with the prayer that he or she, like nature, may enjoy divine compassion. But what does that compassion consist of? The ability to understand and the will to study the *Torah!* This is the mark of the relationship between God and the human being, the Jewish person in particular: that a person's eyes are open to the Torah and that a person's heart is open to the commandments. These are the means of divine service and of reverence and love for God. Israel sees itself as "chosen"—close to God—because of the Torah, and it finds in its devotion to the Torah the marks of its chosenness. The covenant made at Sinai (a contract on Israel's side to do and hear the Torah; on God's side, to be the God of Israel) is evoked by natural events and then confirmed by the deeds and devotion of men.

In the *Shema,* the Torah—revelation—leads Jews to enunciate the chief teaching of revelation:

> Hear, O Israel, the Lord Our God, the Lord is One.

This proclamation is followed by three scriptural passages. The first is Deuteronomy 6:5–9:

> You shall love the Lord your God with all your heart, with all your soul, with all your might.

And further, one must diligently teach one's children these words and talk of them everywhere and always, and place them on one's forehead, doorposts, and gates. The second Scripture is Deuteronomy 11:13–21, which emphasizes that if Jews keep the commandments, they will enjoy worldly blessings; but if they do not, they will be punished and disappear from the good land God gives them. The third is Numbers 15:37–41, the commandment to wear fringes on the corners of one's garments. The fringes are today attached to the prayer shawl worn at morning services by Conservative and Reform Jews and on a separate undergarment for that purpose by Orthodox Jews, and they remind the Jew of *all* the commandments of the Lord.

The proclamation is completed and yet remains open, for having created humanity and revealed his will, God is not unaware of events since Sinai. Humanity is frail, and in the contest between the word of God and the will of humanity, the Torah is not always the victor. We inevitably fall short of what is asked of us, and Jews know that their own history consists of divine punishment for human failure time and again. The theme of redemption, therefore, is introduced.

Redemption—in addition to creation and revelation, the third element in the tripartite worldview—resolves the tension between what we are told to do and what we are able actually to accomplish. In the end, it is the theme of God, not as Creator or Revealer but as Redeemer, that concludes the twice-daily drama:

> You are our King and our father's King,
> Our redeemer and our father's redeemer.
> You are our creator....
> You have ever been our redeemer and deliverer
> There can be no God but You....
> You, O Lord our God, rescued us from Egypt;
> You redeemed us from the house of bondage....
> You split apart the waters of the Red Sea,
> The faithful you rescued, the wicked drowned....
> Then Your beloved sang hymns of thanksgiving....
> They acclaimed the King, God on high,
> Great and awesome source of all blessings,
> The everliving God, exalted in his majesty.
> He humbles the proud and raises the lowly;
> He helps the needy and answers His people's call....
>
> Then Moses and all the children of Israel
> Sang with great joy this song to the Lord:
> Who is like You O Lord among the mighty?
> Who is like You, so glorious in holiness?
> So wondrous your deeds, so worthy of praise!
> The redeemed sang a new song to You;
> They sang in chorus at the sore of the sea,
> Acclaiming Your sovereignty with thanksgiving:
> The Lord shall reign for ever and ever.
> Rock of Israel, arise to Israel's defense!

Fulfill Your promise to deliver Judah and Israel.
Our redeemer is the Holy One of Israel,
The Lord of hosts is His name.
Praised are You, O Lord, redeemer of Israel.[4]

Redemption is both in the past and in the future. That God not only creates but also redeems is attested by the redemption from Egyptian bondage. The congregation repeats the exultant song of Moses and the people at the Red Sea, not as scholars making a learned allusion but as participants in the salvation of old and of time to come. Then the people turn to the future and ask that Israel once more be redeemed.

But redemption is not only past and future. When the needy are helped, when the proud are humbled, and the lowly are raised—in such commonplace, daily events redemption is already present. Just as creation not only is in the beginning but happens every day, morning and night, so redemption is not only at the Red Sea but every day, in humble events. Just as revelation was not at Sinai alone but takes place whenever people study the Torah, whenever God opens their hearts to the commandments, so redemption and creation are daily events.

The great cosmic events of creation in the beginning, redemption at the Red Sea, and revelation at Sinai—these are everywhere, every day near at hand. The Jew views secular reality under the mythical aspect of eternal, ever-recurrent events. What happens to the Jew and to the world, whether good or evil, falls into the pattern revealed of old and made manifest each day. Historical events produce a framework in which future events will find a place and by which they will be understood. Nothing that happens cannot be subsumed by the paradigm.

The myths of creation, the Exodus from Egypt, and the revelation of the Torah at Sinai are repeated, not merely to tell the story of what once was and is no more but rather to re-create out of the raw materials of everyday life the "true being"—life as it was, always is, and will be forever. Streng says, "Myth and ritual recreate in profane time what is eternally true in sacred reality. To live in the myth is to live out the creative power that is the basis of any existence whatever."[5] We see here an illustration of these statements. At prayer the Jew repeatedly refers to the crucial elements of his or her mythic being, thus uncovering the sacred both in nature and in history. We therefore cannot say that Judaic myth does not emphasize a repetition of a cosmic pattern in cyclical or mythical time, for what happens in the proclamation of the Shema is just that: the particular events of creation—sunset, sunrise—evoke in response the celebration of the power and the love of God, of his justice and mercy, and of revelation and redemption.

NOTES

1. Rabbinical Assembly of American Prayerbook Committee, ed., *Weekday Prayer Book* (New York: Rabbinical Assembly, 1962), 42.

2. Ibid., 141.

3. Ibid., 45–56.

4. Ibid., 50*ff.*

5. Frederick J. Streng, *Understanding Religious Man* (Belmont, CA: Dickenson, 1968), 57.

15

Coming Together

The Sanctity of the Family

For the Jew the most intimate occasion—the marriage ceremony—is also intrinsically public. Here a new family begins. Individual lover and beloved celebrate the uniqueness, the privacy of their love. One should, therefore, expect the nuptial prayer to speak of him and her, natural man and natural woman. Yet the blessings that are said over the cup of wine of sanctification are as follows:

> Praised are You, O Lord our God, King of the universe, Creator of the fruit of the vine.
>
> Praised are You, O Lord our God, King of the universe, who created all things for Your glory.
>
> Praised are You, O Lord our God, King of the universe, Creator of Adam.
>
> Praised are You, O Lord our God, King of the universe, who created man and woman in his image, fashioning woman from man as his mate, that together they might perpetuate life. Praised are You, O Lord, Creator of man.
>
> May Zion rejoice as her children are restored to her in joy. Praised are You, O Lord, who causes Zion to rejoice at her children's return.
>
> Grant perfect joy to these loving companions, as You did to the first man and woman in the Garden of Eden. Praised are You, O Lord, who grants the joy of bride and groom.
>
> Praised are You, O Lord our God, King of the universe, who created joy and gladness, bride and groom, mirth, song, delight and rejoicing, love and harmony, peace and companionship. O Lord our God, may there ever be heard in the cities of Judah and in the streets of Jerusalem voices of joy and gladness, voices of bride and groom, the jubilant voices of those joined in marriage under the bridal canopy, the voices of young people feasting and signing. Praised are You, O Lord, who causes the groom to rejoice with his bride.[1]

These seven blessings say nothing of private people and their anonymously falling in love. Nor do they speak of the community of Israel, as one might expect on a public occasion. The blessings speak of archetypical Israel, represented here and now by the bride and groom.

Israel's history begins with creation—first, the creation of the vine, symbol of the natural world. Creation is for God's glory. All things speak to nature, to the physical as much as the spiritual, for all things were made by God. In Hebrew, the blessings end "who formed the *Adam*." All things glorify God; above all creation is Adam. The theme of ancient paradise is introduced by the simple choice of the word *Adam,* so heavy with meaning. The myth of man's creation is rehearsed: man and woman are in God's image, together complete and whole, creators of life, "life God." Woman was fashioned from man together with him to perpetuate life. And again, "blessed is the creator of Adam." We have moved, therefore, from the natural world to the archetypical realm of paradise. Before us we see not merely a man and a woman, but Adam and Eve.

But this Adam and this Eve also are Israel, children of Zion the mother, as expressed in the fifth blessing. Zion lies in ruins, her children scattered:

> If I forget you, O Jerusalem, may my right hand forget its skill…if I do not place Jerusalem above my greatest joy.
> *Psalm 137*

Adam and Eve cannot celebrate together without thought to the condition of the mother, Jerusalem. The children will one day come home. The mood is hopeful yet sad, as it was meant to be, for archaic Israel mourns as it rejoices and rejoices as it mourns. Quickly, then, back to the happy occasion, for we do not let mourning lead to melancholy: "Grant perfect joy to the loving companions," for they are creators of a new line in humanity—the new Adam, the new Eve—and their home: May it be the garden of Eden. And if joy is there, then "praised are you for the joy of bride and groom."

The concluding blessing returns to the theme of Jerusalem. This time it evokes the tragic hour of Jerusalem's first destruction. When everyone had given up hope, supposing with the end of Jerusalem had come the end of time, only Jeremiah counseled renewed hope. With the enemy at the gate, he sang of coming gladness:

> Thus says the Lord:
> In this place of which you say, "It is a waste, without man or beast," in the cities of Judah and the streets of Jerusalem that are desolate, without man or inhabitant or beast,
> There shall be heard again the voice of mirth and the voice of gladness, the voice of the bridegroom and the voice of the bride, the voice of those who sing as they bring thank-offerings to the house of the Lord.…
> For I shall restore the fortunes of the land as at first, says the Lord.
> *Jeremiah 33:10–11*

The closing blessing is not merely a literary artifice or a learned allusion to the ancient prophet. It is rather the exultant, jubilant climax of this acted-out myth: Just as here and now there stand before us Adam and Eve, so here and now in this wedding, the olden sorrow having been rehearsed, we listen to the voice of gladness that is coming. The joy of this new creation prefigures the joy of the Messiah's coming, hope for which is very present in this hour. And when he comes, the joy then will echo the joy of bride and groom before us. Zion the bride, Israel the groom, united now as they will be re-united by the compassionate God—these stand under the marriage canopy.

What is striking is how the theme of Eden and alienation, Land of Israel and exile, is reworked into a new pattern: from the loneliness and exile of the single life to the Eden and Jerusalem of the wedding canopy. The theme of exile and return is recapitulated but now with the message that the joy of the bride and groom (standing, after all, for Israel and God; see Chapter 10) is a foretaste of what is coming. Here the mythic life surfaces, rising above doctrines about Israel and Redemption. The personal and the public join; the individuals before us embody and reenact the entirety of Israel's holy life, past to future.

In classical Judaism, who are Jewish men and women? They are ordinary people who live within a mythic structure and who thereby hold a view of history centered on Israel from the creation of the world to its final redemption. Political defeats of this world are by myth transformed into eternal sorrow. The natural events of human life—here, the marriage of ordinary folk—are by myth heightened into a reenactment of Israel's life as a people. In marriage, individuals stand in the place of mythic figures yet remain, after all, boys and girls. What gives their love its true meaning is the myth of creation, revelation, and redemption, here and now embodied in that love. But in the end, the sacred and secular are in most profane, physical love united.[2]

The wedding of symbol and reality—the fusion and confusion of the two—mark the classical Judaic experience shaped by myths of creation, Adam and Eve, the Garden of Eden, and by the historical memory of the this-worldly destruction of an old, unexceptional temple. Ordinary events, such as a political and military defeat or success, are changed into theological categories such as divine punishment and heavenly compassion. If religion is a means of ultimate transformation, rendering the commonplace into the paradigmatic, changing the here and now into a moment of eternity and of eternal return, then the marriage liturgy serves to exemplify what is *religious* in Judaic existence.

NOTES

1. Jules Harlow, ed., *A Rabbi's Manual* (New York: Rabbinical Assembly, 1965), 45. The seven blessings said at a wedding are printed in traditional Jewish prayer books.

2. I must stress that the marriage ceremony includes provision for the bride and groom to consummate their marriage with sexual intercourse while left in private for an appropriate period. Nowadays the privacy is brief and symbolic, to be sure.

16

Going Forth

Israel, the Holy People and God's First Love

At the festival of Passover, in the spring, Jewish families gather around their tables for a holy meal. There they retell the story of the Exodus from Egypt in times long past. With unleavened bread and sanctified wine, they celebrate the liberation of slaves from Pharaoh's bondage. How do they see themselves?

> *We* were the slave of Pharaoh in Egypt, and the Lord our God brought us forth from there with a mightily hand and an outstretched arm. And if the Holy One, blessed be He, had not brought our fathers forth from Egypt, then surely we, and our children, and our children's children, would be enslaved to Pharaoh in Egypt. And so, even if all of us were full of wisdom and understanding, well along in years and deeply versed in the tradition, we should still be bidden to repeat once more the story of the exodus from Egypt; and he who delights to dwell on the liberation is a man to be praised.[1]

Through the natural eye, one sees ordinary folk, not much different from their neighbors in dress, language, or aspirations. The words they speak do not describe reality and are not meant to. When Jewish people say of themselves, "We were the slaves of Pharaoh in Egypt," they know they never felt the lash; but through the eye of faith that is just what they have done. It is *their* liberation, not merely that of long-dead forebears, that they now celebrate.

To be a Jew means to be a slave who has been liberated by God. To be Israel means to give eternal thanks for God's deliverance. And that deliverance is not at a single moment in historical time. It comes in every generation and is always celebrated. Here again, events of natural, ordinary life are transformed through myth into paradigmatic, eternal, and ever-recurrent sacred moments. Jews think of themselves as having gone forth from Egypt, and Scripture so instructs them. God did not redeem the dead generation of the Exodus alone but the living too—especially the living. Thus, the family states:

> Again and again, in double and redoubled measure, are we beholden to God the All-Present: that He freed us from the Egyptians and wrought His judgment on them; that He sentenced all their idols and slaughtered all their first-born; that He gave their treasure to us and split the Red Sea for us; that He led us through it dry-shod and drowned the tyrants in it; that He helped us through the desert and fed us with the manna; that He gave the Sabbath to us and brought us to Mount Sinai; that He gave the

Torah to us and brought us to our homeland—there to build the Temple
for us, for atonement of our sins.[2]

This is the promise which has stood by our forefathers and stands by us.
For neither once, nor twice, nor three times was our destruction planned;
in every generation they rise against us, and in every generation God delivers us from their hands into freedom, out of anguish into joy, out of
mourning into festivity, out of darkness into light, out of bondage into
redemption.[3]

For ever after, in every generation, *every Israelite must think of himself or
herself as having gone forth from Egypt* [italics added]. For we read in the
Torah: "In that day thou shalt teach thy son, saying: All this is because of
what God did for me when I went forth from Egypt." It was not only our
forefathers that the Holy One, blessed be He, redeemed; us too, the living, He redeemed together with them, as we learn from the verse in the
Torah: "And He brought us out from thence, so that He might bring us
home, and give us the land which he pledged to our forefathers."[4]

Israel was born in historical times. Historians, biblical scholars, and archaeolo-
gists have much to say about that event. But to the classical Jew their findings,
though interesting, have little bearing on the meaning of reality. The redemptive promise that stood by the forefathers and "stands by us" is not a mundane
historical event but a mythic interpretation of historical, natural events. Oppression, homelessness, extermination—like salvation, homecoming, renais-
sance—are this-worldly and profane, supplying headlines for newspapers. The
myth that a Jew must think of him- or herself as having gone forth from Egypt
and as being redeemed by God renders ordinary experience into a moment of
celebration. If "us, too, the living, He [has] redeemed," then the observer no
longer witnesses only historical people in historical time but an eternal return
to sacred time.

The "going forth" at Passover is one sort of Exodus. Another comes morning and night when Jews complete their service of worship. Every synagogue
service concludes with a prayer before going forth, called *Alenu,* from its first
word in Hebrew. Like the Exodus, the moment of the congregation's departure becomes a celebration of Israel's God, a self-conscious, articulated rehearsal of Israel's peoplehood. But now it is the end rather than the beginning
of time that is important. When Jews go forth, they look forward:

Let us praise Him, Lord over all the world;
Let us acclaim Him, Author of all creation.
He made our lot unlike that of other peoples;
He assigned to us a unique destiny.
We bend the knee, worship, and acknowledge
The King of kings, the Holy One, praised is He.
He unrolled the heavens and established the earth;
His throne of glory is in the heavens above;
His majestic Presence is in the loftiest heights.
He and no other is God and faithful King,
Even as we are told in His Torah:

Remember now and always, that the Lord is God;
Remember, no other is Lord of heaven and earth.
We, therefore, hope in You, O Lord our God,
That we shall soon see the triumph of Your might,
That idolatry shall be removed from the earth,
And false gods shall be utterly destroyed.
Then will the world be a true kingdom of God,
When all mankind will invoke Your name,
And all the earth's wicked will return to You.
Then all the inhabitants of the world will surely know
That to You every knee must bend,
Every tongue must pledge loyalty.
Before You, O Lord, let them bow in worship,
Let them give honor to Your glory.
May they all accept the rule of Your kingdom.
May You reign over them soon through all time.
Sovereignty is Yours in glory, now and forever.
So it is written in Your Torah:
The Lord shall reign for ever and ever.[5]

In secular terms, Jews know that in some ways they form a separate, distinct group. In mythical reality, they thank God they enjoy a unique destiny. They do not conclude with thanks for their particular "being" but sing of hope merely that he who made their lot unlike that of all others will soon rule as sovereign over all. The secular difference, the unique destiny, is for the time being only. When the destiny is fulfilled, there will be no further difference. The natural eye beholds a social group with some particular cultural characteristics defining that group. The myth of peoplehood transforms *difference* into *destiny.*

The existence of the natural group means little, except as testimony to the sovereignty of the God who shaped the group and rules its life. The unique, the particular, the private now are no longer profane matters of culture but become testimonies of divine sovereignty, pertinent to all people, all groups. The particularism of the groups is for the moment alone; the will of God is for eternity. When that will be done, then all people will recognize that the unique destiny of Israel was intended for everyone. The ordinary facts of sociology no longer predominate. The myth of Israel has changed the secular and commonplace into a paradigm of true being.

NOTES

1. Maurice Samuel, trans., *Haggadah of Passover* (New York: Hebrew Publishing, 1942), 9.

2. Ibid., 26.

3. Ibid., 13.

4. Ibid., 27.

5. Rabbinical Society of America, ed., *Weekday Prayer Book* (New York: Rabbinical Assembly, 1962), 97–98.

17

The Holy Land and Jerusalem in the Age to Come— and in Our Own Times

THE LAND OF ISRAEL, JERUSALEM, AND DAY-TO-DAY NOURISHMENT

Had Israel not sinned after entering the Promised Land, for Israel, history would have ended; that is our sages' view. But, sages explain, because of sins of various kinds (such as those narrated in the books of Joshua, Judges, Samuel, Kings, and the prophetic writings, Isaiah, Jeremiah, Ezekiel, and the Twelve Minor Prophets), Israel lost the land and went into exile. So the Sabbath Prayerbook states, "On account of our sins we have gone into exile from our land."

Israel's history did not end with the entry into the land of Canaan but rather began. That history, in a worldly sense, consisted of the secular affairs of a seldom important kingdom, able to hold its own only when its neighbors permitted or could not prevent it. In a mythic context, however, Jews looked back on the history of the people as a continuing revelation of divine justice and mercy. Israel, the people, kept the Torah; therefore, they enjoyed peace and prospered. Then Israel sinned, so God called forth instruments of his wrath: the Philistines, Assyrians, Babylonians, Persians, Greeks, Romans—there was no end to the list as time went on. But when Israel was properly chastised, God restored their prosperity and brought them back to the land.

Perhaps the single most powerful worldly experience in the history of Judaism was the destruction of the First Temple in 586 B.C.E., followed by the restoration of Jews to their land by the Persians approximately a half-century later. The worldly motives of the Persians are of no interest here, for they never played a role in the interpretation of historical events put forward by Judaic tradition. What the Jews understood was simply this: God had punished them, but when they repented and atoned, he had forgiven and redeemed them. And they further believed that the prophets who had foretold just this pattern of events were now vindicated, so that much else that they said was likely to be true. From the fifth century B.C.E. to the present, Jews have seen their history within the paradigm of sin, punishment, atonement, reconciliation, and then restoration.

The land entered the Judaic imagination as a powerful—indeed overwhelming—symbol. It was holy, the state for sacred history. We have already noted numerous references to the land, Jerusalem, Zion, and the like. These references all represent concrete exemplifications of myth. Redemption is not an abstract concept, but rather it is what happened when Moses led the people through the Sea of Reeds, or what happened with the return to Zion when the Second Temple was built (circa 515 B.C.E.), or what will happen when God again shines light on Zion and brings the scattered people back to their homes. In classical Judaism, the sanctity of the land, the yearning for Zion, the hope for the restoration of Jerusalem and the Temple cult are all symbols by which the redemption of the past is projected on to the future. The equivalent of the salvation at the sea will be the restoration of Israel to the land and the reconstruction of the Temple and of Jerusalem. The one stands at the beginning of Israel's history; the other, its counterpart, at the end.

How do the several salvific symbols fit together in the larger mythic structure of creation, revelation, and redemption? In the Grace after Meals, recited whenever pious Jews eat bread, we see their interplay. To understand the setting, we must recall that in classical Judaism the table at which meals were eaten was regarded as the equivalent of the sacred altar in the Temple. Judaism taught that each Jew before eating had to attain the same state of ritual purity as the priest in the sacred act of making a sacrifice. So in the classic tradition, the Grace after Meals is recited in a sacerdotal circumstance.

On Sabbaths and festivals, times of eternity in time, Jews first sing Psalm 126: "When the Lord brought back those that returned to Zion, we were like dreamers. Our mouth was filled with laughter, our tongue with singing. Restore our fortunes, O Lord, as the streams in the dry land. They that sow in tears shall reap in joy...." Then they recite the grace:

> Blessed art Thou, Lord our God, King of the Universe, who nourishes all the world by His goodness, in grace, in mercy, and in compassion: He gives bread to all flesh, for His mercy is everlasting. And because of His great goodness we have never lacked, and so may we never lack, sustenance—for the sake of His great Name. For He nourishes and feeds everyone, is good to all, and provides food for each one of the creatures He created.
>
> Blessed art Thou, O Lord, who feeds everyone.
>
> We thank Thee, Lord our God, for having given our fathers as a heritage a pleasant, a good and spacious land; for having taken us out of the land of Egypt, for having redeemed us from the house of bondage; for Thy covenant, which Thou hast set as a seal in our flesh, for Thy Torah which Thou has taught us, for Thy statutes which Thou hast made known to us, for the life of grace and mercy Thou hast graciously bestowed upon us, and for the nourishment with which Thou dost nourish us and feed us always, every day, in every season, and every hour.
>
> For all these things, Lord our God, we thank and praise Thee; may Thy praises continually be in the mouth of every living thing, as it is written. And thou shalt eat and be satisfied, and bless the Lord thy God for the good land which He hath given thee.

Blessed art Thou, O Lord, for the land and its food.

O Lord our God, have pity on Thy people Israel, on Thy city Jerusalem, on Zion the place of Thy glory, on the royal house of David Thy Messiah, and on the great and holy house which is called by Thy Name. Our God, our Father, feed us and speed us, nourish us and make us flourish, unstintingly, O Lord our God, speedily free us from all distress.

And let us not, O Lord our God, find ourselves in need of gifts from flesh and blood, or of a loan from anyone save from Thy full, generous, abundant, wide-open hand; so we may never be humiliated, or put to shame.

O rebuild Jerusalem, the holy city, speedily in our day. Blessed art Thou, Lord, who in mercy will rebuild Jerusalem. Amen.

Blessed art Thou, Lord our God, King of the Universe, Thou God, who art our Father, our powerful king, our creator and redeemer, who made us, our holy one, the holy one of Jacob, our shepherd, shepherd of Israel, the good king, who visits His goodness upon all; for every single day He has brought good, He does bring good, He will bring good upon us; He has rewarded us, does regard, and will always reward us, with grace, mercy and compassion, amplitude, deliverance and prosperity, blessing and salvation, comfort, and a living, sustenance, pity and peace, and all good—let us not want any manner of good whatever.[1]

The context of grace is enjoyment of creation, through which God nourishes the world in his goodness. That we have had this meal, however humble, is not to be taken for granted but rather as a gift. Whenever a person eats, he or she must reflect on the beneficence of the Creator. The arena for creation is the land, which to the ordinary eye is commonplace, small, dry, rocky but to the eye of faith is pleasant, good, spacious. The land lay at the end of redemption from Egyptian bondage. Holding it, enjoying it (as we saw in the *Shema*) is a sign that the covenant is intact and in force and that Israel is loyal to its part of the contract and God to his. The land, the Exodus, the covenant— these all depend on the Torah, statutes, and a life of grace and mercy, here embodied in and evoked by the nourishment of the meal. Thanksgiving wells up, and the paragraph ends with praises for the land and its food.

Then the chief theme recurs—that is, redemption and hope for return, and then future prosperity in the land: "May God pity the people, the city, Zion, the royal house of the Messiah, the Holy Temple." The nourishment of this meal is but a foretaste of the nourishment of the messianic time, just as the joy of the wedding is a foretaste of the messianic rejoicing.

Still, it is not the messianic time, so Israel finally asks not to depend on the gifts of mortal men but only on those of the generous, wide-open hand of God. And then "rebuild Jerusalem." The concluding paragraph summarizes the whole, giving thanks for creation, redemption, divine goodness, every blessing.

In some liturgies creation takes the primary place, as here and in the wedding ceremony. In others, the chief theme is revelation. Redemptive and concrete salvific symbols occur everywhere. So much for the life of the community. What about the life cycle of the year, the events of everyday life? These too express in their manner that same way of the Torah that the public events of worship convey, as we shall see in Chapter 18.

IN OUR OWN TIMES:
ZIONISM AND JUDAISM

The centrality of the holy land and Jerusalem in the worldview of classical Judaism comes to expression in nearly every liturgy. But that is particularly the case in the Grace after Meals, the most common of all prayers, the importance of the land and the city as messianic statements—Israel returns to the Land when the Messiah comes. Through their history from the exile to Babylonia in 586 B.C.E. onward, the Jews sustained the hope of returning to the homeland, and the very heart of their messianic belief—its symbols and fantasies—was shaped by that hope. Some Jews always remained in the Land of Israel, but all Jews until the nineteenth century expected to assemble to witness the resurrection of the dead there.

No account of Judaism, whether in its classical or contemporary formulation, can fail to address the relationship of Zionism to Judaism. Not all Judaists regard Zionism as integral to Judaism, but most do, and contemporary Reform, Conservative, and most of Orthodox Judaisms all deem the advent of the State of Israel, the fulfillment of Zionism, to mark "the beginning of the advent of our redemption," in the language of a commonly recited prayer. What is Zionism, and how does it relate to the sense of place, of a Holy Land belonging to the Holy People, Israel, that marks rabbinic Judaism and its heirs?

Zionism, a political movement founded in 1897 by Theodore Herzl, held that the Jews constitute a this-worldly people, one people, which ought to build its own nation-state. Fifty years later, in November 1947, the United Nations voted to create out of Palestine two nations, the State of Israel and an Arab state. Zionism as a secular, political movement accomplished all of its goals. But because these goals so intimately engaged the entire symbolic and mythic structure of Judaism in its rabbinic form (and in all most other Judaic systems, as a matter of fact), we have to ask how the religion, Judaism, dealt with Zionism. When we reach the study of American Judaism and the practice of Judaism today, we shall return to the matter.

The notion that the Jews form a secular nation, not just a holy people, will have surprised most rabbinic authorities before the end of the nineteenth century. For, as noted in Chapter 2, until modern times, the categories, secular Jew and ethnic Jew, were unknown; no one imagined that a Jew would not also be a Judaist, one who practiced Judaism. The definition of the Jews as a political entity, without regard to supernatural considerations, developed in the late nineteenth century, a by-product of the invention of Judaism as a religion distinct from the secular aspect of life, and therefore the formulation of the Jews as an ethnic (or, in nineteenth-century terms, a racial) and (in due course) a political body.

When Napoleon asked the French rabbinical assembly, called a Sanhedrin, of 1807 whether those Jews born in France regarded France as their native country, the answer of the rabbis could only have been yes. Yet such an answer could not possibly have been a true one, except during the reformation. Ludwig Philippson wrote:

> Formerly the Jews had striven to create a nation…but now their goal was to join other nations.…It was the task of the new age to form a general human society which would encompass all peoples organically. In the same way, it was the task of the Jews not to create their own nation…but rather to obtain from the other nations full acceptance into their society.

Similarly, the West London Synagogue of British Jews heard from its first rabbi in 1845: "To this land [England] we attach ourselves with a patriotism as glowing, with a devotion as fervent, and with a love as ardent and sincere as any class of our British non-Jewish fellow citizens."[2] One could duplicate that statement—and with it, its excessive protest—many times.

The reformation emphasized that Judaism could eliminate the residue of its nationalistic phase that survived in traditional doctrine and liturgy. The reformers saw Messianism not as Zionist doctrine but as a call to the golden age in which a union of nations into one peaceful realm to serve their one true God would take place. The happy optimism that underlay these hopes and affirmations survived among some even after Auschwitz, a death factory in which two million people were killed that serves as a symbol of the Holocaust, that is, after the murder of six million Jews in Europe.

But for the assimilated Western Jews of Paris, Vienna, and London, the rise of virulent scientific and political anti-Semitism during the last third of the nineteenth century raised significant doubts. Nor did the political situation of Eastern Europe Jewry that was characterized by pogroms, repression, and outright murder provide reassurance. Humankind did not seem to be progressing very quickly toward that golden day.

Modern Zionism—the movement to establish a Jewish state in Palestine—represented a peculiar marriage of Western romantic nationalism and Judaic piety. The virtuosi of the movement were mostly Western, but the masses of followers were in the East. The Western Jewish intellectuals found that European culture barred them. Fustel de Coulanges's saying in his book *The Ancient City,* "True patriotism is not love of the soil, but love of the past, reverence for the generations which have preceded us," at once excluded Jews (who were newcomers to French culture and could hardly share love for a French past that included banishment of their ancestors) and invited some of them to rediscover their own patriotism—that is, Zionism. The Jews could not share the "collective being" and could not be absorbed into a nation whose national past they did not share.

The Dreyfus trial of 1893–1894 involved one of the handful of Jewish officers in the French army; he was falsely accused of selling military secrets to

Germany. Because of widespread anti-Semitism, Dreyfus was represented as an example of the bigoted notion that Jews were not loyal citizens. When he was publicly disgraced, the crowds shouted not, "Down with the traitor!" but "Down with the Jews!" That fact forced a clear apprehension on the Viennese reporter Theodore Herzl that the "Jewish problem" could be solved only by complete assimilation or complete evacuation. It occurred to no one in the West that extermination was an option, though the czarist Russians thought of it.

In response to the Dreyfus trial, Herzl published *Der Judenstaat* (*The Jewish State*), from whose appearance in 1896 with the consequent founding of the World Zionist Organization in Basel in 1897 is conventionally dated the foundation of modern Zionism (though there were also some earlier movements). One can hardly overemphasize the secularity of Herzl's vision. He did not appeal to religious sentiments but to modern secular nationalism. His view of anti-Semitism ignores the religious dimension altogether and stresses only economic and social causes. Modern anti-Semitism grows out of the emancipation of the Jews and their entry into competition with the middle classes. The Jews cannot cease to exist as Jews, for affliction increases their cohesiveness.

Herzl's solution was wholly practical: Choose a country to which Jews could go—perhaps Argentina. In fact, Uganda was made available by the British government a few years later, but the Zionist Congress of the day rejected that possibility, opting for Palestine alone. What was important to Herzl was a rational plan: The poor would go first and build the infrastructure of an economy; the middle class would follow to create trade, markets, and new opportunity. The first Zionist Congress was not a gathering of Messianists but of sober women and men. Herzl's statement "At Basel I founded the Jewish state" was not, however, a sober statement, nor was his following one: "The State is already found in essence, in the will of the people of the State." All that remained were mere practicalities.

Herzl's disciple, Max Nordau, held that Zionism resulted from nationalism and anti-Semitism. Had Zionism led to Uganda, one could have believed it. When Herzl proposed Uganda, he was defeated. The masses in the East had been heard from. They bitterly opposed any "Zion" but Jerusalem. To them, Zionism could mean only Zion; Jerusalem was in one place alone. The classical messianic language—much of which was already associated with Zion in the messianic era—was taken over by the Zionist movement, and it evoked a much more than political response in the Jewish hearts. After the mass murder of most of European Jewry, Zionism swept the field, and in the mid twentieth century even the Reform movement affirmed it and contributed some of its major leaders. Only small groups within extreme Reform and Orthodox circles resisted. In the State of Israel today there are, in addition to the Orthodox religious-political party, such as Mizrashi, also Orthodox religious-political parties that are not Zionist and do not affirm the Jewish state.

Most Judaisms in the last half of the twentieth century have treated Zionism as integral to their worldviews and ways of life. From the creation of the

State of Israel forward, "Israel" came to stand not so much for the holy people as for the nation-state. To "go to Israel" meant to take a trip to a place, so "Israel" stood for a location rather than a social entity that flourished in a variety of places. That fact has created complications for Judaic religious discourse, because, for every Judaic religious system, "Israel" stands for the supernatural entity, the holy people, corresponding to Church as the mystical body of Christ, and not for the nation-state. Scripture, the oral Torah, and the liturgy alike all concur on that point. The American Judaism of Holocaust and Redemption reflects some of these complications.

NOTES

1. Judah Goldin, trans., *The Grace after Meals* (New York: Jewish Theological Seminary of America, 1955), 9, 15*ff.*

2. Both quotations are from Joseph L. Blau, *Modern Varieties of Judaism* (New York: Columbia University Press, 1966), 121 and 124, respectively.

18

Life Under the
Law of the Torah

When people think of law, they ordinarily imagine a religion for bookkeepers, who tote up the good deeds and debit the bad and call the result salvation or damnation, depending on the outcome. But life under the Torah brings the joy of expressing love of God through a cycle of celebration. In fact, the Judaic way of life joins three separate cycles: one in the rhythm of the year, the second in the rhythm of the week, the third in the rhythm of a person's life. The Judaic year follows the lunar calendar, so the appearance of the new moon marks the beginning of a month, and that is celebrated. There are two critical moments in the unfolding of the year: the first full moon after the autumnal equinox and the first full moon after the vernal equinox. These mark the time of heightened celebration.

To understand how the rhythm of the year unfolds, however, we begin with the new moon of the month of Tishri, corresponding to September. That marks the New Year, Rosh Hashanah. Ten days later comes the Day of Atonement, commemorating the rite described in Leviticus 16 and marking God's judgment and forgiveness of humanity. Five days afterward is the full moon, which is the beginning of the festival of Tabernacles (in Hebrew, *Sukkot*); that festival lasts for eight days and ends with a day of solemn assembly, Shemini Aseret, and of rejoicing of the Torah, Simhat Torah. So nearly the whole month of Tishri is spent in celebration: eating, drinking, praying, studying, enjoying, and celebrating God's sovereignty, creation, revelation, redemption, as the themes of the festivals and solemn celebrations of the season work themselves out.

The next major sequence of celebration follows the first new moon after the vernal equinox, which begins the month of Nisan and culminates, at its full moon, with Passover (in Hebrew, *pessah*), which commemorates the Exodus of Israel from Egypt and celebrates Israel's freedom, bestowed by God. Fifty days thereafter comes the festival of Pentecost (in Hebrew, *Shavuot*), which commemorates the giving of the Torah at Mount Sinai. Other occasions for celebration exist, but, apart from the Sabbath, the New Year, Day of Atonement, Tabernacles, Passover, and Pentecost are the main holy days.

Just as the Days of Awe, the New Year and the Day of Atonement, and the festivals of Tabernacles, Passover, and Pentecost mark the passage of the lunar year, so the Sabbath marks the movement of time through the week. The sanctification of the Sabbath, observed on the seventh day, Saturday, is one of the Ten Commandments. It is the single happiest moment in Judaism, and, coming as it does every week, the Sabbath sheds its light on the every day. On it people do no servile labor, and they devote themselves to sacred activities, including both worshipping at synagogue and studying the Torah, eating, drinking, relaxing, and enjoying themselves. The song for the Sabbath day, Psalm 92, expresses the spirit of this observance: it is good to give thanks to the Lord. Faithful Jews find in the Sabbath the meaning of their everyday lives.

The passage of the individual's life, from birth to death, marks out the third of the three cycles in the way of Torah, the cycles that convey the spirit of the Torah, or law as the word is translated. The principal points are birth, puberty, marriage, and death (reviewed in later chapters). For males, birth is marked by circumcision on the eighth day. Nowadays in the synagogue, the birth of both sons and daughters is celebrated by a rite of naming the child. The celebration of a child's becoming responsible to carry out the religious duties that are called *mitzvot,* or commandments, entering the status known as *bar mitzvah* for the boy and *bat mitzvah* for the girl, takes place in the synagogue in a simple way. The young woman or man is called to the Torah, which she or he reads, and the prophetic passage of the day also is read by the newly responsible young adult. We have already noted the marriage ceremony; rites of death involve a clear recognition that God rules and is the true and just authority over all humanity. The memorial prayer, or Kaddish for mourners, expresses the worshipper's recognition of God's holiness and dominion and states the hope for the coming of the Messiah. In a few words these events of celebration, which one might call "lifestyle events," define life under the law and explain how Judaists seek to live in accord with God's will, which is that Israel live the holy life in the here and now and await salvation at the end of time.

The word for concrete instruction of one's duty, of the proper way of doing things, is *halakhah,* and when we speak of life under the law, we mean life in accord with the halakhah, the rules and regulations of the holy life. The mythic structure built on the themes of creation, revelation, and redemption finds expression not only in synagogue liturgy but especially in concrete, everyday actions or action symbols—that is, deeds that embody and express the fundamental mythic life of the classical Judaic tradition.

These action symbols are set forth in halakhah. This word, as is clear, is normally translated as "law," for the halakhah is full of normative, prescriptive rules about what one must do and refrain from doing in every situation of life and at every moment of the day. But *halakhah* derives from the root *halakh,* which means "go," and a better translation would be "way." The halakhah is "the way": *the way* people live their lives; *the way* people shape their daily routines into a pattern of sanctity; *the way* people follow the revelation of the Torah and attain redemption.

For the Judaic tradition, this *way* is absolutely central. Belief without the expression of belief in the workaday world is of limited consequence. The purpose of revelation is to create a kingdom of priests and a holy people. The foundation of that kingdom, or sovereignty, is the rule of God over the lives of humanity. For the Judaic tradition, God rules much as people do, by guiding others on the path of life, not by removing them from the land of living.

Creation lies behind; redemption, in the future; the Torah is for here and now. To the classical Jew, the Torah means revealed law or commandment, accepted by Israel and obeyed from Sinai to the end of days.

The spirit of the Jewish way (halakhah) is conveyed in many modes, for law is not divorced from values but rather concretizes human beliefs and ideals. The purpose of the commandments is to show the road to sanctity, the way to God. In a more mundane sense, the following provides a valuable insight:

> Rava [a fourth-century rabbi] said, "When a man is brought in for judgment in the world to come, he is asked, 'Did you deal in good faith? Did you set aside time for study of Torah? Did you engage in procreation? Did you look forward to salvation? Did you engage in the dialectics of wisdom? Did you look deeply into matters?'"
>
> *Babylonian Talmud tractate, Shabbat, p. 31(a)*

Rava's interpretation of the Scripture—"and there shall be faith in thy times, strength, salvation, wisdom and knowledge" (Isaiah 33:6)—provides one glimpse into the life of the classical Jew who followed the way of the Torah. The first consideration was ethical: did the individual conduct him- or herself faithfully? The second was study of the Torah, not at random but every day, systematically, as a discipline of life. Third came the raising of a family, for celibacy and abstinence from sexual life were regarded as sinful; the full use of humanity's creative powers for the procreation of life was a commandment. Nothing God made was evil. Wholesome conjugal life was a blessing. But, fourth, merely living day by day according to an upright ethic was not sufficient. It is true that people must live by a holy discipline, but the discipline itself was only a means. The end was salvation. Hence, the pious people were asked to look forward to salvation, aiming their deed and directing their hearts toward a higher goal. Wisdom and insight—these completed the list, for without them, the way of the Torah was a life of mere routine rather than a constant search for deeper understanding.

19

Hear Our Prayer, Grant Us Peace

L ife under the law means praying—morning, noon, night, and at meals—both routinely and when something unusual happens. To be a Jew in the classical tradition, one lives his or her life constantly aware of the presence of God and always ready to praise and bless God. The way of the Torah is the way of perpetual devotion to God. What is the substance of that devotion? For what do pious Jews ask when they pray?

The answers to these questions tell us about more than the shape and substance of Judaic piety. As noted in Chapter 13, they tell us, too, what manner of person would take shape, for the constant repetition of the sacred words and moral and ethical maxims in the setting of everyday life is bound to affect the personality and character of the individual and the quality of communal life as well. Prayer expresses the most solemn aspirations of the praying community; it is what gives that community a sense of oneness and shared hopes; it embodies the values of the community. But if it is the community in its single most idiomatic hour, it also presents the community at its least particular and self-aware, for in praying, people stand before God without the mediation of culture and ethnic consciousness. But, as we shall see, that does not mean in Judaic prayer we do not find an acute awareness of history and collective destiny. These are very present.

In the morning, noon, and evening prayers are found the Eighteen Benedictions. Some of these, in particular those at the beginning and end, recur in Sabbath and festival prayers. They are said silently. Each individual prays by and for him- or herself, but together with other silent, praying individuals. The Eighteen Benedictions are then repeated aloud by the prayer leader, for prayer is both private and public, individual and collective.

To contemplate the meaning of these prayers, one should imagine a room full of people, all standing by themselves yet in close proximity, some swaying this way and that, all addressing themselves directly and intimately to God in a whisper or a low tone. They do not move their feet, for they are now standing before the King of kings, and it is not meet to shift and shuffle. If spoken to, they will not answer. Their attention is fixed on the words of supplication, praise, and gratitude. When they begin, they bend their knees—so too toward the end—and at the conclusion they step back and withdraw from the presence. These, on ordinary days, are the words they say:

Wisdom—Repentance

You graciously endow man with intelligence;
You teach him knowledge and understanding.
Grant us knowledge, discernment, and wisdom.
Praised are You, O Lord, for the gift of knowledge.
Our Father, bring us back to Your Torah;
Our King, draw us near to Your service;
Lead us back to you truly repentant.
Praised are You, O Lord who welcomes repentance.

Forgiveness—Redemption

Our Father, forgive us, for we have sinned;
Our King, pardon us, for we have transgressed;
You forgive sin and pardon transgression.
Praised are You, gracious and forgiving Lord.
Behold our affliction and deliver us.
Redeem us soon for the sake of Your name,
For You are the mighty Redeemer.
Praised are You, O Lord, Redeemer of Israel.

Heal Us—Bless Our Years

Heal us, O Lord, and we shall be healed;
Help us and save us, for You are our glory.
Grant perfect healing for all our afflictions,
O faithful and merciful God of healing.
Praised are You, O Lord, Healer of His people.
O Lord our God! Make this a blessed year;
May its varied produce bring us happiness.
Bring blessing upon the whole earth.
Bless the year with Your abounding goodness.
Praised are You, O Lord, who blesses our years.

Gather Our Exiles—Reign over Us

South the great shofar to herald [our] freedom;
Raise high the banner to gather all exiles;
Gather the dispersed from the corners of the earth.
Praised are You, O Lord, who gathers our exiles.
Restore our judges as in days of old;
Restore our counsellors as in former times;
Remove from us sorrow and anguish.
Reign over us alone with loving kindness;
With justice and mercy sustain our cause.
Praised are You, O Lord, King who loves justice.

Humble the Arrogant—Sustain the Righteous

Frustrate the hopes of those who malign us;
Let all evil very soon disappear;

Let all Your enemies be speedily destroyed.
May You quickly uproot and crush the arrogant;
May You subdue and humble them in our time.
Praised are You, O Lord, who humbles the arrogant.
Let Your tender mercies, O Lord God, be stirred
For the righteous, the pious, the leaders of Israel,
Toward devoted scholars and faithful proselytes.
Be merciful to us of the house of Israel;
Reward all who trust in You;
Cast our lot with those who are faithful to You.
May we never come to despair, for our trust is in You.
Praised are You, O Lord, who sustains the righteous.

Favor Your City and Your People

Have mercy, O Lord, and return to Jerusalem, Your city;
May Your Presence dwell there as You promised.
Rebuild it now, in our days and for all time;
Re-establish there the majesty of David, Your servant.
Praised are You, O Lord, who rebuilds Jerusalem.
Bring to flower the shoot of Your servant David.
Hasten the advent of the Messianic redemption;
Each and every day we hope for Your deliverance.
Praised are You, O Lord, who assures our deliverance.
O Lord, our God, hear our cry!
Have compassion upon us and pity us;
Accept our prayer with loving favor.
You, O God, listen to entreaty and prayer.
O King, do not turn us away unanswered,
For You mercifully heed Your people's supplication.
Praised are You, O Lord, who is attentive to prayer.
O Lord, Our God, favor Your people Israel;
Accept with love Israel's offering of prayer;
May our worship be ever acceptable to You.
May our eyes witness Your return in mercy to Zion.
Praised are You, O Lord, whose Presence returns to Zion.

Our Thankfulness

We thank You, O Lord our God and God of our fathers,
Defender of our lives, Shield of our safety;
Through all generations we thank You and praise You.
Our lives are in Your hands, our souls in Your charge.
We thank You for the miracles which daily attend us,
For Your wonders and favor morning, noon, and night.
You are beneficent with boundless mercy and love.
From of old we have always placed our hope in You.
For all these blessings, O our King,

We shall ever praise and exalt You.
Every living creature thanks You, and praises You in truth.
O God, You are our deliverance and our help. Selah!
Praised are You, O Lord, for Your Goodness and Your glory.

Peace and Well-Being

Grant peace and well-being to the whole house of Israel;
Give us of Your grace, Your love, and Your mercy.
Bless us all, O our Father, with the light of Your Presence.
It is Your light that revealed to us Your life-giving Torah,
And taught us love and tenderness, justice, mercy, and peace.
May it please You to bless Your people in every season,
To bless them at all times with Your light of peace.
Praised are You, O Lord, who blesses Israel with peace.[1]

The first two petitions pertain to intelligence. The Jew thanks God for mind: knowledge, wisdom, discernment. But knowledge is for a purpose, and the purpose is knowledge of Torah. Such discernment leads to the service of God and produces a spirit of repentance. We cannot pray without setting ourselves right with God, which means repenting for what has separated us from God. The Torah is the way to repentance and return. So knowledge leads to the Torah, the Torah to repentance, and repentance to God. The logical next stop is the prayer for forgiveness. That is the sign of return. God forgives sin; God is gracious and forgiving. Once we discern what we have done wrong through the Torah's guidance, we therefore seek to be forgiven. It is sin that leads to affliction. Affliction stands at the beginning of the way to God; once we have taken that way, we ask for our suffering to end; we beg redemption. This is then specified. We ask for healing, salvation, a blessed year. Healing without prosperity means we may suffer in good health or starve in a robust body. So along with the prayer for healing goes the supplication for worldly comfort.

The individual's task is done. But what of the community? Health and comfort are not enough. The world is unredeemed. Jews are enslaved, in exile, and alien. At the end of days, a great *shofar* (ram's horn) will sound to herald the Messiah's coming. This is now besought. The Jewish people at prayer ask first for the proclamation of freedom, then for the ingathering of the exiles to the Promised Land. Establishing the messianic kingdom, God needs also to restore a wise and benevolent government, good judges, good counselors, and loving justice.

Meanwhile, Israel, the Jewish people, finds itself maligned. As the prayer sees things, arrogant people hating Israel hate God as well. They should be humbled. And the pious and righteous—the scholars, the faithful proselytes, the whole House of Israel that trusts in God—should be rewarded and sustained. Above all, remember Jerusalem. Rebuild the city and dwell there. Set up Jerusalem's messianic king, David, and make him to prosper. These are the themes of the daily prayer: personal atonement, good health, and good fortunes; collective redemption, freedom, the end of alienation, good government, and true justice; the final and complete salvation of the land and of

Jerusalem by the Messiah. At the end comes a prayer that prayer may be heard and found acceptable; then an expression of thanksgiving, not for what may come, but for the miracles and mercies already enjoyed morning, noon, and night. And at the end is the prayer for peace—a peace that consists of wholeness for the sacred community.

People who say such prayers do not wholly devote themselves to this world. True, they ask for peace, health, and prosperity. But these are transient. At the same moment they ask, in so many different ways, for eternity. They arise in the morning and speak of Jerusalem. At noon they make mention of the Messiah. In the evening they end the day with talk of the shofar to herald freedom and the ingathering of the exiles. Living here in the profane, alien world, they constantly talk of going there—to the Holy Land and its perfect society. They address themselves to the end of days and the Messiah's time. The praying community above all seeks the fulfillment and end of its—and humanity's—travail.

NOTE

1. Rabbinical Assembly of America Prayerbook Committee, ed., *Weekday Prayer Book* (New York: Rabbinical Assembly, 1962).

20

Sabbaths for Rest, Festivals for Rejoicing

The classical Jew keeps the Sabbath as both a memorial of creation and a remembrance of the redemption from Egypt. The primary liturgy of the Sabbath is the reading of the Scripture lesson from the Torah in the synagogue service. So the three chief themes—creation, revelation, and redemption—are combined in the weekly observance of the seventh day, that is, from sunset Friday to sunset Saturday.

The Sabbath is protected by negative rules: one must not work; one must not pursue mundane concerns. But the Sabbath is also adorned with less concrete but affirmative laws: one must rejoice; one must rest.

How do pious Jews keep the Sabbath? All week long they look forward to it, and the anticipation enhances the ordinary days. By Friday afternoon they have bathed, put on their Sabbath garments, and set aside the affairs of the week. At home, the family—husband, wife, children—will have cleaned, cooked, and arranged their finest table. It is common to invite guests for the Sabbath meals. The Sabbath comes at sunset and leaves when three stars appear Saturday night. After a brief service the family comes together to enjoy its best meal of the week—a meal at which particular Sabbath foods are served. In the morning comes the Sabbath service—including a public reading from the Torah, the Five Books of Moses, and prophetic writings—and an additional service in memory of the Temple sacrifices on Sabbaths of old. Then home for lunch and very commonly a Sabbath nap, the sweetest part of the day. As the day wanes, the synagogue calls for a late-afternoon service, followed by Torah study and a third meal. Then comes a ceremony, *havdalah* (separation)—effected with spices, wine, and candlelight—between the holy time of the Sabbath and the ordinary time of weekday.

This simple, regular observance has elicited endless praise. To the Sabbath-observing Jew, the Sabbath is the chief sign of God's grace:

> For thou hast chosen us and sanctified us above all nations, in love and favor has given us thy holy Sabbath as an inheritance.[1]

So states the Sanctification of the Sabbath wine. Likewise in the Sabbath morning liturgy:

> You did not give it [Sabbath] to the nations of the earth, nor did you make it the heritage of idolaters, nor in its rest will unrighteous men find a place.

But to Israel your people you have given it in love, to the seed of Jacob whom you have chosen, to that people who sanctify the Sabbath day. All of them find fulfillment and joy from your bounty.

For the seventh day did you choose and sanctify as the most pleasant of days and you called it a memorial to the works of creation.

Here again we find a profusion of themes, this time centered on the Sabbath. The Sabbath is a sign of the covenant. It is a gift of grace, which neither idolaters nor evil people may enjoy. It is the testimony of the chosenness of Israel. And it is the most pleasant of days. Keeping the Sabbath *is* living in God's kingdom:

Those who keep the Sabbath and call it a delight will rejoice in your kingdom.

So states the additional Sabbath prayer. Keeping the Sabbath now is a foretaste of the redemption: "This day is for Israel light and rejoicing." The rest of the Sabbath is, as the afternoon prayer affirms,

a rest granted in generous love, a true and faithful rest.
…Let your children realize that their rest is from you, and by their rest may they sanctify your name.

That people need respite from the routine of work is no discovery of the Judaic tradition. That the way in which they accomplish such a routine change of pace may be made the very heart and soul of their spiritual existence is the single absolutely unique element in Judaic tradition. The word *Sabbath* simply renders the Hebrew *Shabbat;* it does not translate it, for there is no translation. In no other tradition or culture can an equivalent word be found. Certainly those who compare the Sabbath of Judaism to the somber, supposedly joyless Sunday of the Calvinists know nothing of what the Sabbath has meant and continues to mean to Jews.

In his account of the Sabbath, Abraham J. Heschel builds his theology around the meaning of the Sabbath day:

Judaism is a religion of time aiming at the sanctification of time.…Judaism teaches us to be attached to holiness in time, to be attached to sacred events, to learn how to consecrate sanctuaries that emerge from the magnificent stream of a year. The Sabbaths are our great cathedrals, and our Holy of Holies is a shrine that neither the Romans nor the Germans were able to burn.…Jewish ritual may be characterized as the art of significant forms in time as architecture of time.[2]

Heschel finds in the Sabbath "the day on which we are called upon to share in what is eternal in time, to turn from the world of creation to the creations of the world."[3]

From this brief description of what the Jew actually does on the seventh day, we can hardly derive understanding of how the Sabbath can have meant so much as to elicit words such as those of the Jewish prayer book and of Rabbi Heschel. Those words, like the laws of the Sabbath—not to mourn, not to confess sins, not to repent, not to do anything that might lead to unhappiness—describe something only the participant can truly comprehend and feel. Only a family whose life focuses on the Sabbath week by week, year by year, from birth to death, can know the sanctity of which the theologian speaks, the sacred rest to which the prayers refer. The heart and soul of the Judaic tradition as set forth in the rabbinic model, the Sabbath cannot be described—only experienced. For the student of religions, it stands as that element of Judaism that is absolutely unique and therefore a mystery. Indeed, when, in the study of a religion, we reach the point that the faithful find most difficult to express to the outsider, there we stand at the very heart of the matter: Jesus Christ, God Incarnate, for the Christian, the Sabbath for Holy Israel.

The festivals mark the passage of time: not of the week but of the seasons. Earlier we took note of the festivals as expressions of life under the law. Let us now consider precisely how people live out those seasons of sanctification and celebration.

Sukkot, the feast of tabernacles, is the autumnal festival. It marks the end of agricultural toil. The fall crops by then were gathered in from the fields, orchards, and vineyards. The rainy season was about to begin. It was time both to give thanks for what had been granted and to pray for abundant rains in the coming months. Called "festival of the ingathering," it was the celebration of nature par excellence. The principal observance is still the construction of a frail hut, or booth, for temporary use during the festival. In it Jews eat their meals outdoors. The huts are covered with branches, leaves, fruit, and flowers, but light shows through and, at night, the stars. We do not know the origin of the practice. Some have held that during the harvest it was common to build an ordinary shack in the fields for shelter from the heat of the day. In any event, the ancient practice naturally was given a historical context: When the Jews wandered in the wilderness they lived, not in permanent homes, but in frail booths. At a time of bounty it is good to be reminded of people's travail and dependence on heavenly succor.

Passover is the Jewish spring festival, and the symbols of the Passover *seder*—hard-boiled eggs and vegetable greens—are not unfamiliar in other spring rites. But here the spring rite has been transformed into a historical commemoration. The natural course of the year, though important, is subordinated to the historical events remembered and relived on the festival. Called the Feast of Unleavened Bread and the "Season of Our Freedom," the Passover festival preserves very ancient rites in a new framework.

It is, for example, absolutely prohibited to make use of leaven, fermented dough, and the like. The agricultural calendar of ancient Canaan was marked by the grain harvest, beginning in the spring with the cutting of barley and ending with the reaping of the wheat approximately seven weeks later.[4] The farmers would get rid of all their sour dough, which they used as yeast, old bread, and any leaven from last year's crop. The origins of the practice are not clear, but that the Passover taboo against leaven was connected with the agricultural calendar is beyond doubt. Just as the agricultural festivals were historicized, likewise much of the detailed observance connected with them was supplied with historical "reasons" or explanations. In the case of the taboo against leaven, widely observed today even among otherwise unobservant Jews, the "reason" was that the Israelites had to leave Egypt in haste and therefore had to take with them unleavened bread, for they had not time to permit the bread to rise properly and be baked. Therefore, we eat the *matzah,* unleavened bread.

3. The Feast of Weeks, *Shavuot* or Pentecost, comes seven weeks after Passover. In the ancient Palestinian agricultural calendar, it marked the end of the grain harvest and was called the Feast of Harvest. In Temple times, two loaves of bread were baked from the wheat of the new crop and offered as a sacrifice, the firstfruits of wheat harvest. So Shavuot came to be called the Day of the Firstfruits. Pharisaic Judaism added a historical "explanation" to the natural ones derived from the land and its life. The rabbis held that the Torah was revealed on Mount Sinai on that day and celebrated it as "the time of the giving of our Torah."[5] Nowadays, confirmation and graduation ceremonies of religious schools take place on Shavuot.

The three historical-agricultural festivals pertain, in varying ways and combinations, to the themes we have already considered. Passover is the festival of redemption and points toward the Torah revelation of the Feast of Weeks; the harvest festival in the autumn celebrates not only creation but especially redemption.

The New Year, Rosh Hashanah, and the Day of Atonement, Yom Kippur, together mark the Days of Awe, of solemn penitence, at the start of the autumn festival season; they are followed by Sukkot. These are solemn times. In the myth of classical Judaism, at the New Year humanity is inscribed for life or death in the heavenly books for the coming year, and on the Day of Atonement the books are sealed. The synagogues on that day are filled with penitents. The New Year is called the birthday of the world: "This day the world was born." It is likewise a day of remembrance on which the deeds of all creatures are reviewed. On it God asserts his sovereignty, as in the New Year Prayer:

> Our God and God of our Fathers, Rule over the whole world in Your honor…and appear in Your glorious might to all those who dwell in the civilization of Your world, so that everything made will know that You made it, and every creature discern that You have created him, so that all in whose nostrils is breath may say, "The Lord, the God of Israel is king, and His kingdom extends over all."[6]

The themes of the liturgy are divine sovereignty, divine memory, and divine disclosure. These correspond to creation, revelation, and redemption. Sovereignty is established by creation of the world. Judgment depends on law: "From the beginning You made this, Your purpose known…." Therefore, because people have been told what God requires of them, they are judged:

> On this day sentence is passed upon countries, which to the sword and which to peace, which to famine and which to plenty, and each creature

is judged today for life or death. Who is not judged on this day? For the remembrance of every creature comes before You, each man's deeds and destiny, words and way....

The theme of revelation is further combined with redemption; the ram's horn, or shofar, which is sounded in the synagogue during daily worship for a month before the Rosh Hashanah festival, serves to unite the two:

> You did reveal yourself in a cloud of glory....Out of heaven you made them [Israel] hear Your voice....Amid thunder and lightning You revealed yourself to them, and while the shofar sounded You shined forth upon them....Our God and God of our fathers, sound the great Shofar for our freedom. Lift up the ensign to gather our exiles....Lead us happily to Zion Your city, Jerusalem the place of Your sanctuary.

The complex themes of the New Year, the most "theological" of Jewish holy occasions, thus weave together the central mythic categories we have already discovered elsewhere.

The most personal, solemn, and moving of the Days of Awe is the Day of Atonement, Yom Kippur, the Sabbath of Sabbaths. It is marked by fasting and continuous prayer. On it, the Jew makes confession:

> Our God and God of our fathers, may our prayer come before You. Do not hide yourself from our supplication, for we are not so arrogant or stiff-necked as to say before You....We are righteous and have not sinned. But we have sinned.
>
> We are guilt laden, we have been faithless, we have robbed....
>
> We have committed iniquity, caused unrighteousness, have been presumptuous.
>
> We have counseled evil, scoffed, revolted, blasphemed....[7]

The Hebrew confession is built on an alphabetical acrostic following the letters of the Hebrew alphabet, as if by making certain every letter is represented, God, who knows human secrets, will combine them into appropriate words. The very alphabet bears witness against us before God. Then:

> What shall we say before You who dwell on high? What shall we tell You who live in heaven? Do You not know all things, both the hidden and the revealed? You know the secrets of eternity, the most hidden mysteries of life. You search the innermost recesses, testing men's feelings and heart. Nothing is concealed from You or hidden from Your eyes. May it therefore be Your will to forgive us our sins, to pardon us for our iniquities, to grant remission for our transgressions.[8]

A further list of sins follows, built on alphabetical lines. Prayers to be spoken by the congregation are all in the plural: "For the sin which we have sinned against You with the utterance of the lips....For the sin which we have sinned before You openly and secretly...." The community takes upon itself responsibility for what is done in it. All Israel is part of one community, one body, and all are responsible for the acts of each. The sins confessed are mostly against society, against one's peers; few pertain to ritual laws. At the end comes a final word:

> O my God, before I was formed, I was nothing. Not that I have been formed, it is as though I had not been formed, for I am dust in my life, more so after death. Behold I am before You like a vessel filled with shame and confusion. May it be Your will...that I may no more sin, and forgive the sins I have already committed in Your abundant compassion.[9]

So the Jew in the classical Judaic tradition sees him- or herself before God: possessing no merits, yet hopeful of God's love and compassion. To be a classical Jew is to be intoxicated by faith in God, live every moment in God's presence, and shape every hour by the paradigm of the Torah. The day with its worship in the morning and evening, the week with its climax at the Sabbath, the season marked by nature's commemoration of Israel's sacred history all shape life into rhythms of sanctification, and thus make all of life an act of worship. How does an individual enter into and leave that life? That question is addressed in the next chapter.

NOTES

1. Traditional prayer; author's translation from the Hebrew.

2. Abraham J. Heschel, *The Sabbath: Its Meaning for Modern Man* (New York: Farrar, Strauss & Young, 1951), 8.

3. Ibid., 10.

4. Hayyim Schauss, *The Jewish Festivals from Their Beginnings to Our Own Day* (New York: Union of American Hebrew Congregations, 1938), 40*ff.*

5. Ibid., 86*ff.*

6. Traditional prayer; author's translation from the Hebrew.

7. Jules Harlow, trans., *Mahzor* (reprint; New York: Rabbinical Assembly, 1995).

8. Ibid.

9. Ibid.

21

Rites of Passage

Birth, Maturity, Death

Rites for the private person, as distinct from those for the celebration of the holy people as a community, tend to be simple; they ordinarily take place at home and not in the synagogue. The Torah marks these rites of passage and treats them as critical to the formation of the holy people. The individual, not only holy Israel, stands in a covenanted relationship with God. For males that is concrete and physical. The covenant between God and Israel is not a mere theological abstraction, nor is it effected only through laws of community and family life. It is quite literally engraved on the flesh of every male Jewish child through the rite of circumcision, *brit milah* (the covenant of circumcision).

Circumcision must take place on the eighth day after birth, normally in the presence of a quorum of ten adult males. Elijah, the prophet of scriptural record, is believed to be present. A chair is set for him, based on the legend that Elijah complained to God that Israel neglected the covenant (I Kings 19:10–14).[1] God therefore ordered him to come to every circumcision so as to witness the loyalty of the Jews to the covenant. The *mohel,* or circumciser, is expert at the operation. The traditional blessing is said: "Praised are You…who sanctified us with Your commandments and commanded us to bring the son into the covenant of Abraham our father." The wine is blessed:

> Praised are You, Lord our God, who sanctified the beloved from the womb and set a statute into his very flesh, and his parts sealed with the sign of the holy covenant. On this account, Living God, our portion and rock, save the beloved of our flesh from destruction, for the sake of his covenant placed in our flesh. Blessed are You…who makes the covenant.

The advent of puberty is marked by the bar mitzvah rite for a young man and a bat mitzvah rite for a young woman, at which a young person becomes obligated to keep the commandments. *Bar* means son and *bat* means daughter, with the sense that one is subject to, and *mitzvah* means commandment. The young person is called to pronounce the benediction over a portion of the Torah lection in the synagogue and is also given the honor of reading the prophetic passage. In olden times, it was not so important an occasion as it has become in modern America.

Only when a Jew achieves intelligence and self-consciousness, normally at puberty, is he or she expected to accept the full privilege of mitzvah (commandment) and to regard him- or herself as *commanded* by God. Judaism perceives the commandments as expressions of one's acceptance of the yoke of the Kingdom of Heaven and submission to God's will. That acceptance cannot be coerced but requires thoughtful and complete affirmation. The bar or bat mitzvah thus represents the moment that the young Jew first assumes full responsibility before God to keep the commandments.

Rites of death are simple and brief. The natural process of death is treated as a normal chapter of life. At the onset of death, the dying Jew says a confession:

> My God and God of my fathers, accept my prayer....
>
> Forgive me for all the sins which I have committed in my lifetime....
>
> Accept my pain and suffering as atonement and forgive my wrongdoing for against you alone have I sinned....
>
> I acknowledge that my life and recovery depend on You.
>
> May it be Your will to heal me.
>
> Yet if You have decreed that I shall die of this affliction,
>
> May my death atone for all sins and transgressions which I have committed before You.
>
> Shelter me in the shadow of Your wings.
>
> Grant me a share in the world to come.
>
> Father of orphans and Guardian of widows, protect my beloved family....
>
> Into Your hand I commit my soul. You redeem me, O Lord God of truth.
>
> Hear O Israel, the Lord is our God, the Lord alone.
>
> The Lord He is God.
>
> The Lord He is God.[2]

The corpse is carefully washed and always protected. The body is covered in a white shroud, then laid in a coffin and buried. Normally burial takes place on the day of death or on the following day. Once the body has been placed in the grave, three pieces of broken pottery are laid on eyes and mouth as signs of the person's vanity. A handful of dirt from the Land of Israel is laid under the head.[3] The family recites the *kaddish,* an eschatological prayer of sanctification of God's name that looks forward to the messianic age and the resurrection of the dead. The prayer expresses the hope that the Messiah will soon come, "speedily, in our days," and that "he who brings harmony to the heavens will make peace on Earth." The mourners remain at home for a period of seven days and continue to recite the memorial *kaddish* for eleven months.

The life cycle for the private individual is simple, but for the individual as part of Israel, God's holy people, it is rich, absorbing, and encompassing. Life is lived with people, God's people, in God's service.

NOTES

1. Abraham Z. Idelsohn, *The Ceremonies of Judaism* (New York: National Federation of Temple Brotherhoods, 1930), 120.

2. Jules Harlow, ed., *A Rabbi's Manual* (New York: Rabbinical Assembly, 1965), 96.

3. Idelsohn, *The Ceremonies of Judaism,* 133.

22

At the Center of the Holy Way of Life
Study of the Torah

If you have accomplished much in the study of the Torah, do not take pride on that account, for it was to that end that you were created.

RABBAN YOHANAN BEN ZAKKAI

Israel knows God through the Torah, which is God's gift to Israel. We cannot find surprising, therefore, the fact that for the holy way of life, the single most important action is study of the Torah, for that is where holy Israel meets God.

Central to classical Judaism—the worldview of the Torah—is the belief that the ancient Scriptures constituted divine revelation, but only a part of it. At Sinai, God had handed down a dual revelation: the written part known to one and all, and also the oral part preserved by the great scriptural heroes, passed on by prophets to various ancestors in the obscure past, and finally and most openly handed down to the rabbis who created the Palestinian and Babylonian Talmuds. The "whole Torah" thus consisted of both written and oral parts. The rabbis taught that that "whole Torah" was studied by David, augmented by Ezekiel, legislated by Ezra, and embodied in the schools and by the sages of every period in Israelite history from Moses to the present. It is a singular, linear conception of a revelation preserved only by the few, pertaining to the many, and in time capable of bringing salvation to all.

The Torah story as told by rabbinic Judaism further regards Moses as "our rabbi," the first and prototypical figure of the ideal Jew. It holds that whoever embodies the teachings of Moses "our rabbi" thereby conforms to the will of God—and not to God's will alone but also to his *way*. In Heaven God and the angels study the Torah just as rabbis do on Earth. God dons phylacteries like a Jew. He prays in the rabbinic mode. He carries out the acts of compassion called for by Judaic ethics. He guides the affairs of the world according to the rules of the Torah, just as does the rabbi in his court. One exegesis of the creation legend taught that God had looked into the Torah and from it had created the world.

The myth of the Torah is multidimensional. It includes the striking detail that whatever the most recent rabbi is destined to discover through proper exegesis of the tradition is as much a part of the way revealed to Moses as is a sentence of Scripture itself. It therefore is possible to participate even in the giving of the law by appropriate, logical inquiry into the law. God himself, studying and living by the Torah, is believed to subject himself to these same rules of logical inquiry. If an earthly court overrules the testimony, delivered through miracles, of the heavenly one, God would rejoice, crying out, "My sons have conquered me! My sons have conquered me!"

In a word, before us is a mythical–religious system in which Earth and Heaven correspond to one another, with the Torah as the nexus and model of both. The heavenly paradigm is embodied on Earth. Moses "our rabbi" is the pattern for the ordinary sage of the streets of Jerusalem, Pumbedita, Mainz, London, Lvov, Bombay, Dallas, or New York. And God himself participates in the system, for it is his image that, in the end, forms that cosmic paradigm. The faithful Jew constitutes the projection of the divine on Earth. Honor *is* due to the learned rabbi more than to the scroll of the Torah, for through his learning and logic he may alter the very content of Mosaic revelation. He *is* the Torah, not merely because he lives by it but because at his best he forms as compelling an embodiment of the heavenly model as does a Torah scroll itself.

The final element in the rabbinic account of the Torah concerns salvation. It takes many forms. One salvific teaching holds that had Israel not sinned— that is, disobeyed the Torah—the Scriptures would have closed with the story of the conquest of Palestine. From that eschatological time, the sacred community would have lived in eternal peace under the divine law. Keeping the Torah was therefore the veritable guarantee of salvation. The opposite is said in many forms also. Israel had sinned; therefore God had called the Babylonians in 586 B.C.E. and the Romans in 70 C.E. to destroy the Temple of Jerusalem. But in his mercy he would be equally faithful to restore the fortunes of the people when they, through their suffering and repentance, had expiated the result and the cause of their sin.

So in both negative and positive forms, the Torah tells of a necessary connection between the salvation of the people and of the world and the state of Torah among them. For example, if all Israel would properly keep a single Sabbath, the Messiah would come. Of special interest here is the rabbinic saying that the rule of the pagans depends on the sin of Israel. If Israel would constitute a full and complete replication of "Torah" (that is, Heaven), then pagan rule would come to an end. It would end because all Israel then, like some few rabbis even now, would attain to the creative, theurgical powers inherent in the Torah. Just as God had created the world through the Torah, so saintly rabbis could now create a sacred community. When Israel makes itself worthy through its embodiment of the Torah—that is, through its perfect replication of the heavenly way of living—then the end will come.

Learning thus finds a central place in a classical Judaic tradition because of the belief that God had revealed his will to humanity through the medium of a written revelation given to Moses at Mount Sinai, accompanied by oral traditions taught in the rabbinic schools and preserved in the Talmuds and related literature. The text without the oral traditions might have led elsewhere than into the academy, for the biblicism of other groups yielded something quite different from Jewish religious intellectualism. But belief in the text was coupled with the belief that oral traditions were also revealed. In the books composed in the rabbinic academies, as much as in the Hebrew Bible itself, was contained God's will for humanity.

The act of study, memorization, and commentary on the sacred books is holy. The reason is that, when one studies the Torah, the faithful Jew hears God's word and will. The study of sacred text therefore assumes a *central* position in Judaism. Other traditions had their religious experts whose virtuosity consisted in knowledge of a literary tradition; but few held, as does Judaism, that everyone must become such an expert.

Traditional processes of learning are discrete and exegetical. Creativity is expressed not through abstract dissertation but rather through commentary on the sacred writings or, more likely in later times, commentary on earlier commentaries. One might also prepare a code of the laws, but such a code represented little more than an assemblage of authoritative opinions of earlier times, with a decision being offered on those few questions the centuries had left unanswered.

The chief glory of the commentator is his *hiddush* (novelty). The hiddush constitutes a scholastic disquisition on a supposed contradiction between two earlier authorities chosen from any period, with no concern for how they might in fact relate historically, and on a supposed harmonization of their "contradiction." Or a new distinction might be read into an ancient law, on which basis ever more questions might be raised and solved. The focus of interest quite naturally lies on law rather than theology, history, philosophy, or other sacred sciences. But within the law it rests on legal theory, and interest in the practical consequences of the law is decidedly subordinated.

The devotion of the Jews to study of the Torah, as here defined, is held by them to be their chief glory. This sentiment is repeated in song and prayer and shapes the values of the common society. The important Jew is the learned individual. The child many times is blessed, starting at birth. "May he [or in today's world, she] grow in Torah, commandments, good deeds."

One central *ritual* of the Judaic tradition, therefore, is study. But we must clearly distinguish the secular act of learning from the religious act of Torah study. They scarcely intersect, even though they may produce the same result in this-worldly terms: information, understanding. Study as a natural action entails learning of traditions and executing them—in this context, in school or in court. Study becomes a *ritual action* when it is endowed with values *extrinsic* to its ordinary character—that is, when set in a mythic context. When a disciple memorizes the master's traditions and actions, he or she participates in that myth. Study is thereby endowed with the sanctity that ordinarily pertains to prayer or other cultic matters. It loses its referent in intellectual attainment. The act of study itself becomes holy, so that its original purpose, which was mastery of particular information, ceases to matter much. What matters is piety—piety expressed through the rites of studying. Repeating the words of the oral revelation, even without comprehending them, produces reward, just as imitating the master matters, even without really being able to explain the reasons for his actions.

The separation of the value, or sanctity, of the act of study from the natural, cognitive result of learning therefore transforms study from a natural to a ritual action. That separation is accomplished in part by myth and in part by the powerful impact of the academic environment itself. A striking illustration of the distinction between mere learning and learning as part of ritual life derives from the comment of Mar Zutra, a fifth-century c.e. Babylonian rabbi, on Isaiah 14:5: "The Lord has broken the staff of the wicked, the scepter of rulers." He said, "These are disciples of the sages who teach public laws to boorish judges"(Talmud, b. Shabbat, 139a). The fact that the uncultivated judge would know the law did not matter, for he still was what he had been— a boor, not a disciple of the sages. Mere knowledge of the laws does not transform an ordinary person, however powerful, into a sage.

Learning carried with it more than naturalistic valence, as further seen in the saying of Amemar, a contemporary of Mar Zutra: "A sage is superior to a prophet, as Scripture [Psalm 90:12] says, 'And a prophet has a heart of wisdom'" (Talmud, b. Bava Batra, 12a). The sense is that what made a prophet credible was his knowledge of wisdom, and wisdom, in sages' speech, stood for Torah learning. What characterized the prophet was, Amemar said, sagacity. Because the prophet was supposed to reveal the divine will, it was not inconsequential that his revelation depended *not* on gifts of the spirit but on *learning.*

The Talmudic rabbis' emphasis on learning as a ritual act ought not to obscure their high expectations of actual accomplishment in learning. Although they stressed the act of study without reference to its achievement, at the same time they possessed very old traditions on how best to pursue their task. These traditions included much practical advice on how to acquire and preserve learning. Another Babylonian sage, R. Mesharsheya, advised his sons:

> When you wish to come before your teacher to learn, first review your Mishnah and then go to your teacher. When you are sitting before your teacher look at the mouth of your teacher, as it is written, *But thine eyes shall see they teacher* [Isaiah 30:20]; and when you study any teaching, do so by the side of water, for as the water is drawn out, so your learning may be prolonged. Be on the dustheaps of Mata Mehasia [a great center of learning] rather than in the palaces of Pumbedita [where Torah was lacking].
>
> *Babylonian Talmud tractate Keritot, p. 6(a)*

Part of that advice was perfectly reasonable. Reviewing before classes, concentrating on the teacher, staying near the great schools would make sense anywhere. On the other hand, the counsel to study by a body of water "so that your learning may be prolonged" has little to do with the practical problems of memorizing and reasoning. Rather, it reflects the rabbis' view of a correspondence between their own study and those aspects of nature that the rabbis looked on as symbolic of their activities—and they many times compared the Torah to living waters.

What makes an act of learning into Torah study is discipleship. For study of the Torah involves a master, from whom one learns the Torah. Many of the holy books use brief and elliptical language, and only through instruction may we make sense of these notes toward the reconstruction of thought. That is why the oral aspect is so vital: oral instruction from master to disciple forms the chain of tradition.

The sage, called by the title "rabbi" or "my lord," functioned in the Jewish community as judge and administrator. But he lived in a society in some ways quite separate from that of Jewry as a whole. The rabbinic academy was, first, a law school. Some of its graduates served as judges and administrators of the law. The rabbinic school was by no means a center for merely legal study. It was, like the Christian monastery, the locus for a peculiar kind of religious living. Only one of its functions concerned those parts of the Torah to be applied in everyday life through the judiciary. In ancient, medieval, and modern times, these activities and institutions remained remarkably stable.

The school, or *yeshiva* (literally, session), was a council of Judaism, a holy community. In it men learned to live a holy life, to become saints. When they left, sages continued to live by the discipline of the school. They invested great efforts in teaching that discipline by example and precept to ordinary folk. Through the school, classical Judaism transformed the Jewish people into its vision of the true replica of Mosaic revelation. The schools, like other holy communities, imposed their own particular rituals intended, in the first instance, for the disciples and masters. Later, it was hoped, all Jews would conform to those rituals and so join the circle of master and disciples.

As with study, the schools' discipline transformed other ordinary, natural actions, gestures, and functions into rituals—the rituals of "being a rabbi." Everyone ate. Rabbis did so in a "rabbinic" manner. That is, what others regarded as matters of mere etiquette—formalities and conventions intended to render eating aesthetically agreeable—rabbis regarded as matters of "Torah," something to be *learned*. It was "Torah" to do things one way, and it was equally "ignorance" to do them another (though not heresy, for theology was the issue). The master of the Torah, whether disciple or teacher, would demonstrate his mastery not merely through what he said in the discussion of legal traditions or what he did in court. He would do so also by how he sat at the table, by what ritual formulas he recited before eating one or another kind of fruit or vegetable, by how he washed his hands. Everyone had to relieve himself. The sage would do so according to "Torah." The personality traits of men might vary. Those expected of, and inculcated into, a sage were of a single fabric.

23

The Philosopher

TYPES OF RELIGIOUS EXPRESSION

The mark of a successful religion is its power to accommodate diverse types of personality, to make a place for everybody, man and woman, rich and poor, practical and spiritual, simple and brilliant, and the like. For in the nature of things in any community different kinds of people assemble. Catholic Christianity, for instance, finds a place for people who wish to spend their lives at prayer, others who want to serve, and still others who find their vocation in everyday life.

In this section, we take up four different types of human being and how rabbinic Judaism accommodates each of them: the intellectual, the mystic, the ordinary man, and the extraordinary woman. In this way we see how one and the same system makes its impact on quite exceptional sorts of people. Not surprisingly, what we see is how the Torah infuses each type of personality, giving the philosopher problems for thought, the mystic an encounter with the living God, the everyday man the ethics to guide him in ordinary life, and the exceptional woman the promise—fulfilled only in our own day—that she too may find a place in the life of learning God's will and word in the Torah and a life of leadership in Holy Israel.

THE PHILOSOPHICAL FORMULATION
OF THE DUAL TORAH

Up to now we have dealt with those enduring formations of the Judaism of the dual Torah that had come into being in late antiquity, the first seven centuries of the Common Era, from the destruction of the Temple in 70 to the Muslim conquest of the Near and Middle East from 640 onward. However, the Judaism of the dual Torah not only survived the world-historical changes represented by the shift from Christian to Muslim rule of territories in which Jews lived, such as the Land of Israel and Babylonia. The rise of Islam brought important intellectual changes, because of the character of Islamic culture. Specifically, Muslim theologians, who could read Greek or who read Greek philosophy translated into Arabic, developed a mode of thought along philosophical lines, rigorous, abstract, and scientific, with special interest in a close reading of Aristotle. Although in ancient times a school of Judaic philosophy in the Greek-speaking Jewish world, represented by Philo of Alexandria, read

Scripture in the light of philosophical modes of thought, the sages of the Talmud did not follow that generalizing and speculative mode of thought. They read Scripture within a different framework altogether. But as the Judaic intellectuals of Islam faced the challenge of Muslim rationalism and philosophical rigor, they read Scripture and the Oral Torah too in a new way. The task at hand was to reconcile and accommodate the one with the other. For just as today most Judaists—faithful believers all—cannot imagine denying the established truths of science while affirming the revelation of the Torah (no one thinks the world is flat, for instance, and the story of a seven-day creation is also set aside), so in medieval Islam, no Judaic intellectuals could rest easy in the admission that Scripture and science, in its philosophical form, came into conflict.

That is why alongside study of the Torah—meaning spending one's life in learning the Babylonian Talmud and later codes, commentaries, and rabbinic court decisions—a different sort of intellectual-religious life flourished in classical Judaism. It was the study of the tradition through the instruments of reason and the discipline of philosophy.

For the whole history of the classical tradition, "study of Torah" predominated. The philosophical enterprise attracted small numbers of elitists and mainly served their specialized spiritual and intellectual needs. That does not mean the philosophical way was unimportant. Those who followed it included the thoughtful and the perplexed, those who took the statements of the tradition most seriously and, through questioning and reflection, intended to examine and then effect them. The philosophers, moreover, were not persons who limited their activities to study and teaching; they frequently both occupied high posts within the Jewish community and served in the high society of politics, culture, and science outside the community also. Though not numerous, the philosophers exercised considerable influence, particularly over the mind of an age that believed reason and learning, not wealth and worldly power, were what really mattered.

The way of Torah, embodying as it does the recapitulation of the ecology of holy Israel, formed the path everywhere and always. By contrast, the philosophical way proved attractive only at specific times and under unique circumstances, while the way of the Torah was always and everywhere characteristic in premodern times. Philosophy proved uniquely important to Jews living in close contact with other cultures and traditions, such as those of Hellenistic Alexandria in the first century C.E., ninth-century Muslim Baghdad, Spain in the eleventh and twelfth centuries, Christian Germany in the nineteenth century, and in North America in the twentieth century. In such settings, Jews coexisted in an open society with Gentiles—pagans, Muslims, Christians, Zoroastrians. They did not live isolated from or in ignorance of the dominant spiritual currents of the day. On the contrary, each particular group felt called on to explain its chief ideas and doctrines in terms accessible to all others. Reason was conceived as the medium for such discourse.

All groups in the day-to-day encounter of differing cultures and traditions, therefore, attained a high degree of self-consciousness; so that something called Judaism or Christianity or Islam could be defined by contrast to—against the background of—other sorts of "-isms" and "-ities." The total, all-encompassing worldview of the Torah, on the other hand, quite unselfconsciously spoke of "person," in the assumptionx that people were pretty much alike because they were Jews. "The good way" for a human being could be defined in a homogeneous setting. But the heterogeneity of the world of intersecting Islam, Christianity, and Judaism was only one of detail. Philosophy flourished in a world of deep religious conviction—a conviction common to the several disparate communities. The issues of philosophy were set not by lack of belief but by deep faith. Few, if any, denied providence, a personal God, and a holy book revealed by God through his chosen messenger.[1] Everyone believed in reward and punishment, a last judgment, and a settling of accounts.

The Jewish philosopher had to cope with problems imposed not only by the classical faith but also by the anomalous situation of the Jews themselves. Here again, the enduring ecology left no choice: the issues that faced Jews in times past, present, and future would dictate a set of issues that philosophy, too, had to take up. For instance, what was the meaning of the strange, unfortunate history of the Jews? How was philosophy to account reasonably for a homelessness of God's people, who were well aware that they lived as a minority among powerful, prosperous majorities, Christian or Muslim? If the Torah were true, why did different revelations claiming to be based on it—but to complete it—flourish, while the people of the Torah suffered? Why, indeed, ought one to remain a Jew, when every day one was confronted by the success of the daughter religions? For a member of a despised minority, conversion was always a possibility—an inviting one even under the best of circumstances.[2]

These problems pressed on the philosopher in particular—a marginal figure both in Jewry and in the urban civilization of the day. For him, the easy answers—"We are still being punished for our sins" or "We suffer now but our reward will be all the greater later on"—were transparent, self-serving, and unsatisfactory because they were too easy. He was, further, concerned with the eternal questions facing all religious people: Is God just? What is the nature of humanity? What is the meaning of revelation? Where were answers to be found?

The search was complicated by the formidable appeal of Greek philosophy to medieval Christian and Islamic civilization. Its rationalism, its openness, its search for pure knowledge challenged all revelations. Philosophy questioned all assertions of truth verifiable not through reason but only through appeals to a source of truth not universally recognized. Reason thus stood, it seemed, against revelation. Mysterious divine plans came into conflict with allegations of the limitless capacity of human reason. Free inquiry might lead anywhere and so would not reliably lead to the synagogue, church, or mosque. And not merely traditional knowledge but the specific propositions of faith and the assertions of a holy book had to be measured against the results of reason. Faith *or* reason—this seemed to be the choice.

For the Jews, moreover, the very substance of faith—in a personal, highly anthropomorphic God who exhibited traits of character not always in conformity with humanity's highest ideals and who in rabbinic hands looked much like the rabbi himself—posed a formidable obstacle. Classical conundrums of philosophy were further enriched by the obvious contradictions between belief in free will and belief in divine providence. Is God all-knowing? Then how can people be held responsible for what they do? Is God perfect? Then how can he change his mind or set aside his laws to forgive people?

No theologian in such a cosmopolitan, rational age could begin with an assertion of a double truth or a private, relative one. The notion that something could be true for one party and not for another or that faith and reason were equally valid and yet contradictory were ideas that had little appeal. And the holy book had to retain the upper hand: "Scripture as the word of God contained, of course, absolute truth, while philosophy as a human activity could find its truth only in reasoning."[3] The two philosophers we shall now consider represent the best efforts of medieval Judaic civilization to confront these perplexities.

MOSES MAIMONIDES

Moses Maimonides (1141–1205) was at the same time a distinguished student of the Talmud and Jewish law in the classical mode, a community authority, a great physician, and a leading thinker of his day. His achievement was to synthesize a neo-Platonic Aristotelianism with biblical revelation. His *Guide to the Perplexed,* published in 1190, was intended to reconcile the believer to the philosopher and the philosopher to faith. For him philosophy was not alien to religion but identical with it, for truth was, in the end, the sole issue. Faith is a form of knowledge; philosophy is the road to faith.

His proof for the existence of God was Aristotelian. He argued for creation to Creator but accepted the eternity of the world. Julius Guttmann describes Maimonides' view as follows:

> Since, in addition to bodies which are both moving and moved, there are other bodies which are moved and yet are not causes of movement, there must also exist a being which moves without being moved. The second proof is based not on the movement of bodies but on their transition from potency to act: the transition presupposed the existence of an actualizing principle which is external to the being thus changed. The impossibility of an infinite regression of causes, just as it led in the first proof to prime mover, now serves to establish the existence of a first actualizing principle, free of all potentiality and hence also immaterial in nature....Maimonides can prove the origin of the world as a whole, from God, only by deduction from the contingent existence of things.[4]

God becomes, therefore, an "absolutely simple essence from which all positive definition is excluded."[5] One can say nothing about the attributes of God. He is purged of all sensuous elements. One can say only that God is God, nothing more, for God can only be *known* as the highest cause of being.

What then of revelation? Did God not say anything about himself? And if he did, what need for reasonings such as these? For Maimonides, prophecy, like philosophy, depends on the Active Intellect. But in the case of the prophets, "the Active Intellect impresses itself especially upon their imaginative faculty, which is why they express their teachings in a poetic or literary form, rather than in the ratiocinative form of the philosophers."[6] Prophecy is a gift bestowed by God on man. The Torah and commandments are clearly important, but they are not ultimately beyond question or reasonable inquiry. They, however, survive the inquiry unimpaired. The Torah fosters a sound mind and body:

> All its precepts and teachings conspire to guide a man to the greatest benefits, moral and intellectual. Everything in the Torah, whether it be a law or a narrative or genealogy, is significant...intended to inculcate a moral or intellectual truth, to wean men away from wrong beliefs, harmful excesses, or dangerous indulgences. In its entirety, the Law is the supreme means whereby man realizes himself most fully.[7]

The greatest good, however, is not to study the Torah in the sense described earlier but rather to know God—that is, to worship and love him. Piety and knowledge of the Torah serve merely to prepare people for this highest achievement. Study of the Torah loses its character as an end in itself and is rendered into a means to a philosophical goal. This constituted the most striking transformation of the old values. Philosophical knowledge of physical and metaphysical truths "culminates in a purified conception of the nature of God. It is this kind of understanding that engenders the longing for God and the love of him."[8]

Maimonides provided a definition of Judaism—a list of articles of faith he thought obligatory on every faithful Jew. These are as follows:

1. Existence of God

2. His unity

3. His incorporeality

4. His eternity

5. The obligation to worship him alone

6. Prophecy

7. Moses as the greatest of the prophets

8. The divine origin of Torah

9. The eternal validity of Torah

10. God's knowledge of man's deeds

11. His punishing of evil and rewarding of goodness

12. His promise to send a Messiah

13. His promise to resurrect the dead

These philosophical principles were hotly debated and much criticized, but, ironically, they achieved a place in the life of Judaic piety. Although subjected to debate and criticism, in the end they were sung as a prayer in a hymn, *Yigdal,* which is always sung at the conclusion of synagogue prayer.

1. The living God we praise, exalt, adore
    He was, he is, he will be evermore.

2. No unity like unto his can be
    Eternal, inconceivable is he.

3. No form or shape has the incorporeal one
    Most holy he, past all comparison.

4. He was ere aught was made in heaven or earth
    But his existence has no date or birth.

5. Lord of the Universe is he proclaimed
    Teaching his power to all his hand has framed.

6. He gave his gift of prophecy to those
    In whom he gloried, whom he loved and chose.

7. No prophet ever yet has filled the place
    Of Moses, who beheld God face to face.

8. Through him (the faithful in his house) the Lord
    The law of truth to Israel did accord.

9. This Law of God will no alter, will not change
    For any other through time's utmost range.

10. He knows and heeds the secret thoughts of man:
    He saw the end of all ere aught began.

11. With love and grace doth he the righteous bless,
    He metes out evil unto wickedness.

12. He at the last will his anointed send
    Those to redeem who hope and wait the end.

13. God will the dead to life again restore.
    Praised by his glorious name for evermore.[9]

The esoteric words of the philosopher were thus transformed into a message of faith, at once sufficiently complex to sustain critical inquiry according to the canons of the day and simple enough to bear the weight of the faith of ordinary folk and be sung. The "God without attributes" is still guide, refuge, stronghold. It is a strange and paradoxical fate for the philosopher's teachings. Who would have supposed at the outset that the way of the philosopher would lead to the piety of the people?

JUDAH HALEVI

Many, indeed, came to no such supposition. They found the philosophers presumptuous, inadequate, and incapable of investigating the truths of faith. But the critics of "philosophy" were themselves philosophers. The greatest was Judah Halevi (1080–1141), who produced *not* a work of sustained philosophical argument and analysis but a set of dialogues between a king—the King of the Khazars, a kingdom that did, in fact, adopt Judaism several centuries earlier—in search of true religion and the advocates of the several religious and philosophical positions of the day, including Judaism. Halevi, poet and mystic, objected to the indifference of philosophy to the comparative merits of the competing traditions. In philosophy's approach, "the ultimate objective is the knowledge of God. Religion is recommended because it inculcates the proper moral qualities in men, but no attention is paid to the question of *which* system of religious morality one ought to follow."[10] For the majority religions in the West—Islam and Christianity—such an indifference may have been tolerable, but *not* for a minority destined any day to have to die for the profession of faith.

Martyrdom will not be evoked by the unmoved mover, the God anyone may reach either through revelation or through reason. Only for the God of Israel will a Jew give up his or her life. By its nature, philosophy is insufficient for the religious quest: "It starts with assumptions and ends with mere theories."[11] It can hardly compete with, let alone challenge, the *history* of the Jewish people—a history recording extraordinary events starting with revelation. What has philosophy to do with Sinai, with the land, with prophecy? On the contrary, the Jew, expounding religion to the king of the Khazars, begins not like the philosopher with a disquisition on divine attributes, nor like the Christian who starts with the works of creation and expounds the Trinity, nor like the Moslem who acknowledges the unity and eternity of God, but as follows:

> I believe in the God of Abraham, Isaac, and Israel, who led the Israelites out of Egypt with signs and miracles; who fed them in the desert and gave them the Land, after having made traverse the sea and the Jordan in a miraculous way; who sent Moses with His Torah and subsequently thousands of prophets, who confirmed His law by promises to those who observed and threats to the disobedient. We believe in what is contained in the Torah—a very large domain.[12]

The king then asks, Why did the Jew not say he believes in the creator of the world and in similar attributes common to all creeds? The Jew responds that the evidence for Israel's faith is *Israel,* the people, this history and endurance, and not the kinds of reasonable truths offered by other traditions. The *proof* of revelation is the testimony of those who were *there* and wrote down what they heard, saw, and did.

If so, the king wonders, what accounts for the despised condition of Israel today? The Jew compares Israel to the dry bones of Ezekiel:

these bones, which have retained a trace of vital power and have once been the seat of a heart, head, spirit, soul, and intellect, are better than bones formed of marble and plaster, endowed with heads, eyes, ears, and all limbs, in which there never dwelt the spirit of life.[13]

God's people is Israel; he rules them and keeps them in their present status:

Israel amid the nations is like the heart amid the organs: it is the most sick and the most healthy of them all....The relationship of the Divine power to us is the same as that of the soul to the heart. For this reason it is said, *You only have I known among all the families of the earth, therefore I will punish you for all your iniquities* [Amos 3:2]....Now we are oppressed, while the whole world enjoys rest and prosperity. But the trials which meet us serve to purify our piety, cleanse us, and to remove all taint from us.[14]

The pitiful condition of Israel is, therefore, turned into the primary testimony and vindication of Israel's faith. That Israel suffers is the best assurance of divine concern. The suffering constitutes the certainty of coming redemption. In the end, the Jew parts from the king to undertake a journey to the Land of Israel. There he seeks perfection with God:

The invisible and spiritual *Shekhinah* [presence of God] is with every born Israelite of pure life, pure heart, and sincere devotion to the Lord of Israel. And the Land of Israel has a special relation to the Lord of Israel. Pure life can be perfectly lived only there.[15]

To this the king objects. He thought the Jew loved freedom, but the Jew finds himself in bondage by imposing duties obligatory in residing in the Land of Israel. The Jew replies that the freedom he seeks is from the service of men and the courting of their favor. He seeks the service of one whose favor is obtained with the smallest effort: "His service is freedom, and humility before him is true honor." He, therefore, turns to Jerusalem to seek the holy life. He closes his remarks:

Thou shalt arise and have mercy upon Zion; for it is time to favor her, the moment is come. For thy servants love her stones and pity her dust [Psalm 102:14–15].
This means, Jerusalem can only be rebuilt when Israel yearns for it to such an extent that we sympathize even with its stones and its dust.[16]

Here we find no effort to identify Judaism with rational truth but rather the claim that the life of the pious Jew stands above—indeed constitutes the best testimony to—truth.

The source of truth is biblical revelation; it was public, complete, fully in the light of history. History, not philosophy, testifies to the truth and in the end constitutes its sole criterion. Philosophy claims reason can find the way to God. Halevi says that only God can show the way to God, and he does so through revelation, and therefore in history. For the philosopher, God is the object of knowledge.[17] For Halevi, God is the subject of knowledge: "The yearning heart seeks the god of Abraham; the labor of the intellect is directed toward the God of Aristotle."[18] And Israel has a specifically religious faculty that mediates the relationship to God, so we have seen in the references to the role of Israel among the nations as similar to the role of the heart among the limbs.

Halevi seeks to explain the supernatural status of Israel. The religious faculty is its peculiar inheritance and makes it the core of humanity. He thus "predicates...the supernatural religious faculty."[19] But whereas the rest of humanity is subject to the laws of nature, Israel is subject to supernatural, divine providence, manifested in reward and punishment. The very condition of the Jews, in that God punishes them, verifies the particular and specific place of Israel in the divine plan. The teaching of prophecy thus returns in Halevi's philosophy.

CONCLUSION

These two philosophers were part of a number of important thinkers who attempted to meet the challenge of philosophy and reason by constructing a comprehensive theological system. But the uses of reason were not exhausted by the philosophical enterprise. Reason played a central role in Torah study. The settings, however, were vastly different. Still, so far as reasoning power "is one of the modes of human awareness through which man constructs human experience,"[20] the classic Judaic tradition fully explored this mode.

If, in Judaic tradition, salvation was never reduced to a "confession of a creed or theological agreement," still important efforts were made, such as that of Maimonides, to produce just such a creed. It is not, as is often asserted, that Judaism had (or has) no theology. Such a statement is obviously absurd. It is simply that the theological idiom of the Judaic tradition often diverged from that of the Christian West. In Maimonides, we meet a theological mind quite capable of addressing itself to the issues confronting any religious tradition perplexed by philosophical reason.

Although like the Muslim and Christian intellectuals in mentality, the Jewish philosophers had more in common with the Talmudic rabbis than with gentile philosophers. The rabbis accepted the Bible and the Talmud as "the whole Torah," and so did the Jewish philosophers. Both groups devoted themselves to the articulation of the Torah's role in the life of Israel, to the meaning of the fate of Israel and to the effort to form piety and shape faith. And for both, *reason* was the means of reaching into the Torah—of recovering and achieving truth. Both agreed that words could contain and convey the sacred; therefore, reason—the examination of the meaning and referents of words— was the golden measure. They differed only in the object of reason; the one studied law, the other, philosophy. Yet Maimonides, the complete and whole Jew, studied both and made a lasting impact on the formation not only of both sorts of Judaic tradition but also of the pious imagination of the ordinary Jew. He translated his philosophical and theological principles and convictions into his presentation of the concrete, practical law. And it is in the study and practice of the Torah and its law that Judaism finds its being.

NOTES

1. Abraham S. Halkin, "The Judeo-Islamic Age," in *Great Ages and Ideas of the Jewish People,* ed. Leo W. Schwarz (New York: Random House, 1956), 235.

2. Ibid., 238–239.

3. Ibid., 245.

4. Julius Guttmann, *Philosophies of Judaism: The History of Jewish Philosophy from Biblical Times to Franz Rosenzweig,* trans. David Silverman (New York: Holt, Rinehart & Winston, 1964), 158.

5. Ibid.

6. Halkin, "The Judeo-Islamic Age," 251.

7. Ibid.

8. Ibid., 251–252.

9. Alice Lucas, trans., quoted in Bernard Martin, *Prayer in Judaism* (New York: Basic Books, 1968), 84–85.

10. Halkin, "The Judeo-Islamic Age," 253.

11. Ibid.

12. Cited in Isaak Heinemann, "Judah Halevi, Kuzari," in *Three Jewish Philosophers,* ed. Isaak Heinemann, Alexander Altmann, and Hans Lewy (Philadelphia: Jewish Publication Society, 1960), 33.

13. Ibid., 72.

14. Ibid., 75.

15. Ibid.

16. Ibid., 126–129.

17. Guttmann, *Philosophies of Judaism,* 125.

18. Ibid.

19. Ibid., 126.

20. Frederick J. Streng, *Understanding Religious Man* (Belmont, CA: Dickenson, 1968), 92.

24

The Mystic

MYSTICAL KNOWLEDGE AND EXPERIENCE IN RABBINIC JUDAISM

The Judaism of the dual Torah, in ancient and also medieval and modern times, welcomed and placed a high value on mystical experience attained through prayer, asceticism, and devotion to godly service. It furthermore made a place within the Torah for holy books of mystical doctrine. In ancient times, it is clear, a mystical experience involving visions of God in the levels of the firmament, was available to some sages. A continuing tradition of speculation about matters of mystical knowledge and experience flourished from late antiquity forward. That tradition came to its zenith in the most important work of mystical speculation and experience, the *Zohar,* a thirteenth-century work of immense proportions and commensurate influence. It suffices to say that the dual Torah of Judaism encompassed not only Scripture, the Mishnah, and other writings of the oral tradition of the ancient rabbis but also yet a third powerful and important "Torah" as well, the Torah of religious experience of an intense and mystical confrontation with the living God. The *Zohar* is that third component of the Judaism of the dual Torah.

THE *ZOHAR* AND MOSES DE LEON

Although we know that Moses de Leon wrote the *Zohar* in Spain between 1281 and 1286, we cannot be surprised that he speaks in the name of important second-century rabbis. For the mystics before and after the *Zohar* took for granted that their doctrines were Torah and derived from the same authorities who gave them Mishnah and other parts of the oral Torah. The intense inner life of direct encounter through prayer, performance of the commandments, and Torah study thus strengthened the power of the rabbinic Torah myth in the life of the Jewish people and, indeed, generated fructifying, creative forces in the way of the Torah.

Especially important was the conviction that every deed of a human being on Earth has its counterpart in invisible reality in Heaven. The Talmudic stress on practical action elevated concrete deeds into the highest mode of religious expression. What a Jew did affected the profound reality: "Thus I do this *mitzvah* for the sake of the unity of the Holy One, blessed be He" was said by a mystic to help effect the greater unity of the one God. The social effect was to stress the performance of deeds that formed a pattern of religious living—deeds that the nonmystic performed habitually in a more mundane spirit and an attitude of mere conformity. The mystic knew that one does things for a deeper, transcendent reason. The mystic therefore brought new devotion to the old, established way of life. He joined the community ever more concerned to do precisely what everyone else was doing anyhow, but for his own reason.

It is no accident that the greatest lawyers and Talmudists also were among the most profound and influential mystics. For example, the author of the code of Jewish law (*Shulhan Arukh*), Joseph Karo, believed that he received heavenly visitations from the Mishnah incarnate. A great biblical commentator, Nachmanides, introduced into his commentary on the Pentateuch important mystical considerations. The greatest genius of the Talmudic tradition, Elijah, the Gaon of Vilna who lived at the end of the eighteenth century, was a paragon of rabbinic rationality who also gave his best efforts to the study of the *Zohar* and other mystical writings. We cannot, in fact, locate a major legal authority who, after mystic literature became available, did not also devote himself in some measure to the study of mysticism. The reason is that the law and the inner life of the believing Jew were understood to express one and the same pattern. The former was the body and the latter, the spirit; the former was the outer capsule and the latter, the inner meaning. So when the mystics, for their part, undertook ascetic behavior, it was in the form of moral behavior. Ascetic renunciation led less to hair shirts and fasting (though there assuredly was self-torture) than to moral action—that is, giving up one's rights in favor of another. Because the Jewish mystic wanted to love God, he had also to love his neighbor.

THE *BOOK OF THE PIOUS*

A thirteenth-century book of mysticism, the *Book of the Pious,* describes the practical expression of ascetic mysticism in this way:

> At all times you should love your Creator with all your heart and all your soul and take council with your heart and a lesson from man who is but worms; if a person give you ten gold pieces or more, how deeply engraved would his love be in your heart. And if he provides your support and the support of your children and of your household you would certainly think, "This man which I have never seen and who has extended to me such kindness I would not be able to repay for all the goodness he has shown me should I live a thousand years. I would love him with all my heart and with all my soul; he could not command me to do anything that I would not do for him, because both my wealth and my being are his." As with the love of man so with the love of the Holy One, blessed be He, raised and exalted be His fame. It is He who gives sustenance to all, how much better that we should cleave to the love of the Creator, fear

Him, nor transgress His commands whether great or small. For we do not know the reward of each commandment, and the punishment for transgressions though they appear light in our eyes, as it is written, *When the iniquity of my supplanters compasseth me about* (Psalm 49:6). The transgressions to which a man becomes habituated in this world will encompass him on the Day of Judgment. If he is deserving his good deeds will bear witness for him. True and firm it is that we are not to transgress the commandments of our Creator even one of the small ones for a house full of gold and silver. If an individual says, "I will transgress a commandment and with the gold and silver they give me I will fulfill the difficult commandments. With this I will support the poor, invite wayfarers, I will do very many favors." These are the futile thoughts, for perhaps soon after the transgression he will die and not succeed to the gift. Moreover, if he should not die the money would soon be dissipated so that he dies in his sin. Come and see how much you should love your Creator and who does wonderful kindnesses with you, He creates you from a decayed drop, He gives you a soul, draws you forth from the belly, then gives you a mouth with which to speak, a heart to understand, ears to hear the pure words of His mouth, which are refined as silver and pure gold. It is He who leads you on the face of earth, who gives sustenance to all, who causes death and gives life to all. In His hand are the souls of all the living. It is He who distributes your share of bread. What is there to say? For the mouth is unable to speak, the ear unable to hear, for to Him all praise is as silence, there is no end to the length of His days, His years will have no end, He is the King of kings, the Holy One, blessed be His name and His fame. It is He who has created the heavens and earth, sea, and all that is therein. He is the provider of all, for His eyes are open upon all men's paths recompensing each according to his ways and the fruit of his deeds, whether good or bad. Behold it is He who sets forth before men two paths, the path of life and the path of death and says to you, *Choose life* (Deuteronomy 30:19). In spite of all this, we who are filled with worms do not think and do not set our hearts but to fill our appetites freely. We do not think that man's days are numbered, today he is here, tomorrow in the grace, that suddenly he dies. For no man rules over his spirit retaining it (forever). Therefore, it is good for man to remove himself from all appetites and direct his heart to love and fear the Lord with all his heart at all times and revile the life of vanity. For we will not be able to humble ourselves and subdue our passion which thrusts us from the land of the living, except through subduing our heart and returning to our Maker in complete repentance, to serve Him and to do His will with a whole heart. Our sages have said, "Bread and salt shalt thou eat and water in measurement shall you drink and beware of gazing at women which drives a person from the world. Love humans and judge all people in the scale of merit." And this is what the Torah has said, *But in righteousness shalt thou judge they neighbor* (Leviticus 19:15). Be humble before all, busy yourself with Torah, which is whole, pure and upright and do not praise yourself for it, because for this were you created.[1]

Some may ask how this intense religious experience is particularly mystical, because most religious people seek to attain that same unity of life and thought with God.

ABRAHAM JOSHUA HESCHEL'S ACCOUNT
OF MYSTICISM IN JUDAISM

Indeed, the main purpose of mysticism for Judaism is that God is very real, and the desire of the mystic is "to feel and to enjoy Him; not only to obey but to approach Him." So says Abraham J. Heschel, the great theologian of Judaism in the twentieth century, who goes on: "They want to taste the whole wheat of spirit before it is ground by the millstones of reason. They would rather be overwhelmed by the symbols of the inconceivable than wield the definitions of the superficial."[2] What, then, is the mystic doctrine of God in Judaism? According to Heschel:

> Mystic intuition occurs at an outpost of the mind, dangerously detached from the main substance of the intellect. Operating as it were in no-mind's land, its place is hard to name, its communications with critical thinking often difficult and uncertain and the accounts of its discoveries not easy to decode. In its main representatives, the Kabbalah teaches that man's life can be a rallying point of the forces that tend toward God, that this world is charged with His presence and every object is a cue to His qualities. To the cabbalist, God is not a concept, a generalization, but a most specific reality; his thinking about Him full of forceful directness. But He who is "the Soul of all souls" is "the mystery of all mysteries." While the cabbalists speak of God as if they commanded a view of the Beyond, and were in possession of knowledge about the inner life of God, they also assure us that all notions fail when applied to Him, that He is beyond the grasp of the human mind and inaccessible to meditation. He is the *En Sof,* the Infinite, "the most Hidden of all Hidden." While there is an abysmal distance between Him and the world, He is also called All. "For all things are in Him and He is in all things…. He is both manifest and concealed. Manifest in order to uphold the all and concealed, for He is found nowhere. When He becomes manifest He projects nine brilliant lights that throw light in all directions. So, too, does a lamp throw brilliance in all directions, but when we approach the brilliance we find there is nothing outside the lamp. So is the Holy ancient One, the Light of all Lights, the most Hidden of all Hidden. We can only find the light which He spreads and which appears and disappears. This light is called the Holy Name, and therefore All is One."
>
> Thus, the "Most Recondite One Who is beyond cognition does reveal of Himself a tenuous and veiled brightness shining only along a narrow path which extends from Him. This is the brightness that irradiates all."

The *En Sof* has granted us manifestations of His hidden life: He had descended to become the universe; He has revealed Himself to become the Lord of Israel. The ways in which the Infinite assumes the form of finite existence are called *Sefirot*. These are various aspects or forms of Divine action, spheres of Divine emanation. They are, as it were, the garments in which the Hidden God reveals Himself and acts in the universe, the channels through which His light is issued forth.[3]

Obviously, in so fresh and original a system, all the antecedent symbols and conceptions of Judaism are going to be revised and given new meanings. The single most striking revision is in the very definition of the Torah. We know that for classical Judaism the Torah means revelation, and revelation is contained in various documents—some of them written down and handed on from Sinai, others transmitted orally, also from Sinai. But for the mystic, the Torah also becomes a "mystic reality," as Heschel explains:

The Torah is an inexhaustible esoteric reality. To enter into its deep, hidden strata is in itself a mystic goal. The Universe is an image of the Torah and the Torah is an image of God. For the Torah is "the Holy of Holies"; it consists entirely of the name of the Holy One, blessed be He. Every letter in it is bound up with that Name."

The Torah is the main source from which man can draw the secret wisdom and power of insight into the essence of things. "It is called Torah (lit.: showing) because it shows and reveals that which is hidden and unknown; and all life from above is comprised in it and issues from it." "The Torah contains all the deepest and most recondite mysteries; all sublime doctrines both disclosed and undisclosed; all essences both of the higher and the lower grades, of this world and of the world to come are to be found there." The source of wisdom is accessible to all, yet only few resort to it. "How stupid are men that they take no pains to know the ways of the Almighty by which the world is maintained. What prevents them? Their stupidity, because they do not study the Torah; for if they were to study the Torah they would know the ways of the Holy One, blessed be He."

The Torah has a double significance: literal and symbolic. Besides their plain, literal meaning, which is important, valid and never to be overlooked, the verses of the Torah possess an esoteric significance, "comprehensible only to the wise who are familiar with the ways of the Torah." "Happy is Israel to whom was given the sublime Torah, the Torah of truth. Perdition take anyone who maintains that any narrative in the Torah comes merely to tell us a piece of history and nothing more! If that were so, the Torah would not be what it assuredly is, to wit, the supernal Law, the Law of truth. Now if it is not dignified for a king of flesh and blood to engage in common talk, much less to write it down, is it conceivable that the most high King, the Holy One, blessed be He, was short of sacred subjects with which to fill the Torah, so that He had to collect such commonplace topics as the anecdotes of Esau, and Hagar, Laban's talks to Jacob, the words of Balaam and his ass, those of Balak, and of Zimri, and such-like, and make of them a Torah? If so, why is it called the 'Law of Truth'? Why do we read *The Law of the Lord is perfect....The testimony of the Lord is sure....The Ordinances of the Lord are true....More to be desired are they than gold, yea, than much fine gold* (Psalm 19:8–11). But assuredly each word of the Torah signifies sublime things, so that this or that narrative, besides its meaning in and for itself, throws light on the all-encompassing Rule of the Torah."[4]

In Heschel's statement here, we see how the long, influential tradition of mysticism in Judaism was able to reinforce and vivify rabbinic Judaism in its Talmudic mode. It is clear that the mystic finds in the Torah meanings and dimensions not perceived in the earlier phases of Talmudic Judaism. In many ways, the mysterious power of the mystic is to see what lesser eyes cannot perceive. But the perception is there, and to the mystic and his audience it was very real. So the Torah took on a richer meaning that it had had, even for the rabbi. Thus, it came to include both the literal meaning of the words and the deeper or symbolic meaning—the level of meaning far more profound than meets the eye. The Torah was made to yield the meanings not solely of its sentences, but now of each and every individual letter.

GERSHOM G. SCHOLEM'S ACCOUNT
OF MYSTICISM IN JUDAISM

The essence of the mystic way is not contained within the notion of the deeper layers of meaning to be found within the Torah. Rather, the essence of mysticism is the inquiry into the very essence of God. What made mysticism a powerful force in Judaism is the vivid encounter with God made possible in mysticism as it was not in any other mode of Judaism or Judaic religiosity. This is how Gershom C. Scholem, founder of the academic study of Judaic mysticism, explains the mystic encounter with God:

> The mystic strives to assure himself of the living presence of God, the God of the Bible, the God who is good, wise, just and merciful and the embodiment of all other positive attributes. But at the same time he is unwilling to renounce the idea of the hidden God who remains eternally unknowable in the depths of His own Self, or, to use the bold expression of the Kabbalists "in the depths of his nothingness." This hidden God may be without special attributes—the living God of whom the Revelation speaks, with whom all religion is concerned, must have attributes, which on another plane represent also the mystic's own scale of moral values: God is good, God is severe, God is merciful and just....The mystic does not even recoil before the inference that in a higher sense there is a root of evil even in God. The benevolence of God is to the mystic not simply the negation of evil, but a whole sphere of divine light, in which God

manifests Himself under this particular aspect of benevolence to the contemplation of the Kabbalist.[5]

In many ways, then, mysticism must be seen as the ultimate, logical conclusion of that mode of Judaism that took shape in the aftermath of the messianic disasters of the first and second centuries. For the encounter with God outside history and time—the direct realization of the knowledge of God, who in some measure is hidden and unknowable in the depths of his nothingness—removes the mystic from the one thing that rabbinic Judaism to begin with proposed to neutralize—namely, the vagaries of history. The essentially ahistorical quality of mystical thinking accounts for the ready home provided to mysticism by that form of Judaism that began with the Mishnah and the Talmud and, we now see, came to fruition and fulfillment—in the minds of many great Talmudists—in the mystical realization of the encounter with God's hidden self.

To what degree did the values of the rabbis of the Talmud and the great philosophers and mystics actually influence the lives of ordinary folk? Were Jews truly the "people of Torah" that the rabbis, philosophers, and mystics wanted them to be? Next we turn to an ordinary Jew, and then we shall look at the spiritual traits of two extraordinary women, both of whom lived when Judaism in its classical form predominated. When, at the end, we discover in the writing of a pious and traditional woman an essentially fresh aspiration, we shall know that it is time to ask what has changed in the modern period in the history of Judaism, and why that change has taken place.

NOTES

1. Scholom Alchanan Singer, trans., *Medieval Jewish Mysticism: The Book of the Pious* (Northbrook, IL: Whitehall, 1971), 37–38.

2. Abraham J. Heschel, "The Mystical Elements of Judaism," in *The Jews: Their History, Culture, and Religion,* ed. Louis Finkelstein (New York: Harper & Row, 1971).

3. Ibid., 284–285.

4. Ibid., 292–293.

5. Gershom G. Scholem, "Major Trends in Jewish Mysticism," in *Understanding Rabbinic Judaism,* ed. J. Neusner (New York: Ktav, 1977), 253–254.

25

An Ordinary Jew

In rabbinic Judaism, to be "Israel" means to model life in the image, after the likeness, of God. But in the everyday world, Jews are subjected to negative stereotypes, and Judaism has also been denigrated. Any negative experience one may have with an individual of Jewish origin, whether or not a practitioner of Judaism, is taken to represent all the Jews and Judaism too. In a university classroom in New Zealand, for instance, Judaism was represented as "not a religion so much as a certain attitude toward money,"[1] and the same sort of denigration of the faith and people of Israel are common everywhere. Christian anti-Semites have described life under the law, that is, under the Torah, in derogatory terms, denying that any true piety can emerge under the burden of so many petty rules and regulations. Secular anti-Semites attribute to the fault of the Jews everything they find wrong with the world.

The kind of human being the Torah (that is, "Judaism") means to nurture therefore requires attention. When we examine the statements of ordinary people, we find rich evidence of a profound ethical life with God: women and men devoted to the holy way of life because they love God and want to live their lives and form their communities in accord with the covenant that God made with Israel at Mount Sinai. Life under the law has rightly been characterized by the New Testament scholar, E. P. Sanders, as a life of "covenantal nomism," meaning that Israel keeps the Torah in obedience to the covenant made by God with the holy people through the Torah.[2]

What of the common folk who lived out their days in a community shaped by the values of the Torah? What were their ideals? One insight is to be derived from the "ethical wills" written by fathers for their children. In the ethical will, the legator would divide not his earthly property but his highest ideals. He would ask his heirs to carry out those ideals. Such wills obviously present the father at his best, for, facing the prospect of death and judgment, the father hoped to show his best side and urge on his children the highest and noblest ideals. But that is what makes the ethical wills interesting, for they mirror ordinary folks' ideals at an extraordinary moment. The ideals of an average Jew are represented by the testament of Eleazar of Mainz, who died in 1357:

> These are the things which my sons and daughters shall do at my request. They shall go to the house of prayer morning and evening, and shall pay special regard to the Prayer and the *Shema*. So soon as the service is over, they shall occupy themselves a little with the Torah, the Psalms, or with works of charity.
>
> Their business must be conducted honestly, in their dealing both with Jew and gentile.

They must be gentle in their manners, and prompt to accede to every honorable request. They must not talk more than is necessary, by this will they be saved from slander, falsehood and frivolity.

They shall give an exact tithe of all their possessions; they shall never turn away a poor man empty-handed, but must give him what they can, be it much or little. If he beg a lodging overnight, and they know him not, let them provide him with the wherewithal to pay an innkeeper. Thus shall they satisfy the needs of the poor in every possible way.

My daughters must obey scrupulously the rules applying to women; modesty, sanctity, reverence, should mark their married lives. Marital intercourse must be modest and holy, with a spirit of restraint and delicacy, in reverence and silence. They shall be very punctilious and careful with their ritual bathing. They must respect their husbands, and must be invariably amiable to them. Husbands, on their part, must honor their wives more than themselves, and treat them with tender consideration. If they can by any means contrive it, my sons and daughters should live in communities, and not isolated from other Jews, so that their sons and daughters may learn the ways of Judaism. Even if compelled to solicit from others the money to pay a teacher, they must not let the young, of both sexes, go without instruction in the Torah. Marry your children, O my sons and daughters, as soon as their age is ripe, to members of respectable families.

Every Friday morning, they shall put themselves in careful trim for honoring the Sabbath, kindling the lamps while the day is still great, and in winter lighting the furnace before dark, to avoid desecrating the Sabbath (by kindling fire thereon). For due welcome to the Sabbath, the women must prepare beautiful candles.

In their relation to women, my sons must behave continently, avoiding mixed bathing and mixed dancing and all frivolous conversation, while my daughters ought not to speak much with strangers, nor jest nor dance with them. They ought to be always at home, and not be gadding about. They should not stand at the door, watching whatever passes. I ask, I command, that the daughters of my house be never without work to do, for idleness leads first to boredom, then to sin. But let them spin, or cook, or sew.

I earnestly beg my children to be tolerant and humble to all, as I was throughout my life. Should cause for dissension present itself, be slow to accept the quarrel; seek peace and pursue it with all the vigor at your command. Even if you suffer loss thereby, forbear and forgive, for God has many ways of feeding and sustaining His creatures. To the slanderer do not retaliate with counter-attack; and though it be proper to rebut false accusations, yet is it most desirable to set an example of reticence. You yourselves must avoid uttering any slander, for so will you win affection. In trade be true, never grasping at what belongs to another. For by avoiding these wrongs—scandal, falsehood, money-grubbing—men will surely find tranquility and affection. And against all evils, silence is the best safeguard....

Whatever happiness befalls you, be it in monetary fortune or in the birth of children, be it some signal deliverances of any other of the many blessings which may come to you, be not stolidly unappreciative, like dumb cattle that utter no word of gratitude. But offer praises to the Rock who has befriended you, saying: "O give thanks unto the Lord, for He is good, for His mercy endureth for ever. Blessed art Thou, O Lord, who are good and dispenses good." Besides thanking God for His bounties at the moment they occur, also in your regular prayers let the memory of these personal favors prompt your hearts to special fervor during the utterance of the communal thanks. When words of gratitude are used in the liturgy, pause to reflect in silence on the goodness of God to you that day. And when ye make the response: "May Thy great Name be blessed," call to mind your own personal experiences of the divine favor.

Be very particular to keep your houses clean and tidy. I was always scrupulous on this point, for every injurious condition, and sickness and poverty, are to be found in foul dwellings. Be careful over the benedictions; accept no divine gift without paying back the Giver's part; and His part is man's grateful acknowledgment.

Every one of these good qualities becomes habitual with him who studies the Torah; for that study indeed leads to the formation of a noble character. Therefore, happy is he who toils in the Law! For this gracious toil fix daily times, of long or short duration, for it is the best of all works that a man can do....

Be of the first ten in Synagogue, rising betimes for the purpose. Pray steadily with the congregation, giving due value to every letter and word, seeing that there are in the *Shema* 248 words, corresponding to the 248 limbs in the human body.

I beg of you, my sons and daughters, my wife and all the congregation, that no funeral oration be spoken in my honor. Do not carry my body on a bier but in a coach. Wash me clean, comb my hair, trim my nails, as I was wont to do in my life-time, so that I may go clean to my eternal rest, as I went clean to Synagogue every Sabbath day. If the ordinary officials dislike the duty, let adequate payment be made to some poor man who shall render this service carefully and not perfunctorily. At a distance of thirty cubits from the grave, they shall set my coffin on the ground, and drag me to the grave by a rope attached to the coffin. Every four cubits they shall stand and wait awhile, doing this in all seven times, so that I may find atonement for my sins. Put me in the ground at the right hand of my father, and if the space be a little narrow, I am sure that he loves me well enough to make room for me by his side. If this be altogether impossible, put me on his left, or near my grandmother, Yuta. Should this also be impractical, let me be buried by the side of my daughter.[3]

Where did the "way of Torah" lead? The human being before us clearly shapes his life and values by what the Torah was supposed to mean. He stresses a life of prayer, study, and good deeds. A disciple of the sages should not bring the

Torah into disrepute by false dealing, and no distinction is made between Jew and gentile. The disciple must be gentle and modest, not talk too much, and be careful to avoid slander. Tithing is encouraged, as is generously receiving the poor. Daughters must be modest, and sons, solicitous. Jews must live with other Jews, so as to sustain one another during the long exile. Living as a nation within other nations, governed by their own laws and under their own administrations, Jews had best seek one another out. Above all, one should borrow—even impoverish oneself—to make certain children study the Torah. The Sabbath comes next in order of interest and then an appeal for modesty, sobriety, and tolerance. Life is to be lived as a gift from God. Whatever happens, one must thank God, in public and private worship, on every possible occasion. The difference between humans and beast is *gratitude*. And once more, all these virtues are the habits of the student of the Torah. Study leads not to learning but to nobility. As to the rituals of death, they should be humble—even degrading—so that penance on Earth may produce felicity in Heaven.

You may well doubt that any ordinary person could live up to these high ideals. Indeed, the homely touch at the end of Eleazar's testament reminds us of his humanity: "Put me in the ground at the right hand of my father…he loves me well enough to make room…or near my grandmother…[or] by the side of my daughter." Life under Torah law was meant to produce a saint. Being of flesh and blood, Jews cannot be thought everywhere and always to have replicated the values of the Torah; what is important is that these values set the standard.[4] Until modern times, no others were widely adopted. Studying the Torah, living in the traditional community, following the stable and serene way of life from Sabbath to Sabbath and season to season—these were what it meant to be a Jew. It was a sweet life—sweeter than honey—full of piety, reverence, and beauty. So the pious Jew prayed, and continues to pray, day by day, "How good our lot! How pleasant our portion!"

NOTES

1. Norman Symes, Waikato University, Hamilton, New Zealand, personal communication.

2. E. P. Sanders, *Paul and Palestinian Judaism* (Philadelphia: Fortress, 1975).

3. Israel Abrahams, *Hebrew Ethical Wills* (Philadelphia: Jewish Publication Society of America, 1948), vol. 2, 207–218.

4. For an excellent account of medieval Jewish life, see Cecil Roth, "The European Age," in *Great Ages and Ideas of the Jewish People,* ed. Leo W. Schwarz (New York: Random House, 1956), 267–314.

26

Two Extraordinary Women

In concluding our examination of how Jews from the second to nineteenth centuries explored the way of Torah, we return to the position of women, for two reasons. First, the matter is intrinsically important. We cannot understand a religion unless we make some sense of the role and position that religion accords to half its adherents—women—just as we must attend to the values and ideals shaped for that religion's male adherents. Second, and still more important, one of the principal traits of the advent of the new era in the history of Judaism will be a shift in the status and role of women, on the one side, and in women's aspirations for such a shift to take place, on the other.

We may point to important roles taken by women in Israelite politics, culture, and religion in biblical times. The Hebrew Scriptures speak of women who were important political figures, such as generals, heads of state, and prophets. Women form the center of important biblical narratives from the time of Miriam, the sister of Moses, through Deborah to Ruth, Esther, Bathsheba, and others. So within the complexities of a mosaic of biblical documents, one continuing trait is undoubtedly that women may come to the center of the stage and play a leading role. That this was so in exceptional circumstances—that men generally were the heads of state, prophets, generals, and other important political figures—is beside the point. Women could and did attain prominence.

There was one institution in ancient times in which women were afforded no role whatsoever and from which, in fact, women were essentially excluded. That was the Temple and, with it, the priesthood, which was no mean exclusion. The priestly law codes contained within Leviticus and Numbers take women very seriously and devote much attention to their status within the priesthood. But women's status was solely dependent on the priests, all of whom were males, and it was principally a vehicle for the sanctification of the priesthood. Although some rites (for example, those performed after childbirth) were defined for women, no rites could be performed by women, who were not permitted into the holier part of the Temple buildings and were kept out in a women's courtyard. We cannot now speculate on why the imagination of the priesthood should have excluded all roles for women, whereas, by contrast, the royal house could put forward queens as well as kings, the prophetic movement could put forward a Hulda along with a Jeremiah, and the great writers could pay attention to a Ruth and an Esther as much as to a David and a Solomon. We must recognize that exclusion from Temple and priesthood as a fact.

When, in the first and second centuries, movements took shape out of the priesthood and around the priestly ideals, the consequence of that fact became clear. Just as the priesthood excluded women, so its successor, the rabbinate, found little place for women. After the second century, we hear of a few, if any women in the all-male society of the rabbinic schools (*yeshivot*). And for the next eighteen hundred years not a *single* woman is associated with the writing of a commentary to the Talmud, the conduct of a rabbinic court, or the administration of the Jewish community as a rabbinic authority.

The exclusion of women from the centers of learning and leadership does not, of course, mean that women were abused or disgraced. The contrary is the case. Every effort was made to preserve the rights, property, and dignity of women. But women could not preserve their own rights, property, or dignity. They formed a subordinated caste within the community of rabbinic Judaism.

GLÜCKEL OF HAMELN

Now we must ask, Does the fact of their subordination mean women were alienated by the classical system? In the writings of Glückel of Hameln (1646–1724), we find that was not so. Indeed, if we now compare Glückel's letter to her children with the ethical will of Eleazar of Mainz (written three hundred years earlier!) we find pretty much the same beliefs and ethical values. Glückel's message is the same and expresses precisely the same religious worldview as Eleazar's:

> In my great grief and for my heart's ease I begin this book in the year of Creation 5451—God soon rejoice us and send us His redeemer soon. Amen.
>
> With the help of God, I began writing this, my dear children, upon the death of your good father in the hope of distracting my soul from the burdens laid upon it, and the bitter thought that we have lost our faithful shepherd. In this way I have managed to live through many wakeful nights, and springing from my bed have shortened the sleepless hours.
>
> I do not intend, my dear children, to compose and write for you a book of morals. Such I could not write, and our wise men have already written many. Moreover, we have our holy Torah in which we may find and learn all that we need for our journey through this world to the world to come. Of our beloved Torah we may seize hold....We sinful men are in the world as if swimming in the sea and in danger of being drowned. But our great, merciful and kind God, in His great mercy, has thrown ropes into the sea that we may take hold of them and be saved. These are our holy Torah where is written what are the rewards and punishments for good and evil deeds....
>
> I pray you this, my children: be patient, when the Lord, may He be praised, sends you a punishment, accept it with patience and do not cease to pray to Him; perhaps He will have mercy upon you....Therefore, my dear children, whatever you lose, have patience, for nothing is our own, everything is only a loan....We men have been created for nothing else

but to serve God and to keep His commandments and to obey the Torah, "for that is thy life, and the length of the days."

The kernel of the Torah is: "Thou shalt love thy neighbour as thyself." But in our days we seldom find it so, and few are they who love their fellowmen with all their heart. On the contrary, if a man can contrive to ruin his neighbour nothing pleases him more....

The best thing for you, my children, is to serve God from your heart without falsehood or deception, not giving out to people that you are one thing while, God forbid, in your heart you are another. Say your prayers with awe and devotion. During the time for prayers do not stand about and talk of other things. While prayers are being offered to the Creator of the world, hold it a great sin to engage another man in talk about an entirely different matter—shall God Almighty be kept waiting until you have finished your business?

Moreover, set aside a fixed time for the study of the Torah, as best you know how. Then diligently go about your business, for providing your wife and children with a decent livelihood is likewise a mitzvah—the command of God and the duty of man. We should, I say, put ourselves to great pains for our children, for on this the world is built, yet we must bear in mind that if children did as much for their parents, the children would quickly tire of it.

A bird once set out to cross a windy sea with its three fledglings. The sea was so wide and the wind so strong that the father bird was forced to carry his young, one by one, in his claws. When he was half-way across with the first fledgling the wind turned to a gale, and he said: "My child, look how I am struggling and risking my life in your behalf. When you are grown up, will you do as much for me and provide for my old age?" The fledgling replied: "Only bring me to safety, and when you are old I shall do everything you ask of me." Whereat the father bird dropped his child into the sea, and it drowned, and he said: "So shall it be done to such a liar as you." Then the father bird returned to the shore, set forth with his second fledgling, asked the same question, and receiving the same answer, drowned the second child with the cry "You, too, are a liar!" Finally he set out with the third fledgling, and when he asked the same question, the third and last fledgling replied: "My dear father, it is true you are struggling mightily and risking your life in my behalf, and I shall be wrong not to repay you when you are old, but I cannot bind myself. This though I can promise: when I am grown up and have children of my own, I shall do as much for them as you have done for me." Whereupon the father bird said: "Well spoken, my child, and wisely; your life I will spare and I will carry you to shore in safety."

Above all, my children, be honest in money matters, with both Jews and Gentiles, lest the name of Heaven be profaned. If you have in hand money or goods belonging to other people, give more care to them than if they were your own, so that, please God, you do no one a wrong. The first question put to a man in the next world is, whether he was faithful in his business dealings. Let a man work ever so hard amassing great wealth dishonestly, let him during his lifetime provide his children fat dowries and upon his death a rich heritage—yet woe, I say, and woe again to the wicked man who for the sake of enriching his children has lost his share in the world to come! For the fleeting moment he has sold Eternity.[1]

If we look in vain for evidence that Glückel is discontented with her status as a woman, it is because, within the system, her work is as important as her husband's. She is one who shapes and transmits Judaism, as much as her husband, but she does it in a different context; she has a different job to do. And she carried out her work unselfconsciously and in a thoroughly accepting spirit.

HENRIETTA SZOLD

A dramatic, profound shift took place in the consciousness and culture of the Jewish people of Europe and North America in the nineteenth and twentieth centuries, and an example of that shift is captured in a single document—a letter written by one woman in 1906. One symptom of the great changes of modern times is the fact that women became conscious of their subordinated and secondary role in Judaism and undertook to change that role.

One of the earliest and most effective leaders in this movement was Henrietta Szold, who founded the Women's Zionist Movement (*Hadassah*) and formed it into the single most important organization in American and world Zionism. When her mother died, she insisted on saying the memorial prayer (kaddish) in her mother's memory and refused the offer of a well-meaning male to say it in her behalf:

It is impossible for me to find words in which to tell you how deeply I was touched by your offer to act as "*Kaddish*" for my dear mother. I cannot even thank you—it is something that goes beyond thanks. It is beautiful, what you have offered to do—I shall never forget it.

You will wonder, then, that I cannot accept your offer. Perhaps it would be best form not to try to explain to you in writing, but to wait until I see you to tell you why it is so. I know well, and appreciate what you say about, the Jewish custom; and Jewish custom is very dear and sacred to me. And yet I cannot ask you to say *Kaddish* after my mother. The *Kaddish* means to me that the survivor publicly and markedly manifests his wish and intention to assume the relation to the Jewish community which his parent had, and that so the chain of tradition remains unbroken from generation to generation, each adding its own link. You can do that for the generations of your family, I must do that for the generations of my family.

I believe that the elimination of women from such duties was never intended by our law and custom—women were freed from positive duties when they could not perform them, but not when they could. It was never intended that, if they could perform them, their performance of them should not be considered as valuable and valid as when one of the male sex performed them. And of the *Kaddish* I feel sure this is particularly true.

My mother had eight daughters and no son; and yet never did I hear a word of regret pass the lips of either my mother or my father that one of us was not a son. When my father died, my mother would not permit others to take her daughters' place in saying the *Kaddish,* and so I am sure I am acting in her spirit when I am moved to decline your offer. But beautiful your offer remains nevertheless, and, I repeat, I know full well that it is much more in consonance with the generally accepted Jewish tradition than is my or my family's tradition. You understand me, don't you?[2]

It would not be possible to adduce a more eloquent statement of the shift toward modernity, represented by the change in the consciousness and aspirations of Jewish women, than this simple, deeply traditional statement. In the modern age some women would no longer accept the role, assigned to them in classical Judaism, of silent partner and member of a protected but subordinated caste. What other changes took place? And how shall we account for them?

NOTES

1. Franz Kobler, *A Treasury of Jewish Letters* (Philadelphia: Jewish Publication Society of America, 1954), vol. 2, 565–567.

2. "The Jewish Woman: An Anthology," *Response* (1973) 18:76.

PART III

Classical Judaism
in Modern Times

27

Modern Times

CHRISTIANITY AND JUDAISM TOGETHER
MEET COMPETITION IN SECULARISM

Political change in the world in which both Christianity and Judaism had flourished takes the critical role in shaping theological discourse. When Christianity no longer governed as the sole arbiter of the social order, the political life and therefore also the symbolic transactions of Europe and its overseas diaspora, the Judaism that had taken shape in response to triumphant Christianity and had so long and successfully sustained the life of Israel, the Jewish people, confronted skeptical questioning among people now standing essentially outside its system of truths. New Judaisms took shape, dealing with other agenda of urgent questions and answering those questions in ways self-evidently right for those who believed. Each of these Judaisms claimed to continue in linear succession the Judaism that had flourished for so long, to develop in an incremental succession and so to connect, through the long past, to Sinai. But, in fact, each one responded to contemporary issues deemed urgent among one or another group of Jews.

The birth of the Judaism described in Part II—which bears the adjectives *rabbinic,* because of the title accorded its authorities; *normative,* because of its definitive standing for so long; or *classical,* because of its endurance—symbolically took place in the year 312, the year of Constantine's vision at the Milvian Bridge of a cross and the words "By this sign you will conquer." In Western, Christian civilization, that same Judaism met formidable competition and so ceased to impress nearly all Jews as self-evidently true in the year 1789, with the American Constitution and the French Revolution. These immense turning points for the first time established in the West a politics and a cultural realm distinct from that of Christianity. In a very short time, the changes they brought about produced the same new politics among the Jews. And Judaisms, too, responded.

The rabbinic Judaism that flourished addressed the agenda of Christianity and gave answers that, for holy Israel, proved self-evidently valid. Christianity in the West, like Islam in North Africa and the Near and Middle East, defined the world to which each Judaism responded, the world that made Judaism relevant for holy Israel. Then, when Christianity's agenda competed with secular ones, other Judaisms took shape, and just as Christianity faced competition from secularism, communism, Nazism, nationalism, and hedonism (among others), so those same competing views of the world provoked the formation of Judaisms in response. Placing into context what we call "modern times," which, in the case of Western Judaism begins with the American Constitution and the French Revolution, requires some attention, therefore, to the context in which rabbinic Judaism began its long, successful life but came, in the nineteenth and twentieth centuries, to have to confront alternative Judaisms, including especially the secular, ethnic system of Jewishness described in Chapter 2.

In this section, we deal with only the three Judaisms that carried forward rabbinic Judaism, each in its own claim forming the natural and legitimate next step in the ongoing life of that Judaism. When we examine them, we shall want to see how they make explicit their claim to stand in a linear, unitary, harmonious relationship with the dual Torah of Sinai, to form the necessary development of the Torah. At the same time, we shall observe how each of these three Judaisms negotiated issues of secularity, on the one side, and social and cultural and political change, on the other. None affirmed an essentially secular view, nor did any one of them formulate its systemic statement outside the framework of the dual Torah. In the final unit, we shall compare these Judaisms with the American Judaism of Holocaust and redemption, which has framed for itself a worldview and a way of life utterly disconnected from the dual Torah. Only then will the comparison and contrast among Judaisms place into accurate perspective the history of Judaism set forth in these pages.

THE PRINCIPAL JUDAISMS
OF MODERNITY: REFORM,
ORTHODOX, CONSERVATIVE

The three main Judaisms born in the aftermath of the advent of modern politics now must be specified. All of them continued the Torah as set forth in rabbinic Judaism and adopted the Torah as their generative symbol and myth, its law as their norms, its theology as their touchstone. Between 1800 and 1850, all had taken shape.

First in time is Reform Judaism, coming to expression in the early part of the nineteenth century and making changes in liturgy, then in doctrine and way of life of the received Judaism of the dual Torah. Reform Judaism recognized the legitimacy of making changes and regarded change as reform, yielding Reform.

Second was the reaction to Reform Judaism, called Orthodox Judaism, which in many ways was continuous with the Judaism of the dual Torah but in some ways as selective of elements of that Judaism as was Reform Judaism. Orthodox Judaism reached its first systematic expression in the middle of the nineteenth century. It addressed the same issue, that of change, and held that Judaism lies beyond history; it is the work of God; it constitutes a set of facts of the same order as the facts of nature. Hence, change is not reform, and Reform Judaism is not Judaism—so Orthodoxy.

Third in line and somewhat after Orthodox Judaism was positive Historical Judaism, known in North America as Conservative Judaism, which occupied the center between the two other Judaisms of continuation of the dual Torah. This Judaism maintained that change could become reform, but only in accord with the principles by which legitimate change may be separated from illegitimate change. Conservative Judaism would discover those principles through historical study. In an age in which historical facts were taken to represent theological truths, the historicism of Conservative Judaism bore compelling weight.

All three Judaisms claim to constitute "Judaism, pure and simple." So we wish to compare them to find grounds for their views of themselves. All recognized other Judaisms and explicitly rejected their Torah. So our task also is to contrast the three principal Judaisms of modern times. How? We must ask two things. First, what questions do the three Judaisms address, and why do these questions matter? Second, how did each of the Judaisms link its worldview and way of life and theory of the social entity, "Israel," to those of the received and familiar system of the dual Torah? This latter question is of a different order from the former. Because the questions found urgent in the last two centuries derive not from the challenge of Christianity but from other political challenges altogether, the systems of the age had to mediate between answers to questions people no longer were asking and a program of thought and action people deemed self-evidently right and appropriate. We define the Judaisms and propose to characterize their principal issues: urgent questions, self-evident answers.

All the new Judaisms made ample use of the heritage of the prior (and continuing) rabbinic Judaism. No nascent Judaism of modern times, for example, ever ignored the Hebrew Scriptures. But rare are the Judaisms that concur on which passages in those Scriptures demand attention and articulation. Just as Christianity and Judaism shared common Scriptures but read different portions of those same Scriptures, so was the case in modern Judaisms. To state matters simply, everyone concedes that people know what they wish to prove before they go in search of proof texts. So the fact that they find what they seek presents no surprises, but it also proves nothing about the incremental character of the new Judaisms, let alone the traditional power of the old. What then is the indicator that people make choices, so give birth to new Judaisms?

The masks of innovation—appeals to tradition and precedent and "historical fact"—conceal the creative power of picking and choosing. When people make decisions, therefore choices, their selections of the past invariably compose a new formation. Of still greater consequence, the very act of making choices ratifies change that has already taken root. For the Judaism of the dual Torah accommodated change but made no provision for making choices, claimed to recapitulate in the here and now the eternal holiness of Israel but never accommodated rehearsal of a past perceived as a stage. So the claim to tradition bears its own disproof. Someone who knows there is tradition can never be traditional. Such a person can only pick and choose, even selecting the whole of the matter. Once the given demands to be received, acceding to that demand requires an act of self-consciousness. Choosing to live by "tradition" then constitutes an act of deliberation, therefore imagination and creative power. And the thing received no longer stands as self-evidently true.

POLITICAL CHANGE AND RELIGIOUS TRANSFORMATION

The ecology of Judaism requires attention once again, because the modern period marked a radical change in the environment in which Judaisms would take shape, and much that happened makes best sense when we consider how the several Judaisms addressed the ecological crisis (a political ecology, not a natural one) that overtook "Holy Israel" and turned it into "the Jews." In the nineteenth century, sweeping changes in political and economic circumstances made urgent issues that formerly had drawn slight attention and rendered inconsequential claims that had for so long demanded response. The Jews had formerly constituted a distinct group. Now in the West they formed part of an undifferentiated mass of citizens, all of them equal before the law, all of them subject to the same law. The Judaism of the dual Torah rested on the political premise that the Jews were governed by God's law and formed God's people. The two political premises—the one of the nation-state, the other of the Torah—scarcely permitted reconciliation. The consequent Judaic systems, Reform Judaism, Orthodox Judaism, positive Historical Judaism (in the United States, Conservative Judaism), each of them addressing issues regarded as acute and not merely chronic, in the nineteenth century alleged that they formed the natural next step in the unfolding of "the tradition," meaning the Judaic system of the dual Torah.

From the time of Constantine to the nineteenth century, Jewry in Christendom sustained itself as a recognized, ordinarily tolerated minority. The contradictory doctrines of Christianity—the Jews as Christ killers to be punished, the Jews as witnesses to be kept alive and ultimately converted at the second coming of Christ—held in an uneasy balance. The pluralistic character of some societies (for instance, that in Spain) and the welcome accorded entrepreneurs in opening territories (for instance, Norman England, Poland and Russia, White Russia and Ukraine) in the early centuries of development account still more than doctrine for the long-term survival of Jews in Christian Europe. The Jews, like many others, formed not only a tolerated religious minority but something akin to a guild, specializing in certain occupations (for instance, crafts and commerce in the East). True, the centuries of essentially ordinary existence in the West ended with the Crusades, which forced Jewry to migrate to the eastern frontier of Europe. But, until the twentieth century, the Jews formed one of the peoples permanently settled in Europe, first in the West, later in the East. But only in modern times did the Jews as a whole find, or even aspire to, a position equivalent to that of the majority population in European societies.

Before that time the Jews were subjected to legal restrictions as to where they might live and how they might earn a living. They enjoyed political and social rights of a most limited character. In the East, where most Jews lived, they governed their own communities through their own administration and law. They spoke their own language, Yiddish; wore distinctive clothing; ate only their own food; controlled their own sector of the larger economy and ventured outside it only seldom; and, in all, formed a distinct and distinctive group. Commonly, the villages in which they lived found Jews and Christians living side by side, but in many of those villages Jews formed the majority of the population. These facts made for long-term stability and autonomy. In the West, the Jews formed only a tiny proportion of the population but, until modern times, lived equally segregated from the rest of the country, behind the barriers of language, custom, and economic calling. So the Jews for a long time formed a caste, a distinct and clearly defined group—but within the hierarchy ordered by the castes of the society at hand.

"EMANCIPATION"

A process called "emancipation," part of a larger movement of emancipation of serfs, women, slaves, Catholics (in Protestant countries, for instance, England and Ireland), also encompassed the Jews. Benzion Dinur defines this process of emancipation as follows:

> Jewish emancipation denotes the abolition of disabilities and inequities applied specially to Jews, the recognition of Jews as equal to other citizens, and the formal granting of the rights and duties of citizenship. Essentially the legal act of emancipation should have been simply the expression of the diminution of social hostility and psychological aversion toward Jews in the host nation…but the antipathy was not obliterated and constantly hampered the realization of equality even after it had been proclaimed by the state and included in the law.[1]

The political changes that fall into the process of the Jews' emancipation began in the eighteenth century and, in a half-century, affected the long-term stability that had characterized the Jews' social and political life from Constantine onward. These political changes raised questions not previously found urgent and, it follows, also precipitated reflection on problems formerly neglected. The answers to the questions flowed logically and necessarily from the character of the questions themselves.

Dinur traces three periods in the history of the Jews' emancipation, from 1740 to 1789, ending with the French Revolution; then from 1789 to 1878, from the French Revolution to the Congress of Berlin; and from 1878 to 1933, from the Congress of Berlin to the rise of the Nazis to power in Germany. The adoption of the American Constitution in 1787 confirmed the U.S. position on the matter. Jewish males enjoyed the rights of citizens, along with all other whites. The first period marks the point at which the emancipation of the Jews first came under discussion. The second denotes the period in which Western and Central European states accorded to the Jews the rights of citizens. The third brought to the fore a period of new racism that in the end simply wiped out Jewish communities in vast parts of Europe where Jews had lived for more than a thousand years and came very close to annihilating all the Jews of Europe.[2]

In the first period, advocates of the Jews' emancipation maintained that religious intolerance accounted for the low-caste status assigned to the Jews. Liberating the Jews would mark another stage in overcoming religious intolerance. During this first period, the original ideas of Reform Judaism came to expression, although the important changes in religious doctrine and practice were realized only in the earlier part of the nineteenth century. In the second period, the French Revolution brought Jews political rights in France, Belgium, the Netherlands, Italy, Germany, and Austria-Hungary. As Germany and Italy attained unification and Hungary independence, the Jews were accorded the rights and duties of citizenship. Dinur explains: "It was stressed that keeping the Jews in a politically limited and socially inferior status was incompatible with the principle of civic equality . . . 'it is the objective of every political organization to protect the natural rights of man,' hence, 'all citizens have the right to all the liberties and advantages of citizens, without exception.'"[3]

Jews at that time entered the political and cultural life of the Western nations, including their overseas empires (hence Algerian Jews received French citizenship). During this second period, Reform Judaism reached its first stage of development, beginning in Germany. It made it possible for Jews to hold together the two things they deemed inseparable: their desire to remain Jewish and their wish also to be one with their "fellow citizens." By the middle of the nineteenth century, Reform had reached full expression and had won the support of a sizable part of German Jewry. In reaction against Reform ("the excesses of..."), Orthodoxy came into existence. As we shall see, Orthodoxy no less than Reform asked how "Judaism" could coexist with "German-ness," meaning citizenship in an undifferentiated republic of citizens. Theologians worked out a centrist position, mediating between Reform and Orthodoxy, in what was then called the Historical School and what, in twentieth-century America, took the name of Conservative Judaism.

The period from the French Revolution to the Congress of Berlin therefore saw the full efflorescence of all of the Judaisms of political modernization. All of these Judaisms characterized the Jews of Western Europe and, later, North America. But in North America, Reform, Orthodoxy, and the Historical School or Conservative Judaism radically changed in character, responding to the urgent issues of a different circumstance, producing self-evidently

valid answers of a character not compatible with the nineteenth-century statements of those same systems.

In the third period, anti-Semitism as a political and social movement attained power. Jews began to realize that, in Dinur's words, "the state's legal
recognition of Jewish civic and political equality does not automatically bring
social recognition of this equality."[4] The Jews continued to form a separate
group; they were racially "inferior." The impact of the new racism would be
felt in the twentieth century. As we shall see in the next part, the Judaisms of
the twentieth century raised the questions of political repression and economic
dislocation, as these faced the Jews of Eastern Europe and North America.

Clearly, in the nineteenth century, particularly in Western countries, a
new order revised the political settlement covering the Jews, in place for nearly
the entire history of the West. From the time of Constantine forward, the
Jews' essentially autonomous life as a protected minority had raised political
questions that found answers of an essentially supernatural and theological
character. But now the emancipation redefined those questions, asking about
Jews not as a distinct group but as part of some other polity altogether than
the Jewish one. Those Jews who simply passed over retain no interest for us;
Karl Marx, converted to Christianity at an early age, produced no ideas important in the study of Judaism(s). But vast numbers of Jews in the West determined to remain Jewish and also to become something else. Their urgent
question addressed the issue of defining Israel, now in a new formulation of
the ecological crisis of the age: how to be both Jewish and something else—a
citizen of Germany or France or Britain. This issue would not confront the
Jews of the Russian Empire until World War I, and, together with the Jews of
the Austro-Hungarian Empire, Rumania, and other Eastern European areas,
these formed the vast majority of the whole.

SYMBOL CHANGE AND SOCIAL CHANGE:
THE ADVENT OF HISTORICISM

Even now, we recognize the force of historical fact in the thinking of the
framers of the modern Judaisms. History turned into doctrine: if we can show
it really happened, then the event bears self-evident moral meaning. If we can
show it did not happen, then the event is dismissed as null. For Christianity,
the "quest for the historical Jesus" (meaning the specification of the things
Jesus "really" said out of the many things attributed to him by the Gospels)
formed a counterpart. "Historicism" in theology appeals to historical fact in
determining theological truth and serves as a medium for validating change,
which, after all, is the one thing historical study is well equipped to uncover.

The change to which historicism formed the response was, as we realize,
political in character. But the same change bore deep implications for the conduct of the cultural life of Jewry. The Jews of the West, preoccupied with
change in their political position, formed only a small minority of the Jews of

the world—the Western frontier (extending to California in the farthest west of all) of the Jewish people. But their confrontation with political change proved paradigmatic. They were the ones to invent the Judaisms of the nineteenth century.

Each of these Judaic systems exhibited three characteristic traits. First, it asked how one could be both Jewish and something else, that is, also a citizen, a member of a nation. Second, it defined "Judaism" (that is, its system) as a religion, so leaving ample space for that something else, namely, nationality, whether German ("*Deutschtum und Judentum,*" German-ness and Jewish-ness), or British, or French, or American. Third, it appealed to history to prove the continuity between its system and the received Judaism of the dual Torah. The resort to historical fact, the claim that the system at hand formed the linear development of the past, the natural increment of the entire "history" of Israel, the Jewish people, from the beginning to the new day—that essentially factual claim masked a profound conviction concerning self-evidence. The urgent question at hand—the political one—produced a self-evidently correct answer out of the history of politics constituted by historical narrative.

That appeal to history, particularly historical fact, characterizes all three Judaisms. The Reformers stated explicitly that theirs would be a Judaism built on fact. The facts of history, in particular, would guide Jews to the definition of what was essential and what could be dropped. History then formed the court of appeal but also the necessary link, the critical point of continuity. Conservative Judaism, which in Europe called itself the Historical School, took the same position but reached different conclusions. History would show how change could be effected, and the principles of historical change would then govern. Orthodoxy met the issue in a different way, maintaining that "Judaism" was above history, not a historical fact at all. But the Orthodox position would also appeal most forcefully to the past in its claim that Orthodoxy constituted the natural and complete continuation of "Judaism" in its true form.

The importance of history in the theological thought of the nineteenth-century Judaisms derives from the intellectual heritage of the age, with its stress on the nation-state as the definitive unit of society and on history as the mode of defining the culture and character of the nation-state. Furthermore, history as an instrument of reform had served the Protestant Reformation, with its appeal to Scripture as against (mere) tradition, its claim that it would restore Christianity to its (historical) purity. Finally and most important, the supernaturalism of the inherited Judaism of the dual Torah—with its emphasis on God's active intervention in history, on miracles, on a perpetual concern for the natural implications of the supernatural will and covenant—contradicted the rationalism of the age. The one thing the Jewish thinkers wished to accomplish was to show the rationalism, the reason, the normality of the Judaisms they constructed. Appealing to (mere) facts of history, versus the unbelievable claims of a Scripture, placed on a positive and this-worldly foundation that religious view of the world that, in the received system of the dual Torah, rested on a completely supernatural view of reality.

COMPARING JUDAISMS

Earlier we recognized the need to compare and contrast the Judaisms. We now ask questions of four kinds: (1) the context of that Judaism: where, when, how come it came into being; (2) a description of the worldview at hand, with special reference to the urgent question to which a given Judaic system responds; (3) an account of the way of life; and (4) the basis for the allegation that the system at hand enjoys the status of self-evidence: why do the faithful of a system deem the system self-evidently true?

The three Judaisms of the age, which we see as continuous in important ways, took as their task the demonstration of how they formed out of the received and unwanted old Judaism something new, different, and acceptable. The nineteenth-century Judaisms were born in the matrix of the received system of the dual Torah, among people who themselves grew up in a world in which *that* Judaism defined what people meant by Judaism. Thus, the questions of analysis address the fact that the framers of the Judaisms of continuation could not evade the issue of continuity. They wished both to continue and also to innovate—and to justify innovation. And that desire affected Orthodoxy as much as Reform. In making changes, they appealed to the past for justification. But they pointed to those changes also as proof that they had overcome an unwanted past. The delicate balance between tradition and change attained by each of the Judaisms of continuation marks the genius of its inventors. All worked out the same equation: Change, but not too much, whatever the proportion a group found excessive.

When we analyze the Judaisms of continuity, each one alleging itself to form the necessary next step of history, we therefore want to know in what ways that allegation corresponds to fact. Do the Judaic systems that came into being in the nineteenth century claim to renew the received Judaism of the dual Torah, or do they allege that they invent a Judaism? And if they allege that they stand as the natural next step in "the tradition," does that claim stand? The Judaic systems answered through (to devotees) self-evidently right doctrine questions that none can escape or ignore. And the questions before all three important Judaisms of the nineteenth century were the same, the answers of the three systems remarkably congruent to one another.

The view, from a later perspective, that the Judaisms of the nineteenth century look remarkably alike would have surprised their founders and framers, for they fought bitterly among themselves. But, as noted, the three Judaisms of continuity exhibit striking traits in common. All looked backward, at the received system of the dual Torah. All sought justification in precedent out of a holy and paradigmatic past. All viewed the documents of that system as canonical, differing, of course, on the relative merit of the several components. They concurred that texts to prove propositions deemed true should derive from those canonical writings (or from some of them). All took for granted the enduring, God-given authority of those writings. None doubted that God had revealed the (written) Torah at Sinai. All looked for validating precedent in the received canon. Differing on issues important to both worldview and way of life, all three Judaisms agreed on the importance of literacy in the received writings, the lasting relevance of the symbolic system at hand, the pertinence of the way of life (in some, if not every, detail), and the power of the received Judaism of the dual Torah to stand in judgment on whatever, later, would serve to continue that Judaism.

True, the differences among the three Judaisms impressed their framers, and with good reason. The Reformers rejected important components of the Judaism of the dual Torah and said so. Written Torah, yes; oral Torah, no. The Orthodox explicitly denied the validity of changing anything, insisting on the facticity, the givenness, of the whole. The Conservatives, in appealing to historical precedent, shifted the premise of justification entirely. Written Torah, yes, oral Torah, maybe. They sought what the Orthodox thought pointless and the Reform inconsequential—namely, justification for making some few changes in the present in continuation of the processes that had effected development in the past. None of these points of important difference proved trivial. But all of them, all together, should not obscure the powerful points of similarity that mark all three Judaisms as continuators of the Judaism of the dual Torah.

Continuators, but not lineal developments, not the natural next step, not the ineluctable increment of history—all claimed to be, each with good reason, and, of course, all wrong. The points at which each Judaism took its leave from the received system do not match. In the case of Reform, the break proved explicit: change carried out by articulate, conscious decision, thus change as a matter of policy, enjoys full legitimacy.

Although the differences in the grounds of separation from the received system prove formidable, still more striking and fresh are the several arguments adduced once more to establish a firm connection to the Judaism of the dual Torah, or, more accurately, to "the tradition" or to "Judaism." For the Judaisms of continuation characteristically differ in the several ways in which each, on its own, proposed to establish its continuity with a past perceived as discontinuous. All three Judaisms enjoyed ample justification for the insistence, each in its way, that it carried forward the entire history of Judaism and took the necessary and ineluctable step beyond where matters had rested before its own formation. Reform in this regard found itself subjected to vigorous criticism, but in saying that "things have changed in the past, and we can change them too," Reform established its primary position. It, too, pointed to precedent and took as implicitly conceded the power of the received system to stand in judgment. All the more so did the Orthodox and Conservative theologians affirm that same power and place themselves under the judgment of the Judaism of the dual Torah. All three established a firm position within the continuation of that Judaism. And all three flourish today wherever Judaism is practiced.

NOTES

1. Benzion Dinur, "Emancipation," *Ency-clopaedia Judaica* (Jerusalem: Keter, 1971) 6696, col. 696.

2. This matter can be followed up in a simple way. The *Encyclopaedia Judaica,* published in 1971, scarcely twenty-five years after the gas chambers at Auschwitz were blown up by the retreating Germans to hide what they had done, has a write-up on nearly every location in Europe where Jews ever lived. For all the towns and cities in the territories occupied by the Germans, the entries follow the same pattern: Jews first came in such and such a time, they lived in such and such a way, and then what happened in the Holocaust is described to the day and to the hour: the German army came and, upon arrival, did thus and so; then the Jews were forced into a tiny area ("ghetto") and kept there to starve and die of disease; then, on such and such a day, there was a round-up and the Jews were forced to dig a mass grave and were then machine-gunned; or the Jews were rounded up and shipped off to..., with the death factory to which the Jews of that place were shipped then named. That encyclopedia forms the detailed monument to nearly every event in the Holocaust; in scholarship, it represents an amazing achievement in so short a time.

3. Ibid.

4. Dinur, "Emancipation."

28

Reform Judaism

THE BIRTH OF THE FIRST
JUDAISM OF MODERN TIMES

The reform of Judaism began with some modest changes in the liturgy but ended up as Reform Judaism, the single most important, influential, and effective Judaism of the nineteenth century in Central Europe and of the later twentieth century in North America. More important, Reform Judaism achieved enormous influence over all other Judaisms, because it was the first Judaic religious system to address the critical issue of modern times: should the Jews integrate into their native countries or remain a completely segregated social entity? That meant, can the Jews, a secular, ethnic group, find a neutral definition of themselves, or will holy Israel, a religious community, define all possibilities of community life for the group?

Nearly all Judaisms in the United States and Canada, including most of Orthodoxy, have accepted the integrationist premises of Reform Judaism—that Jews should live pretty much like everybody else, fully participating in the politics and culture of their native countries, and should differ from other Americans or Canadians or Europeans only or mainly in matters of religion. Only the tiny sector comprised by segregationist Orthodoxy, a small number in North America, a considerable number in the State of Israel, and little pockets in Western Europe (in Belgium, Britain, and Switzerland) reaffirm the received social policy of rabbinic Judaism, which treats the Jews as separate—holy, sanctified to God—and aims at complete cultural, linguistic, social, residential, and economic segregation.

So the reason for its remarkable success in North America (as in nineteenth- and twentieth-century Germany) is that Reform Judaism forthrightly and articulately faced the political changes that redefined the conditions of Jews' lives and presented a Judaism, closely tied to the inherited system of the dual Torah, fully responsive to those changes. The Jews in some nations were offered the status of undifferentiated citizens of nations (in theory, at least) by political change in the late eighteenth and nineteenth centuries. Wherever the political revolution represented by the American Constitution and the French Revolution reached, so redefining the political circumstances in which Jews made their lives, there Reform Judaism found a favorable hearing. Where, as in most of Central and Eastern Europe and the Muslim world, the Jews lived in segregated communities, speaking a Jewish language (Yiddish or Judeo-Arabic), practicing a Jewish profession or calling (for example, diamond cutting or tailoring), dressing in a Jewish manner, eating only Jewish food, there Reform answered questions no one was asking.

Constructive and intellectually vital in its day, Reform Judaism said what it would do and did it. Still more interesting, because it was a movement that confronted the issues of the day and the Jews' condition, Reform Judaism found itself able to change itself, its own deepest concerns and values. So Reform Judaism not only responded to the questions many asked but turned about and set the issues for debate from then to our own day. That explains why no Judaism in the past two hundred years exercised deeper influence in defining the issues Jews would debate; none made a richer or more lasting contribution to the program of answers Jews would find self-evident.

SYSTEM CONSTRUCTION, STARTING WITH WHO AND WHAT IS "ISRAEL"

Every Judaism begins by defining its "Israel," that is, by explaining the existence of the social group of Jews that that Judaism frames. For Reform Judaism in the nineteenth century, the full and authoritative statement of the system—its worldview, with profound implications on its way of life and its theory of who is Israel—came to expression not in Europe but in the United States, in an assembly in Pittsburgh in 1885 of Reform rabbis. At that meeting of the Central Conference of American Rabbis, the Reform Judaism of the age, by now about a century in aborning, took up the issues that divided the Judaism and made an authoritative statement on them, one that most people could accept. Because we understand that a Judaic religious system will commence its work by defining the "Israel" to which it speaks, we may not find surprising a heavy emphasis on who is Israel. That doctrine exposes the foundations of the way of life and worldview that these rabbis had formed for the Israel they conceived:

> We recognize in the Mosaic legislation a system of training the Jewish people for its mission during its national life in Palestine, and today we accept as binding only its moral laws and maintain only such ceremonies as elevate and sanctify our lives, but reject all such as are not adapted to the views and habits of modern civilization....We hold that all such Mosaic and rabbinical laws as regular diet, priestly purity, and dress originated in ages and under the influence of ideas entirely foreign to our present mental and spiritual state....Their observance in our days is apt rather to obstruct than to further modern spiritual elevation....We recognize in the modern era of universal culture of heart and intellect the approaching of the realization of Israel's great messianic hope for the establishment of the kingdom of truth, justice, and peace among all men. We consider ourselves no longer a nation but a religious community and therefore expect neither a return to Palestine nor a sacrificial worship under the sons of Aaron nor the restoration of any of the laws concerning the Jewish state....

The Pittsburgh Platform takes up each component of the system in turn. Who is Israel? What is its way of life? How does it account for its existence as a distinct and distinctive group? Israel once was a nation ("during its national life"), but today is not a nation. It once had a set of laws that regulate diet, clothing, and the like. These no longer apply, because Israel now is not what it was then. Israel forms an integral part of Western civilization. The reason to persist as a distinctive group was that the group has its work to do, namely, to realize the messianic hope for the establishment of a kingdom of truth, justice, and peace. For that purpose, Israel no longer constitutes a nation. It now forms a religious community.

What that means is that individual Jews do live as citizens in other nations. Difference is acceptable at the level of religion, not nationality, a position that accords fully with the definition of citizenship of the Western democracies. The worldview then lays heavy emphasis on an as-yet unrealized but coming perfect age. The way of life admits to no important traits that distinguish Jews from others, because morality, in the nature of things, forms a universal category, applicable in the same way to everyone. The theory of Israel then forms the heart of matters, and what we learn is that Israel constitutes a "we," that is, that the Jews continue to form a group that, by its own indicators, holds together and constitutes a cogent social entity.

All this in a simple statement of a handful of rabbis forms a full and encompassing Judaism, one that, to its communicants, presented truth of a self-evident order. But it was also a truth declared, not discovered, and the self-evidence of the truth of the statements competed with the self-awareness characteristic of those who made them. For they could recognize the problem that demanded attention: the reframing of a theory of Israel for that Israel that they themselves constituted, that "we" that required explanation. No more urgent question faced the rabbis, because, after all, they lived in a century of opening horizons, in which people could envision perfection. World War I would change all that, also for Israel. By 1937 the Reform rabbis, meeting in Columbus, Ohio, would reframe the system, expressing a worldview quite different from that of the half-century before.

Let us briefly summarize this picture of the program of urgent issues and self-evident responses that constituted the first of the new Judaisms of the nineteenth century. Questions we find answered fall into two categories: first, why "we" do not keep certain customs and ceremonies but do keep others; second, how "we relate to the nations in which we live." So the system of Reform Judaism explained both why and why not—that is, why this, not that—the mark of a fully framed and cogent Judaism. The affirmative side covered why the Jews would persist as a separate group; the negative would account for the limits of difference.

These two questions deal with the same urgent problem, namely, working out a mode of Judaic existence compatible with citizenship in (for these rabbis) North America. Jews do not propose to eat or dress in distinctive ways. They do seek a place within "modern spiritual elevation . . . universal culture of heart and intellect." They impute to that culture the realization of "the messianic hope," a considerable stake. And, explicit to the whole, the Jews no longer constitute a nation. They therefore belong to some other nation(s). Political change has changed the entirety of "Judaism," but the Judaism at hand has the power to accommodate to that change.

WHAT IS REFORM JUDAISM?

The original and enduring Judaic system of Reform correctly appeals to Moses Mendelssohn for its intellectual foundations, and Mendelssohn presented, in the words of Michael A. Meyer, an appeal "for a pluralistic society that offered full freedom of conscience to all those who accepted the postulates of natural religion: God, Providence, and a future life."[1] Issues dominant from Mendelssohn's time forward concerned what was called "emancipation" (discussed in the preceding chapter), meaning the provision, for Jews, of the rights of citizens. Reform theologians took the lead in the struggle for such rights. To them it was self-evident that Jews not only should have civil rights and civic equality. It also was obvious that they should want them. A Judaism that did not explain why the Jews should want and have full equality as part of a common humanity ignored the issues that preoccupied those who found, in Reform Judaism, a corpus of self-evident truths. To those truths, the method—the appeal to historical facts—formed a contingent and secondary consideration.

Reform Judaism dates its beginnings to the nineteenth century with changes, called reforms and regarded as the antecedents of Reform, in trivial aspects of public worship in the synagogue.[2] The motive for these changes derived from the simple fact that many Jews rejected the received system. People were defecting from the synagogue. Giving up the faith was taken for granted as meaning surrendering all ties to the group, so the beginning of change made reform and ultimately Reform address two issues at one time: (1) making the synagogue more attractive so that (2) defectors would return and others would not leave. Here is an important example in which the interplay of the ethnic and the religious accounts for the development of a Judaism. The enemies of reform called Reform Judaism a path to apostasy. But the founders of Reform Judaism claimed, with considerable justification, that only through reform would Jews stay Jewish. To this the critics replied (in other terms, to be sure) perhaps Jewish, but not Judaic!

LEGITIMATING CHANGE
BY CALLING IT "REFORM"

The issue involved not politics but merely justification for changing anything at all. But that issue asked the wrong question in the wrong way. The Reformers maintained that change was alright because historical precedent proved that change was alright. But change long had defined the constant in the ongoing life of the Judaism of the dual Torah. Generative causes and modes of effecting change marked the vitality of the system. The Judaism of the dual Torah endured, never intact but always unimpaired, because of its power to absorb and make its own the diverse happenings of culture and society. So long as the structure of politics remained the same, with Israel an autonomous entity, subordinated but recognized as a cogent and legitimate social group in charge of some of its own affairs, the system answered the paramount question. The trivial ones could work their way through and become part of the consensus, to be perceived in the end as "tradition," too. A catalogue of changes that had taken place over fifteen hundred years, from the birth of Judaism to its death, therefore will list many more dramatic and decisive sorts of change than those matters of minor revision of liturgy (for example, sermons in the vernacular) that attracted attention at the dawn of the age of change become Reform.

We must wonder, therefore, what made the difference, then, so that change could be perceived as reform and transformed into the Reform of Judaism, hence, Reform Judaism. When people could take a stance external to the received mode and effect change as a matter of decision and policy rather than as a matter of what is restorative and purported to be timelessly appropriate, we know that, for those people, Judaism in its received form had already died. For the received system no longer defined matters but now became subject to definition. And that marks the move from self-evidence to self-consciousness.

What had brought about the demise of the received system as definitive and normative beyond all argument is something we do not know. Nothing in the earliest record of reform of liturgy tells us. The constructive efforts of the first generation, only later recognized not as people who made changes or even as reformers but as founders of Reform Judaism, focused on synagogue worship. The services were too long; the speeches were in a language foreign to participants; the singing was not aesthetic; the prayers were in a language no one understood. But that means some people recited the prayers as a matter of duty, not supplication; did not speak the language of the faith; formed other than received opinions on how to sing in synagogue; saw as alien what earlier had marked the home and hearth. Those people no longer lived in that same social world that had for so long found right and proper precisely the customs now seen as alien.

When the heritage forms an unclaimed, unwanted legacy, people nonetheless accept it out of duty. So the changes called reform that produced Reform Judaism introduced a shortened service, a sermon in the language people spoke, a choir and an organ, prayers in the vernacular. Clearly, a great deal of change had taken place before the recognition that something had changed. People no longer knew Hebrew; they no longer found pleasing received modes of saying the prayers. We look in vain to the consequent reforms for answers to the question of why people made these changes, and the reasons adduced by historians settle no interesting questions.

The more interesting question concerns why the persistence of engagement and concern. For people always had the option, which many exercised, of abandoning the received Judaism of the two Torahs and all other Judaisms, too. Among those for whom these cosmetic changes made a difference, much in the liturgy, and far more beyond, retained powerful appeal. The premise of change dictated that Jews would say the old prayers in essentially the old formulation. And that premise carried much else: the entire burden of the faith, the total commitment to the group, in some form, defined by some indicators, if not the familiar ones, then some others. So we know that Reform Judaism, in its earliest manifestation in Germany in the early nineteenth century, constituted an essentially conservative, profoundly constructive effort to save for Jews the received Judaism by reforming it in some (to begin with) rather trivial ways.

REFORM'S HISTORICIST THEOLOGY: REFORM AS THE NATURAL NEXT STEP IN THE HISTORY OF JUDAISM

What formed the justification for these changes was the theory of the incremental history of a single, linear Judaism, which played a powerful role in the creative age of Reform Judaism. The ones who made changes (it is too soon to call them Reformers or the changes, reforms) rested their case on an appeal to the authoritative texts. Change is legitimate, and these changes in particular wholly consonant with the law, or the tradition, or the inner dynamics of the faith, or the dictates of history, or whatever out of the past worked that day. The laypeople who made the changes tried to demonstrate that the changes fit the law of Judaism. They took the trouble because Reform even at the outset claimed to restore, to continue, to persist in the received pattern.

The justification of change always invoked precedent. People who made changes had to show that the principle that guided what they did was not new, even though the specific things they did were. So to lay down a bridge between themselves and their past they laid out beams resting on deep-set piles. The foundation of change was formed of the bedrock of precedent. And more still: change restores, reverts to an unchanging ideal. So the Reformer claims not to change at all but only to regain the correct state of affairs, one that others, in the interval, themselves have changed. That forms the fundamental attitude of mind of the people who make changes and call the changes Reform. The appeal to history, a common mode of justification in nineteenth-century politics and theology, therefore defined the principal justification for the new Judaism: it was new because it renewed the old and enduring, the golden Judaism of a mythic age of perfection. Arguments on precedent drew the Reformers to the work of critical scholarship, as they settled all questions by appeal to the facts of history.

We cannot find surprising, therefore, the theory that Reform Judaism stood in a direct line with the prior history of Judaism. Judaism is one. Judaism has a history, that history is single and unitary, and it was always leading to its present outcome: Reform Judaism. Others would later challenge these convictions. Orthodox Judaism would deny that Judaism has a history at all. Conservative, or positive Historical, Judaism would discover a different goal for history from that embodied by Reform Judaism. But the mode of argument, appealing to issues of an historical and factual character, and the premises of argument, insisting that history proved or disproved matters of theological conviction, characterized all the Judaisms of the nineteenth century. This point presents no surprises, considering that the Judaisms of the age took shape in the intellectual world of Germany, with its profoundly philosophical and historical mode of thought and argument.

So the challenge of political change carried with it its own modes of intellectual response: in the academic, scholarly framework. The challenges of the twentieth century exhibited a different character altogether. They were not intellectual but wholly political, and they concerned not matters of political status but issues of life or death. The Judaic systems of the age then would respond in their own way: through forming instrumentalities of collective action, political power, not theory.

Reform began in Germany, and the earliest theologians had before them the precedent of Martin Luther, the leader of the Protestant Reformation. The very premise—integration is not only possible but also right—explains the pertinence of the Christian model. Whether Luther demanding reversion to the pure and primitive faith of the Gospels or the earliest generation of Reform leaders appealing to the Talmud as justification for rejecting what others thought the contemporary embodiment of the Talmud's requirements, the principle remains the same. Reform renews, recovers the true condition of the faith, selects, out of a diverse past, that age and that moment at which the faith attained its perfect definition and embodiment. Not change but restoration and renewal of the true modes, the recovery of the way things were in that perfect, paradigmatic time, that age that formed the model for all time—these deeply mythic modes of appeal formed the justification for change, transforming mere modification of this and that into Reform. But, confronted with dubious allegations as to matters of faith and fact, the leaders of change took on the mantle of Reform, for they revised not only a few lines of a prayer but the entire worldview expressed in the accepted liturgy.

To Judaists, and nearly all Jews at the beginning of modern times who practiced Judaism, the condition of Israel in exile formed a self-evident fact of politics and culture alike. Speaking their own language, pursuing occupations distinctive to their group, living essentially apart from other peoples of the same time and place (who themselves formed not a uniform nation but a mosaic of equivalent social entities, that is, religion-nations, each with its language and its economy and its distinct society), Jews knew who they were. They were a nation in exile. When, therefore, the early changes encompassed rewording the liturgy so as to shade off the motifs of the return to Zion and restoration of the cult, they signaled that much else already had undergone revision and still more would have to change as well. Reform ratified change now a generation old, proposed to cope with it, to reframe and revise the received "tradition" as to mark out new limbs for self-evident truth.

The original changes, in the first decades of the nineteenth century, pro-duced a new generation of rabbis. Some forty years into the century, these rabbis gave to the process of change the name of Reform and created those institutions of Reform Judaism that would endow the inchoate movement with a politics of its own. In the mid-1840s, a number of rabbinic conferences brought together the new generation of rabbis. Trained in universities, rabbis who came to these gatherings turned backward, justifying the changes in prayer rites long in place, effecting some further, mostly cosmetic changes in the observance of the Sabbath and the laws covering personal status through marriage and divorce. In 1845, a decision to adopt for some purposes German in place of Hebrew led to the departure of conservative Reformers, who founded what they called the Historical School in Germany and Conservative Judaism in the United States. But the Reformers appealed for their apologia to the received writings, persisting in their insistence that they formed a natural continuation of the processes of the "tradition." Indeed, that point of insistence—that Judaism—formed the centerpiece of the nascent Judaism at hand.

REFORM MOVEMENTS IN JUDAISM: THE APPEAL TO HISTORICAL PRECEDENT

Let us consider a concrete example of historicist theology as Reform Judaism practiced it. In his preface to Abraham Cronbach's *Reform Movements in Judaism*,[3] Jacob Rader Marcus, a principal voice in Reform Judaism in the twentieth century, provides a powerful statement of the Reform view of its place in history. Marcus recognizes that diverse Judaisms have flourished in the history of the Jews. What characterizes them all is that each began as a reform movement but then underwent a process we might characterize as "traditionaliza-tion." Change becomes not merely reform but tradition, and the only constant in the histories of Judaisms is that process of transformation of the new to the conventional or, in theological language, the traditional. Acording to Marcus:

> All [Judaisms] began as rebellions, as great reformations, but after receiv-ing widespread acceptance, developed vested 'priestly' interests, failed their people, and were forced to retreat before the onslaught of new rebel-lions, new philosophies, new challenges.

So the fundamental theological method of Reform Judaism in its initial phase, the appeal to facts of history for the validation of theological propositions, en-dures. But the claim that everything always changes yields a challenge, which Marcus forthrightly raises:

> Is there then nothing but change? Is change the end of all our history and all our striving? No, there is something else, the desire to be free....In the end [the Jew] has always understood that changelessness is spiritual death. The Jew who would *live* must never completely surrender himself to one

truth, but…must reach out for the farther and faint horizons of an ever Greater God….This is the meaning of Reform.

Marcus thus treats as self-evident—obvious because it is a fact of history—the persistence of change. And, denying that that is all there is to Reform, at the end he affirms the simple point that change sets the norm. It comes down to the same thing. The something else of Marcus's argument presents its own problems. Appeal to the facts of history fails at that point at which a constructive position demands articulation. "The desire to be free" bears a predicate: free of what? Free to do, to be what? If Marcus fails to accomplish the whole of the theological task, however, he surely conveys the profoundly constructive vision that Reform Judaism afforded to its Israel.

WHAT DO WE LEARN ABOUT JUDAISM FROM REFORM JUDAISM?

From the perspective of the political changes taking place from the American and French Revolutions onward, in responding to the challenge of not citizenship but triumphant Christianity, the received system of the Judaism of the dual Torah simply answered the wrong questions. For the issue no longer found definition in the claims of regnant Christianity. A new question, emerging from forces not contained within Christianity, demanded attention from Jews affected by those forces. For those Jews, the fact of change derived its self-evidence from shifts in political circumstances. When the historians began to look for evidence of precedents for changing things, it was because their own circumstance had already persuaded them that change matters—change itself effects change (so to speak). What they sought, then, was a picture of a world in which they might find a place, and, it went without saying, that picture would include a portrait of a Judaic system—a way of life, a worldview, a definition of the Israel to live the one and believe the other.

The issue confronting the new Judaism derived not from Christianity, therefore, but from political change brought about by forces of secular nationalism, which conceived of society as the expression not of God's will for the social order under the rule of Christ and his Church or anointed king (emperor, czar) but of popular will for the social order under the government of the people and their elected representatives—a considerable shift. When society does not form the aggregate of distinct groups, each with its place and definition, language and religion, but rather undifferentiated citizens (male, white, wealthy, to be sure), then the Judaism that Jews in such a society will have to work out also will account for difference of a different order altogether. That Judaism will have to frame a theory of who is Israel consonant with the social situation of Jews who will to be different, but not so different that they cannot also be citizens. Reform set forth one answer; the Orthodoxy that affirmed Jews' integration into the nation-state gave a different answer.

NOTES

1. Michael A. Meyer, *The Origins of the Modern Jew: Jewish Identity and European Culture in Germany, 1749–1824* (Detroit: Wayne State University Press, 1967), 48.

2. Jakob J. Petuchowski, "Reform Judaism," in *Encyclopaedia Judaica* (Jerusalem: Keter, 1971), vol. 14, 23–28.

3. Pp. 7–9 (New York: Bookman, 1963).

29

Orthodox Judaism

ORTHODOXY AND "THE TRADITION"

All Orthodox Judaisms break down into two camps: the segregationist, rejecting accommodation with the politics and culture of the secular world, and integrationist, maintaining that total adherence to the Torah also allowed for participation in everyday politics, culture, and economic life. Many people reasonably identify all "traditional" or "observant" Judaism with Orthodoxy, and they furthermore take for granted that all traditional Judaisms are pretty much the same. But "tradition" stands for many things, and so does the term *Orthodox Judaism*. Some Orthodox Judaists reaffirmed self-segregation; others maintained that they could practice "the tradition" and also integrate themselves into the politics and culture of their native countries. Segregationist Orthodoxy persisted where political change did not lend urgency to the issue of integration. Integrationist Orthodox flourished in countries where Jews had reason to hope for political emancipation. The State of Israel today shelters both kinds of Orthodoxy and differentiates among them. In the United States, segregationist Orthodoxy is dominated by highly sectarian Hasidic communities, that is, Judaists who, in addition to the dual Torah, value a heritage of mysticism centered around holy men, or *rebbes,* as the nexus between God and the world.

The difference between segregationist and integrationist Orthodoxy appropriately came to public debate in matters of learning: the Torah and/or secular education. When Jews who kept the law of the Torah, for example, as it dictated food choices and use of leisure time (to speak of the Sabbath and festivals in secular terms), sent their children to secular schools in addition to or instead of solely Jewish ones, or when they included in Jewish schools' curriculum subjects outside the sciences of the Torah, they crossed the boundary between the received and the new Judaism. For the notion that science or German or Latin or philosophy deserved serious study in the nineteenth century struck as wrong those for whom the received system remained self-evidently right. Those Jews did not send their children to gentile schools and did not include in Jewish schools' curriculum subjects other than Torah study.

Orthodox Judaism arose (predictably) in Germany, in the middle of the nineteenth century. It came to articulated expression among Jews who rejected Reform and made a self-conscious decision to remain within the way of life and worldview that they had known and cherished all their lives. They framed the issues in terms of change and history. The Reformers held that Judaism could change and that Judaism was a product of history. The Orthodox opponents denied that Judaism could change, insisting that Judaism derived from God's will at Sinai and was eternal and supernatural, not historical and artificially made. In these two convictions, of course, the Orthodox recapitulated the convictions of the received system. But in their appeal to the given, the traditional, they found more persuasive some components of that system than they did others, and in the picking and choosing, in the articulation of the view that Judaism formed a religion to be seen as distinct and autonomous of politics, society, and "the rest of life," they entered that same world of self-conscious believing that the Reformers also explored.

DEFINING ORTHODOX JUDAISM IN ITS WESTERN POLITICAL CONTEXT

Integrationist Orthodox Judaism does two things. First, it maintains the worldview of the received dual Torah, constantly citing its sayings and adhering with only trivial variations to the bulk of its norms for the everyday life. Second, Orthodoxy holds that Jews adhering to the dual Torah may wear clothing that non-Jews wear and do not have to wear distinctively Jewish (even Judaic) clothing, live within a common economy and not practice distinctively Jewish professions (however, in a given setting, these professions may be defined), and, in diverse ways, take up a life not readily distinguished in important characteristics from the life lived by people in general.

So, for Orthodoxy, a portion of holy Israel's life may prove secular, in that the Torah does not dictate and so sanctify all details under all circumstances. Because the Judaism of the dual Torah presupposed not only the supernatural entity, Israel, but also a way of life that in important ways distinguished that supernatural entity from the social world at large, the power of Orthodoxy to find an accommodation for Jews who valued the received way of life and worldview and also planned to make their lives in an essentially integrated social world proves formidable. The difference between Orthodoxy and the system of the dual Torah therefore comes to expression in social policy: integration, however circumscribed, versus the total separation of the holy people.

The term *Orthodoxy* takes on meaning only in the contrast to Reform, so in a simple sense, integrationist, or Western, or Modern, Orthodoxy owes its life to Reform Judaism. The term first surfaced in 1795[1] and covers all Jews who believe that God revealed the dual Torah at Sinai and that Jews must carry out the requirements of Jewish law contained in the Torah as interpreted by the sages through time. Obviously, so long as that position struck as self-evident the generality of Jewry at large, Orthodoxy as a distinct and organized Judaism did not exist. It did not have to. What is interesting is the point at which two events took place: first, the recognition of the received system, "the tradition" as Orthodoxy; second, the specification of the received system as religion. The two, of course, go together. So long as the Judaism of the dual Torah enjoys recognition as a set of self-evident truths, those truths add up not to something so distinct as special as "religion" but to a general statement of how things are: all of life explained and harmonized in one whole account.

The former of the two events—the view that the received system was "traditional"—came first. The matter of the self-aware recognition of "Judaism" as "religion" comes later. That identification of truth as tradition came about when the received system met the challenge of competing Judaisms. Then, on behalf of the received way of life and worldview addressed to supernatural Israel, people said that the Judaism of the dual Torah was established of old, the right, the only way of seeing and doing things, how things have been and should be naturally and normally: "tradition." But that is a category that contains within itself an alternative, namely, change, as in "tradition and change."

When the system lost its power of self-evidence, it entered, among other apologetic categories, the classification "tradition." And that came about when Orthodoxy met head-on the challenge of change become Reform. We understand why the category of tradition, the received way of doing things, became critical to the framers of Orthodoxy when we examine the counter-claim. That is, just as the Reformers justified change, the Orthodox theologians denied that change was ever possible. As Walter Wurzburger states, "Orthodoxy looks upon attempts to adjust Judaism to the 'spirit of the time' as utterly incompatible with the entire thrust of normative Judaism which holds that the revealed will of God rather than the values of any given age are the ultimate standard."[2]

The issue important to the Reformers, the value of what was called "emancipation" (meaning the provision to Jews of civil rights) defined the debate. When the Reform Judaic theologians took a wholly one-sided position affirming Emancipation, numerous Orthodox ones adopted the contrary view. The position outlined by those theologians followed the agenda laid forth by the Reformers. If the Reform made minor changes in liturgy and its conduct, the Orthodox rejected even those that, under other circumstances, might have found acceptance. Saying prayers in the vernacular, for example, provoked strong opposition. But everyone knew that some of the prayers, said in Aramaic, in fact were in the vernacular of the earlier age. The Orthodox thought that these changes, not reforms at all, represented only the first step of a process leading Jews out of the Judaic world altogether, so, as Wurzburger says, "The slightest tampering with tradition was condemned."[3]

If we ask where did the received system of the dual Torah prevail and where, by contrast, did Orthodoxy come to full expression, we may follow the spreading out of railway lines, the growth of new industry, the shifts in political status accorded to, among other citizens, Jews, changes in the educational system—in all, the entire process of political change, economic and social, demographic and cultural shifts of a radical and fundamental nature. Where the changes came first, there Reform Judaism met them in its way—and Orthodoxy in its way. Where change came later in the century, as in the case of Russian Poland, the eastern provinces of the Austro-Hungarian Empire, and Russia itself, there, in villages contentedly following the old ways, the received system endured.

Again, in an age of mass migration from Eastern Europe to North America and other Western democracies, those who experienced the upheaval of leaving home and country met the challenge of change either by accepting new ways of seeing things or articulately and in full self-awareness reaffirming the familiar ones, once more, Reform or Orthodoxy. We may, therefore, characterize the received system as a way of life and worldview wedded to an ancient peoples' homelands, the villages and small towns of Central and Eastern Europe, and Orthodoxy as the heir of that received system as it came to expression in the towns and cities of Central and Western Europe and North America. That rule of thumb, with the usual exceptions, allows us to distinguish between the piety of a milieu and the theological conviction of a self-conscious community. Or we may accept the familiar distinction between tradition and articulate Orthodoxy, a distinction with its own freight of apologetics, to be sure.

When, therefore, we explain by reference to political and economic change the beginnings of Reform Judaism, we also understand the point of origin of Orthodoxy as distinct and organized and articulated. Clearly, the beginnings of Orthodoxy took place in the areas where in response to fundamental political change, Reform made its way, hence in Germany and Hungary. In Germany, where Reform attracted the majority of numerous Jewish communities, the Orthodox faced a challenge indeed. Critical to their conviction was the notion that "Israel," all of the Jews, bore responsibility to carry out the law of the Torah. But the community's institutions in the hands of the Reform did not obey the law of the Torah as the Orthodox understood it. So, in the end, Orthodoxy took that step that marked it as a self-conscious Judaism. Orthodoxy separated from the established community altogether. The Orthodox set up their own organization and seceded from the community at large. The next step prohibited Orthodox from participating in non-Orthodox organizations altogether. Isaac Breuer, a leading theologian of Orthodoxy, would ultimately take the position that "refusal to espouse the cause of separation was interpreted as being equivalent to the rejection of the absolute sovereignty of God."[4]

The matter of accommodating to the world at large, of course, did not allow for so easy an answer as mere separation. The specific issue—integration or segregation—concerned preparation for life in the large politics and economic life of the country, which meant secular education, involving not only language and science but history and literature, matters of values. Orthodoxy proved diverse, with two wings to be distinguished: one rejecting secular learning as well as all dealing with non-Orthodox Jews, the other cooperating with non-Orthodox and secular Jews and accepting the value of secular education. That position in no way affected loyalty to the law of Judaism (for example, belief in God's revelation of the one whole Torah at Sinai). The point at which the received system and Orthodox split requires specification. In concrete terms, we know the one from the other by the evaluation of secular education. Proponents of the received system never accommodated themselves to secular education, whereas the Orthodox in Germany and Hungary persistently affirmed it. That represents a remarkable shift, since central to the received system of the dual Torah is study of Torah, not philosophy.

Explaining where we find the one and the other, Katzburg works with the distinction we have already made, between an unbroken system and one that has undergone a serious caesura with the familiar condition of the past. He states:

> In Eastern Europe until World War I, Orthodoxy preserved without a break its traditional ways of life and the time-honored educational framework. In general, the mainstream of Jewish life was identified with Orthodoxy, while Haskalah [Jewish Enlightenment, which applied to the Judaic setting the skeptical attitudes of the French Enlightenment] and secularization were regarded as deviations. Hence there was no ground wherein a Western type of Orthodoxy could take root.... European Orthodoxy in the nineteenth and the beginning of the twentieth centuries was significantly influenced by the move from small settlements to urban centers...as well as by emigration. Within the small German communities there was a kind of popular Orthodoxy, deeply attached to tradition and to local customs, and when it moved to the large cities this element brought with it a vitality and rootedness to Jewish tradition.[5]

Katzburg's observations provide important guidance. He authoritatively defines the difference between Orthodoxy and "tradition." So he tells us how to distinguish the received system accepted as self-evident from an essentially selective, therefore by definition new, system called Orthodoxy. He guides us in telling the one from the other and where to expect to find, in particular, the articulated, therefore, self-conscious affirmation of "tradition" that characterizes Orthodoxy but does not occur in the world of the dual Torah as it glided in its eternal orbit of the seasons and unchanging time.

OLD AND NEW IN ORTHODOXY

The urban Orthodox experienced change, daily encountered Jews unlike themselves, and no longer lived in that stable Judaic society in which the received Torah formed the given of life. Pretense that Jews faced no choices scarcely represented a possibility. Nor did the generality of the Jews propose, in the West, to preserve a separate language or renounce political rights. So Orthodoxy made its peace with change, no less than did Reform. The educational program that led Jews out of the received culture of the dual Torah, the use of the vernacular, the acceptance of political rights, the renunciation of Jewish garments, education for women, abolition of the power of the community to coerce the individual—these and many other originally Reform positions characterized the Orthodoxy that emerged, another new Judaism, in the nineteenth century.[6]

If we ask, How new was the Orthodox system? we find ambiguous answers. In conviction, way of life, and worldview, we may hardly call it new at all. For the bulk of its substantive positions found ample precedent in the received dual Torah. From its affirmation of God's revelation of a dual Torah to its acceptance of the detailed authority of the law and customs, from its strict observance of the law to its unwillingness to change a detail of public worship, Orthodoxy rightly pointed to its strong links with the chain of tradition. But Orthodoxy constituted a sect within the Jewish group. Its definition of the "Israel" to whom it wished to speak and the definition characteristic of the dual Torah hardly coincide. The Judaism of the dual Torah addressed all Jews, and Orthodoxy recognized that it could not do so. Orthodoxy acquiesced, however, in a situation that lay beyond the imagination of the framers of the Judaism of the dual Torah.

True, the Orthodox had no choice. Their seceding from the community and forming their own institutions ratified the simple fact that they could not work with the Reformers. But the upshot remains the same. That supernatural entity, Israel, gave up its place and a natural Israel, a this-worldly political fact, succeeded. Pained though Orthodoxy was by the fact, it nonetheless accommodated the new social reality—and affirmed it by reshaping the sense of Israel in the supernatural dimension. Their Judaism no less than the Judaism of the Reformers stood for something new, a birth not a renewal—a political response to a new politics. True enough, for Orthodoxy the politics was that of the Jewish community, divided as it was among diverse visions of the political standing of Israel, the Jewish people. For the Reform, by contrast, the new politics derived from the establishment of the category of neutral citizenship in an encompassing nation-state. But the political shifts flowed from the same large-scale changes in Israel's consciousness and character, and, it follows, Orthodoxy as much as Reform represented a set of self-evident answers to political questions that none could evade.

To claim that the Orthodox went in search of proof for a system formed and defined in advance, of course, misrepresents the reality—but not by much. For once the system of a self-conscious and deliberate Orthodoxy took shape, much picking and choosing, assigning of priorities to some things and not others, would follow naturally. The upshot of it all remains the same: a new system, a way of life much like the received one, but readily differentiated; a worldview congruent to the received one, but with its own points of interest and emphasis; and, above all, a social referent, an "Israel" quite beyond the limits of the one posited by the dual Torah. Orthodoxy represents the most interesting challenge to the hypothesis announced at the outset.

Each Judaism begins on its own, defining the questions it wished to answer and laying forth the responses it found self-evidently true, only then going back to the canon of received documents in search of proof. Every Judaism therefore commences in the definition (to believers, the discovery) of its canon. Orthodoxy surely forms an enormous exception to such a proposed rule. For its canon recognized the same books, accorded the same status and authority. Yet, as we shall now see, that is hardly the case. Orthodoxy produced books to which the received system of the dual Torah could afford no counterpart, and vice versa. Orthodoxy addressed questions impertinent to the received system or to the world that it constructed. Its answers violated, of course, important givens of the received system. The single most significant trait of Orthodoxy is its power to see the "Torah" as "Judaism," the category shift that changed everything else (or that ratified all other changes).

JUDAISM ENTERS THE CATEGORY "RELIGION"

The category "religion," with its counterpart "secular," recognizes as distinct from "all of life" matters having to do with the church, the life of faith, the secular versus the sacred. Those distinctions were lost on the received system of the dual Torah, of course, which legislated for matters we should today regard as entirely secular or neutral, for example, the institutions of state (king, priest, army). We have already noted that in the received system as it took shape in Eastern and Central Europe, Jews wore garments regarded as distinctively Jewish, and some important traits of these garments indeed derived from the Torah. They pursued sciences that only Jews studied—for instance, the Talmud and its commentaries. In these and other ways, the Torah encompassed all of the life of Israel, the holy people. The recognition that Jews were like others, that the Torah fell into a category into which other and comparable matters fell, was long in coming.

For Christians it had become a commonplace in Germany and other Western countries to see "religion" as distinct from other components of the social and political system. While the church in Russia identified with the czarist state or with the national aspirations of the Polish or Ukrainian peoples, two churches in Germany, for example, Catholic and Lutheran, competed. The terrible wars of the Reformation in the sixteenth and seventeenth centuries, which ruined Germany, had led to the uneasy compromise that the prince might choose the religion of his principality, and, from that self-aware choice, people understood that "the way of life and worldview" in fact constituted a religion and that one religion might be compared with some other. By the nineteenth century, moreover, the separation of church and state ratified the important distinction between religion, where difference would be tolerated, and the secular, where citizens were pretty much the same.

That fact of political consciousness in the West reached the Judaic world only in the late eighteenth century for some intellectuals, and in the nineteenth century for large numbers of others. It registered, then, as a fundamental shift in the understanding and interpretation of "the Torah," now seen, in Orthodox as much as in Reform, as "Judaism," an -ism along with other -isms. A mark of the creative power of the Jews who formed the Orthodox Judaic system derives from their capacity to shift the fundamental category in which they framed their system. The basic shift in category is what made Orthodoxy a Judaism on its own, not simply a restatement, essentially in established classifications, of the received system of the dual Torah.

If we ask how Orthodox Judaism, so profoundly rooted in the canonical writings and received convictions of the Judaism of the dual Torah, at the same time provided for the issues of political and cultural change at hand, we recognize the importance of the shift in category contributed by Orthodoxy. For Orthodoxy, within the sector of the received system, made provision for the difference between sacred and secular, so within Judaic systems it identified as a religion, Judaism, what the received system had called the Torah, encompassing and symmetric with the whole of the life of Judaic society. Specifically, Orthodox Judaism took the view that one could observe the rules of the Judaic system of the ages and at the same time keep the laws of the state.

More important, Orthodox Judaism took full account of the duties of citizenship, so far as being a good citizen imposed the expectation of conformity in certain aspects of everyday life. So a category, "religion," could contain the Torah, and another category, "the secular," could allow Jews a place in the accepted civic life of the country. Many Orthodox Jews would die defending Germany in World War I. The importance of the category shift therefore lies in its power to accommodate the political change so important, also, to Reform Judaism. The Jews' differences from others would fit into categories in which difference was acceptable (in Jews' minds, at any rate) and would not violate those lines to which all citizens had to adhere.

The received system, giving expression to the rules of sanctification of the holy people, did entail wearing Jewish clothing, speaking a Jewish language, and learning only, or mainly, Jewish sciences. So clothing, language, and education now fell into the category of the secular, whereas other equally important aspects of everyday life remained in the category of the sacred. Integrationist Orthodox Judaism, as it came into existence in Germany and other Western countries, therefore found it possible by recognizing the category of the secular to accept the language, clothing, and learning of those countries.

These matters serve to exemplify a larger acceptance of gentile ways, not all but enough to lessen the differences between the holy people and the nations. Political change of a profound order, which made Jews question some aspects of the received system (if not most or all of them, as would be the case for Reform Judaism), presented to Jews who gave expression to Orthodox Judaism the issues at hand: how separate, how integrated? And the answers required picking and choosing—different things, to be sure—just as much as, in principle, the Reform Jews picked and chose. Both Judaisms understood that some things were sacred, others not, and that understanding marked these Judaisms off from the system of the dual Torah.

Once the category shift had taken place, the difference was to be measured in degree, not kind. For integrationist Orthodox Jews maintained those distinctive beliefs of a political character in the future coming of the Messiah and the reconstitution of the Jewish nation in its own land that Reform Jews rejected. But, placing these convictions in the distant future, the same type of Orthodox Jews nonetheless prepared for a protracted interim of life within the nation at hand, like the Reform different in religion, not in nationality as represented by citizenship. What follows for our inquiry is that Orthodoxy, as much as Reform, signals remarkable changes in the Jews' political situation and—more important—aspiration. They did want to be different, but not so different as the received system would have made them.

Still, Orthodoxy in its nineteenth-century formulation laid claim to carry forward, in continuous and unbroken relationship, "the tradition." That claim assuredly demands a serious hearing, for the things that Orthodoxy taught, the way of life it required, the Israel to whom it spoke, the doctrines it deemed revealed by God to Moses at Sinai, all conformed more or less exactly to the system of the received Judaism of the dual Torah as people then knew it. So any consideration of the issue of a linear and incremental history of Judaism has to take at face value the character, and not merely the claim, of Orthodoxy. But we do not have without reflection to concede that claim. Each Judaism, after all, demands study not in categories defined by its own claims of continuity, but in those defined by its own distinctive and characteristic choices. For a system takes shape and then makes choices—in that order. But the issue facing us in Orthodoxy is whether Orthodoxy can be said to make choices at all. For is it not what it says it is, "just Judaism"? Indeed so, but the dual Torah of the received tradition hardly generated the base category, "Judaism." And "Judaism," Orthodox or otherwise, is not "Torah."

That is the point at which making self-conscious choices enters the discourse. For the Orthodoxy of the nineteenth century (that is, the Judaism that named itself "Orthodox") exhibited certain traits of mind that marked its framers as distinctive, as separate from the received Judaism of the dual Torah as the founders of Reform Judaism. To state the matter simply: By adopting for themselves the category "religion" and by recognizing a distinction between religion and the secular, the holy and other categories of existence, the founders of Orthodoxy performed an act of choice and selectivity. And that fact defines them as self-conscious, rendering the received system for them not self-evident, therefore definitive of the very facts of being as it was for those for whom it was self-evident.

The Torah found itself transformed into an object, a thing out there, a matter of choice, deliberation, affirmation. In that sense, Orthodoxy recognized a break in the line of the received "tradition" and proposed to repair the break: a self-conscious, modern decision. The issues addressed by Orthodoxy and the questions its framers found ineluctable take second place. The primary consideration in our assessment of the claim of Orthodoxy to carry forward, in a straight line, the incremental history of a single Judaism, carries us to the fundamental categories within which Orthodoxy pursued its thought, but the Judaism of the dual Torah did not. How so? The Judaism of the dual Torah had no word for Judaism, and Orthodoxy did (and does).

To the Jews who abided within the received Judaism of the dual Torah, the discovery of "Judaism," "religion," and "Orthodoxy" as categories therefore represented an innovation, a shift from the self-evident truths of the Torah. For their word for Judaism was *Torah* (as in the title of this book!), and when they spoke of the whole all at once, they used the word *Torah*—and they also spoke of different things from the things encompassed by Judaism. For the received Judaism of the dual Torah did not use the word the nineteenth-century theologians used when speaking of the things of which they spoke when they said, Juda-*ism*. The received system not only used a different word but in fact referred to different things. The two categories, Judaism and Torah, which are supposed to refer to the same data in the same social world, in fact encompass different data from those taken in categorically by Judaism. So we contrast the two distinct categories, Judaism and Torah.

Judaism falls into the classification of a philosophical or ideological or theological one, a logos, a word; whereas *Torah* falls into the classification of a symbol, a symbol that in itself encompassed the whole of the system that the category at hand was meant to describe. The species -ism falls into the classification of the genus, logos, whereas the species Torah, though using words, transcends words. It falls into a different classification, a species of the genus symbol. How so? The -ism category does not invoke an encompassing symbol but a system of thought. Judaism is an it, an object, a classification, an action. Torah, for its part, is an everything in one thing, a symbol. I cannot imagine a more separate and unlike set of categories than Judaism and Torah, even though both encompass the same way of life and worldview and address the same social group. So Torah as a category serves as a symbol, everywhere present in detail and holding all the details together. Judaism as a category serves as a statement of the main points: the intellectual substrate of it all.

The conception of Judaism as an organized body of doctrine, as in the sentence "Judaism teaches" or "Judaism says," derives from an age in which people further had determined that Judaism belonged to the category of religion, and, of still more definitive importance, a religion was something that *teaches* or *says.* That is, Judaism is a religion, and a religion to begin with (whatever else it is) is a composition of beliefs. That age is the one at hand, the nineteenth century, and the category of religion as a distinct entity emerges from Protestant theological thought. For in Protestant theological terms, one is saved by faith. But the very components of that sentence—"one" (individual, not the people or holy nation), "saved" (personally, not in history; and saved, not sanctified), and "faith" (not commandments of God) in fact prove incomprehensible in the categories constructed by Torah. Constructions of Judaic dogmas, the specification of a right doctrine—an ortho-doxy—and the insistence that one can speak of religion apart from such adventitious matters as clothing and education (for the Orthodox of Germany who dressed like other Germans and studied in Universities, not only in yeshivas) or food (for the Reform) testify to the same fact: the end of self-evidence, the substitution of the distinction between religion and secularity, the creation of *Judaism* as the definitive category.

In fact, in the idiomatic language of Torah speech, one cannot make such a statement in that way about, or in the name of, Judaism—not an operative category at all. In accord with the modes of thought and speech of the received Judaism of the dual Torah, one has to speak as subject of Israel, not one, to address not only individual life but all of historical time, so *saved* by itself does not suffice. Furthermore, one must invoke the verb, because the category of sanctification, not only salvation, must find its place. Finally, one native to the speech of the Torah will use the words of commandments of God, not of faith alone. So the sentence serves for Protestant Christianity but not for the Torah. Of course "Judaism," Orthodox or Reform, for its part will also teach things and lay down doctrines, even dogmas.

The counterpart, in the realm of self-evidence comprised by the received Judaism of the dual Torah, of the statement "Judaism teaches" can only be "The Torah requires," and the predicate of such a sentence would not be "…that God is one" but "…that you say a blessing before eating bread." The category "Judaism" encompasses, classifies, and organizes doctrines: the faith, which, by the way, an individual adopts and professes. The category "Torah" teaches what "we," God's holy people, are and what "we" must do. The counterpart to the statement of Judaism, "God is one," then is "…who has sanctified us by his commandments and commanded us to…." The one teaches, that is, speaks of intellectual matters and beliefs; the latter demands social actions and deeds of us, matters of public consequence—including, by the way, affirming such doctrines as God's unity, the resurrection of the dead, the coming of the Messiah, the revelation of the Torah at Sinai, and on and on. "We" can rival the Protestants in heroic deeds of faith. So it is true, the faith demands deeds, and deeds presuppose faith. But, categorically, the emphasis is what it is: Torah on God's revelation, the canon, to Israel and its social way of life; Judaism on a system of belief. That is a significant difference between the two categories, which, as I said, serve a single purpose, namely, to state the thing as a whole.

Equally true, one would (speaking systemically) also *study Torah*. But what one studied was not an intellectual system of theology or philosophy but rather Scripture, the Mishnah, the Talmud, the midrash—a document of revealed Scripture and law. That is not to suggest that the nineteenth-century theologians of Judaism, Orthodox or Reform, did not believe that God is one or that the philosophers who taught that "Judaism teaches ethical monotheism" did not concur that, on that account, one has to say a blessing before eating bread. But the categories are different and, consequently, so too the composites of knowledge. A book on Judaism explains the doctrines, the theology or philosophy, of Judaism. A book of the holy Torah expounds God's will as revealed in "the one whole Torah of Moses, our rabbi," as sages teach and embody God's will. I cannot imagine two more different books, because they represent totally different categories of intelligible discourse and of knowledge. Proof, of course, is that the latter books are literally unreadable. They form part of a genuinely oral exercise, to be cited sentence by sentence and expounded in the setting of other sentences, from other books, the whole made cogent by the speaker. That process of homogenization is how Torah works as a generative category. It obscures other lines of structure and order.

True, the two distinct categories come to bear upon the same body of data, the same holy books. But the consequent compositions—selections of facts, ordering of facts, analyses of facts, statements of conclusion and interpretation, and above all, modes of public discourse, meaning who says what to whom—bear no relationship to one another, none whatsoever. Indeed, the compositions more likely than not do not even adduce the same facts or even refer to them.

How is it that the category that was imposed, extrinsic, and deductive, namely, "Judaism," attained the status of self-evidence? Categories serve because they are self-evident to a large group of people. In this case, therefore, Judaism serves because it enjoys self-evidence as part of a larger set of categories that are equally self-evident. In all of these categories, religion constitutes a statement of belief distinct from other aspects and dimensions of human existence, so religions form a body of well-composed -isms. So whence the category "Judaism"? The source of the categorical power of "Judaism" derives from the Protestant philosophical heritage that has defined scholarship, including category formation, from the time of Kant onward. *"Juda"* + *"ism"* do not constitute self-evident, let alone definitive, categories—except where they do. Judaism constitutes a category asymmetric to the evidence adduced in its study. The category does not work because the principle of formation is philosophical and does not emerge from an unmediated encounter with the Torah. Orthodoxy can have come into existence only in Germany and, indeed, only in that part of Germany in which the philosophical heritage of Kant and Hegel defined the categories of thought, also, for religion.

WHAT DO WE LEARN ABOUT
JUDAISM FROM ORTHODOX JUDAISM?

Continuity or new creation? Both—but, therefore, by definition, new creation. Piety selected is by definition piety invented, and Samson Raphael Hirsch (the first voice of integrationist Orthodoxy, a German rabbi of the mid–nineteenth century) emerges as one of the intellectually powerful creators of a Judaism. "Torah and secular learning" defined a new worldview, dictated a new way of life, and addressed a different Israel, from the Judaism of the dual Torah. To those who received that dual Torah as self-evident what the Torah did not accommodate was secular learning. The Torah as they received it did not approve changes in the familiar way of life and did not know an Israel other than the one at hand. So the perfect faith of Orthodoxy sustained a wonderfully selective piety. And the human greatness of Hirsch and the large number of Jews who found self-evident the possibility of living the dual life of Jew and German or Jew and American? It lay in the power of the imagination to locate in a new circumstance a rationale for inventing tradition.

The human achievement of Orthodoxy demands more than routine notice. Living in a world that only grudgingly accommodated difference and did not like Jews' difference in particular, the Orthodox followed the rhythm of the week to the climax of the Sabbath, of the seasons to the climactic moments of the festivals. They adhered to their own pattern of daily life, with prayers morning, noon, and night. They married only within the holy people. They ate only food that had been prepared in accord with the rules of sanctification. They honored philosophy and culture, true, but these they measured by their own revealed truth as well. It was not easy for them to keep the faith when so many within Jewry, and so many more outside, wanted Jews to be pretty much the same as everyone else.

The human costs cannot have proved trivial. To affirm when the world denies, to keep the faith against all evidence—that represents that faith that in other settings people honored. It was not easy for either the integrationist Orthodox of Germany or the immigrant Jews of North America, who in an ocean voyage moved from the world of self-evident faith to the one of insistent denial of the faith. But Jews throughout the Western world did respond to the agenda of political change in a manner radically different from the response of Reform Judaism. Integrationist Orthodoxy has remained predominant in post-Holocaust Europe and, though overshadowed by segregationist Orthodox Judaisms, still deeply influential in the State of Israel also. What we learn about Judaism from Orthodoxy is what we learn about humanity from religion, which is, different people reach different conclusions about the same questions. Religion cannot be reduced to a function of politics or economics or even culture. It is an independent variable.

NOTES

1. Nathaniel Katzburg and Walter S. Wurzburger, "Orthodoxy," *Encyclopaedia Judaica* (Jerusalem: Keter, 1971), vol. 12, 1486–1493.

2. Ibid., col. 1487.

3. Ibid.

4. Ibid., col. 1488.

5. Ibid., col. 1490.

6. Ibid., col. 957.

30

Conservative Judaism

TRADITION AND SELECTIVITY:
HISTORICISM FORMS A JUDAISM

The Historical School, a group of a nineteenth-century German scholars, and Conservative Judaism, a twentieth-century Judaism in North America, took the middle position, each in its own context. We treat them as a single Judaism, because they share a single viewpoint: moderation in making change, accommodation between "the tradition" and the requirements of modern life, and above all, adaptation to circumstance.

The Historical School began among German Jewish theologians who advocated change but found Reform extreme. They parted company with Reform on some specific issues of practice and doctrine—observance of the dietary laws and belief in the coming of the Messiah, for example. But they also found Orthodoxy immobile. Conservative Judaism in North America in the twentieth century carried forward this same centrist position and turned a viewpoint of intellectuals into a Judaism: a way of life, worldview, addressed to an Israel. The Historical School shaped the worldview, and Conservative Judaism later on brought that view into full realization as a way of life characteristic of a large group of Jews, nearly half of all American Jews by the middle of the twentieth century.

The Historical School in Germany and Conservative Judaism in America affirmed a far broader part of the received way of life than Reform, while rejecting a much larger part than did Orthodoxy of the worldview of the system of the dual Torah. Calling itself "the Historical School,"[1] the Judaism at hand concurred with the Reformers in their basic position. The Reformers had held that change was permissible and claimed that historical scholarship would show what change was acceptable and what was not. But the proponents of the Historical School differed in matters of detail. The emphasis on historical research in settling theological debates explains the name of the group. Arguing that its positions represent matters of historical fact rather than theological conviction, Conservative Judaism maintained that "positive historical scholarship" will prove capable, on the basis of historical facts, of purifying and clarifying the faith, joined to far stricter observance of the law than the Reformers required.

Toward the end of the nineteenth century, rabbis of this same centrist persuasion organized the Jewish Theological Seminary of America in 1886–1887, and from that rabbinic school the Conservative Movement developed. The order of the formation of the several Judaisms of the nineteenth century therefore is, first, Reform, then Orthodoxy, finally, Conservatism: the two extremes, then the middle. Reform defined the tasks of the next two Judaisms to come into being. Orthodoxy framed the clearer of the two positions in reaction to Reform, but, in intellectual terms, the Historical School in Germany met the issues of Reform in a more direct way.

THE MIDDLE POSITION:
WHEN IS A BOOK NOT A JUDAISM?

In trying to understand the middle position, we have to sort out a measure of confusion, for two reasons. First, the centrist viewpoint had one name, the Historical School, in Germany, another, Conservative Judaism, in North America. The second and more important is that the Historical School in Germany did not constitute a Judaism but a body of ideas. A Judaism must take shape within an "Israel" and come to expression in an organized community. But the Historical School added up to a handful of scholars writing books, and a book is not a Judaism, only the intellectual basis for a Judaic community, which forms a Judaism. In North America, by contrast, the Conservative Movement in Judaism (as it sometimes called itself to avoid setting up a sect on its own) or Conservative Judaism did reach full realization in a way of life characteristic of large numbers of Jews, a worldview that, for those Jews, explained who they were and what they must do, a clearly articulated account of who is Israel—a Judaism. But the center's fundamental definition of the urgent issues and how they were to be worked out in both nineteenth-century Germany and twentieth-century North America proved remarkably uniform, beginning to the present.

The stress of the Historical School in Europe and Conservative Judaism in North America lay on two matters: first, scholarship, with historical research assigned the task of discovering those facts of which the faith would be composed; second, observance of the rules of the received Judaism. A professedly free approach to the study of the Torah, specifically through what was called "critical scholarship," therefore would yield an accurate account of the essentials of the faith. But the scholars and laypeople alike would keep and practice nearly the whole of the tradition just as the Orthodox did.

The ambivalence of Conservative Judaism, speaking in part for intellectuals deeply loyal to the received way of life but profoundly dubious of the inherited worldview, came to full expression in the odd slogan of its intellectuals and scholars: "Eat kosher and think *traif.*" *Traif* refers to meat that is not acceptable under Judaic law, and the slogan announced a religion of orthopraxy: do the right thing, and what you believe does not matter. That statement meant people should keep the rules of the holy way of life but ignore the convictions that made sense of them. *Orthopraxy* is the word that refers to correct action and unfettered belief, versus *orthodoxy,* right doctrine. Some would then classify Conservative Judaism in North America as an orthoprax Judaism defined through works, not doctrine. Some of its leading voices even denied that Judaism set forth doctrine at all in what is called "the dogma of dogmaless Judaism."

The middle position then derived in equal measures from the two extremes. The way of life was congruent in most aspects with that of the Orthodox; the worldview, with that of the Reform. The two held together in the doctrine of Israel that covered everyone. Conservative Judaism laid enormous stress on what the people were doing, on the consensus of what one of its founders called "catholic Israel," meaning the whole ethnic-religious group. Conservative Judaism saw the Jews as a(nother) people, not merely a(nother) religious community, as Reform did, or a unique and holy people, as Orthodoxy did. That Judaism celebrated the ethnic as much as the more narrowly religious side to the Jews' common life. Orthodoxy took a separatist and segregationist position, leaving the organized Jewish community in Germany as that community fell into the hands of Reform Jews. Reform Judaism, for its part, rejected the position that the Jews constitute a people, not merely a religious community. Conservative Judaism emphasized the importance of the unity of the community as a whole and took a stand in favor of Zionism as soon as that movement got under way.

What separated Conservative Judaism from Reform was the matter of observance. Fundamental loyalty to the received way of life distinguished the Historical School in Germany and Conservative Judaism in the United States from Reform Judaism in both countries. When considering the continued validity of a traditional religious practice, the Reform asked why; the Conservatives, why not. The Orthodox, of course, would ask no questions to begin with. The fundamental principle, that the worldview of the Judaism under construction would rest on (mere) historical facts, came from Reform Judaism. Orthodoxy could never have concurred. The contrast to the powerful faith despite the world, exhibited by integrationist Orthodoxy's stress on the utter facticity of the Torah, presents in a clear light the positivism of the Conservatives, who, indeed, adopted the name "the *positive* Historical School."

The emphasis on research as the route to historical fact, and on historical fact as the foundation for both theological change and also the definition of what was truly authentic in the theological tradition, further tells us that the Historical School was made up of intellectuals. In the United States and Canada, too, a pattern developed in which essentially nonobservant congregations of Jews called on rabbis whom they expected to be observant of the rules of the religion. As a result, many of the intellectual problems that occupied public debate concerned rabbis more than laypeople, because the rabbis bore responsibility (so the community maintained) for not only teaching the faith but, on their own, embodying it. I describe this Judaism as "Orthodox rabbis serving Conservative synagogues made up of Reform Jews."

But in a more traditional liturgy, in an emphasis on observance of the dietary taboos and the Sabbath and festivals—which did, and still does, characterize homes of Conservative more than of Reform Jews—Conservative Judaism in its way of life as much as in its worldview did establish an essentially mediating position between Orthodoxy and Reform Judaisms. And the conception that Conservative Judaism is a Judaism for Conservative rabbis in no way accords with the truth. That Judaism for a long time enjoyed the loyalty of fully half of the Jews in the United States and Canada, and, though losing ground, today still retains the center and the influential position of Judaism there. The viewpoint of the center predominates even in the more traditional circles of Reform and the more modernist sectors of Orthodoxy.

RESPONDING TO REFORM JUDAISM

The point of movement of the viewpoint of a school into the status of a Judaism is not difficult to locate. The school—the Historical School in Germany, a handful of moderate rabbis in the United States and Canada—defined itself as a movement in Judaism (in my terms, a Judaism) in response to a particular event. It was the adoption, by the Reform rabbis, of the Pittsburgh Platform of 1885, cited earlier. At that point a number of European rabbis now settled in North America determined to break from Reform and establish what they hoped would be simply "traditional" Judaism. In 1886, they founded the Jewish Theological Seminary of America, which is when Conservative Judaism as a religious movement began. The actual event was simple. The final break between the more traditional and the more radical rabbis among the non-Orthodox camp produced the formation of a group to sponsor a new rabbinic school for "the knowledge and practice of historical Judaism."[2]

The power of Reform Judaism to create and define the character of its own opposition—Orthodoxy in Germany, Conservative Judaism in the United States and Canada—tells us how accurately Reform had outlined the urgent questions of the age. Just as Reform had created Orthodoxy, it created Conservative Judaism. Reform, after all, had treated as compelling the issue of citizenship ("emancipation") and raised the heart of the matter. How could Jews aspire to return to the Holy Land and form a nation and at the same time take up citizenship in the lands of their birth and loyalty? Jews lived a way of life different from that of their neighbors, with whom they wished to associate. A Judaism had to explain that difference.

The answers of all three Judaisms accepted the premises framed, to begin with, by Reform. That is why Reform Judaism was, and remains, the single most powerful and successful Judaism in modern times, dominant in North America in particular, even though, in the State of Israel and Europe, Australia, and South Africa, Orthodoxy defines the institutional norms. Orthodoxy maintained one could accept citizenship and accommodate political change but also adhere loyally to the Torah. To Orthodoxy certain changes, necessary in context, represented trivial and unimportant matters, even though, as we have noted, these matters—secular education being the most significant—did not strike other "traditionalists" as trivial at all. Conservative Judaism in its German formulation took up a midposition, specifying as essential fewer aspects of the received way of life than did Orthodoxy but more than Reform. In many ways, therefore, Reform Judaism defined the agenda for all of the Judaisms of the nineteenth century, and its success lies in imposing its fundamental perspective on its competition.

The urgent issue of the age, then, lay in the address to political change. If we want to understand Conservative Judaism, we have to follow its mode of sorting out the legitimate changes from the unacceptable ones, for that method marked the middle off from the extremes on either side. The way in which the Historical School coped with political change, particularly the secularization of politics and the challenge to reframe the political teleology (and associated way of life and worldview—of Judaism), lay through historical study. The search for precedent need hardly surprise us because the Reformers took the same route. The fundamental premise of the Conservatives' emphasis on history rested on the conviction that history demonstrated the truth or falsity of theological propositions.

We should look in vain in all of the prior writings of Judaic systems for precedent for that fact, self-evident to the nineteenth- and twentieth-century system builders. The appeal to historical facts was meant to lay on firm, factual foundations whatever change was to take place. In finding precedent for change, the Conservatives sought reassurance that some change, if not a great deal of change, would not endanger the enduring faith they wished to preserve. But there was a second factor. The laws and lessons of history would then settle questions of public policy near at hand.

Both in Germany in the middle of the century and in North America at the end, the emphasis throughout lay on "knowledge and practice of historical Judaism as ordained in the law of Moses expounded by the prophets and sages in Israel in Biblical and Talmudic writings," so the articles of Incorporation of the Jewish Theological Seminary of America Association stated in 1887. Calling themselves "traditionalists" rather than "Orthodox," the Conservative adherents accepted for most Judaic subjects the principles of modern critical scholarship. Conservative Judaism therefore exhibited traits that linked it to Reform but also to Orthodoxy, a movement very much in the middle. Precisely how the Historical School related to the other systems of its day— the mid- and later-nineteenth century—requires attention to that scholarship that, apologists insisted, marked the Historical School off from Orthodoxy.

HISTORY AND RELIGION: THE POWER OF HISTORICISM

The principal argument in validation of the approach of the Historical School and Conservative Judaism derived from these same facts of history. Change now would restore the way things had been at that golden age that set the norm and defined the standard. So by changing, Jews would regain that true Judaism that, in the passage of time, had been lost. The Lutheran model governed, as noted in Chapter 18. Reform added up to more than mere change to accommodate the new age, as the Reforms claimed. This kind of reform would conserve, recover, restore. That is what accounts for the basic claim that the centrists would discover how things had always been. By finding out how things had been done, what had been found essential as faith, in that original and generative time, scholarship would dictate the character of the Judaic system. It would say what it was and therefore what it should again become, and, it followed, Conservative Judaism then would be "simply Judaism."

Reform identified its Judaism as the linear and incremental next step in the unfolding of the Torah. The Historical School and Conservative Judaism later on regarded their Judaism as the reversion to the authentic Judaism that in time had been lost. Change was legitimate, as the Reform said, but only that kind of change that restored things to the condition of the original and correct Judaism. That position formed a powerful apologetic, because it addressed the Orthodox view that Orthodoxy constituted the linear and incremental outgrowth of "the Torah" or "the tradition," hence, the sole legitimate Judaism. It also addressed the Reform view that change was alright. Conservative Judaism established a firm criterion for what change was alright: the kind that was, really, no change at all. For the premise of the Conservative position was that things should become the way they had always been.

Here we come to the strikingly secular character of the several Judaisms moving beyond the limits of the dual Torah: their insistence that religious belief could be established on a foundation of historical fact. The category of faith, belief in transcendent things, matters not seen or tangible but nonetheless deeply felt and vigorously affirmed—these traits of religiosity hardly played a role. Rather, fact, ascertained by secular media of learning, would define truth. And truth corresponded to here-and-now reality: how things were. Scholarship would tell how things had always been and dictate those changes that would restore the correct way of life, the true worldview, for the Israel composed of pretty much all the Jews—the center. Historical research therefore provided a powerful apologetic against both sides.

That is why history was the ultimate weapon in the nineteenth century in the struggle among the Judaisms of the age. We therefore understand how much authority was carried by the name "the Historical School" in the Germany of the mid-nineteenth century. The claim to replicate how things always had been and should remain thus defined as the ultimate weapon historical research, of a sort. That weapon was, specifically, a critical scholarship that did not accept at face value as history the stories of holy books but asked whether and how they were true, and in what detail they were not true. That characteristically critical approach to historical study would then serve as the instrument for the definition of Conservative Judaism, the Judaism that would conserve the true faith but also omit those elements, accretions of later times, that marred that true faith.

At issue in historical research into secular facts, out of which the correct way of life and worldview would be defined, was the study of the Talmudic literature, that is, the oral Torah. The Hebrew Scriptures enjoyed immunity. Both the Reformers and the Historical School theologians stipulated that the written Torah was God given. The Conservatives and Reformers concurred that God gave the written Torah, people made the oral Torah. So the two parties of change, Reformers and Historical School alike, chose the field of battle, declaring the Hebrew Scriptures to be sacred and outside the war. They insisted that what was to be reformed was the shape of Judaism imparted by the Talmud, specifically, and preserved in their own day by the rabbis whose qualification consisted in learning in the Talmud and approval by those knowledgeable therein.

That agreement on the arena for critical scholarship is hardly an accident. The Reform and Historical School theologians revered Scripture. Wanting to justify parting company from Orthodox and the received tradition of the Oral Torah, they focused on the Talmud because it formed the sole and complete statement of the one whole Torah of Moses our rabbi, to which Orthodoxy and, of course, the traditionalists of the East, appealed. Hence, in bringing critical and skeptical questions to the Talmud but not to the Hebrew Scriptures, the Conservatives and Reformers addressed scholarship where they wished, and they preserved as revealed truth what they in any event affirmed as God's will. That is why the intellectual program of the Historical School in Germany and Conservative Judaism in North America consisted of turning the Talmud, studied historically, into a weapon turned against two sides: against the excessive credulity of the Orthodox, but also against the specific proposals and conceptions of the Reformers.

The role of scholarship being critical, Conservative Judaism looked to history to show which changes could be made in the light of biblical and rabbinic precedent, "for they viewed the entire history of Judaism as such a succession of changes," Arthur Hertzberg explains.[3] The continuity in history derives from the ongoing people. The basic policy from the beginning, however, dictated considerable reluctance at making changes in the received forms and teachings of the Judaism of the dual Torah. The basic commitments to the Hebrew language in worship, the dietary laws, and the keeping of the Sabbath and festivals distinguished the Historical School in Europe and Conservative Judaism in North America from Reform Judaism. The willingness to accept change and affirm the political emancipation of the Jews as a positive step marked the group as different from the Orthodox. So far as Orthodoxy claimed to oppose all changes of all kinds, Conservative Judaism did take a position in the middle of the three.

THE BIRTH OF A JUDAISM

In its formative century, Conservative Judaism carried forward the received way of life; hence, it set forth a Judaism professedly continuous with its past. But in its forthright insistence that no single worldview could delimit and define that way of life, Conservative Judaism imposed a still more radical break than did Reform Judaism between itself and the received tradition. Above all, Conservative Judaism denied the central fact of its system: its own novelty. It claimed to form "the tradition" while thoroughly ethnicizing the religion, Judaism.

So if we ask, Incremental development or new beginning? the answer is self-evident. Conservative Judaism formed a deeply original response to a difficult human circumstance. In its formative century, it solved the problem of alienation: people who had grown up in one place, under one set of circumstances, now lived somewhere else, in a different world. They cherished the past, but they themselves had initiated the changes they now confronted. In the doctrine of orthopraxy, they held on to the part of the past they found profoundly affecting, and they made space for the part of their present circumstance they did not, and could not, reject. A Judaism that joined strict observance to free thinking kept opposed weights in equilibrium—to be sure, in an unsteady balance.

By definition such a delicate juxtaposition could not hold. Papered over by a thick layer of words, the abyss between the way of life, resting on supernatural premises of the facticity of the Torah, and the worldview, calling into question at every point the intellectual foundations of that way of life, remained. But how did the successor generation propose to bridge the gap, so to compose a structure resting on secure foundations?

We look for the answer to a representative Conservative theologian of the second generation, active from the 1920s to the 1970s, the high tide of Conservative Judaism. The claim of Reform Judaism to constitute an increment of Judaism, we recall, rested on the position that the only constant in "Judaism" is change. The counterpart for Conservative Judaism comes to expression in the writings of Robert Gordis (a professor at the Jewish Theological Seminary of America), which, for their day, set the standard and defined the position of the center of the religion. Specifically, we seek Gordis's picture of the Judaism that came before and how he proposes to relate Conservative Judaism to that prior system. We find a forthright account of "the basic characteristics of Jewish tradition" as follows:

> The principle of development in all areas of culture and society is a fundamental element of the modern outlook. It is all the more noteworthy that the Talmud...clearly recognized the vast extent to which rabbinic Judaism had grown beyond the Bible, as well as the organic character of this process of growth....For the Talmud, tradition is not static—nor does this dynamic quality contravene either its *divine origin* or its *organic continuity* [all italics in the original]....Our concern here is with the historical fact, intuitively grasped by the Talmud, that *tradition grows.*[4]

Gordis's appeal is to historical precedent. Without the slightest concern for anachronism, the Conservative theologians found in the tradition ample proof for precisely what they proposed to do, which was, in Gordis's accurate picture, to preserve in a single system the beliefs in both the divine origin and the "organic continuity" of the Torah: that middle-ground position, between Orthodoxy and Reform, that Conservative Judaism so vastly occupied. For Gordis's generation, the argument directed itself against both Orthodoxy and Reform. In the confrontation with Orthodoxy, Gordis points to new values, institutions, and laws "created as a result of new experiences and new felt needs."

But to Reform, Gordis points out "instances of accretion and of reinterpretation, which...constitute the major modes of development in Jewish tradition." That is, change comes about historically, gradually, over time, and change does not take place by the decree of rabbinic convocations. The emphasis of the positive Historical School on the probative value of historical events, we now recognize, serves the polemic against Reform as much as against Orthodoxy. To the latter, history proves change; to the former, history dictates modes of appropriate change.

Gordis thus argues that change deserves ratification after the fact, not deliberation beforehand: "Advancing religious and ethical ideals were inner processes, often imperceptible except after the passage of centuries." Gordis, to his credit, explicitly claims, on behalf of Conservative Judaism, origin in an incremental and continuous, linear history of Judaism. He does so in an appeal to analogy:

> If tradition means development and change…how can we speak of the continuity or the spirit of Jewish tradition? An analogy may help supply the answer. Biologists have discovered that in any living organism, cells are constantly dying and being replaced by new ones.…If that be true, why is a person the same individual after the passage of…years? The answer is twofold. In the first instance, the process of change is gradual.…In the second instance, the growth follows the laws of his being. At no point do the changes violate the basic personality pattern. The organic character and unit of the personality reside in this continuity of the individual and in the development of the physical and spiritual traits inherent in him, which persist in spite of the modifications introduced by time. This recognition of the organic character of growth highlights the importance of maintaining the method by which Jewish tradition…continued to develop.[5]

The incremental theory follows the modes of thought of Reform, with their stress on the continuity of process. Here too, just as Marcus saw the permanence of change as the sole continuity, so Gordis sees the ongoing process of change as permanent. The substance of the issues, however, accords with the stress of Orthodoxy on the persistence of a fundamental character to Judaism. The method of Reform then produces the result of Orthodoxy, at least so far as practice of the way of life would go forward.

WHAT DO WE LEARN ABOUT JUDAISM
FROM CONSERVATIVE JUDAISM?

Like Orthodoxy, Conservative Judaism defined itself as Judaism, pure and simple. But it did claim to mark the natural next step in the slow evolution of "the tradition," an evolution within the lines and rules set forth by "the tradition" itself. Appeals to facts proved by scholars underline the self-evidence claimed on behalf of the system in its fully articulated form. The incapacity to discern one's own anachronistic reading of the past in line with contemporary concerns further sustains the claim that, at hand, we deal with a system of self-evidence. What truths Conservative theologians hold to be self-evident they have uncovered through a process of articulated inquiry. The answers may strike them as self-evident. But they themselves invented the questions. And they knew it.

The appeal to an incremental and linear history, a history bonded by a sustained method and enduring principles that govern change, comes long after the fact of change. Assuredly, Conservative Judaism forms a fresh system, a new creation, quite properly seeking continuity with a past that has been abandoned. For processes of change discerned after the fact and in the light of change already made or contemplated are processes not discovered but defined, then imputed by a process of deduction to historical sources that, read in other ways, scarcely sustain the claim at hand. The powerful scholarship of Conservative Judaism appealed to a reconstructed past, an invented history: a perfect faith in a new and innovative system, a Judaism discovered by its own inventors.

Conservative Judaism solved a profound human problem rather than answering an urgent question. The problem was how to make a graceful and dignified exit from a worldview and way of life that people now found alien. As between the two, they abandoned the worldview—ideas are cheap, words do not have to mean much—but they sustained the way of life, imparting to it all sorts of fresh meanings, as best they could. The insistence on continuity yielded a certain cynicism, a going-through of motions. But the human anguish for a generation deeply loyal to a world it rejected cannot escape our notice. What marks Conservative Judaism in its formulation as orthopraxy? It is its transience.

As the movement of reversion, discussed in Chapter 32, gathered strength, diverse movements of a more Orthodox and uncompromising character would serve to express the yearning of people who wished not to enshrine but to overcome alienation. The middle did not hold. In the mid-1950s, Conservative Judaism was the largest Judaism in the United States and Canada, encompassing one half of the entire Judaic population of North America. At the end of the twentieth century, it had fallen to second place, behind Reform Judaism, and held scarcely a third. The elite of Conservative Judaism found its way to Orthodoxy, and the masses, to Reform Judaism. The differences between Conservative and Reform Judaisms mattered to the virtuosi, mostly rabbis; but to ordinary folk, the two Judaisms said mostly the same things to the same people, and that sufficed.

NOTES

1. Arthur Hertzberg, "Conservative Judaism," *Encyclopaedia Judaica* (Jerusalem: Keter, 1971), vol. 5, 901–906.

2. Ibid., col. 902.

3. Ibid., col. 901.

4. Robert Gordis, *Understanding Conservative Judaism,* ed. Max Gelb (New York: Rabbinical Assembly, 1978), 26–27.

5. Ibid., 39–40.

31

The American Judaism of Holocaust and Redemption

WHAT IS "THE AMERICAN JUDAISM OF HOLOCAUST AND REDEMPTION"?

The American Judaism of Holocaust and Redemption sets forth a distinctive worldview, way of life, and definition of "Israel." The worldview appeals to the murder of millions of European Jews ("Holocaust") and the creation of the State of Israel as the center and self-evident meaning of Jews' distinctive character as a group; defines a way of life of Holocaust-memorializing and pro-Israel political activities; and when it speaks of "Israel," it means "the State of Israel." It is a Judaism wholly outside the framework of the inherited Torah, however received and interpreted, and it is a Judaism meant to answer through a political response the unanswerable question of the Holocaust. Indeed, the American Judaism of Holocaust and Redemption defines a theory of the Jewish social order that scarcely relates to, or can be classified as, a religion at all; it is essentially a system of ethnic Jewishness and shows us that not all Judaic religious systems need to take shape within the framework of religions at all, though most have. Here is the point at which the development of the ethnic and secular Jew impinges on the history of Judaisms.[1] For once Jews continued as an identifiable social group not defined by religion, or defined only partially by religion, then some Jews would identify themselves as a social entity that was Jewish but not religious and formulate a worldview and a way of life to match their sense of ethnic identification, that is, to realize their particular version of "being Israel."

Once more the issue of the ecology of Judaism faces us: under what circumstances did the issue of the Holocaust and the State of Israel become the urgent question facing a community of Jews, and what question did the self-evident answer of this Judaism settle? This Judaism's worldview stresses the unique character of the murders of European Jews, the providential and redemptive meaning of the creation of the State of Israel. The way of life requires active work in raising money and political support for the State of Israel. Different from Zionism, which held that Jews should live in a Jewish State, this system serves, in particular, to give Jews living in North America a reason and an explanation for being Jewish. This Judaism lays particular stress on the complementary experiences of mid-twentieth-century Jewry: the mass murder in death factories of six million of the Jews of Europe, and the creation of the State of Israel three years after the end of the massacre. These events, together seen as providential, bear the names Holocaust, for the murders, and redemption, for the formation of the State of Israel in the aftermath. The system as a whole presents an encompassing myth, linking one event to the other as an instructive pattern, and moves Jews to follow a particular set of actions, rather than other sorts, as it tells them why they should be Jewish.

Holocaust-and-Redemption Judaism thus finds its generative myth in two historical facts: the murder of six million Jewish children, women, and men in Europe in 1933 through 1945 by the Germans, and the creation of the State of Israel in 1948, in the aftermath of the Holocaust. This Judaic system flourishes in North America and forms the principal force in the lives of American Jews overall. That is shown by the heavy emphasis, within Jewish-ethnic and Judaic-religious life, on the matched events of mass murder and national regeneration. Measured by communal investment, the creation of Holocaust memorials in the United States and the raising of funds and political support for the State of Israel predominate, occupying the best energies of the organized Jewish communities of North America (and the rest of the diaspora as well). Not only so, but (outside Orthodox circles) sales of books on those two subjects vastly outnumber sales of books on all other Judaic subjects. Public events devoted to one of those two subjects will draw mass audiences; no other public events can do so, except for the synagogue services on the Days of Awe.

To understand the power and importance of the Judaic system of Holocaust and Redemption, we have to focus on American Jews of the third generation after the mass immigration of 1880–1920, that is, those who came of age in the years 1960–2000 (thus, the second, 1920–1960, and the third, 1960–2000). That generation held very strong convictions about how they would continue to be Jews in the setting of American life, but they treated religion as instrumental to that goal rather than as a goal in itself. Most of them hoped their children would marry within the Jewish community. Most of them joined synagogues and did so because they wanted their children to grow up as Jews. Above all, most of them regarded the fact that they are Jewish as bearing great significance.

So American Jews of the third generation continued to see everyday life in terms different from their gentile neighbors, beginning with the fact that to them, if not to their neighbors, their being Jewish seems an immensely important fact of life. The words they used to explain that fact, the symbols by which they expressed it, were quite different from those of the Judaism of the dual Torah and its continuators. They spoke, for example, of Jewishness, not Torah. They were obsessed with a crisis of identity rather than with the tasks and responsibilities of "Israel." They are deeply concerned by the opinion of gentiles.

In all, they were eager to be Jewish—but not too much so, not so much that they could not also take their place within the undifferentiated humanity of which they fantasized. They confronted a crisis not merely of identity but of commitment, for they did not choose to resolve the dilemma of separateness within an open society. In preferring separateness, they seemed entirely within the archaic realm; in dreaming of an open society, they evidently aspired to a true accomplishment of the early promise of political emancipation (which accounts for the enormous influence of Reform and Conservative Judaisms). The underlying problem was understanding what the ambiguous adjective *Jewish* is supposed to mean when the noun *Judaism* had been abandoned in its received meanings. It was the system of Holocaust and Redemption that answered the questions "Who are you? What should you do? What do you make of the other?"

TO WHOM DOES AMERICAN JUDAISM OF HOLOCAUST AND REDEMPTION PRESENT SELF-EVIDENT TRUTHS?

The Judaism of Holocaust and Redemption forms an important creation of the third and fourth generation of Jewish Americans, that is, the grandchildren and great-grandchildren of the wave of immigrants who came to the United States in the great migration of 1880–1920. The immigrants produced diverse Judaisms. But they found "being Jewish" a self-evident fact of life; they exhibited the traits of a highly distinctive and coherent ethnic group. The numerous immigrants of the later nineteenth and early twentieth centuries (from 1880 to 1920, more than 3.5 million Jews came to the United States from Russia, Poland, Rumania, Hungary, and Austria) spoke Yiddish all their lives. They pursued a limited range of occupations. They lived mainly in crowded Jewish neighborhoods of a few great cities. So the facts of language, occupation, and residence reinforced their separateness. Their several Judaisms then explained it. In this period, moreover, other immigrant groups, together with their churches, likewise found themselves constituting tight enclaves of the old country in the new.

The children of the immigrants, that is, the second generation in America, by contrast, adopted the American language and American ways of life. Its Judaisms included Conservative Judaism, which thrived in the areas to which the second generation moved, as well as Reform Judaism, which vastly changed in character and definition on account of the immigrants' children. Zionism, the Jewish national movement aiming at creating a Jewish State in the Land of Israel, a.k.a. Palestine, exercised a great attraction for a portion of that generation as well. The second generation grew up and lived in a period of severe anti-Semitism at home and in Europe, especially in the 1930s and 1940s. While trying to forget the immigrant heritage, the second generation found the world a school for Jewish consciousness, and that of a distinctively negative sort. They did not have to go to class to learn what it meant to be a Jew. Like many other groups, they were excluded, vilified, placed in a pariah caste (among many pariah castes of the multiethnic time). Jews learned their lessons (they are Jewish and it matters!) in the streets and marketplaces. Coming to maturity during the depression and World War II, the second generation did not have to decide whether to "be Jewish," nor were many decisions about what "being Jewish" demanded of them.

That set of decisions, amounting to the framing of a situation of genuine free choice, awaited the third generation, reaching its maturity some time after World War II. The years before and during and immediately after 1945 were marked by virulent anti-Semitism in the United States. Only in the later 1950s, as part of the larger reform marked by the civil rights movement, did the exclusion of the Jews from elite universities and industries (Yale and banking, for instance) ease. That generation, coming of age in about 1960, found little psychological pressure, such as had faced its predecessors, in favor of "being Jewish." Surveys of anti-Semitic opinion turned up progressively diminishing levels of Jew hatred. More important, whereas the second generation had strong memories of Yiddish-speaking parents and lives of a distinctively Jewish character, the third generation in the main did not. For in line with Marcus Lee Hanson's law, which says that the third generation wants to remember what the second generation tried to forget, the second generation made a vigorous effort to forget what it knew. The third generation had to make a decision to learn what it did not know, indeed, what it had no natural reason, in its upbringing and family heritage, to know.

American Judaism of Holocaust and Redemption is the creation of that third generation, the result of its conscientious effort to remember what its parents equally deliberately forgot. The decision was made in a free society and represented free and uncoerced choice. So the third generation forms the first generation of Judaism in a very long sequence of centuries to have the right to decide in an open society whether to be Jewish. More interesting, it is the first generation to define for itself what "being Jewish" would consist of, and how Judaism, as an inherited and received religious tradition, would be taken over as part of this definition.

THE WORLDVIEW OF "HOLOCAUST-AND-REDEMPTION" JUDAISM

A Judaism may bear its worldview in the form not of theological propositions but of a myth, a mode of conveying deep truth and abiding meaning in the form of a story. Let me recount the salvific story of Holocaust and Redemption as it is nearly universally perceived by American Jews. We refer to the reading of the experience of the community as a whole, that is, how the myth sees things. But the power of the myth, the story at hand, profoundly grips not those about whom the story is told but those to whom the story bears meaning. So we speak of a long past, but we mean the present. But here is how the story might go, as I would attempt to tell the tale:

> Once upon a time, when I was a young man, I felt helpless before the world. I was a Jew, when being Jewish was a bad thing. As a child, I saw

my old Jewish parents, speaking a foreign language and alien in countless ways, isolated from America. And I saw America, dimly perceived to be sure, exciting and promising, but hostile to me as a Jew. I could not get into a good college. I could not aspire to medical school. I could not become an architect or an engineer. I could not even work for an electric utility.

When I took my vacation, I could not go just anywhere, but had to ask whether Jews would be welcome, tolerated, embarrassed, or thrown out. Being Jewish was uncomfortable. Yet I could not give it up. My mother and my father had made me what I was. I could hide, but could not wholly deny, not to myself even if to others, that I was a Jew. And I could not afford the price in diminished self-esteem of opportunity denied, aspiration deferred, and insult endured. Above all, I saw myself as weak and pitiful. I could not do anything about being a Jew nor could I do much to improve my lot as a Jew.

Then came Hitler and I saw that what was my private lot was the dismal fate of every Jew. Everywhere Jew hatred was raised from the gutter to the heights. Not from Germany alone, but from people I might meet at work or in the streets I feared that being Jewish was a metaphysical evil. "The Jews" were not accepted but debated. Friends would claim we were not all bad. Enemies said we were. And we had nothing to say at all.

As I approached maturity, a still more frightening fact confronted me. People guilty of no crime but Jewish birth were forced to flee their homeland, and no one would accept them. Ships filled with ordinary men, women, and children searched the oceans for a safe harbor. And I and they had nothing in common but one fact, and that fact made all else inconsequential. Had I been there, I should have been among them. I too, should not have been saved at the sea.

Then came the war and, in its aftermath, the revelation of the shame and horror of holocaust, the decay and corrosive hopelessness of the displaced person camps where survivors of the war were warehoused, the contempt of the nations who would neither accept nor help the saved remnants of hell.

At the darkest hour came the dawn. The State of Israel saved the remnant and gave meaning and significance to the inferno. After the dawn, the great light: Jews no longer helpless, weak, unable to decide their own fate, but strong, confident, decisive.

And then came the corrupting doubt: if I were there, I should have died in hell, but now has come redemption and I am here, not there.

How much security in knowing that if it should happen again I shall not be lost. But how great a debt paid in guilt for being where I am and who I am!

This story gives meaning and transcendence to the petty lives of ordinary people. The story recapitulates the most profound traits of myths capable of nearly universal appeal. It forms Judaic example of the myth of the darkness followed by light, of passage through the netherworld and past the gates of hell, then, purified by suffering and by blood, into the new age. The myth conforms to the supernatural structure of the classic myths of salvific religions from time immemorial.

And well it might, for a salvific myth has to tell the story of sin and redemption, disaster and salvation, the old being and the new, a vanquishing of death and mourning, crying and pain, the passing away of former things. This is the myth—the narrative expression of the worldview—that shapes the mind and imagination of American Jewry, supplies the correct interpretation and denotes the true significance of everyday events, and turns workaday people into saints. This is the myth that transforms commonplace affairs into history, makes writing a check into a sacred act. So the generations that lived through disaster and triumph, darkness and light, understand the world in terms of a salvific myth. The generations that have merely heard about the darkness but have daily lived in the light take for granted the very redemption that lies at the heart of the salvific myth.

So much for the Holocaust, transformed from the mundane murders of millions into a tale about cosmic evil, unique and beyond all comparing. We come to the other half, the Redemption, which is symbolized by the use of the word *Israel*—the State of Israel, the Jewish State. The Holocaust formed the question; Redemption in the form of the creation of the State of Israel, the answer. It is that simple.

Why so simple? Because nearly all American Jews identify with the State of Israel and regard its welfare as more than a secular good but a metaphysical necessity: the other chapter of the Holocaust. Nearly all American Jews not only are supporters of the State of Israel. They also regard their own "being Jewish" as inextricably bound up with the meaning they impute to the Jewish State. But critical to the way of life of the system of American Judaism is scarcely a single important component of Zionism in its own systemic formulation. American Judaism absorbs and reworks for its own systemic purposes the creation of the State of Israel. American Judaism is not a Zionism. For Zionism always insisted, and the State of Israel today maintains, that immigration to the State of Israel forms the highest goal, indeed the necessary condition, for true Zionism.

And nearly six million American Jews, including a great many deeply engaged by the Judaic system at hand, presently exhibit not the slightest intention of migrating anywhere, though they gladly pay visits. But that is not Zionism. So what way of life does give substance to the doctrine? And how does a story of a tragedy of incalculable sorrow on one continent, finding a happy ending in the creation of a new nation on a second continent, find so deep meaning for Jews living two oceans away, on yet a third continent? That seems to me the analytical fulcrum of the Judaism of Holocaust and Redemption: why the formation of Jewish Americans, whence the power of self-evidence to people utterly alien—in their personal lives—to the experiences by which they interpret their existence.

THE WAY OF LIFE OF "HOLOCAUST-AND-REDEMPTION" JUDAISM

Let us begin once again with a picture of an individual and ask what that person does to carry out in everyday life the expectations of the worldview at hand. We deal with a Judaism that makes an ample place for women. Before us stands the president of a federation or a synagogue or a Hadassah chapter (Women's Zionist Organization). He or she has devoted most of his or her spare time—and much time that could not be spared—to the raising of funds for these and similar good causes for twenty years or more. If a woman, she has given up many afternoons and nights to the business of her organization; has attended conferences of states, regions, and "national"; has badgered speakers to speak for nothing and merchants to contribute to rummage sales—and all for the good cause. If a man, he has patiently moved through the chairs of the communal structure, on the board of this client agency, president of that one, then onward and upward to lead a "division" of a "campaign," then to head a campaign, to sit on the board. Above all, both men and women have found for their lives transcendent meaning in the raising of funds for Jewish causes.

"Mr. President," "Madam Chairwoman"—both have exhibited not only selflessness but also iron determination. They have enjoyed the good conscience of those for whom the holy end justifies all legitimate secular means. They worked for a salvation of which they were certain, and it was, despite appearances, not of this world. The makers of American Judaism have seen a vision and kept alive its memory. They have dedicated their lives to the realization of their holy vision, just as much as the students of Torah in another place and time gave their lives to the study of Torah—for all, a salvific enterprise, an exercise in the realized eschaton, in Heaven on Earth. They did not see their lives as trivial, their works as unimportant, because their lives were spent on significant things. Not for them the beaches of Florida, the gambling tables of Nevada. Their works were for a sacred goal. Superficially, these claims seem extravagant.

What transcendent importance is to be located in the eleemosynary activities of the mattress makers' division of the local Federation of Jewish philanthropies, devoted to raising money for the State of Israel and domestic Jewish purposes also? Of what salvific consequence the leisure-time activities of a pants manufacturer in Hoboken? What great goals are perceived by men who spend their lives filling holes in teeth, litigating negligence claims, or running a store? How has Madam Chairwoman attained the end of days, merely by meeting her quota? These are the types of questions confronting an interpretation of the Judaism of Holocaust and Redemption.

What do devotees of the Judaic system of American Judaism actually do to deserve my commendation as people who do things that save the world? They engage in a life of organizing for the accomplishment of good works. They raise vast sums of money for domestic and overseas support. For one example, in addition to their work of sustaining their community here at home and also a myriad of philanthropic activities in Jewish communities abroad and in the State of Israel, they select particular, poor neighborhoods in Israeli towns. These they make their own, through visits and personal concern. Again, because political action forms a vital part of support for the State of Israel, they work hard in political affairs, seeking friends for the Jewish community and the State of Israel. In so doing, they undertake selfless commitments that demand much of their energy and time: they are women and men who live for others.

What then defined the great goal? Preserving the safe place for Jews to live out their lives—if they need it. In many ways these Jews every day of their lives relive the terror-filled years in which European Jews were wiped out—*and every day they do something about it*. It is as if people spent their lives trying to live out a cosmic myth and, through rites of expiation and regeneration, accomplished the goal of purification and renewal. Highfalutin language for humble deeds? True. But appropriate words as well.

The participants in American Judaism rightly claim to have helped improve the world. But they themselves claim to be more than merely good and useful people. They see themselves as engaged in serving a cause of salvific valence, whose righteousness confers on them enviable certainty, a sense of worth beyond doubt or measure. These saints are as certain of their vision of the world—a vision of the work of redemption following the near-victory of evil—as were the saints of the olden days. Enjoying the certainty of a self-validating vision of the world, possessed of the security derived from the right understanding of perceived history, illuminated by an all-encompassing view of Jewish realities, they are the saved. What characterizes group life in modern times is the development of specialists for various tasks, the organization of society for the accomplishment of tasks once performed individually and in an amateur way, the growth of professionalism, the reliance on large institutions. The way of life of American Judaism requires joining and supporting organizations—thus the so-called "culture of organizations."

THE SELF-EVIDENCE OF "HOLOCAUST-AND-REDEMPTION" JUDAISM AS A JUDAISM

The worldview of Holocaust-and-Redemption Judaism and the way of life persuade participants before, and without, sustained argument. The worldview so closely corresponds to, and yet so magically transforms and elevates, reality that people take vision and interpretation for fact. They do not need to believe in or affirm the myth, for they know it to be true. In that they are confident of the exact correspondence between reality and the story that explains reality, they are the saved—the saints, the witnesses to the end of days. "We know this is how things really were and what they really meant." At what point did the Judaism of Holocaust and Redemption take a position of paramount importance among the Jews of North America and become the self-evident Judaism of the bulk of the organized Jewish community?

Three factors, among the Jews, reinforced one another in turning the Judaism of Holocaust and Redemption into a set of self-evident and descriptive facts, truths beyond all argument: (1) the Six Day War of 1967, (2) the reethnicization of American life, and (3) the transformation of the mass murder of European Jews into an event of mythic and world-destroying proportions.

Why date the birth of the Judaism of Holocaust and Redemption so precisely to the 1967 war? People take as routine the importance of the State of Israel in American Jewish consciousness. But in the 1940s and 1950s, American Jewry had yet to translate its deep sympathy for the Jewish State into political activity, on the one side, and the shaping element for local cultural activity and sentiment, on the other. So too the memory of the destruction of European Jewry did not right away become "the Holocaust," as a formative event in contemporary Jewish consciousness. In fact, the reethnicization of the Jews could not have taken the form that it did—a powerful identification with the State of Israel as the answer to the question of "the Holocaust"—without a single, catalytic event.

That event was the 1967 war between the State of Israel and its Arab neighbors. When, on June 5, after a long period of threat, the dreaded war of "all against one" began, American Jews feared the worst. Six days later they confronted an unimagined outcome, with the State of Israel standing on the Jordan River, the Nile, and the outskirts of Damascus. The trauma of the weeks preceding the war, when the Arabs promised to drive the Jews into the sea and no other power intervened or promised help, renewed for the third generation the nightmare of the second. Once more the streets and newspapers became the school for being Jewish. On that account the Judaism in formation took up a program of urgent questions—and answered them.

In the trying weeks before June 5, 1967, American Jewry relived the experience of the second generation and the third. In the 1930s and 1940s, the age of Hitler's Germany and the murder of the European Jews in death factories, every day's newspaper brought lessons of Jewish history. Everybody knew that were he or she in Europe, death would be the sentence on account of the crime of Jewish birth. And the world was then indifferent. No avenues of escape were opened to the Jews who wanted to flee, and many roads to life were deliberately blocked by anti-Semitic foreign service officials. The contemporary parallel? In 1967 the Arab states threatened to destroy the State of Israel and murder its citizens. The Israelis turned to the world. The world again ignored Jewish suffering, and a new "Holocaust" impended. But now the outcome was quite different. The entire history of the century at hand came under a new light. A moment of powerful and salvific weight placed into a fresh perspective everything that had happened from the beginning to the present.

The third generation now had found its memory and its hope, as much as Zionism had invented a usable past. It now could confront the murder of the Jews of Europe, along with its parents' and its own experience of exclusion and bigotry. No longer was it necessary to avoid painful, intolerable memories. Now what had happened had to be remembered, because it bore within itself the entire message of the new day in Judaism. That is, putting together the murder of nearly six million Jews of Europe with the creation of the State of Israel transformed both events. One became "the Holocaust," the purest statement of evil in all of human history. The other became salvation in the form of "the first appearance of our redemption" (as the language of the Jewish prayer for the State of Israel has it). Accordingly, a moment of stark epiphany captured the entire experience of the age and imparted to it that meaning and order that a religious system has the power to express as self-evident. The self-evident system of American Judaism, then, for the third generation encompassed a salvific myth deeply and personally relevant to the devotees. That myth made sense at a single instant equally of both the world and the self, of what the newspapers had to say, and of what the individual understood in personal life.

THE ETHNICIZATION OF RELIGION

The distinctively American form of Judaism under description here clearly connects to the Judaism of the dual Torah. But it is not at all continuous with it. In that regard it is profoundly different from Orthodox, Reform, and Conservative Judaisms, all of them efforts at negotiating with that Judaism and its holy books. American Judaism draws on some of the received religious tradition and claims to take up the whole of it. But in its stress on the realization, in the here and now, of ultimate evil and salvation, and in its mythicization of contemporary history, this American Judaism offers a distinctively American and ethnic reading of the received tradition. This is by definition. For when Jews have come to speak of fully realized salvation and an end of history, the result has commonly proved to be a new Judaism, a religious system, connected to but not continuous with the received religion of Judaism. Here, by contrast, the urgent questions and the self-evidently valid answers address the condition of an ethnic group and do nothing to transform that condition into cosmic and transcendental terms. We deal with a this-worldly answer to a political question.

Specifically, we ask what urgent questions find their answers in the system at hand. To answer that question, we have to turn back, once more, to an earlier period, before the public recognition of the self-evidence of the Judaism of Holocaust and Redemption. From 1945 to about 1965, the Holocaust was subsumed under the "problem of evil." The dominant theological voices of the time did not address themselves to "radical evil" and did not claim that something had happened to change the classical theological perspective of Judaism. The theologians of the day wrote not as if nothing had happened but as if nothing had happened to impose a new perspective on the whole past of Jewish religious experience. To be sure, the liberal, world-affirming optimism of the old theological left was shaken. But the Holocaust was part, not the whole, of the problem. The evil of humanity in conventional rhetoric came to realization in more than that one way. Indeed, few called to mind the murder of European Jewry, and "the Holocaust" did not yet exist.

Clearly, something happened between the end of the 1950s and the beginning of the 1970s. This was an experience so fundamental as to impart to the massacre of European Jewry a symbolic meaning, self-evident importance, and mythic quality. Jews had been put to death in unimaginably dreadful circumstances. What happened was a sequence of events, some general, some particular to the Jews: the assassination of President Kennedy, the disheartening war in Southeast Asia—Vietnam, Laos, and Cambodia—and a renewed questioning of the foundations of religious and social polity. "Auschwitz" became a Jewish code word for all the things everyone was talking about, a kind of Judaic key word for the common cause. People found a number of problems—the tragic murders of political leaders, the two Kennedys and King in particular; the unwanted war in Vietnam; unrest in urban ghettos—a whole host of national disappointments that added up to a malaise. And the Jews' code word for that malaise was "Auschwitz," which stood for everything troubling everybody but made it all particular to the Jews. That—and nothing more. The Jewish theologians who claim that from Holocaust events one must draw conclusions essentially different from those reached after the destruction of the Second Temple or other tragic moments posit that "our sorrow is unlike any other, our memories more searing." But they say so in response not to the events of which they speak but through those events, to a quite different situation—their own.

What turned a historical event into a powerful symbol of contemporary social action and imagination was a searing shared experience. For millions of Jews, the dreadful weeks before the 1967 war gave a new vitality to the historical record of the years 1933–1945—the war and its result. But the story of the extermination of European Jewry could not serve as the foundation for a usable myth of "Holocaust" without one further component. No myth is serviceable if people cannot make it their own and through it explain their own lives; no story of a life can end in gruesome death. A corollary of "Holocaust," therefore, had to be redemption. The extermination of European Jewry could become "the Holocaust" only on June 9, when, in the aftermath of a remarkable victory, the State of Israel celebrated the return of the people of Israel to the ancient wall of the Temple of Jerusalem. On that day, the extermination of European Jewry attained the—if not happy, at least viable—ending that served to transform events into a myth and to endow a symbol with a single, ineluctable meaning.

As is clear from the reference to the murders of the Kennedys and King, the tragedy of Southeast Asia, and the unrest in the United States that marked the 1960s and early 1970s, the questions answered by American Judaism are two separate and distinct ones, the first addressed to the particular world of the Jews, the second to the world at large. The first question is, Why should I be different? Why should I be Jewish? The second is, How should I relate to the world at large? The Judaism of Holocaust and Redemption made available a powerful and critical experience in answer to the question of why be Jewish: "Because you have no choice." That same Judaism explained that "Israel" should relate to the world at large in its own state and nation overseas—and in its distinctive and distinct communities at home. So the two questions answered by American Judaism speak to the inner world and to the policy toward the outer world as well.

But the two questions are not unrelated, for both of them emerge from the special circumstances of the American of Jewish origin whose grandparents or great-grandparents immigrated to this country. For that sort of American Jew, there is no common and acknowledged core of religious experience by which "being Jewish" may be explained and interpreted. Because anti-Semitism as a perceived social experience has become less common than it was from the 1920s through the early 1950s, there is also no common core of social alienation to account for the distinctive character of the group and explain why it continues, and must continue, to endure. Indeed, many American Jews, though they continue to affirm their Jewishness, have no clear notion of how they are Jewish or what their Jewish heritage demands of them. Judaism is, for this critical part of the American Jewish population, merely a reference point, one fact among many. For ideologists of the Jewish community, the most certain answer to the question of the third generation must be "There is no real choice." And "the Holocaust" provides that answer: "Hitler knew you were Jewish. So you too should know, and affirm, you are Jewish. So what? That's what." Here we listen to the voice of ethnicity for its own sake.

The formative experiences of "the Holocaust" are now immediately accessible through emotions unmediated by sentiment or sensibility. No person can encounter the events of 1933–1945 without entering into them in imagination. It is better to understate the matter. The experience of "the Holocaust" is not something that ended in 1945; it ends when I wake up in the morning, and it is renewed when I go to sleep. And so it is for all of us. These "Judaizing experiences," then, take the place of Sinai in nurturing an inner and distinctive consciousness of "being Jewish." So the first of the two questions before us, the inner one, is the question of who "we" are and why we are what we are and not something else. "The Holocaust" is made to answer that question.

The second is a social question. Let us phrase it in the discourse of the people who participate: Who are we in relationship to everybody else? The utility of "the Holocaust" in this context is not difficult to see, once we realize that the TV counterpart to "Holocaust" is *Roots.* It follows that, for American Jews, "the Holocaust" is that ethnic identity available to a group of people so far removed from culturally and socially distinctive characteristics as to be otherwise wholly "assimilated." "The Holocaust" is the Jews' special thing: it is what sets them apart from others while giving them a claim on those others. That is why Jews insist on "the uniqueness of the Holocaust." If blacks on campus have soul food, the Jews will have kosher meals, even if they do not keep the dietary laws under ordinary circumstances. Unstated in this simple equation, *Roots* = "Holocaust," is the idea that being Jewish is an ethnic, not primarily a religious, category. For nearly a century, American Jews have persuaded themselves and their neighbors that they fall into the religious—and therefore acceptable—category of being "different," and not into the ethnic—and therefore crippling and unwanted—category of being "different." Now that they have no Jewish accent, they are willing to be ethnic.

So a profound inner dilemma and a difficult matter of social differentiation and identification work themselves out within the myth of "Holocaust." As to the "redemption" chapter of the story, the State of Israel tells the same truths to American as it does to Israeli Jews. But because American Jews do not, and cannot, infer the same consequences from that story of redemption that Israeli Jews must infer, a certain incongruity has arisen between the two versions. After all, it is difficult to speak much about a redemption that we do not really wish to experience. A salvation that works for others and not for oneself is, in the end, not of much value. Thus, the "Holocaust" part of the myth tends to play a larger part in this country than it does in the State of Israel.

The human dimension of the Judaic system of Holocaust and Redemption finds its measure in the North America of the 1960s and 1970s. Third-generation American Jews found in the continuator-Judaisms of the synagogue something conventional and irrelevant. To make of those Judaisms the model for viable life—an explanation of the world, an account of how to live—Jews found they had to give what they did not have. What was required was either memories few possessed or the effort to locate a road back that few found the will to invest. The world of the everyday did not provide access to so subtle and alien a worldview as that of the Judaism of the dual Torah and its conception of humanity and of Israel, let alone to the way of life formed within that worldview.

How, then, to engage the emotions without the mediation of learning in the Torah? And how to define a way of life that imparted distinction without much material difference? To state matters in a homely way, what distinctively Judaic way of life would allow devotees to eat whatever they wanted anyhow? The answer to both questions—access to the life of feeling and experience, to the way of life that made one distinctive without leaving the person terribly different from everybody else—emerged in the Judaic system of Holocaust and Redemption. This system presented an immediately accessible message, cast in extreme emotions of terror and triumph, its round of endless activity demanding only spare time. In all, the system of American Judaism of Holocaust and Redemption realizes in a poignant way the conflicting demands of Jewish Americans to be intensely Jewish, but only once in a while, and not exacting much of a cost in meaningful difference from others.

NOTE

1. Another such point is the advent, for the first time in the history of the Jews, of apostates from Judaism who wish to belong to the Jewish community. Until the end of the twentieth century, when Jews converted to another religion—for instance, Christianity—they cut their ties to Jewry and excluded themselves. They went to church, raised their children as Christians, and desired no further

affiliation with the Jewish group. In the final decades of this millennium, by contrast, "Jews for Jesus," practicing "Messianic Judaism," converted to Christianity but wanted to remain active members of the (secular) Jewish community; converts to Christianity migrated to the State of Israel and claimed citizenship under the Law of Return that accords automatic citizenship to all (ethnic) Jews, without religious test. Converts to Christianity in San Antonio remained on the board of Hadassah, the Women's Zionist Organization, and in Utica remained office holders of the synagogue itself. These are some of the complications for the life of Jewry brought about by the secularization and ethnicization of the category of rabbinic Judaism, Holy Israel.

32

How Jews Practice Judaism in North America

WHAT THE BOOKS SAY, WHAT THE PEOPLE DO

The holy books say one thing about a religion, the people who believe in and practice that religion do quite another. Because religion defines the meaning of life for most Americans and shapes community life for many, bridging the gap between religion as described and religion as lived demands our attention. In fact, trying to understand the difference between official religion and believed and practiced religion defines a central problem in making sense of religion as we see it in today's world. Apart from small circles of the truly and consistently pious, people do make choices about what counts and what does not, or, more to the point, what can be compromised or neglected, and what is going to matter.

What makes the problem interesting for the study of religion is simple: the same Catholic who practices birth control goes to confession and Mass, and Baptists who drink beer Saturday night sing with a full voice and love of God Sunday morning, and in many instances Jews who eat unkosher food out eat only kosher food at home. All of these choices make of religion something strange and wonderful, original and incomprehensible, but they demand attention: how do we explain the difference, how do people know the difference between what is required and what—acceptably, amiably, with all the good will in the world—is actually done? And, more to the point of an introduction to Judaism, what do we learn about Judaism from the choices people make?

WHAT THE JEWISH PEOPLE IN NORTH AMERICA DO: THE SOCIAL SCIENCE PORTRAIT OF JUDAISM

To describe the generality of Jews' conduct in religious matters, some data outlining a broad consensus, excluding only the fringes, may be helpful. These are in two directions. On the one side are the total integrationists, on the far side of Reform Judaism, who retain only a residual connection with Judaism by reason of birth (and, if male, possibly, though not unanimously, circumcision) but have opted out of Jewry. Such people locate themselves out of reach of social scientific study, because there is no way of identifying them by any actions generally defined as Judaic in character (for example, synagogue attendance) or Jewish in ethnicity (for example, giving money to a Jewish charity or supporting the State of Israel in politics). Doing none of the things that are measurable, they also do not count when we ask about the things they do not do. It is not for us to declare them no longer Jews; but in any study of Judaism as a religion, they do not wish to be included, and so the data they provide concern the sociology of Jewry but not the morphology of Judaism.

On the other side are the total segregationists, on the far side of Orthodox Judaism, who have chosen to live so far as they can entirely outside of the framework of American life. Their Judaism is not described in accounts of the generality of American Jews, because they form too small a percentage to matter.

Current social studies of Judaism in North America yield a consensus that all surveys have produced.[1] Among the many religious occasions and obligations set forth by the Torah, American Jews in the aggregate do practice some and not others. Take demography for starters. The United States counts as a "Jewishly identified population" some 6,840,000. Of these, 4.2 million identify themselves as born Jews with the religion Judaism. They embody all the Judaisms that flourish in North America. Another 1.1 million call themselves born Jews with no religion. Adults of Jewish parentage with some other religion than Judaism are 415,000. Born of Jewish parents, raised as Jewish, and converted to some other religion number 210,000. Jews by choice ("converts") are 185,000. Children under 18 being raised in a religion other than Judaism are 700,000.[2] It follows that the "core Jewish population" is 5.5 million, of which approximately 80 percent—4.4 million—are Jews by religion.

The distinction between the ethnic and the religious, with which we began our study of Judaism, takes on weight when we examine popular opinion on whether the Jews are a religious group, an ethnic group, a cultural group, or a nationality. A 1991 report states, "Being Jewish as defined by cultural group membership is the clear preference of three of the four identity groups [Jews by birth, religion, Judaism; Jews by choice, converts; Jews by birth with no religion; born and raised Jewish, converted out; adults of Jewish parentage with another current religion]. Definition in terms of ethnic group was the second highest and was cited more frequently than the religious concept by every Jewish identity group."[3] Jews who thought of themselves as a religious group were 49 percent of those who said they were born Jews, religion Judaism; 35 percent of born Jews with no religion; 56 percent of born and raised Jews who converted out; and 40 percent of adults of Jewish parents with another current religion.

The further figure that affects our study (besides the 4.4 million, which defines its parameters) concerns intermarriage patterns. At this time, 68 per-

cent of all currently married Jews by birth (1.7 million) are married to someone who was also born Jewish. However:

> The choice of marriage partners has changed dramatically over the past few
> decades. In recent years just over half of born Jews who married, at any age,
> whether for the first time or not, chose a spouse who was born a Gentile
> and has remained so, while less than 5 percent of these marriages include a
> non-Jewish partner who became a Jew by choice. As a result, since 1985,
> twice as many mixed couples, that is, born Jew with gentile spouse, have
> been created as Jewish couples (Jewish with Jewish spouse). This picture...
> tends to underestimate the total frequency, because it does not include cur-
> rently born-Jews divorced or separated from an intermarriage nor Jew-Gen-
> tile unmarried couple relationships and living arrangements.[4]

Wertheimer, too, comments on the matter of intermarriage, in these terms:
"Intermarriage has exploded on the American Jewish scene since the mid-
1960s, rapidly rising in incident to the point where as many as two out of five
Jews who wed marry a partner who was not born Jewish."[5] In Reform Judaism, he reports, 31 percent of the lay leaders of Reform temples reported
having a child married to a non-Jewish spouse. So the first thing that captures
our attention is that the single most important building block of Judaism, the
family—expression in the here and now of the sacred genealogy of Israel, that
is, "the children of Israel"—wobbles.

Restricting our attention to the Judaists and the ethnic Jews (Kosmin et
al.'s born Jews, religion Judaism, and born Jews with no religion), what do we
learn about religious beliefs?

1. The Torah is the actual word of God: 13 percent concur (but 10 percent
   of born Jews with no religion do, too—not a very impressive differential).

2. The Torah is the inspired word of God, but not everything should be
   taken literally word for word: 38 percent of Judaists concur, and 19 percent of the ethnicists.

3. The Torah is an ancient book of history and moral precepts recorded by
   man: 45 percent of the Judaists, 63 percent of the ethnicist Jews concur.

4. Finally, 4 percent of the Judaists and 8 percent of the ethnicists had no
   opinion.

It follows that, by the criterion of belief in the basic proposition of the Judaism of the dual Torah, the Torah is the word of God, 13 percent of the Judaists concur; another 38 percent agree that the Torah is the inspired word of
God but not literally so; and another 45 percent value the Torah. If we were
to posit that these numbers represent Orthodox, Conservative, and Reform
Judaisms, we should not be far off the mark.

In fact, the denominational figures that Kosmin et al.'s report gives are as follows (current Jewish denominational preferences of adult Jews by religion are equivalent to our Judaists):

Denomination	Proportion of Those Polled (%)	Proportion of Households (%)
Orthodox	6.6	16
Conservative	37.8	43
Reform	42.4	35
Reconstructionist	1.4	2
"Just Jewish"	5.4	Not available

Of the Judaists, 80 percent are Reform or Conservative, approximately 7 percent, Orthodox. The comparatively high level of identification with Orthodoxy is strictly a phenomenon in the greater New York City area. Elsewhere, the percentage of Orthodox Jews in the community of Judaists is still lower.[6] The denominational choice of the rest is scattered. A slightly earlier study by Kosmin (for 1987) divided the Jews in general as follows: 2 percent Reconstructionist, 9 percent Orthodox, 29 percent Reform, 34 percent Conservative, and 26 percent "other" or "just Jewish." It is not clear whether the distinction between Jews and Judaists is reflected in these figures, but the upshot is not in doubt.[7] Kosmin et al. further observe that there is "a general trend of movement away from traditional Judaism. While one quarter of the born Jewish religion Judaism group was raised in Orthodox households, only 7 percent report themselves as Orthodox now." Not only so, but

> nearly 90 percent of those now Orthodox were raised as such, thus indicating any movement toward Orthodoxy is relatively small. In contrast to the Orthodox, the Conservative and Reform drew heavily from one or both of the major denominations; one third of the Conservatives were raised as Orthodox, and one-quarter of the Reform as Conservative, with an additional 12 percent having been raised Orthodox.[8]

Wertheimer also observes that the trend is away from Orthodoxy and Conservatism and toward Reform Judaism: "Nationally, the Conservative movement still commands the allegiance of a plurality of Jews, albeit a shrinking plurality. The main beneficiary of Orthodox and Conservative losses seems to be the Reform movement."[9] As to synagogue affiliation, "Synagogue affiliation is the most widespread form of formal Jewish connection, but it characterized only 41 percent of the entirely Jewish households."[10] Furthermore, a discrepancy between calling oneself Reform and belonging to a Reform temple is noted: "The distribution of the 860,000 households reporting synagogue membership across the denominations shows that the Reform plurality, which was evidence for denominational preferences, does not translate directly into affiliation. By contrast, the Orthodox are more successful in affiliating their potential constituency."[11]

How about religious practice of the Judaists, the center of concern for this inquiry? Here the figures cover only three matters:

Fast on the Day of Atonement	61 percent
Attend synagogue on high holidays	59 percent
Attend synagogue weekly	11 percent

Every study for several decades has replicated these results: lots of people go to Passover seders, a great many also observe the so-called High Holy Days (in the Torah, "the Days of Awe"—that is, Rosh Hashanah, the New Year, and Yom Kippur, the Day of Atonement). So why do people who do not pray weekly (or daily) in community come to synagogue worship for the New Year and the Day of Atonement? In other words, why do approximately half of the Judaists who worship in community at all do so only three days a year? How do they know what is fit and proper: this day, not that?

As to rites at home and household practices, Kosmin and his colleagues shift to entirely Jewish households, as against mixed Jewish and gentile households—that is, from the Judaist to the Jewish (and a sensible shift at that):

Attend Passover seder	86 percent
Never have Christmas tree	82 percent
Light Hanukkah candles	77 percent
Light Sabbath candles	44 percent
Belong to a synagogue	41 percent
Eat kosher meat all the time	17 percent

What makes Passover different from all other holidays? Clearly, that question must come up first. What makes Sabbath candles (all the more so, the weekly Sabbath as a holy day of rest) only half so important as Hanukkah candles (one week out of the year)?

Because the Torah devotes considerable attention to the foods that may sustain the life of holy Israel, and because the ethnic Jews too identify foods as particularly Jewish, we may ask about the matter of observance of dietary rules in Conservative Judaism, which affirms them and regards them as a key indicator of piety. Charles S. Liebman and Saul Shapiro report[12] that among the Conservative Jews they surveyed, 5 percent of the men and 6.4 percent of the women report that they observe the dietary laws both at home and away (by the standards of Conservative Judaism, which are somewhat more lenient than those of Orthodoxy); 29.2 percent of the men and 28.8 percent of the women have kosher homes but do not keep the dietary taboos away from home. Approximately a third of the Conservative homes, then, appear to be conducted in accord with the laws of kosher food.

Liebman and Shapiro comment that the home of the parents of those in this group also was kosher, and observance of the dietary laws correlates with Jewish education:

Of the children receiving a day school education, 66 percent come from kosher homes; of all those who attended Camp Ramah [a Jewish education summer camp run by the Conservative movement], 53 percent came from kosher homes; this despite the fact that only 34 percent of the parents report their homes are kosher. The differences are even more dramatic if one bears in mind that a disproportionate number of older Conservative synagogue members have kosher homes, which means that their children were educated at a time when day school education was much less widespread in the Jewish community.

Along these same lines, Steven M. Cohen introduces the metaphor of "an artichoke syndrome," in which

> the outer layers of the most traditional forms of Jewish expression are peeled away until only the most essential and minimal core of involvement remains, and then that also succumbs to the forces of assimilation...according to assimilationist expectations, ritual observance and other indicators of Jewish involvement decline successively from parents to children.[13]

But current studies do not "support a theory predicting uniform decline in ritual practice from one generation to the next. Rather, they suggest intergenerational flux with a limited movement toward a low level of observance entailing Passover Seder attendance, Hanukkah candle lighting, and fasting on Yom Kippur."[14] In yet other studies, Cohen speaks of "moderately affiliated Jews," who nearly unanimously "celebrate High Holidays, Hanukkah and Passover, belong to synagogues when their children approach age 12 and 13, send their children to afternoon school or Sunday school, and at least occasionally support the Federation [that is, UJA] campaigns."[15] Cohen speaks of "broad affection for Jewish family, food, and festivals."

Here, Cohen's report provides especially valuable data. He explains "why Jews feel so affectionate toward their holidays":

> One theme common to the six items [celebrated by from 70 to over 90 percent surveyed] is family. Holidays are meaningful because they connect Jews with their family-related memories, experiences, and aspirations. Respondents say that they want to be with their families on Jewish holidays, that they recall fond childhood memories at those times, and that they especially want to connect their own children with Jewish traditions at holiday time. Moreover, holidays evoke a certain transcendent significance; they have ethnic and religious import; they connect one with the history of the Jewish people, and they bear a meaningful religious message. Last, food...constitutes a major element in Jews' affection for the holidays.[16]

The holidays that are most widely celebrated in this report remain the same as in the others: Passover, Hanukkah, and the High Holy Days. By contrast, "relatively few respondents highly value three activities: observing the Sabbath, adult Jewish education, and keeping kosher." The question comes to the fore once again: why those rites and not others, why those rites in preference to others?

How about Israeli matters? Among the Judaists, 31 percent have visited the State of Israel, 35 percent have close family or friends living there; among the ethnic Jews (not Judaists), the figures are 11 percent and 20 percent, respectively. Here is another question: What makes the State of Israel so important to the Judaists? Along the same lines comes charity, including Israel-centered charity (UJA, for instance) (once more speaking of entirely Jewish households):

Contributed to a Jewish charity in 1989	62 percent
Contributed to UJA/Federation campaign in 1989	45 percent
Celebrate Israeli independence day	18 percent

And, for comparison:

Contributed to a secular charity in 1989	67 percent
Contributed to a political campaign in 1988–1990	36 percent

Remarking on the Kosmin report, one commentator said, "In a radical change from just a generation ago, American Jews today are as likely to marry non-Jews as Jews. But even as this assimilation accelerates, Jews are clinging to religious traditions....These trends—one away from tradition, the other maintaining tradition—are spelled out."[17]

Covering a variety of issues, Wertheimer proposes to "evaluate the state of contemporary Jewish religious life," with special attention to changing patterns of religious observance, which concern this inquiry into the contrast between book Judaism and practiced Judaism.[18] Orthodoxy, conceded by all parties to be closest in popular observance to the Judaism described in the holy books, retains its young people but at the same time loses its older population, a disproportionately large component of its numbers, to death, with from two to three times as many Orthodox Jews over age 65 as between 18 and 45. Thus, the gap between the books as lived by everyday Jews and the conduct of the generality of Jews is in fact growing wider. Synagogue attendance rates vary but decline. In the early 1980s, Wertheimer says, approximately 44 percent of Americans claimed they attended services weekly, and 24 percent of American Jews did; but that figure is high. Wertheimer says, "In most communities between one third and one half of all Jews attend religious services either never or only on the High Holy Days."[19]

Dividing the country by communities (for example, New York, Philadelphia, Baltimore Washington, St. Louis, Miami, and the like) yields various statistics on diverse religious practices. For the sake of simplifying the picture (for the variations are not formidable), we shall review Wertheimer's "practice of selected observances, by community"[20] (see the table on p. 246).

The figures show a fair amount of variation but, overall, confirm the impressions formed in the Kosmin study. Some religious practices are widespread, others not. Not only so, but if we distinguish, as Kosmin does, between those who say they are Jews by religion and those who say they are not, the probability that the percentages of Judaists who practice the rites listed here is probably higher than indicated.

Wertheimer's "Practice of Selected Observances, by Community"

	New York (%)	Philadelphia (%)	St. Louis (%)	Phoenix (%)	Rochester (%)
Attends seder	89	89	71	81	80
Lights Hanukkah candles	76	78	80	78	78
Has mezuzah	70	71	76	57	—
Fasts on Yom Kippur	67	67	—	—	63
Lights Sabbath candles	37	32	28	—	33
Buys only kosher meat	36	—	19	—	—
Uses two sets of dishes, meat and dairy	30	16	15	9	23
Handles no money on the Sabbath	12	—	—	4	—
Refrains from transport on the Sabbath	—	5	5	4	—
Has Christmas tree (sometimes or frequently)	—	—	—	—	15

The available figures rarely tell us about other rites—for instance, what percentage of Jews who marry other Jews and who also identify as Judaists marry in a Judaic rite, and what percentage do not? What percentage of Jews circumcise their sons? If they do, do they do so eight days after birth, through the offices of a ritual circumciser (mohel), or do they use a doctor and pass on the religious rite altogether? Here we have some intriguing data. Cohen notes that a large proportion, 55 percent, of respondents say it is extremely important that their children have sons ritually circumcised; another 18 percent say it is very important.[21] These proportions far exceed those on marrying another Jew—33 percent say marrying another Jew is extremely important for their children, as opposed to the 55 percent for circumcising their grandsons. The upshot is somewhat curious: grandparents are more concerned that their grandsons be circumcised than that their sons marry Jewish women; because the child of a gentile woman is, in the law of Judaism, gentile, it turns out that these grandparents favor the circumcision of (specified) gentiles as part of what "a good Jew" wants.

What percentage of Jews are buried by a rabbi and in a Jewish cemetery, what percentage of Judaists have Judaic last rites, and so forth? Here we rely on guesswork, but one's first inclination strongly suggests that most Jews who marry other Jews have a religious rite for the wedding; most Judaists are buried with Judaic rites; the rite of circumcision tends, among Reform Jews, to be transformed into a (merely) surgical operation, but it is exceedingly common among American Jews. These and other impressions do not have the same authority as the results of the surveys just now quoted. They suffice to suggest that Judaists practice rites of passage: circumcision or some other rite at the birth of a child (synagogue service for naming sons and daughters, for instance); bar or bat mitzvah (for boys and girls, respectively); marriage by a rabbi and a cantor under a Judaic marriage canopy; burial. Add to this very high levels of observance of Passover, Hanukkah, and some other home rites, and we form the impression of a religion that enjoys substantial everyday observance of rites that involve the family (rites of passage) and the home (Passover).

But it would be a considerable error to ignore certain broadly practiced activities that characterize Jews in North America and form a major, public component of their community (philanthropic and political activities, for instance) under a deeply Judaic aspect, frequently explained within the framework of Judaism. So there is a public and communal Judaism, as much as a Judaism for home and family, and that too demands description and explanation.

If, then, we wish to describe the large center of American Jews, those who are both ethnically Jewish and religiously Judaic—estimated by Cohen to number about half of the American Jews—we may do so in the terms Cohen has provided. He gives these generalizations that pertain to our problem:[22]

The moderately affiliated are proud of their identity as Jews, of Jews generally, and of Judaism.

They combine universalist and particularist impulses; they are ambivalent about giving public expression to their genuinely felt attachment to things Jewish.

They are especially fond of the widely celebrated Jewish holidays as well as the family experiences and special foods that are associated with them.

They celebrate High Holidays, Hanukkah and Passover as well as most major American civic holidays....

They vest importance in those Jewish activities they perform; and they regard those activities they fail to undertake as of little import. Accordingly, they are happy with themselves as Jews; they believe they are "good Jews."

Their primary Jewish goal for their children is for them to maintain Jewish family continuity....

The Holocaust and anti-Semitism are among the most powerful Jewish symbols....

The moderately affiliated believe God exists, but they have little faith in an active and personal God.

They are voluntarists, they affirm a right to select those Jewish customs they regard as personally meaningful, and unlike many intensive Jews, most of the moderately affiliated reject the obligatory nature of halakhah [laws, norms].

They endorse broad, abstract principles of Jewish life (such as knowing the fundamentals of Judaism) but fail to support narrower, more concrete normative demands (such as regular text study or sending their children to Jewish day schools).

The moderately affiliated prefer in-marriage but fail to oppose out-marriage with a great sense of urgency.

They support [the State of] Israel, but only as a subordinate concern, one lacking any significant influence on the private sphere of Jewish practice.

To the moderately affiliated, "good Jews" are those who affiliate with other Jews and Jewish institutions.

We have before us the description of a mass of Judaists, who in some ways conform and in others do not to book Judaism. Their religion presents us with a problem of interpretation: how do these people know the difference between what matters and what does not, not only Passover versus Pentecost (Shabuot) fifty days later, but circumcision versus intermarriage, the Holocaust and anti-Semitism versus the State of Israel, the existence of God versus God's active caring? The key lies in Cohen's description: "they affirm a right to select."

WHY THIS, NOT THAT?

North American Jews practice two Judaisms: one at home, the other in public. The rites of the Judaism of the dual Torah, Reform, Conservative, and Orthodox Judaisms alike, prevail in the home, inclusive of rites of the life cycle. Passover, bar mitzvah, marriage, and burial—these are defined by Judaism. But large numbers of people do not come together regularly for public worship. For when it comes to the corporate, ethnic Jewish community, the rites of the American Judaism of Holocaust and Redemption are practiced, and the public and corporate rites of Judaic religious origin are not.

1. *Personal, private, familial Judaism.* American Jews identify with the religious world of the Judaism of the dual Torah, individual experiences that are plausibly transformed in rites of passage and events in the home and family into encounters with transcendence. That is why the social imagination of Jewry engages with Judaism in its narrative of the rites of the passage through life, on the one side, and of a social experience mediating between home and family and the sheltering world, on the other. Circumcision and the Passover banquet, seder, bear in common a single social referent: family, home, and experiences of essentially private life. The theological message of the rites corresponds to the social experience of the faithful that practice those rites.

2. *Public, corporate, communal Jewishness.* Rites that focus on community and public affairs, by contrast, fail because they invoke in common another social referent: society beyond individual and family. So one set of social experience corresponds to the myth and ritual of individual, home, and family; another set of social experiences corresponds to the transcendent tale and ritual of corporate Jewry, Israel all together. And they do not seem to match—intersecting

in many people to be sure, but hardly corresponding in the essentials of symbol, myth, and ritual.

The rites of the Judaism of the dual Torah that bear deep meaning speak of resentment against a social order and of freedom (Passover) or of Adam and Eve in Eden (the wedding rite), to take two among several solid cases. The rites of the Judaism of Holocaust and Redemption that attain the compelling force of self-evidence speak of resentment and fear, the shared experience of an uncomfortable minority. That is what the successes of the two Judaisms have in common—that, and one other thing. Neither speaks of *must* but only *may;* both sets of choices preserve freedom to choose; and concerning covenant and obligation and the God who commands and the Israel that obeys, neither Judaism (as shaped by the people out there, not the books in here) says nothing. Out of what the two Judaisms say, as much as out of what they do not say, we hear the message "This is plausible, that not; good Jews do this but don't have to do (or believe) that."

What is personal and private imposes no discipline, no objective obligation. What people do at home, they do because they want to. What they do in the synagogue, in public, they do in response to norms they cannot, on their own, shape. The difference between "Why this?" and "Why not that?" takes shape at the dividing point between the optional and the obligatory or, in the language of Judaism, on the frontier of the norm for behavior, halakhah. To state matters simply: Why this? Because I want to; why not that, because (if that) I have to. Mordecai M. Kaplan, the theologian of Judaism who founded Reconstructionist Judaism, states forthrightly, "mitzvot [commandments] yes, averot [transgressions] no," meaning, yes to religious duty, no to religiously defined transgression. If there is no obligation, there also can be no transgression.

The "why not" then rejects what is obligatory or subject to public regulation. The premise of what the people do is that religion is a matter of one's own definition and choice—hence the centrality of home and family, rites of passage, and subjective liturgy. And the Judaism of Holocaust and Redemption depends on the willing obedience of the faithful, obedience given by choice or withheld by one's own will, as much as the Judaism of rites of passage and celebration at home depends on options taken. So the differentiating criteria that tell people what they need not do is very simple: "You don't have to...." And there is no "You do have to" to which all "good Jews" respond, except because they feel like it.

Now what is it in the experience of the social order that renders the "ought" of the Torah's commandments implausible, therefore irrelevant? In Jewry (and not there alone), people experience a cogent social world, one of integrity and inner coherence, beginning and ending with family. Society presents diversities, both within Jewry and beyond, such that people cannot refer to a cogent religious life (so far as they define religion as personal, not political) beyond family. It is simply not there. Quite to the contrary, the plurality of society in general, the diversity of Jewry in particular, prevent the formation of that sense of corporate existence beyond the individual in family that would lay foundations for a shared experience of transformation, through rites' enchantment, of the given into a gift. To be sure, there is a corporate experience of being Israel, and it does yield a cogent system of a wholly political and public character.

JUDAISM IN THE AMERICAN PROTESTANT MODEL: RELIGION IN PRIVATE, POLITICS IN PUBLIC

What we learn concerns what it means to be religious in North America in the democratic and Protestant West. Here in Protestant North America people commonly see religion as something personal and private; prayer, for example, therefore speaks for the individual. Public life, politics, and corporate, community activity are separate from religion. No wonder, then, that those enchanted words and gestures that, for their part, Jews adopt transform the inner life, recognize life's transitions, and turn them into rites of passage. It is part of a larger prejudice that religion and rite speak to the heart of the particular person. What can be changed by rite then is first of all personal and private, not social, not an issue of culture, not affective in politics, not part of the public interest. For Jews the public is ethnic; the private, religion, which explains what people do and also what they refrain from doing within the received Judaisms of today.

What people do when they respond to religion, therefore, affects an interior world—a world with little bearing on the realities of public discourse: what, in general, should we do about nuclear weapons, or, in terms of Judaism, how should we organize and imagine society? The transformations of religion do not involve the world, or even of the self as representative of other selves, but mainly the individual at the most unique and unrepresentative. If God speaks to the individual in particular, then the message, by definition, is mine, not someone else's. Religion, the totality of these private messages (within the present theory), therefore does not make itself available for communication in public discourse. Religion plays no public role. It is a matter not of public activity but of what people happen to believe or do in private, a matter mainly of the heart.

When religion addresses what actually happens to people living together, and when the message it conveys conforms to their sense of self-evidence (that is, the same thing twice), then religion governs. What the books say will accurately describe what the people do. When religion pertains but its message jars, what happens? People may do what the books say, but they may not do it in the way the books direct. Or they may not do what the books say at all. And they can always tell the difference—and the reason why. That defines (their) Judaism. And when the social order and the religious system do not correspond at all, then people will conclude "good Jews do this, not that."

So what we learn is that religion lives in the perceived, social experience that people have; its ideas prove not right or wrong, not even persuasive or implausible, but self-evidently true because they are descriptive, or obviously irrelevant because they are not descriptive, of the world as lived out in the social world. Conscience is the creation of community, theological truth subject to the disposition of common sense—that is, a sense of what is fitting and just made common by being shared.

This brings us back to the question of the ecology of Judaism: how the world outside of Jewry dictates the shape of the Judaic religious (and ethnic) systems that Jews formulate. When we ask (now in general terms) why the split occurs between (1) the personal and the familial, subjected to the Judaism of the dual Torah, perceived as religion, and (2) the public and civic, governed by the Judaism of Holocaust and Redemption, perceived as politics, we turn outward. For the explanation lies in the definition of permissible difference in North America and the place of religion in that difference. Specifically, in North American society, defined as it is by Protestant conceptions, it is permissible to be different in religion, and religion is a matter of what is personal and private.

Hence, Judaism as a religion encompasses what is personal and familial. But that definition of religion proves insufficient to cover Judaic religious systems that flourish. The Jews as a political entity then put forth a separate system, one that concerns not religion, which is not supposed to intervene in political action, but public policy. Judaism in public policy produces political action in favor of the State of Israel, or Russian Jewry, or other important matters of the corporate community. Judaism in private affects the individual and the family and is not supposed to play a role in politics at all. That pattern conforms to the Protestant model of religion, and the Jews have accomplished conformity to it by the formation of two Judaisms.

Judaism in North America conforms to the Protestant pattern, which separates not the institutions of church from the activities of the state. Ethnic Jewishness comes to expression in activities of a secular and political character. But the public life of Jewry, reaching religious statement in the Judaism of Holocaust and Redemption, is not trivial, not private, not individual, not a matter only of the heart. Religion is public, political, social. To understand Judaism, we have both to distinguish the ethnic from the religious and also to investigate the relationship between the ethnic and the religious. But we must also recognize that Judaism exercises a power of its own.

NOTES

1. I rely mainly on Steven M. Cohen, *Content or Continuity? Alternative Bases for Commitment* (New York: American Jewish Committee, 1991); Jack Wertheimer, "Recent Trends in American Judaism," in *American Jewish Yearbook, 1989,* ed. David Singer (New York: American Jewish Committee and Jewish Publication Society, 1989); and Barry A. Kosmin, Sidney Goldstein, Joseph Waksberg, Nava Lerer,

Ariella Keysar, and Jeffrey Scheckner, *Highlights of the CJF* [Council of Jewish Federations] *1990 National Jewish Population Survey* (New York: Council of Jewish Federations, 1991). The latter work is cited in the text as "the Kosmin study."

2. Kosmin et al., *Highlights,* 4.

3. Ibid., 28.

4. Ibid., 14–15.

5. Wertheimer, "Recent Trends," 39.

6. Ibid., 80.

7. Ibid., 80–81.

8. Kosmin et al., *Highlights,* 32.

9. Wertheimer, "Recent Trends," 80.

10. Kosmin et al., *Highlights,* 37.

11. Ibid.

12. Material from Liebman and Shapiro cited here comes from *A Survey of the Conservative Movement and Some of Its Religious Attitudes,* unpublished manuscript, September 1979, Library of the Theological Seminary of America, 3080 Broadway, New York, NY.

13. Steven M. Cohen, *American Assimilation of Jewish Revival* (Bloomington: Indiana University Press, 1988), 80.

14. Ibid., 81.

15. Cohen, *Content or Continuity?* 4. Cohen distinguishes between the Jewish-identity patterns of the more involved and passionate elites from those of the more numerous, marginally affiliated Jews, those with roughly average levels of Jewish involvement and emotional investment…. One may be called "commitment to content" and the other "commitment to continuity," alternatively…"commitment to ideology" versus "commitment to identity."

16. Ibid., 14–15.

17. Ari L. Goldman, *New York Times,* June 7, 1991.

18. Wertheimer, "Recent Trends," 63.

19. Ibid., 85.

20. Ibid., 88*ff.*

21. Cohen, *Content or Continuity?* 21.

22. Ibid., 41–42.

33

Reversionary Judaisms
Forward to "Tradition"?

The last third of the twentieth century has witnessed a vast movement of "return to tradition," or reversion, affecting all of the Judaic systems of the past two hundred years, from Orthodoxy to Reform, inclusive of American, European, and Israeli Jewry. Quite what people meant by "tradition" was not always clear, but, in general, the movement involved formerly secular and nonobservant Jews, often quite divorced from Jewish social life, undertaking some type of religious observance, adopting a religious viewpoint, and moving from the secular and ethnic to the religious and theological framework of (a) Judaism. Sometimes the pattern of reversion brought a Reform Jew into a Conservative rabbinic seminary or a Conservative Jew into an Orthodox yeshiva (a center for full-time Torah study, comparable to a monastery in its providing for a holy way of life for all participants). Sometimes reversion meant that a formerly indifferent ("assimilated") Jew discovered his or her Jewishness and determined to engage with the organized Jewish community. Reversion came about for some in a personal crisis; for others, in an event involving the State of Israel. In general, the pattern of reversion is marked by the movement from the life of an isolated individual to participation in a Jewish social entity ("the community"). In this way, personal and private religiosity or utter secularity lost their hold, and public and social religiosity took over.

The Judaic system of reversion therefore encompasses large numbers of Jews who have moved from an essentially secular and naturalist to a profoundly religious and supernatural view of Israel, God's people, and also of themselves; so they have adopted the way of life of the received Judaism of the dual Torah or of one of its continuators, whether Reform, Orthodox, or Conservative systems of Judaism. The single most striking trait of the contemporary Judaic religious world, in all its diversity, is the return to Judaism on the part of formerly secular Jews, on the one side, or the movement from less rigorous to more complete observance of the holy way of life, on the other. All together, the diverse phenomena fall under the category of reversion, that is, "return to tradition," in the theological language of the matter, or renewed religiosity, in more descriptive terms. Reversion both marks a movement and also defines a particular Judaic system.

Let me make this picture of the return to Judaism more concrete. When, as happens not uncommonly, Jews in North America make a decision to observe the dietary laws and the Sabbath, to say prayers every day and to identify with a Torah study circle in a yeshiva, they adopt a way of life and a world-view new to them. For the generality of American Jews have defined their lives in other terms. Reversion marks the entry of Jews not born and brought up within the Judaic system of the dual Torah into the way of life defined by the dual Torah and the adoption of the viewpoint and values of that same Torah. Reversioners enter into the Israel to whom the dual Torah speaks, entering an intense social life lived in a round of daily and Sabbath prayers, study sessions, celebrations. Leaving Judaic systems that favor or accommodate integration, they choose a Judaic system that, in effect if not in articulated policy, creates a life of segregation. The shift from world to world marks entry into a stunningly powerful Judaic system.

Yet in interpreting the Judaic mode and system of reversion, we may not take for granted that we witness a mere "return to tradition." Some maintain that the "return" is exactly that. Quite to the contrary, whatever is meant by "tradition," reversioners in their context represent new, not traditional choices. The reversioners do undertake to redefine—for themselves, but they are exemplary—that way of life and worldview that they received as traditional from their parents. But that was *not* the received system of the dual Torah, its world-view, its way of life. So to the reversioners the new is what (they say) is old, even as what was old is new to them. Accordingly, our analysis requires us to treat as fresh not the received system but the way the reversioners receive it: a system of reversion is fresh, even though that to which people return draws them (in its own terms) upward to Sinai.

Extant Judaisms of the last third of the twentieth century all bear the marks of reversion; when people wished to find their way home, they generally moved over one chair. That could mean from total estrangement from the synagogue to involvement with a Reform temple, or it could mean from one Orthodox yeshiva, of a less segregated character, to another one, which totally rejected secular learning. All the Judaic systems of the past thirty years bore the marks of a renewal of observance and a return to more classical formulations of the faith. But a particular reversionary system also took shape, the one that led utterly secular but searching young Jews into one or another of the Orthodox Judaic systems of the age, in both North America and in the State of Israel. Described first here will be the movement that imparted a style of its own to existing Judaisms, all of which have seen themselves as "more traditional" than they had earlier been.

Reversion to Judaism in North America began with the third generation in the mid-1960s, that is, with the grandchildren of the immigrant generations of the period 1880–1920, when millions of East European Jews came to this country. But it reached its height with the fourth and beyond, and reversion will mark the formation of Judaic systems into the twenty-first century.

Reversion uses the language of "return," which in Hebrew, as *teshuvah*, bears the further sense of repentance. The Judaic systems of return or repentance invoke profoundly moral and theological dimensions, not characteristic of the four movements just reviewed. For all of the Judaic systems of the late nineteenth and twentieth centuries explained a process of distance, that is, a movement away from "the Tradition," whereas the Judaic style and system of the present propose to account for the opposite: a return, a closing of the gap between the Jew and the Torah.

That is the explanation for the word choice at hand: *return* to the Judaic way of life and worldview in one of its religious formulations rather than its secular ones. Why stress return? The worldview of reversionary Judaisms sees Israel as God's people, who *by nature and by definition* should keep the Torah. All Jews who do not ought to return to their true calling and character as the people of the Torah. So the title of the movement expresses its worldview and its theory of who is Israel and what it is natural for Israel to become. The worldview of the movement perceives the Jews as alienated from "the Tradition" to which they must "return." The way of life, on the surface, is simply that mode of behavior prescribed by "the Tradition" for whatever chair the reversioner chooses to occupy.

We may wonder why Jews growing up in secular circumstances opt for a religious Judaism. And, more important, we want to know how that tendency on the part of individuals became a movement and generated a Judaism, the Judaic system(s) of return, indeed, the one fresh Judaism as we approach the twenty-first century. To answer these questions, we must take note of the highly secular character of American Judaism, that is, a Judaism that overall stresses institutions and organizations rather than the inner life of faith, learning, and observance. That system has provided a mode of "being Jewish" in the context of an open and free society, when one wanted to be both Jewish and also part of an undifferentiated society. It involved essentially secular activity—fund-raising, political organizing—and left untouched the inner life and values of the participants. But the success of American Judaism had an unexpected effect. People took seriously the powerful emotions elicited by the appeals, characteristic of fund-raising and organizational propaganda (for instance, rehearsals of "the Holocaust" and engagement with the ongoing crises of the State of Israel). They were sold, and they find later that they have bought a partial and incomplete Judaism.

As the 1970s unfolded, the stress of the community at large on a high level of emotion, joined to only occasional activity and then activity of an essentially neutral character, affected younger people in a curious way. People sold on the centrality of "being Jewish" in their lives required modes of expression that affected their lives more deeply, and in more ways, than the rather limited way of life offered by American Judaism. Searching for values, rejecting what they deemed the superficial, merely public Jewish activities of their parents, they resolved that tension between being Jewish and not being too Jewish that American Judaism generated for the third generation. They were sold on "being Jewish" and looked not for activity but for community, not for an occasional emotional binge but for an enduring place and partnership: a covenant.

In the United States and Canada, reversioners have come from Reform or secular backgrounds, Conservative or Orthodox ones. It hardly matters. In all cases we find a conversion process, a taking up of a totally new way of life and a rejection of the inherited one, the parents' way of life. In the State of Israel, reversioners derive from three different sources of Jews: North America, Israelis of European background, and Israelis of Asian or African origin.[1]

But reversion has formed not only a style for Judaic systems of all sorts but also a Judaic system on its own. The definitive chronicle of the matter, by Janet Aviad, provides a systematic picture of the ideology, way of life, and a synoptic portrait of the movement as a whole. Still, enough is in hand to generalize. The movement's American component derived, she says, from the youth rebellion of the 1960s:

> Protesting a war they regarded as immoral, a situation that permitted terrible injustices to ethnic minorities, what appeared as a wasteful directionless use of technology, youth struck out in various directions. One direction was toward new forms of a religious life.[2]

Involved was a rejection of the "tradition of skeptical, secular intellectuality which has served as the prime vehicle for three hundred years of scientific and technical work in the West." The reversioners described here had earlier in the 1960s experimented with diverse matters, including drugs, poetry, and religion. And, among the religions, some Jews tried out Judaism. The quest involved travel, and Judaism "was often only the end station of a long search."[3] Coming to Judaism occurred by chance meetings with rabbis or religious Jews, but staying there was because of the yeshivas that received the reversioners.

Yet another group of reversioners derived from Reform and Conservative synagogues; they came to improve their knowledge and raise their level of practical observance of piety. A further group, Israelis of Western background compared overall with this second group. They had seen themselves as secular but sought to become, in Israeli terms, religious. Their search for meaning brought them to the yeshivas ready to receive them. The final group that Aviad surveys were Israelis of poorer and Asian or African origin, and to them, too, reversion represented a religious conversion, from life "experienced as empty or meaningless to one experienced as fully, whole, and holy."[4]

In all, we deal with a Jewish expression of a common, international youth culture of the 1970s and 1980s, just as much as we found in American Judaism a version, in a Judaic idiom, of a larger cultural development in American life of the 1960s and early 1970s. The massive rise in the birth rate following World War II suggested, among other things, the youth culture that would emerge twenty years later. When we find that Jews rejected the values they deemed secular and shallow and opted for a new way of life they found authentic and Godly, we may wonder whether, in other groups, young people were reaching the same conclusions. A generation in search, a shared quest for something to transcend the ("merely") material achievements—that generation grew up in the prosperity that followed the end of World War II.

Children of successful parents with leisure and resources to go in quest turned to drugs, others to social concerns, still others to a search for a faith that would demand more than the (to them shallow, compromising) religiosity of their parents. Whether Roman Catholic Pentecostalism, Protestant biblical affirmation (called "fundamentalism"), Judaic reversion, Islamic renewal from Malaya to Morocco (also called "fundamentalism" or "extremism"), the international youth movement exhibits strikingly uniform traits: young people in rebellion against the parents' ways, in search of something more exacting and rigorous. If, as we noticed, the Judaism of the dual Torah insists that Jews are not only Jews all the time but never anything else, then we may characterize as a return to that theory of Israel the movement of reversion. But it is only in that sense. For as an acutely contemporary movement, part of a large-scale rejection of secular, humanistic, and liberal values of a generation concerned to live an affable life, the reversion to Judaism presented much that was fresh, unprecedented, but, above all, selective.

The reversioners under discussion in fact formed part of a larger world movement, a youth movement of resentment of the parents' generation and affirmation of the children's—a Jewish equivalent of the Cultural Revolution of China. They expressed in the Judaic idiom an international message and viewpoint, no less than did Jewish socialism, Yiddishism, Zionism, and, in their ways, Reform, Orthodox, and Conservative Judaisms. The first of these movements formed the Jews' part of international socialism, the second, a Jewish idiomatic expression of romantic linguistic nationalism; the third, the Jewish statement of ethnic nationalism. The fourth, fifth, and sixth presented little more than Judaic versions of Protestant historicistic theology in the aftermath of Kant and Hegel. So all constituted Judaic systems composed within categories available, so to speak, in the larger world of humanity. And so did the reversionary Judaisms of the later decades of the twentieth century.

The system of reversion drew its categories, its values, its goals from a larger setting, too. These it then adapted to the Judaic circumstance: a totally fresh, totally new, totally autonomous Judaic system. A Judaism invented or discovered? Both, but to begin with, invented. In her description of the reversion in the State of Israel, Aviad, whom I shall cite at length, uses such language as this: "who turned outward…who noticed a change in the spiritual climate." That is a mark of invention, I think. But then, assuredly it was also a Judaism discovered and recovered. So the idiom, as Aviad says, may have proved new, but the content was more than welcome: it was what they had brought with them. The worldview of returning to Judaism as an ideology (an -ism) in the present form constitutes part of a larger and international style, a Judaic statement of what a great many people were saying, all of them in the language and categories of their own.

The movement of reversion flourishes throughout the Jewish world. It attains realization as a system, however, in the yeshivas. The ones in the State of Israel lead the movement of reversion and give full expression to its worldview and way of life. But, interestingly, the yeshivas that succeed in embodying the ideals of reversion derive not from Israeli Orthodox rabbis but from American ones living in Jerusalem. It was American Orthodox rabbis trained in yeshivas who saw the opportunity and the issue. They understood as self-evident that all Jews should live by the Torah and study it; but they had the wit to recognize a generation of young Jews who were prepared to revert to that way of life and worldview. And they further undertook to give form and full expression to the system of reversion. The yeshivas that received the newcomers came into being because of American rabbis settled in Jerusalem:

> They discerned a new openness to religion....They felt strongly that Orthodox Judaism would appeal to the young Jews being drawn to non-Jewish religious groups....The problem seemed merely technical: how to make young people aware of orthodox values and beliefs as a way of life.[5]

What these rabbis found points to the freshness of the movement at hand, for in fact the established yeshivas took no interest in the possibilities at all. They did not think they could absorb the types of students coming their way. So the rabbis founded autonomous schools.

That fact alerts us to the presence of an innovative system. A system that finds itself rejected and ignored by another system of the same family will have difficulty in claiming to form an incremental outcome of the system whose institutions prove—by their own word—utterly incompatible. In the movement of reversion, as well as in the systemic formulations of "return," a transvaluation of that critical value occurs: gifts of the spirit take priority and endow the gifted with status out of all relationship to his (or her) intellectual attainment. The addition of the "or her," of course, provides another signal of a system aborning, for the familiar yeshiva world makes slight provision for women's participation in its Judaism. But the Judaic system of reversion worked out within the Judaic system of the dual Torah flourishing in the State of Israel founded yeshivas for women and understood the importance of equality, within the received system, for them, an astounding and important mark of innovation and renewal.

The initiative involved in identifying the opportunity further provides solid evidence that a new system is under way. The total negation of Western culture that forms the centerpiece of the worldview at hand finds no ample precedents in the received dual Torah, which found itself entirely at home in diverse circumstances and drew both deliberately and unselfconsciously on the world in which it flourished. We need hardly point to obvious precedents for a policy of selecting what was appropriate. The policy of rejecting the entire world beyond, moreover, finds few precedents and, in the balance, presents an egregious exception to a long history of not integration but mediation. But if we look toward another wellspring for the view at hand, we readily discern it. The worldview of reversion, resting on the principle of total rejection of "Western culture," in fact corresponded point by point with the worldview of comparable movements of its time and circumstance. It was the youth revolution of the 1960s. Rejecting the parents and their values, the authority of their youth, the conventions of society, the juvenile revolutionaries sought radical change, finding it in politics, music, clothing, food, drugs, and, for some, religion.

The view that the reversion was a homecoming, that the values of reversionism simply replicated, for the occasion, the theology of the Judaic system of the dual Torah, contradicts the particular structure and points of value and emphasis of reversionism. The questions at hand come from the circumstance; the answers derive from a process of selection and arrangement of evidentiary texts provided by the canonical writings, on the one side, and (if truth be told) the everyday way of life of the dual Torah's Judaic system, on the other. The whole then compares to other wholes, other Judaic systems: a work of selection along lines already determined, a system dictated by its own inventive framers to answer questions urgent particularly to themselves, a Judaism.

The matter of context requires attention. Reversionist Judaism came about at exactly the same time marked by massive out-marriage, apostasy to other religions, a turning away from engagement with Jewry in any terms. At the end of World War II, British Jewry numbered approximately 500,000; had natural growth taken place, the community would be substantially larger than its present number of approximately 300,000–350,000! Moreover, World War II left the Jews as a group decimated, about one third of all the Jews in the world alive in 1939 having been murdered by 1945. These demographic facts raised the question, Are we the end? And the question confronted individuals as well: Am I the last Jew on Earth, as Arthur A. Cohen's *Days of Simon Stern* puts matters? So the Jews' natural ecology once more defined a crisis, and the response of one sector of the Jews was to revert to (a) Judaism, to (a formulation of) tradition—to reaffirm Israel in the face of extinction.

To conclude this introduction to the twenty-first century, let me specify why I single out the reversion movement as the key to what lies ahead. I do so because I find in the contemporary mode evidence of renewal and regeneration, whether within Reform or far-out Orthodoxy. The source of the rebirth is the world as it is, the motive and the power, the teachings of the Torah. For the reversionary Judaisms begin in a mix of resentment of a social present with a right and natural reflection on an awful, near-at-hand past. The reversion to the dual Torah marked the generations beyond the murder of the Jews of Europe, facing the demographic loss. It affected the generations that made the State of Israel, addressing the perpetual insecurity of the bastion-become-beleaguered fortress. It touched deeply the great-grandchildren of the immigrants who formed American Jewry, the children of the framers of American Judaism, looking backward at integration fully realized and forward toward what they feared would be no future at all. With no family untouched by out-marriage (whether demographically advantageous), and with many families' lives framed out of all relationship with distinctively Judaic or even culturally Jewish activity (however defined), the future came under doubt. The reversionary Judaic systems for their part say no to two hundred years of Judaic system building. They reject the premises and programs not only of the Judaic systems of an essentially economic and political character (socialism and Zionism, for example) but also the ones that affirm religious viewpoints and ways of life. Because these systems by definition come into being as the creation of children—great-great-grandchildren, really—of the nineteenth-century reformers, they mark the conclusion of the age of modernization.

The pressing problem the Judaic systems address seems to me clear. The Jews en route to the dual Torah once more ask very profound, very pressing human problems. They want to know the answers to such questions as, Why do I live? What do I do to serve God? What should I do with my life? No wonder Orthodoxy cannot cope with them. The reversioners come to study Torah as God's word, not as a source of historical facts. They take up a way of life quite alien to that they knew from their parents as an act of conversion to God, not as a means of expressing or preserving their Jewishness. They repudiate, yes, but only to affirm.

If I had to explain, in a single sentence, the remarkable power of reversionary Judaisms—whether to Reform or to Israeli yeshiva Orthodoxy—I would invoke a single consideration. The one question ignored by the former Judaic systems, the human question, found its answer in the reversionist movement. After two hundred years of change, the final turning of the wheel brought up the original issue afresh.

For what questions had the Judaic system of the dual Torah set at the center of discourse, if not the ones of living a holy and a good life? The Jews for those long centuries in which Christianity defined the frame of reference for all Western society understood that that question pressed, that its answers demanded attention. The Judaism of the dual Torah addressed that Jew who was always a Jew and who was only a Jew, delivering the uncompromising lesson that God demanded the human heart, that Israel was meant to be a kingdom of priests and a holy people, and that the critical issues of life concerned conduct with God, the other, and the self. That piety that explained from day to day what it meant to be a mensch, a decent human being, answered that question that through the Christian centuries the West understood as critical: how shall I live so as to die decently. For all of us owe God one death, and the worthy make it a good one: one out of a good life.

The issues of modern times shifted from the human questions framed by humanity in God's image and likeness to an altogether different set of urgent concerns. These had to do with matters of politics and economics. The received Torah echoed with the question: Adam, where are you? The Torahs of the nineteenth century answered the question, Jew, what *else* can you become? For millennia Jews had not wanted to be more than they were, and now the Jewish question, asked by gentiles and Jews alike, rested on the premise that to be Jewish did not suffice. Now Jews wished not totally to integrate but also not entirely to segregate themselves. They no longer had in mind a place where a people dwells alone. The Judaic systems of the twentieth century, with their stress on politics for professionals, ephemeral enthusiasm for everybody else, reconstituted the people that dwells alone—for fifteen minutes at a time. No wonder then that, at the end of two hundred years, the heirs of a set of partial systems would go in search of a whole and complete one: one that provided what all the established ones did not, that same sense of center and the whole that, for so long, was precisely what Jews did not want for themselves. The protracted love affair over, some Jews reengaged the received Torah, the one in two parts, in a long-term union. Not many, not experienced, sometimes awkward, often forced and unnatural, they in time would find their path and, in ways they could not imagine or approve, lead the Jewish world.

The capacity of Judaic systems drawing on the Judaism of the dual Torah to come to grips with the acutely contemporary issues of Jews' lives forms the source of their remarkable power to change lives, to bring about what in secular terms one would call conversion and, in Judaic terms, return. The reversionary Judaisms—including Reform, Orthodoxy, Conservatism, each one in its many formulations—take up today's concerns and draw them into the framework of an enduring program of lively reflection. That capacity to form a relationship between the individual, here and now, and the social entity, holy, supernatural Israel, in the far reaches of time and unto eternity, takes the measure of Judaic systems. By that criterion, the systems of reversion, however limited their actual effect in numbers, exercise moral authority and therefore enjoy remarkable success. I discern only one source of that success: the Judaic system of the dual Torah, its enduring power to address the human condition of Israel, the Jewish people everywhere, in God's name. "And he believed the Lord, and he reckoned it to him as righteousness."

NOTES

1. Janet Aviad, *Return to Judaism: Religious Renewal in Israel* (Chicago: University Press, 1983), ix.

2. Ibid., 2.

3. Ibid., 4.

4. Ibid., 10.

5. Ibid., 16.

Glossary

Adon Olam Lord of the World: hymn containing dogmas of divine unity, timelessness, providence.

aggadah lit. telling, narration; generally: lore, theology, fable, biblical exegesis, ethics.

ahavah love; *Ahavah rabbah:* great love; first words of prayer preceding Shema.

Alenu It is incumbent on us: first word of prayer cited in "Going Forth."

aliyah going up; migration to the Land of Israel.

Am HaAres lit.: people of the land; rabbinic usage: boor, unlearned, not a disciple of the sages.

Amidah lit.: standing; the main section of obligatory prayers morning, afternoon, and evening, containing nineteen benedictions: (1) God of the fathers, (2) praise of God's power, (3) holiness, (4) prayer for knowledge, (5) prayer for repentance, (6) prayer for forgiveness, (7) prayer for redemption, (8) prayer for healing the sick, (9) blessing of agricultural produce, (10) prayer for ingathering of dispersed Israel, (11) prayer for righteous judgment, (12) prayer for punishment of wicked and heretics, (13) prayer for reward of pious, (14) prayer for rebuilding Jerusalem, (15) prayer for restoration of the house of David, (16) prayer for acceptance of prayers, (17) prayer of thanks, (18) prayer for restoration of Temple service, and (19) prayer for peace.

amora rabbinic teacher in Palestine and Babylonia in Talmudic times (ca. 200–500 C.E.).

Apikoros Hebrew for Epicurus; generally: belief in hedonism.

archetype original pattern or model

Ashkenaz (–im) European Jews, those who follow the customs originating in medieval German Judaism.

Ashré "Happy are they," Psalm 145; read in morning and afternoon worship.

assimilation taking on the cultural traits of a culture different from the one in which a person is born

Av, Ninth of Day of Mourning for destruction of Jerusalem Temple in 586 B.C.E. and 70 C.E.

B.C.E. before the common era; used in place of B.C.

Baal Shem Tov (ca. 1700–1760): Master of the Good Name, Founder of Hasidism.

bar mitzvah ceremony at which a thirteen-year-old boy becomes an adult member of Jewish community; an adult male Jew who is obligated to carry out the commandments (*mitzvah/mitzvot*).

bat mitzvah adult female Jew who is obligated to carry out commandments; marked by ceremony as for *bar mitzvah*.

Berakhah benediction, blessing or praise.

Bet Am house of people; early word for *synagogue*.

Bet Din court of law judging civil, criminal, religious cases according to halakhah.

Bet Midrash house of study.

Bimah place from which worship is led in synagogue.

Birkat HaMazon blessing for food; Grace after Meals.

brit milah covenant of circumcision; removal of foreskin of penis on eighth day after birth.

C.E. common era; used instead of A.D.

canon officially recognized set of holy books.

Central Conference of American Rabbis association of Reform rabbis.

code an organized system of rules and laws.

cohen/kohen priest.

Conservative Judaism religious movement, reacting against early Reform; attempts to adapt Jewish law to modern life on the basis of principles of change inherent in traditional laws.

credo confession of faith.

creed a formula or accepted system of religious belief.

cult a system of religious worship, a mode of serving God, not to be confused with another use of the word *cult,* a religious group that is unconventional.

dayyan judge in Jewish court.

decalogue Ten Words; the Ten Commandments (Hebrew: *'Aseret HaDibrot).*

Derekh Eretz lit.: the way of the land; normal custom, correct conduct; good manners, etiquette.

diaspora dispersion, exile of Jews from the Land of Israel.

dichotomy division into two parts.

dietary laws pertaining to animal food; pious Jews may eat only fish that have fins and scales, animals that part the hoof and chew the cud (sheep, cows, but not camels, pigs). Animals must be ritually slaughtered (Hebrew: *shehitah),* following a humane method of slaughter accompanied by a blessing of thanks. Jews may not eat shellfish, worms, snails, flesh torn from a living animal, and so forth. Any mixture of meat and milk is forbidden; after eating meat, one may not eat dairy products for a period of time (one to six hours, depending on custom). Fish are neutral (*pareve).* See *kosher.*

dogma beliefs that faithful are expected to affirm.

dynamic system a religious system that develops and changes over time.

El, Elohim God, divinity.

erev evening, sunset, beginning of a holy day.

eschatology theory of the end of time, death, judgment, world to come, Messianic era, resurrection of the dead.

etrog citron, one of four species carried in synagogue on *Sukkot;* from Leviticus 23:40, "fruit of a goodly tree."

exegesis critical explanation of Scripture or other holy books.

exilarch head of the exile; Aramaic: *Resh Galuta;* head of the Jewish community in Babylonia in Talmudic and medieval times.

gaon eminence, excellency; title of head by Babylonian academies; later on, distinguished Talmudic scholar.

Gedaliah, fast of third day of autumn month of *Tishri,* commemorating assassination of Gedaliah (II Kings 25, Jeremiah 40:1).

Geiger, Abraham (1870–1874) early reformer in Germany; produced modern prayer book; wanted Judaism to become a world religion.

gemara completion; comments and discussions of Mishnah. Mishnah + *Gemara* = Talmud.

get bill of divorce, required to dissolve Jewish marriage.

golus Ashkenazic pronunciation of *galut*: exile; life in *diaspora*; discrimination, humiliation.

Hadassah U.S. women's Zionist organization.

halakhah "the way things are done," from *halakh:* go; more broadly, the prescriptive, legal tradition.

Haskalah Jewish Enlightenment, eighteenth-century movement of rationalists.

havdalah the rite that at sundown at the end of the Sabbath or Festival marks the separation of the holy time of the Sabbath or festival to the secular or profane time of the everyday week; see *Kiddush.*

Hebrew Union College Jewish Institute of Religion; founded in Cincinnati in 1875; center for training Reform rabbis, teachers; campuses in Los Angeles, Cincinnati, New York City, and Jerusalem.

heder room; elementary school for early education.

hiddush novella; new point, insight, given as a comment on classical text. Often ingenious; sometimes hairsplitting.

Hillel first-century Pharisaic leader; taught "Do not unto others what you would not have them do unto you."

Hillul HaShem profanation of God's name; doing something to bring disrepute on Jews, Judaism—particularly among non-Jews.

Hillul Shabbat profanation of the Sabbath.

Hol HaMoed intermediate days of festivals of Passover, Sukkot.

Holocaust the mass murder of more than six million Jews in Europe by Germany and its allies from 1933, when the German National Socialist Workers Party (Nazis) came to power, to 1945, when the Allies vanquished Germany.

huppah marriage canopy, under which ceremony takes place.

inculcate instill

Jehovah transliteration of Divine name, based on misunderstanding of Hebrew letters *YHWH.* Jews did not pronounce name of God; referred to the name as *Adonai*, Lord. Translators took vowels of *Adonai* and added them to consonants *JHVH*; hence, JeHoVaH.

Jewish Theological Seminary founded 1888; center for training conservative rabbis, teachers; in New York City, Los Angeles, Jerusalem.

Judah the Patriarch head of Palestinian Jewish community, 200 C.E.; promulgated Mishnah.

kabbalah lit.: tradition; later, the mystical Jewish tradition.

kaddish doxology said at end of principal sections of Jewish service; praise of God with congregational response "May his great name be praised eternally." Eschatological emphasis; hope for speedy advent of Messiah. Also recited by mourners.

Karaites eighth- to twelfth-century Middle Eastern Jewish sect; rejected oral Torah; lived by written one alone.

kehillah Jewish community.

Keneset Israel assembly of Israel; Jewish people as a whole.

Keriat Shema recital of Shema.

ketuvah marriage contract specifying obligations of husband to wife.

Ketuvim writings; biblical books of Psalms, Proverbs, and so forth.

kibbutz galuyyot gathering together of the exiles; eschatological hope that all Israel will be restored to land; now applied to migration of Jewish communities to State of Israel.

kibbutz collective settlement in State of Israel where property is held in common.

Kiddush HaShem sanctification of the name of God; applies to conduct of Jews among non-Jews that brings esteem on Jews, Judaism; in medieval times: martyrdom.

kiddush sanctification, generally of wine, in proclamation of Sabbath, festival.

Kol Nidré all vows; prayer opening Yom Kippur eve service, declaring that all vows made rashly during the year and not carried out are null and void.

kosher lit.: fit, proper; applies to anything suitable for use according to Jewish law.

Lag BeOmer thirty-third day in seven-week period of counting the Omer, from second day of Passover to Pentecost (Leviticus 23:15); day of celebration for scholars.

Lamed Vav thirty-six men of humble vocation not recognized, but by whose merit the world exists; they bring salvation in crisis.

liturgy religiously prescribed prayers

lulav palm branch used on Sukkot.

Maariv evening service.

Magen David Shield of David; six-pointed star; distinctive Jewish symbol after the seventeenth century.

Mah Nishtannah "Wherein is this night different from all others"; opening words of four questions asked by child at Passover seder.

mahzor prayer book for New Year and Day of Atonement.

Malkhuyyot sovereignties, section of New Year Additional Service devoted to theme of God's sovereignty.

Maoz Tsur "Fortress, Rock of My Salvation"; Hanukkah hymn.

maror bitter herbs, consumed at Passover seder in remembrance of bitter life of slaves.

mashgiah supervisor of rituals, particularly ritual slaughter; must be expert in laws, pious, and God fearing. An ignorant person, motivated by financial gain, cannot supervise religious rites.

maskil enlightened person, follower of *Haskalah* (Enlightenment).

masorah tradition.

matzah unleavened bread; used for Passover.

mazzal lit.: constellation, star.

mazzal tov good luck.

megillah scroll; usually, scroll of Esther, read at Purim.

Melavveh Malkah accompanying the Queen; the Sabbath meal held at end of holy day to prolong Sabbath celebration.

menorah candelabrum; nine-branched menorah is used at Hanukkah; seven-branched menorah was used in ancient Temple.

Messiah eschatological king to rule in end of time.

Mezuzah parchment containing first two paragraphs of Shema, rolled tightly and placed in case, attached to doorposts of home.

midrash exegesis of Scripture; also applied to collection of such exegeses.

mikveh ritual bath for immersion to wash away impurity; baptism.

minhah afternoon prayers.

minyan number needed for quorum for worship; ten.

Mishnah code of law promulgated by Judah the Patriarch (ca. 200 C.E.); in six parts, concerning agricultural laws, festival and Sabbath law, family and personal status, torts, damages, and civil law, laws pertaining to the sanctuary and to rules of ritual cleanness.

mitnaged opponent; opposition to Hasidism on the part of rationalists, Talmudists.

mitzvah commandments; technical sense: scriptural or rabbinic injunctions; later on, also used in sense of good deed; every human activity may represent an act of obedience to divine will.

moed festival.

mohel ritual circumciser.

Mosaic what pertains to Moses or to the writings attributed to him—for example, Mosaic law.

Musaf additional service on Sabbath and festivals, commemorating additional offering in Temple times.

musar lit.: chastisement; instruction in right behavior; movement in modern Judaism emphasizing study and practice of ethical traditions, founded by Israel Salanter (1810–1883).

mystic someone who has experiences of direct encounter with God's presence.

nasi prince.

navi prophet.

neder vow.

Neilah closing service at end of Yom Kipper, at nightfall when fast ends.

niggun melody, traditional tune for prayer.

Olam Hazeh, Olam Haba this world, the world to come.

omer sheaf cut in barley harvest.

Oneg Shabbat Sabbath delight.

Orthodoxy traditional Judaism; belief in historical event of revelation at Sinai of Oral and written Torah, binding character of Torah, and the authority of Torah sages to interpret Torah.

paradigm example, pattern

Passover (Hebrew: *Pesah*) festival commemorating Exodus from Egypt, in spring month of Nisan (April).

peot corners; Leviticus 19:27 forbids removing hair at corners of head, meaning not to cut earlocks.

peshat literal meaning of Scripture; distinct from *derash*, or homily.

Pharisee (from Hebrew *Parush*) separatist; party in ancient Judaism teaching Oral Torah revealed at Sinai along with written one, preserved among prophets and sages down to the Pharisaic party; espoused prophetic ideals and translated them to everyday life of Jewry through legislation. Distinctive beliefs according to Josephus: (1) immortality of the soul, (2) existence of angels, (3) divine providence, (4) freedom of will, (5) resurrection of the dead, (6) oral Torah.

philosophy rational investigation of truths concerning being, ethics, conduct, knowledge.

pilpul dialectical reasoning in study of oral law.

piyyut synagogue poetry.

pogroms race riots against the Jews, involving looting, destruction of property, violence against persons, and murder; common in nineteenth-century Russia and twentieth-century Germany; a foretaste of the Holocaust.

profane secular, not sanctified; not to be confused with *profane* as profanity.

Purim festival commemorating deliverance of Persian Jews from extermination in fifth century B.C., as related in Scroll of Esther; on fourteenth of Adar, generally in March.

rabbi "my master"; title for teacher of oral Torah.

Rabbinical Assembly association of conservative rabbis.

Rabbinical Council association of Orthodox rabbis in United States.

Rashi a name for R. Solomon Isaac (1040–1105), composed of *Rabbi Shlomo Yzhak*; hence *Rashi*. He was the writer of the most widely consulted of all commentaries on the Bible and Talmud.

rationalism belief that reason governs opinion, serves as a reliable source of knowledge.

Rava fourth-century Talmudic master, head of Babylonian school at Mahoza.

recondite hidden, concealed.

reconstructionism movement to develop modern, naturalist theology for Judaism; founded by Mordecai M. Kaplan (1881–1982); emphasizes Jewish peoplehood, sees Judaism as natural outgrowth of Jewish people's efforts to ensure survival and answer basic human questions.

Reform religious movement advocating change of tradition to conform to conditions of modern life. Holds halakhah to be human creation, subject to judgment of humanity; sees Judaism as historical religious experience of Jewish people.

Rosh Hashanah New Year, first day of Tishri (September).

Rosh Yeshivah head of Talmudic academy.

Sabbateanism Movement of followers of Sabbetai Zevi (1626–1676), messianic leader who became an apostate. Followers believed this apostasy was part of divine plan.

Sabbetai Zevi (1626–1676) Messiah, kabbalist; made mystical revelations; announced himself as Messiah in Smyrna (Turkey) synagogue in 1665; went to Constantinople to claim his kingdom from sultan; was imprisoned; converted to Islam.

Sadducees sect of Temple priests and sympathizers; stressed written Torah and the right of the priesthood to interpret it against Pharisaic claim that oral tradition held by Pharisees was means of interpretation; rejected belief in resurrection of the dead, immortality of soul, angels, divine providence.

salvific having to do with salvation.

Sanhedrin Jewish legislative-administrative agency in Temple times.

secular everyday affairs, not sanctified.

seder order; Passover home service.

sefer Torah Scroll of Torah.

Selihot penitential prayers, recited before New Year.

semikhah laying on of hands; ordination.

Sephardi(m) descendants of Spanish Jewry, generally in Mediterranean countries.

shaharit morning service; dawn.

shalom peace.

Shammai colleague of Hillel, first-century Pharisaic sage.

Shavuot feast of weeks; Pentecost; commemorates giving of Torah at Mount Sinai.

shehitah ritual slaughter; consists in cutting through both windpipe and gullet by means of sharp knife, examining to see both have been cut through.

Shekhinah presence of God in world.

Shema proclamation of unity of God: Deuteronomy 6:4–9, 11:13–21, Numbers 15:37–41.

Shemini Atzeret eighth day of solemn assembly (Numbers 30:35); last day of Sukkot. This is a holy day in itself.

Sheva Berakhot seven blessings recited at wedding ceremony.

shiva seven days of mourning following burial of close relative.

shofar ram's horn, sounded during high holy day period, from a month before New Year until end of Yom Kipper.

Shoferot *Shofar*—verses, concerning revelation, read in New Year Additional Service.

shohet ritual slaughterer.

Shulhan Arukh prepared table; code of Jewish law by Joseph Karo, published 1565; authoritative for orthodox Jewry.

Siddur Jewish prayer book for all days except holy days.

simhah celebration.

Simhat Torah rejoicing of law; second day of *Shemini Atzeret,* on which the Torah reading cycle is completed; celebrated with song and dance.

sukkah booth, tabernacle.

Sukkot autumn harvest festival, ending high holy day season.

synagogue Greek translation of Hebrew *bet hakeneset* (house of assembly); place of Jewish prayer, study, assembly.

taboo any prohibition based on religious concerns.

takkanah decree, ordinance issued by rabbinic authority.

tallit prayer shawl; four-cornered cloth with fringes (Numbers 15:38) worn by adult males in morning service.

Talmid Hakham disciple of the wise.

Talmud Torah study of Torah; education.

Talmud Mishnah (see definition earlier) plus commentary on the Mishnah produced in rabbinic academies from about 200 to 500 C.E. (called *Gemara)* form the Talmud. Two Talmuds were produced—one in Palestine, the other in Babylonia. From 500 C.E. onward, Babylonian Talmud was the primary source for Judaic law and theology.

Tanakh Hebrew Bible; formed of Torah, Nevi'im, Ketuvin, Pentateuch, Prophets, Writings; hence, TaNaKh.

tanna one who studies and teaches; a rabbinic master mentioned in Mishnah is called a tanna.

Tannaite an authority of the Mishnah or of the same period as the Mishnah, up to about 200.

tefillin phylacteries worn by adult males in morning service, based on Exodus 13:1, 11, Deuteronomy 6:4–9, 11:13–21. These passages are written on parchment, placed in leather cases, and worn on the left arm and forehead.

Tehillim psalms.

tekiah sounding of shofar on New Year.

tenet opinion, principle, doctrine

teref, terefa lit.: torn; generally: unkosher food.

theology systematic statement of religious faith in proportionate and coherent presentation.

Torah lit.: revelation. At first, the Five Books of Moses; then Scriptures as a whole; then the whole corpus of revelation, both written and oral, taught by Pharisaic Judaism. Talmud Torah: study of Torah. Standing by itself, *Torah* can mean "study," the act of learning and discussion of the tradition.

Tosafot novellae on the Talmud, additions generally to the commentary of Rashi. The *Tosafists,* authorities who produced Tosafot, flourished during the twelfth and thirteenth centuries in northern France.

Tosefta supplements to the Mishnah.

tractate a subdivision of the Mishnah; the Mishnah is divided into six divisions, and these, in turn, are divided into tractates, each with its own topic. A tractate, then, is a topical exposition of the Mishnah, a commentary on the Mishnah in the Toseft, or one of the two Talmuds.

transcendent what goes beyond the ordinary limits of this world.

tzaddik righteous man; in Hasidism, intermediary, master of Hasidic circle.

tzedakah righteousness; used for charity, philanthropy.

Tzidduk HaDin justification of the judgment; prayer of a dying person.

tzitzit fringes of tallit.

virtuoso a person who has special knowledge or skill; an expert, specialist.

Wissenschaft des Judentums science of Judaism; scientific study using scholarly methods of philology, history, and philosophy of Jewish religion, literature, and history; founded in nineteenth-century Germany.

yahrzeit anniversary of death of relative.

Yahveh see *Jehovah.*

Yamim Noraim Days of Awe; Rosh Hashanah, intervening days, and Yom Kippur; ten in all.

yeshiva session; Talmudic academy.

Yetzer HaRa, Yetzer Tov evil inclination, good inclination.

Yigdal hymn that contains the thirteen principles of faith formulated by Maimonides; sung at the end of synagogue worship as the creed of Judaism.

Yiddish Jewish language of Eastern Europe, now used in the United States, Israel, Argentina, and Mexico, in addition to vernacular; originally a Judeo-German dialect, with several Hebrew and Slavic words.

Yom Kippur Day of Atonement; fast day for penitence.

zikhronot remembrances, prayers on theme of God's remembering his mercy, covenant, in New Year Additional Service.

Zionism movement to secure Jewish state in Palestine; founded in 1897 by Theodor Herzl.

Zohar medieval kabbalistic (mystical) book, completed by fourteenth century in Spain; mystical commentary on biblical passages; stories of mystical life of the tanna Simeon b. Yohai.

Subject Index

Index to Biblical and Talmudic References

Bible